BEYOND THE SNOW LEOPARD

BEYOND THE SNOW LEOPARD

BILL CROZIER

Published by Carlow Books,
an imprint of Schwartz Books Pty Ltd
Wurundjeri Country
22–24 Northumberland Street
Collingwood VIC 3066, Australia
enquiries@blackincbooks.com
www.blackincbooks.com

9781760645229 (paperback)
9781743823729 (ebook)

A catalogue record for this book is available from the National Library of Australia

Cover design by Beau Lowenstern
Text design and typesetting by Aira Pimping
All photographs by the author

For Paula, Nicola, Madeleine, George and Jake

CONTENTS

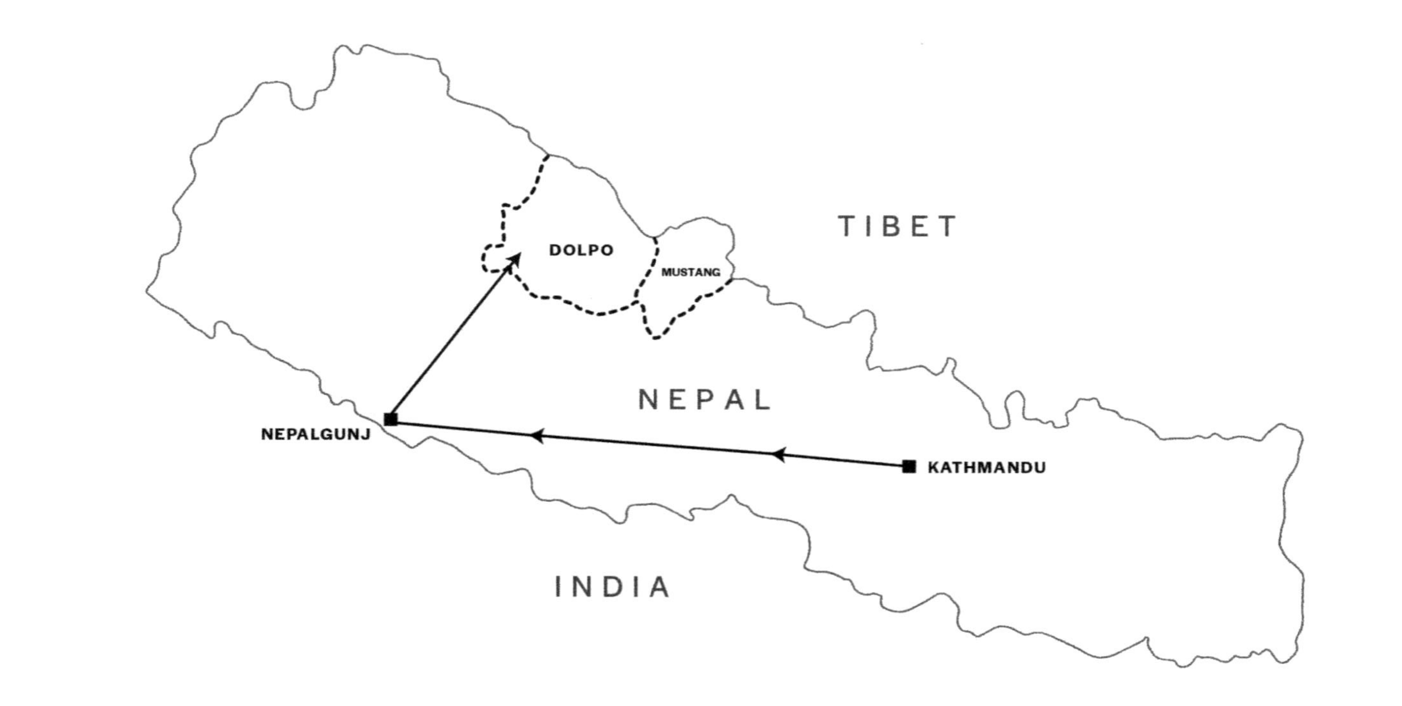
TIBET
DOLPO
MUSTANG
NEPAL
NEPALGUNJ
KATHMANDU
INDIA

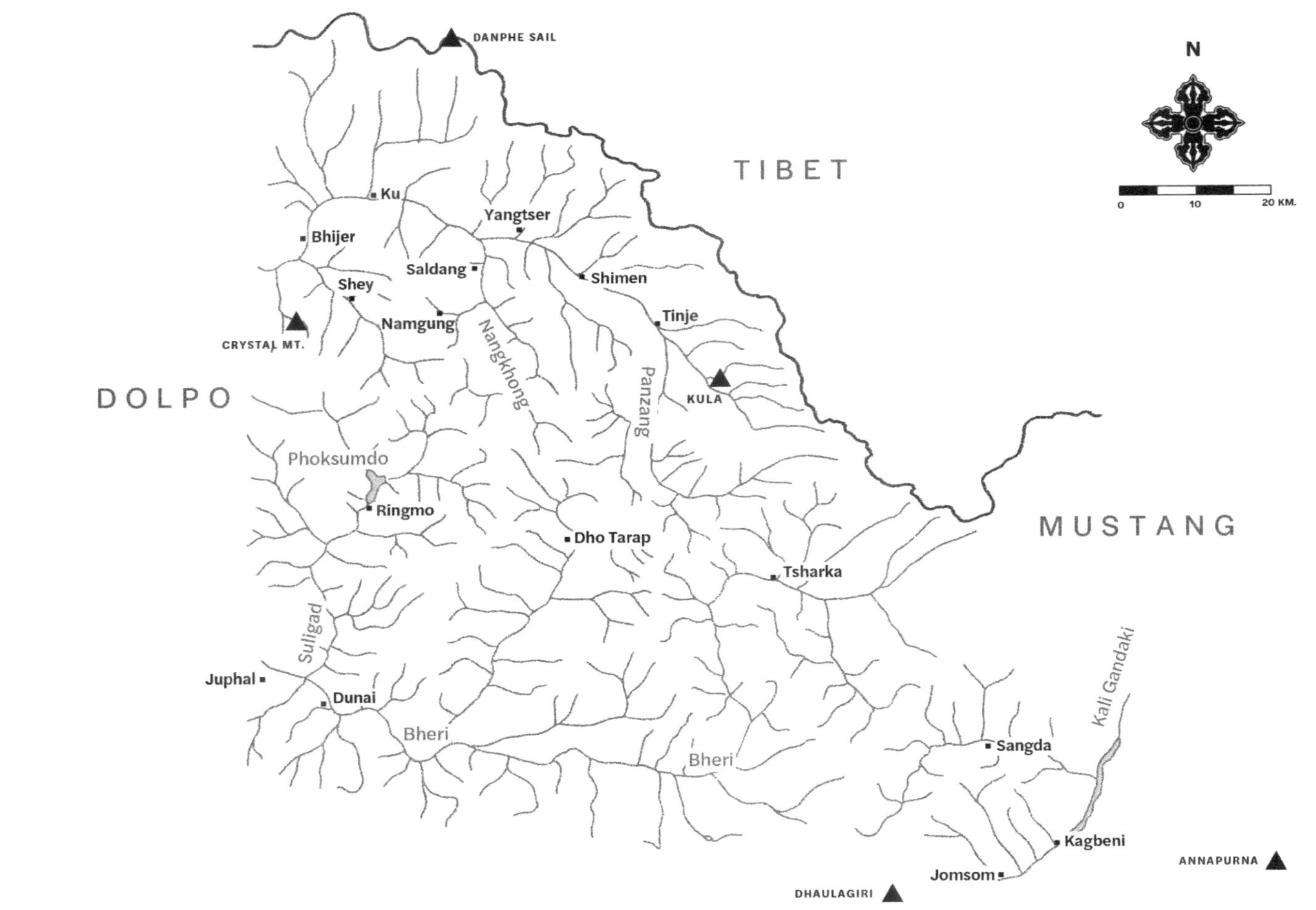
DANPHE SAIL
N
0
10
20 KM.
TIBET
Ku
Yangtser
Bhijer
Saldang
Shimen
Shey
Tinje
Namgung
CRYSTAL MT.
Nangkhong
Panzang
KULA
DOLPO
Phoksumdo
Ringmo
Dho Tarap
MUSTANG
Tsharka
Suligad
Juphal
Dunai
Kali Gandaki
Bheri
Sangda
Bheri
Kagbeni
ANNAPURNA
Jomsom
DHAULAGIRI

MOUNTAIN SONNET

Sky above. Air below. The link with ground
Is tenuous as muscles scream in pain.
The fear, the cold, need stuff as yet unfound
Within our mortal flesh and air starved brain.
A step. A breath. The throat burns on thin air
And the need to get higher makes the mind
Recite George's mantra 'Because it's there'
Yet this sentiment is not why we find
Ourselves on this uncaring cliff. The fire
In the human heart drives us on to fight
Our fears whence we gain the peak of desire,
Alone to gaze in tranquil evening light,
To reflect once more upon our own worth
And our place, if any, on this wondrous earth

—Bill Crozier, 2010

2013

LADAKH

1
LADAKH

I woke suddenly into a world of total darkness as my tent shook noisily.

'Bed tea, Sahib?' said the voice over my head.

It was still night and a frigid –20°C.

This was day fifteen of our winter trek in Ladakh, in the Indian Himalaya, and it was the morning we were to see the snow leopard tracks.

A quick gear-packing session to warm up, breakfast in the mess tent and then we were off again. The sun had risen and the sky was bright blue overhead but we remained chilled in the lingering shadows of the high mountains around us. Climbing down a narrow rocky ledge led us once more onto the frozen Zanskar River, and we strode confidently back onto the ice. There had been a few centimetres of snow overnight so our guide, Lobsang, was out in front tapping the ice with a pole and listening for the clues as to the thickness and stability of our insecure walkway.

After half an hour of walking I saw that Phil, up ahead, had stopped and was snapping photos.

'Snow leopard!' he shouted back to me.

I soon caught up and there, at our feet, were the clear and distinctive prints of large paws in the fresh snow. They were heading in the opposite direction to us but had clearly been made that morning. Every now and again we could see the drag mark of the animal's massive tail. I looked all around us and realised that in the grey light and the shadows the legendary Himalayan cat could easily be watching us, undetectable, from even a few metres away. Tracing the tracks back I could see where the beast had criss-crossed the trail. At one point he'd clearly leapt down from some rocks, and a little further on we could see where he'd made a massive jump up onto that low crag. I took off my sunglasses and put them next to the prints to give some scale to my photos. The pawprint was as wide as my face. This was definitely a fully grown snow leopard.

For six weeks of every year the Zanskar River, a tributary of the Indus, freezes over and presents a highway connecting the Ladakhi capital, Leh, with the more remote villages at a time when the usual high passes are completely blocked by snow. The locals call this icy road 'the Chadar' and for hundreds of years it has been the only winter trade route.

I'd been in touch with my friend Ade Summers a few months before, telling him that I'd like to do something a bit different for my next trek.

'You should come with me to do the Chadar,' he'd said.

Ade is a Welshman in his fifties who is a professional climber and trek leader. He has vast experience in the mountains and a pleasant, calm attitude with a wry sense of humour. He suggested this icy adventure, which he was leading. I jumped at the opportunity and, as it transpired, there were to be just three of us. I first met up with the other trekker, Phil Metzger, at Delhi Airport. He was a tall, rugged-looking American who'd just retired as a surgeon at the Mayo Clinic's Florida campus. We took a short pre-dawn flight up into the mountains and an hour or so later we rendezvoused with Ade in the terminal at Leh. The sun had just risen and it was a brisk –15°C.

Leh is the ancient capital of Ladakh and lies at an altitude of 3500 metres (11,482 feet). It is on the old trade routes between Tibet, to the north and east, and Kashmir and Baltistan to the south and west. The town is largely unspoiled by modern development, and it remains dominated by the nine-storey, seventeenth-century Leh Palace. Behind this, soaring much higher, the Namgyal Tsemo Gompa sits magnificently on its rocky peak surrounded by thousands of colourful prayer flags.

The altitude was immediately apparent when scaling the stairs in the hotel or bending over to tie shoelaces. Simply walking the 2 kilometres into town and back was exhausting. We spent two full days acclimatising before the jeep ride out to our starting point. A three-hour drive past the junction of the Zanskar and the Indus took us deep into the Zanskar Gorge. The last settlement was the aptly named hamlet of Chilling. At the end of the trail, we met our porter team and their *sirdar*, or head guide, Lobsang who was a large man of Tibetan origin. As impressive as the man himself was the stunning sheepskin jacket he was wearing. This had apparently been sent to him by relatives in Tibet and was worn 'fur side in'. It was dyed green, with a flamboyant colourful silk trim and embroidery. The instant the car stopped the porters began unloading our gear and soon our bags were on the ice about 20 metres below us and being dragged on makeshift sledges towards our first camp. We scrambled down and clumsily followed, but with much trepidation. All our lives we instinctively stay away from frozen bodies of water, preferring not to, literally, 'skate on thin ice'. Counterintuitive though it was, we soon adapted to the essential shuffling gait we'd employ for the next three weeks.

The camp we were heading for was visible on the opposite riverbank, just over a kilometre away. The exertion of ice-walking kept us warm and we guzzled down the hot tea awaiting us on our arrival. Throwing gear into the tents we got out all our down clothing and settled in to eat. Deep in the gorge there is little sunlight and night slams down quickly. It becomes bone-chillingly cold. Our down sleeping bags were the only real refuge.

Each day's walking presented spectacular views as we slowly made our way around each bend of the river. We were on ice most of the time but it varied dramatically in its nature: sometimes thick, sometimes thin. The colour ranged from pure white to grey to blue, but it was often absolutely clear and we could watch the water flowing visibly under our feet. In places the ice was too broken or wet to cross, so we climbed up the rocky riverbank to regain the river-ice a little further along. Where the gorge was narrow, the ice was especially thick and there was no indication of the raging torrent below. When the river widened, there was open rushing water with a narrow ledge of ice clinging to the cliff. This was often less than a metre wide and we'd have to push our backpacks ahead of us as we gingerly crawled on hands and knees. Our ever-cheerful porters would race ahead and set up camp. We always had a fire and hot tea waiting for us on arrival. Amazingly our Ladakhi friends didn't use tents but would build an open fire in one of the many shallow caves along the riverbank and settle around the flames, nestled in their Indian army sleeping bags.

Nights were intensely cold and dark, but the skies were generally cloudless with startlingly clear views of the stars and Milky Way. My inflatable mattress and down sleeping bag, with my down jacket thrown on top, kept me cosy. Intermittently during the night there'd be a thunderous crack or crushing noise as the river ice succumbed to the massive natural forces imposed upon it. Morning 'bed tea' was always welcome and at breakfast we'd stock up on carbs – porridge with sugar and honey, coffee with plenty of sugar, eggs and *chapati*. We had a variety of breads: *naan*, *chapati* and delicious 'Tibetan cakes' which were remarkably like English 'rock buns'. We were impressed at their freshness and availability. Lobsang explained that each night he'd prepare the dough and put it into a plastic bag. By keeping it warm in his sleeping bag, the dough would rise and be ready to bake by the morning.

On our third day of trekking we had a large dump of snow and this obscured the ice underfoot making our trekking even more precarious. In the afternoon we approached some prayer flags and a *chorten*, a religious monument, perched high on the hillside. Round the next bend was a frozen waterfall about 30 metres high, giving a spectacular display of the various hues of ice – deep blue, cream, turquoise, pale blue, grey. Then, above us, was a rickety wooden bridge spanning the chasm. This carried the track leading to the village of Nerak, about 2 kilometres away. We stood on the ice in complete silence, surrounded by these human artefacts – *chortens*, prayer flags, the bridge – hardly able to imagine what it must be like in the spring when the melt would unleash a torrent of white water, of monumental and deafening proportions, in the exact spot where we now lingered.

Six days brought us to the end of the Chadar, where we climbed above the river and took to the road. We'd managed between 10 and 14 kilometres on each of the last five days and had now reached the end of the gorge leading to the wider Zanskar Valley. A completely iced-over, single-track road led to the towns beyond. On a glaringly bright and frigidly cold day we slogged 17 kilometres to the small village of Pidmo, a tiny hamlet nestled close to the mountains. It had a welcoming *chorten*, a *gompa*, a school and about twenty houses. We spent the night there in a traditional homestead. Living rooms upstairs, yaks and goats on the ground floor. We three shared a room with a central wood-burning stove made from an old oil can with a tin-pipe chimney leading up through the ceiling. We spread our sleeping bags around and settled in for afternoon tea. I was able to inspect a couple of fingers on my right hand which had some frost-nip on the tips:

white, hard flesh with blisters forming already but fortunately no long-term damage. It's impossible to have gloves that are too good! The children of the household couldn't restrain their curiosity and came into our room to simply sit and stare. The more adventurous among them touched our backpacks or sleeping bags as though they were exotic artefacts.

The next day we travelled on to the further settlement of Zangla. This was a larger but more spread-out town, which had a nunnery, a *gompa*, and a ruined old fort known as the King's House. We were staying once again in a traditional Tibetan farmhouse. We arrived on this clear and bitterly cold day, beards solidly festooned with icicles of frozen breath, to be met by a barking hound on a chain and the lady of the household. She looked about eighty, but in reality could have been anywhere between forty and ninety. She had greasy black hair, a grey knitted yak-wool hat, Tibetan jewellery of silver, coral and turquoise, few teeth, but a great smile. Our room was brilliantly sunny, with several rugs and a central stove. The walls were roughly painted a Tiffany blue, with the window frames bright pink and rather messily done. It was a welcome, cosy home for the next three nights.

Besides having a break from the ice and cold, the main reason for using Zangla as a base was to be able to visit and restock at Padum, the main town of the Zanskar Valley, with a population of about 1000. We took a jeep there for the day and were able to buy a leg of yak, rice, and other supplies for the return journey. We also had a morning at the beautiful Karsha Gompa. It floated ethereally above an icy river mist, directly across the valley, and was set solidly into the cliff face. The spiritual leader of this monastery is Tendzin Choegyal, the youngest brother of the Dalai Lama. The drive up the hill to this dramatic place was remarkable – until the jeep suddenly ground to a halt on the ice. The diesel had become too cold and viscous, a problem easily solved by firing up the petrol stove we used for making tea and sitting the naked hissing flame directly under the fuel tank for a quarter of an hour. Once we got going again, and after a minor crash into a wall, we were able to take the walk up through the monastery buildings to the main *gompa* and chat with the monks. There was a school for the very young monks, and the teenage ones were keen to pose for photographs wearing my shiny blue Ray-Bans.

A free day in Zangla allowed Ade, Phil and me some time to wander round and say hello to the locals. The village had many *chortens* and a large population of sheep, goats, dogs and yaks that seemed as keen as the people to pose for our photos. A long climb up to the King's House fort gave us sensational views of the valley and afforded Ade the perfect place to fly some prayer flags he'd brought specifically to commemorate the life of a friend's mother.

Later in the day the jeeps delivered us back to the beginning of the gorge, where we spent a numbingly cold night in the workers' huts.

Next morning we were back on the ice, by now relaxed and comfortable with the concept of not necessarily falling through. We made good speed. That this was a well-used highway was evident by the groups of Ladhakis, whole families, travelling in both directions with their goods. There were also several large groups of Indian trekkers, all wearing the kind of cheap rubber boots widely available in Leh.

On our second last day we were confronted by a long stretch of broken and slushy ice. We used ropes over certain areas and several times had to climb high above the river to a more stable area further downstream. That night a spectacular full moon rose above the mountain ridge, but it was far too cold to stay out and admire for more than a couple of minutes.

Our last day on the ice highway left us feeling rather sad, as we approached the end of this beautiful trek. Ade and I walked the last few kilometres slowly, taking plenty of photographs. About 1 kilometre from our camp we could hear the racket of the hammer drills from the building of the new road. This track carved out of the cliffs would link Pidmo with Leh and was to be finished in the next couple of years. It would be the winter highway for Zanskar and would mean dramatic change to the conditions and culture of the Zanskar area.

A couple of rest days back in Leh were more than welcome and provided the opportunity to visit the main Chowkhang Gompa in the centre of town and climb up to the fort and higher to Namgyal Tsemo Gompa on the summit behind. The view from here, looking down on the medieval city of Leh with its ancient polo ground and *chortens*, was breathtaking. The sound of the monks chanting and drumming rose from the *gompa* in the middle of town. Directly south stood the Stok range of snow-covered mountains, with the simply beautiful peak of Stok Kangri (6153 metres; 20,187 feet) dead centre. A scramble down a zigzag trail ended with a welcome lunch of *momos* and tea in a Tibetan restaurant in the main street of Leh.

A few days later Ade and I were back in Delhi and Phil had begun his long journey back to the States. Over a final curry in the hotel, with a decent Aussie wine, we reminisced about the trip.

'You should come with me to Dolpo next year,' said Ade.

I required no further encouragement. Dolpo was the land of the snow leopard, immortalised by the American author Peter Matthiessen. Without hesitation I said I would go. I wanted to follow in Matthiessen's footsteps, and I even dared to hope that I might see a snow leopard myself.

2014

TO DOLPO

2
OF SNOW LEOPARDS AND MEN

The only snow leopard I had seen was in Taronga Zoo in Sydney. I dislike most zoos and was saddened and strangely ashamed to be in the presence of this majestic mountain creature in its tropical Australian prison. Nevertheless, I also felt a deep sense of privilege to have been in such close proximity to this otherworldly, magnificent feline.

The snow leopard, *Panthera uncia*, is well catalogued in the zoological literature. It is described as a beautiful, endangered, enigmatic predator living in the high regions of central Asia. It is a medium-sized member of the cat family and weighs between 25 and 50 kilograms. It has a body length of up to 130 centimetres and its thick furry tail is the same length again. The fur is a smoky grey colour and the whole body patterned with open rosettes of a dark, charcoal grey. Snow leopards blend in well with their rocky surrounds and are seldom seen, even by the people who share their habitat.

The Snow Leopard Trust, an American-based charity, estimates that there are only 3500 to 6000 animals left in the wild. They are so elusive that no one really knows the true number. Their range covers an area the size of Greenland and is spread over twelve central Asian countries.

Peter Matthiessen's much-celebrated book *The Snow Leopard* is about a journey he made to the remote Nepalese district called Dolpo. I'd read this travel narrative a few years earlier and had a second read as soon as

I returned to Australia from Ladakh. It is an iconic tome, part travelogue, part Buddhist introspection and pilgrimage. It paints a beautiful picture of a remote and untrammelled part of the world with an unsullied Tibetan tradition preserved by the sheer geographical isolation of the land which is Dolpo.

Matthiessen was born on 22 May 1927 in New York. He developed an early interest in nature and wildlife, which stayed with him throughout his life. After service in the US Navy in the 1940s he graduated in English at Yale in 1950 and resolved to become a writer.

He married Patsy Southgate in 1951 and, shortly after, they moved to Paris. It was there in 1953 that Matthiessen helped found *The Paris Review*. It was later revealed that during this period he was working for the CIA. Patsy and he had two children together: Luke, born in Paris, and Sara, born in 1954 after their return to the States. Peter and Patsy were divorced in 1958.

In 1963 he married the writer Deborah Love and they both began practising Zen Buddhism. In 1965 Peter wrote a novel about American missionaries meeting a primitive tribe in South America. It was entitled *At Play in the Fields of the Lord* and was later made into a Hollywood movie. Peter and Deborah had a tumultuous relationship but eventually they reconciled and made a deep commitment to each other. Soon after that, she was diagnosed with cancer. Deborah died towards the end of 1972, only one year before Peter undertook his expedition to Dolpo. They had two children. Peter had adopted Love's daughter, Rue, and their son Alex had been born in 1964. In *The Snow Leopard*, Matthiessen refers frequently to his wife's death and how much he is missing his children.

Peter had always travelled a lot and it was while in Africa, in the Serengeti in 1969, that he first met George Schaller.

George Beals Schaller was born in 1933 in Berlin and moved to the United States when he was in his teens. He'd obtained his primary degree from the University of Alaska in 1955 and earned his PhD in 1962. As early as 1959, at the age of twenty-six, he went off to Central Africa to study the mountain gorillas. This would later provide motivation to the renowned primatologist and conservationist Dian Fossey in her studies of the large primates.

In 1966 George and his wife, Kay, set off for Tanzania to live in the Serengeti and study the lion population there. When Matthiessen and he met in Africa in 1969 they made a loose arrangement to travel together in the near future to the Himalaya, where George was planning his next studies.

Peter knew that if he could accompany George on one of his scientific explorations, he would be able to observe the Tibetan version of Buddhism firsthand.

It was several years later, in September 1973, when Peter was forty-seven, that they met up in Kathmandu to begin the journey which would be narrated in *The Snow Leopard*. The travelogue wasn't destined to be published until 1978. Matthiessen and Schaller set out to observe and document the behaviour of the herds of blue sheep, or *bharal*, and with the help of several groups of porters they trekked from Kathmandu to Pokhara. From there they travelled south of the Dhaulagiri massif and turned northwards up the valley of the Bheri River, then followed the Suli Gad River to Phoksumdo Lake and finally to Shey Gompa. Matthiessen was most certainly on a journey of self-discovery directly related to the recent death of his wife and his deeply felt Zen Buddhist convictions. It was a cathartic trip for him, and the book spells out his feelings as he confronts the discomforts of the journey and delights in the beauty of inner Dolpo and its people. He also wrote of his travelling companions, including 'GS', as he called Schaller. The pair employed guides who were sherpas from the Khumbu Valley north-east of Kathmandu. Jang-Bu the head sherpa, Phu-Tsering the cook, and Gyaltsen and Dawa, camp assistants, were all around thirty years old. Two more lowly paid porters were Bimbahadur and Tukten, who were a bit older and veterans of the British Gurkha Regiment.

On rereading *The Snow Leopard* it became clear that George Schaller must also have come to know the land of Dolpo well. He spent six weeks there in 1973, twice as long as Matthiessen's three weeks. He'd written many books concerning his studies of wildlife all over the world. In 1988 he'd published *Stones of Silence: Journeys in the Himalaya*, which included an account of that same expedition he'd shared with Peter Matthiessen fifteen years earlier.

I ordered *Stones of Silence* online and it turned out to be another satisfying and entertaining read, but of a more serious scientific bent than *The Snow Leopard*. Schaller himself said early in the chapter on Dolpo, 'in spite of our disparate reasons for being here, Peter on an inner search, I on a scientific quest, we are nevertheless travellers on similar paths'.

However, it was in Schaller's book that I first read of the earliest foreigners to venture into the remote Himalayan region. Nepal had been closed to outsiders until 1950 and Dolpo until even later. Schaller had to get a special permit and was always concerned that the authorities in places like Pokhara and Dunai would block his journey. Matthiessen had said next to nothing on the topic of those travellers who'd preceded Schaller and himself into Dolpo. Indeed, his only concession towards those 'who'd gone before' was a single sentence: 'Seeking Shey Gompa in May of 1956, a scholar of Tibetan Buddhism (whose fine book enables me to speak about the iconography of this region with an authority that is not mine) made camp further up.' A number guides the reader to the endnotes at the back of *The Snow Leopard*, where it simply says 'David Snellgrove. Himalayan Pilgrimage'.

Schaller was much more generous in his acknowledgement of their few predecessors and in particular enthused about the Englishman David Snellgrove. He gave much credit to him for his earlier and more extensive explorations in the region of Dolpo.

Only seven years older than Matthiessen, David Snellgrove was born in Portsmouth, England, on 29 June 1920. He spent his early years living in the Hampshire countryside, then attended school at Christ's Hospital in Sussex. He studied languages at Southampton University before being called up for wartime military service attached to the Royal Engineers. He was able to join a newly formed unit called the Wireless Intelligence Group, and in 1943 he was on a ship to India. After succumbing to the vicissitudes of the tropical heat, he was sent to recuperate at a hospital in the hills at Lebong, beyond Darjeeling. It was here that he first visited a series of Buddhist monasteries and began teaching himself Tibetan from the classic text *Grammar and Dictionary of Colloquial Tibetan* by Sir Charles Bell. He subsequently spent his leave back near Darjeeling and made a friend of a young Tibetan called Pasang, who helped him make speedy progress in his spoken Tibetan language studies.

Snellgrove was assigned to a new unit and some special mission took him, in March 1944, to Ceylon, where he was able to visit many of the major Buddhist centres in the island's interior. The rest of his time in the subcontinent allowed him to make repeated visits to Sikkim and the hills, all the time improving his command of spoken Tibetan.

Upon his demobilisation from the army, he undertook three years of study in Cambridge, plus a year in Rome with Professor Giuseppe Tucci, after which he was appointed to the School of Oriental and African Studies at the University of London. He was then able to plan his next journey to India, the Himalaya and, this time, the newly opened country of Nepal. This expedition, from the end of 1953 to 1954 was written about in *Asian Commitment: Travels and Studies in the Indian Subcontinent and South-East Asia*, and more specifically in *Buddhist Himalaya*. I had wholeheartedly enjoyed the latter with its clear explanation of the development and spread of Buddhism throughout India before the message was then conveyed to every corner of Asia.

Snellgrove's next visit to Nepal was largely by way of completing his initial journey, which had not taken him west of Kathmandu. From January to March 1956 he spent his time documenting the Buddhist monasteries of Patan, Kathmandu and Bhadgaon (Bhaktapur). Then, from March to October, he undertook an eight-month exploration of Nepal, starting at the Indian border at Nepalgunj. From there he trekked northwards up the Bheri to ascend the Suli Gad and reach the magical blue Phoksumdo Lake. The route took him over the Kang La, a track which Matthiessen and Schaller were to retrace seventeen years later, and into 'Inner Dolpo'. He explored Shey, the 'Crystal Monastery', and the remote valleys of the area, before heading east, passing north of Dhaulagiri to enter the valley of the Kali Gandaki River at Kagbeni. He then carried on north of Annapurna and Manaslu, reaching Kathmandu via the Buri Gandaki River at the end of his eight-month trip.

This epic journey was recounted in his book *Himalayan Pilgrimage*. I again searched online and managed to get a copy shipped from the States. It was a revelation to me, as it was packed with information about the route we would soon be taking into Dolpo. It said much about the villages, the monasteries and, above all, the people, their customs and their lifestyle. Snellgrove also acknowledged the earliest foreigner to pass through Dolpo, the Japanese monk Ekai Kawaguchi, who in July 1900 had travelled through its eastern parts in his attempt to surreptitiously reach Tibet. His account of this journey was published in 1909 as *Three Years in Tibet*.

Snellgrove's *Himalayan Pilgrimage* was to be my guidebook. I packed it in a waterproof bag and pulled it out most evenings on the trip as I wrote up my diary and compared what we'd seen that day with what Snellgrove had experienced a veritable fifty-eight years before us.

Yet the 1956 trip wasn't the end of Snellgrove's explorations. He was committed to the idea of experiencing what it would be like to over-winter in Dolpo. At the end of 1960, just before the onset of winter, he began his journey via Pokhara and the Kali Gandaki, then climbed up to Sangda, entering Dolpo from the east. It was only when he was staying with his old friend Nyima Tschering, the headman of the village of Saldang, that he discovered some aged documents relating the lives of several of the medieval abbots who had lived in the region. These were vibrant accounts of daily life and death in the fifteenth to seventeenth centuries. He decided that these historical documents should be translated and in 1967 he published *Four Lamas of Dolpo*, which included a detailed account of his journey and the difficulties of his three-month stay in the Nangkhong Valley.

On Snellgrove's 1960–61 journey, as his intentions were to be focused entirely on his literary interests, he was keen to have as his travelling companion an anthropologist to observe the seasonal activity and economy of the Dolpo-pa, the people of Dolpo. He found a willing person in the form of Monsieur Corneille Jest of the Musée de l'Homme in Paris. Jest was born in 1930 and had much experience in the Himalaya. He ended up spending a whole year in Dolpo and wrote several books, in French, about his sojourn. One of his books wasn't published until 1998 and was subsequently translated into English. Called *Tales of the Turquoise: A Pilgrimage in Dolpo*, it recounts his three-week journey with a Tibetan man from near Dho Tarap. This man, Karma, had a reputation as a storyteller and was marvellous company on the trek. Jest made note of his stories and fables and combined the travel narrative with them to write the book. It provides a cultural insight into the traditions and attitudes of the hardy Tibetans who live in Dolpo.

In many respects Peter Matthiessen, in *The Snow Leopard*, had only touched on the complexity of the countryside and culture which is Dolpo; but with Matthiessen, Schaller, Snellgrove and Jest as my guides, and with additional material from authors and movie-makers of more recent times, I felt my travels in Dolpo would be fully informed and provide a depth of experience far beyond a mere stroll in the hills.

3
THE LAMA

I made my first journey to Nepal in 2004.

The Singapore Airlines jet began descending steeply into the Kathmandu Valley. We were startlingly close to the hilltops. The steep slopes were engraved with the curved parallel lines of narrow green and yellow farming terraces and dotted with tiny buildings. It was dazzlingly picturesque as the plane started its gut-churning 180° turn. As my side of the craft began to face north, I beheld my first view of the Himalaya. Rank upon rank of starkly beautiful snow-covered precipices reaching as high as we were flying and brilliantly white in the afternoon sun.

Kathmandu got closer. A veritable Legoland of red brick buildings. Dozens of tall chimneys testament to the many brickworks scattered throughout the valley. It was my first visit to this fabled place. What did I really know of it?

'There's a one-eyed yellow idol to the north of Khatmandu' proclaims the poem cataloguing the downfall of one 'Mad Carew'. Besides the historical British army connection via the Gurkhas, Kathmandu was the end of the trail for legions of 1960s hippies. It was a place where, in 2001, a new king was enthroned because his nephew had massacred most of the royal family. It was a Hindu kingdom, but with a strong Buddhist presence. Yet in this 'peaceful' kingdom an estimated 12,000 people had recently been killed because of a brutal Maoist terrorist insurgency.

Naturally I'd bought all the guidebooks and spent hours studying them.

I couldn't wait to immerse myself in this mesmerising place and see what it was really like. It didn't disappoint.

Many visits later and Kathmandu had become one of my favourite towns in the world. A feast for the senses. A kaleidoscopic visual extravaganza with all the smells of the East, both good and bad. An endless cacophony of traffic noise, bells, chanting, hawkers, beggars. In 2007 Nepal Airlines sacrificed a pair of goats on the tarmac in front of a Boeing 757-200 to appease the Hindu sky god Akash Bhairab and 'help solve some of its aircraft maintenance issues'. Pilgrims, the famous bookshop, was now sadly gone, having burned down in 2013. Each street corner had a shrine to a Hindu god, and all day long prayers and offerings were being made. The Buddhist pantheon was also well represented. Its most massive incarnation is the Great Stupa at Boudhanath. This white hemisphere surmounted by the all-seeing pairs of eyes facing in the four cardinal directions is an oasis of tranquillity in the maelstrom of the city. A slow stroll around, in traditional clockwise fashion, takes twenty minutes or so, involving the spinning of some of the hundreds of prayer wheels. The simple circumambulatory procession indulges some of my basic Buddhist leanings.

My father, George Crozier, known all his life as 'Cherry Crozier', spent almost two years in India between 1944 and 1946. He was a sergeant in the British Army's Royal Corps of Signals. He'd spent most of his war years on a motorbike as a 'dispatch rider' and had quite a rough time in Africa and Italy. He was sent to India in 1944 on his way to fight the Japanese in Burma, but the atomic bomb brought an end to hostilities. He spoke of his time in India in the most glowing terms. He loved a good curry and said that one of the highlights of his life was when he saw Gandhi leading a procession.

When my brother and I were young, he told us an astonishing and scarcely believable story. Soon after he'd arrived in India, he and his military unit took part in a parachute exercise on the edge of the Himalaya which went badly awry. As the plane, a Dakota, approached the mountains, a storm blew up. The craft was thrown around in the most violent manner, was blown way off course and began losing height. Everyone was ordered to bail out as an emergency, and the soldiers were scattered far and wide. The pilot was a hero and went down with his plane. Dad landed his parachute in a snow drift but was within sight of a village high on the mountainside. The villagers took him in and gave him some hot chai. Almost as soon as he'd warmed up, he was escorted to the bedside of a sick young man who was feverish and delirious. Dad told us that all he had was some aspirin and, by breaking open his compass, a little alcohol. He gave these to the young man and by the next morning his fever had broken and the villagers thought it nothing short of miraculous. It turned out that the patient was a Tibetan lama and over the next two weeks, before Dad was able to rejoin his unit, they became close friends. The lama was extremely grateful, and before they parted promised my father that he would be his spiritual guide and would always be there for him in times of trouble. Dad said that they often communicated by thought alone! My brother and I were incredulous, but the power of the lama was clear. Every time we did something naughty, Dad somehow always knew we were up to no good. On every occasion he seemed to know who had caused the damage or who had left the lights burning. 'How did you know it was me?' I'd ask and he'd reply, 'Ah! The lama told me.' He'd back up his tale by regaling us with the story of *Lost Horizon*. He'd seen the original movie and, to us, it strongly reinforced his credibility that Hollywood had seen fit to tell a similar tale. It certainly made us think twice before transgressing. How could we compete with that kind of insider knowledge? Fiction it may have been, but it kept us honest until we were old enough to force the confession out of Dad that it was all made up. He was much amused that we'd fallen for it for so long. Nevertheless, it was my first introduction to the concept of the Buddhist lamas and of a mysticism and spirituality so markedly different to the formal and dour Christianity being thrust upon we young innocents at primary school.

This was back in the days of morning assembly with prayers and hymns each day. I was of a scientific bent, and as I grew older became more critical, even scornful, of the Christian myth, especially as represented by the grandiose and dogmatic Anglican and Catholic churches. My scientific education soon led me to reject the concept of an all-powerful deity. However, my later work as a doctor meant having to understand and appreciate the deeper, more spiritual, attitudes of many people. I may personally have become an atheist but the more I discovered and read about Buddhism over the years the more I began to love the philosophy and iconography of the Buddha.

I first became aware of the Buddha in the late 1990s. I'd studied medicine at Guy's Hospital in London and become a specialist in anaesthesia. I'd spent two years teaching at Johns Hopkins Hospital in Baltimore and the

UK health service no longer held me in its thrall. I moved to Australia and completely enjoyed my practice there and bringing up my family as young Aussies. In 1999 I was invited on a medical working trip to Ho Chi Minh City in Vietnam with an organisation called Interplast – the International Plastic Surgery Association. We were to spend two weeks operating alongside Vietnamese doctors performing reconstructive surgery in a learning/teaching exercise. I'd immersed myself in the history of the place and was more than pleasantly surprised to find that the Vietnam War, which is known there as 'the American War', really had become history – brutal as it had been – and that there was a rich and exotic culture dating back 4000 years which I knew little about. I visited several beautiful Buddhist temples and was stunned by their colour, atmosphere and vibrancy. These were living places full of people going about their daily business, not like the massive, silent and oppressive European cathedrals full of tourists. I saw the Jade Emperor Pagoda with its turtle pond and hundreds of doves and pigeons, the Le Van Duyet Temple, and the Xa Loi Pagoda with its two-storey-high golden Buddha statue. I paused in quiet contemplation at the spot in old Saigon where Thich Quang Duc self-immolated in 1963 and thus gave rise to one of the world's most iconic photographs – one which was instrumental in turning people's opinions against the war. My reading continued apace and I became deeply enamoured with the simple story of Buddhism. Its 'middle path' approach, the emphasis on calm, its consideration of others and the concept that happiness comes from within were all enormously appealing.

Another Interplast trip to Sri Lanka in early 2004 allowed me to see another side of Buddhism, the Theravada school this time. A visit to the town of Kandy, in the centre of the island, overlooked by a massive hilltop statue of Buddha, demonstrated how Buddhism had developed to accommodate many cultures and values. It adapted its ways to various societies, but it was also able to modify those same societies. The Temple of the Tooth in central Kandy is the repository of a piece of jawbone with one or two teeth said to have been plucked from the funeral pyre of the latest Buddha, Siddhārtha Gauthama. It is enshrined in its sanctuary and once a year is placed on the back of the leading elephant in a parade of sixty or more of them and displayed around the streets of Kandy.

A team of us had been working in the capital, Columbo, performing a variety of surgical procedures, again under the auspices of Interplast. We mainly dealt with cleft palates in children, burns, and one or two injuries from the civil war. At the end of these trips we usually left our disposable items such as gloves and syringes, endotracheal tubes and some drugs with the local doctors. It was easier than shipping them back to Australia, and these items would be of great use to the local teams. When I handed over a pile of children's endotracheal tubes to the chief anaesthetist, this delightful Sri Lankan lady was quite overwhelmed and she said, tearfully, 'Oh thank you. You have gained much merit.' It was my turn to feel overwhelmed. I realised that the simple act of giving is of much greater cultural importance and symbolism than we Westerners, with our materialistic ways, seem to understand. I enjoyed the fact that in some way I had 'gained merit', but I also understood that this Buddhist concept is not scoring points on some celestial scoreboard with a view to later entry through pearly gates. It is the idea that one can feel a sense of calm, satisfaction and wellbeing from performing an effortless act of kindness.

A few months after the trip to Sri Lanka I was heading off to trek to Everest Base Camp with my cousin Phil Crozier. The prospect of seeing the Nepalese Buddhist culture, of the Mahayana school, was a part of my trip that I was very much looking forward to. I'd read of Swayambhunath, the Monkey Temple, and Boudhanath, the largest *stupa* in the country. And what of Tengboche, the 'Thyangboche' of the tale of Everest 1953? Would I be able to reach it?

My first Nepalese trek was an unqualified success. We reached Everest Base Camp and climbed up to the minor peak of Kala Pattar, where the air is exactly half the density of sea-level air and one's lips are tinged blue. But just as distinct and pleasurable in my memory of that trip was the cultural high of walking around the Great Stupa, the monkey temple, the *mani* walls and *chortens* along the trail, and the monasteries at Pangboche and Tengboche. I met and received a blessing from the reincarnated Abbot of Tengboche. In every sense it was a higher plane. There was much more. The colours, the smells of incense and the smiling, red-robed monks. Spinning prayer wheels. Purchasing prayer flags for home. Buying my first *thangka*, a Buddhist painting. The philosophy, attitudes and iconography of Buddhism and the nature of the people living the Buddhist lifestyle had completely drawn me in, and I obsessed henceforth on the Buddhist homeland in the Himalaya.

4
TO THE START

The journey to the start of my travels in Dolpo was long.

I was born in a place called Wallsend in the north of England. It was quite literally the end of the ancient Roman Hadrian's Wall. My upbringing in 1960s Newcastle upon Tyne wasn't as austere as might be imagined. I went to good schools, and the lure of the magnificent Northumbrian countryside and proximity of the Lake District meant I spent many weekends camping and hiking with Rutherford Grammar School's Outdoor Activities Club. The school even sent me on an Outward Bound Course for a month to the Moray Firth in Scotland when I was sixteen. I learned the ropes of some basic rock-climbing and was taught to kayak and sail. The weather was invariably inclement but it didn't matter. It was away from the city and outside in the wide, open spaces. It was never a simple escape from the city but a genuine desire and hunger for the beauty and grandeur of nature, which has endured.

I breezed through grammar school and my A-levels and, those behind me, I went off to London at the age of eighteen to study medicine at Guy's Hospital. In the 1970s London was still 'swinging' and was a tremendous place to live, and the medical course itself was pure enjoyment. We studied anatomy, physiology and biochemistry for two years then were let loose on the general public to try to glean some clinical skills. One of the highlights of the course was the so-called 'Elective Period', three months when we could study medicine anywhere in the world. Many of the students went to the United States or Australia, but a friend of mine called Iain Nicholson and I went to East Africa. Idi Amin was running and ruining Uganda at the time, and Iain ended up in Tanzania while I spent most of my time in Kenya. I was placed just outside a town called Nyeri, about 150 kilometres north of Nairobi, at a small mission hospital named Tumutumu. There I was able to see cases of malaria, tetanus, rabies, leprosy and so on, the likes of which were never seen in British medical practice. It was a massive learning experience for me. The ride up to Tumutumu from Nairobi in a *matatu*, a local taxi, was alongside eight or nine Kikuyu tribesmen and a few rampant chickens. As we jolted our way along the red murram roads, past exotic jacaranda and flame trees, which were totally new to me, I was half expecting lions and wildebeest to leap out at any second. In the late afternoon of an overcast and muggy day I arrived at my accommodation within the hospital grounds. It was a tiny wooden hut with a bed and a bath and a small table. I'd only been there a few minutes before I heard a knock on the door and was amazed to find standing outside a slim blonde European girl with a distinct Scottish accent. This was Una MacAskill, who was to become a good friend. She even lent me her *piki-piki*, her motorbike. She'd come to invite me for dinner, and I was treated to a meal of local maize and beans by Una and her friend Joyce Burini.

After a night of disturbed and restless sleep from being in a strange new environment, involving as it did some bizarre animal noises, all my apprehensions were dispelled in an instant the next morning when I pulled back the curtains. I had awoken to a crystal clear and completely unobstructed view of Mount Kenya about 30 kilometres to the north-east. The mountain extended right across my window's field of view and it had broad, gently sloping and symmetrical shoulders with the central collection of peaks like a giant fang. And there, on top, to my absolute surprise and delight, was gleaming, brilliant, pure white snow crowning Africa's second-highest mountain, which sits exactly on the equator.

Forty-five years before my stay in Tumutumu, the legendary English climber Eric Shipton was living just outside Nyeri as a farmer on a large coffee estate. His farm was also about 30 kilometres from the 5199-metre-high mountain. He had an uncannily similar experience on his first morning in Nyeri, which he described in his book *Upon That Mountain*. He said, 'The whole northern horizon was filled with a gigantic cone of purple mist.

The cone was capped by a band of cloud. Above this band, utterly detached from the Earth, appeared a pyramid of rock and ice, beautifully proportioned, hard and clear against the sky. The sun, not yet risen, had already touched the peak, throwing ridge and corrie into sharp relief, lighting here and there a sparkling gem of ice.'

A year after his arrival in East Africa, in 1929, Shipton made the first ascent of Nelion, the subsidiary peak of Mount Kenya, with Percy Wyn-Harris. In 1930 he met and teamed up with another coffee planter, called Bill Tilman, and they completed their first climb together on Mount Kenya, making the first traverse of the mountain.

During my East African sojourn I'd occasionally meet up with Iain and we'd go off on safari to places like Amboseli and Serengeti and even Zanzibar. Towards the end of our time in Africa I spent a month in Dar es Salaam delivering babies. I took a ten-hour bus ride from there to meet up with Iain in Arusha in northern Tanzania and together we climbed Kilimanjaro. We were both twenty-one years old and quite fit. This was in 1974 and in the twenty-one years since Everest had first been climbed only thirty-seven people had stood on the summit of the world's highest peak. The whole process of acclimatisation was much less well understood than today. I seem to recall worrying more about getting cold than the issues of altitude. Naturally, being young and with little sense of vulnerability, we just about ran up the lower slopes. Indeed, I wore 'trainers' the whole way as I had no stout boots, and after three days we found ourselves with a bit of a headache at Kibo Hut (4730 metres; 15,520 feet). We had had only tiny amounts to drink in the previous twenty-four hours as the landscape on the mountain's saddle is desert-like, with no running water. From the hut it was an early morning climb up to Gilman's Point (5681 metres; 18,638 feet). It took about five hours to follow the zigzag path up the 900-metre climb. We were now quite unwell but didn't realise how much. We reached the edge of the crater well after sunrise and Iain spent most of his time there vomiting. I counted my pulse by just tallying up the rapid pounding in my head. It was 200 per minute. We started down as soon as we could and within a quarter of an hour felt better and just kept on going all the way back to Arusha.

And that was my first, unpleasant, experience of high altitude. I went on to finish my medical degree and stayed in London. I worked in the emergency department at Guy's for a year, then did a stint in cardiology.

I even became a ship's doctor for a couple of months in the Arctic. However, I ultimately decided on a specialist career in anaesthesia, with its six years of postgraduate study. During that time I was to marry, have a family and, in the end, emigrate to Australia. Apart from a few skiing holidays in the Alps I'd effectively written off the mountains. Sailing seemed, at one time, to be the occupation of my dreams. But I'd always loved the stories of climbing. Those early explorers' tales; Mallory and Irvine, Shipton and Tilman, Heinrich Harrer in *The White Spider*, Bonington's *Everest, the Hard Way*. These were genuine adventures. Real men battling the elements and recounting their tales, invariably with eloquence, humour and passion.

My first trip to Nepal and Everest Base Camp in 2004 was conceived in a curry restaurant in Lancaster with my cousin Phil Crozier. In the English summer of 2003 my wife, Paula, and myself had a trip to catch up with family and friends back in the UK. Phil and I had grown up together in Newcastle, but I hadn't seen him for many years and we had a lot of catching up to do. We settled into the gaudily decorated Indian restaurant which looked out, incongruously, onto the splendid floodlit gateway of ancient Lancaster Castle. Lubricated with Tiger beers, we talked the talk.

'So how are the Wainwrights going?' I asked.

'Almost finished them, then I can start doing them again,' said Phil of the 214 Lakeland Fells documented in the famous Alfred Wainwright series *A Pictorial Guide to the Lakeland Fells*. 'I get up to the Lakes as often as I can. It's my back garden. I was up at Reghed a couple of weeks back,' he continued.

I knew of Reghed. It was an exhibition centre in Cumbria, which was running, at that time, a display of the artefacts found on the body of George Mallory on Everest a few years earlier.

'I'd love to go there,' I said. 'We won't manage it this trip, but I've read all the books about Mallory and how they found him. It's a great story.'

'I've got loads of books on Everest. I even got some of them signed by Chris Bonington and Doug Scott at a lecture not so long ago,' said Phil.

'Oh wow! I'm jealous. I bought *Everest, the Hard Way* the week it came out, in 1976.' I knew the year because I'd just qualified and was working as a 'houseman' on the English south coast at the time. I hadn't realised that Phil was such a Himalayan enthusiast.

'In fact,' said Phil, 'I'm thinking of doing the trip to Everest Base Camp next year.'

Whoa! Without a second thought I said, 'Oh that would be sensational. I'll come with you.' I turned to Paula. 'What do you think? Would you mind if I went?'

'Of course not. I think it's a great idea,' she said.

And so the game was afoot. I'd told Phil of my discomfort on Kilimanjaro, but by then we knew a little more about the acclimatisation process. We'd be alright, wouldn't we?

And, sure enough, we were.

The trek we planned and enthused about that night was the beginning of a love affair with the mountains in all their guises – friendly, treacherous, agonisingly beautiful, dangerous, exhausting, even deadly, but constantly enticing and beckoning – my femmes fatales of rock and snow.

In the years after my first Himalayan trek I travelled time and time again to Nepal, Tibet, India, Bhutan, Pakistan, even Borneo and New Zealand, trying to achieve greater highs on the mountain but, in reality, benefiting more from meeting people and delving into their culture, and I was especially enjoying gaining a deeper knowledge of the Buddhist societies.

The Buddhist ideals had become quite special, indeed useful, to me and to be able to travel and absorb the major historical sites was scarcely credible. However, one could not have a developing interest in Buddhism without becoming fully aware of the plight of the Tibetan people and the suppression of their culture and religion. I resolved to travel to Tibet and see it for myself. In 2006 I arranged a trek to see the north side of Everest and to attempt a climb of Lhakpa Ri, a 7000-metre mountain near Everest.

I am still incredulous knowing that I've been to the Tibetan plateau and its fringe of Himalayan giants. That I've stood on the rooftop of the Potala Palace in Lhasa, seen the Jowo statue in the Jokhang, and admired the four-storey high, gold-encased statue of Buddha at Tashilhunpo Monastery in Shigatse. Despite the magnificence of these buildings and objects, it's the more personal, sometimes tragic, stories that linger in my memory more than the tourist destinations.

5

INTO TIBET

In 2006 China was preparing for the Beijing Olympic Games, due to be held in August 2008. In September of 2006 I trekked to the Advanced Base Camp on Everest's north side and enjoyed the thin air at 6400 metres while revelling in the unbeatable views of the North Face, the North Col, the second step and the summit of Chomolungma itself. On our way there we'd flown into Lhasa and, by necessity, spent a few days acclimatising.

Lhasa sits at 3650 metres and simply climbing the hotel stairs or bending over to tie shoelaces is instantly exhausting. By the bedside in the hotel was a coin-operated oxygen concentrator and mask. Our guide was a Tibetan man in his early thirties called Sonam. His English was excellent as he'd been brought up in Dharamsala and educated at the Tibetan Children's Village. He'd been desperately keen to trace his family back in Tibet and was thrilled, a few years before, to hear from the Tibetan authorities that they'd found his mother. To meet up with her all he had to do was come to Lhasa. This was, of course, straightforward entrapment. He arrived in Lhasa and was promptly arrested. There was no mother to be reunited with. He was held in prison for four months. He was beaten up and his right leg was broken. Time after time they asked him questions about the Dalai Lama. Had he met him? How often did he see him? What was the Dalai Lama's daily routine? He had little to add to what the Chinese already knew. Once released from prison he realised that his excellent English-speaking skills placed him in a good position to become a guide and he decided to stay in Tibet.

Our trip, on our second day in Lhasa, to visit the Potala Palace was certainly marred by the fact that our friend and guide wasn't allowed to enter the building with us. Native Tibetans simply weren't allowed into the Potala. Sonam had to walk around and meet us at the exit.

The following day we went to the large monastery at Drepung, in a valley to the north-west of Lhasa. This used to be home to over 7000 monks – and at times 10,000. At the time of our visit there were fewer than 500. The monastery was spectacular in both situation and design. Prayer wheels, carved mantras and fluttering prayer flags were everywhere. We visited the soot-stained kitchens with massive cauldrons capable of boiling enough rice for the thousands of residents. Our new friend, our Tibetan guide, was allowed in this time and he gave us a good tour. He took us, at one point, up to the abbot's quarters. It was a large room with an altar. In the centre of the quarters a tall freestanding basin was, in fact, a butter lamp filled with molten yak butter, with a dozen flickering wicks kept burning at all times. Doors led off to the sleeping quarters and to a bathroom. Quietly, in a corner, Sonam told me the story of the abbot. Drepung had always been looked upon by the Chinese as a wellspring of dissent and unrest. About eighteen months before our visit, some intolerable limit of acceptable behaviour had been reached and an example had to be made. The abbot was locked into his bathroom and not allowed out. It took over six weeks for him to die of starvation. I was appalled and incredulous but assured that this had really happened and in the most recent past. A week later, when we'd reached Base Camp, we had another young Tibetan guide. This fellow had been a monk until he was turned out of his monastery. I asked him about Drepung and he had no hesitation in confirming the authenticity of the story of the abbot's death.

On our overland drive from Lhasa to the Rongbuk Valley near Everest we stopped at Shigatse and Gyantse, both breathtakingly beautiful old religious centres. Our visit to Tashilhunpo Monastery in Shigatse, the traditional seat of the Panchen Lama, coincided with what was clearly a large ceremony. Monks were filing into the main *gompa*, leaving a pile of red felt boots outside. A crowd of onlookers was gathering and after a short time a group of shiny black limousines pulled up. A traditional parasol was taken over to the lead car and clearly someone of importance was being escorted out. A tall pale young man was wearing a traditional high and curved yellow hat and red robes. Our guide told us it was the Panchen Lama.

In January 1989 the tenth Panchen Lama died in Shigatse at the age of fifty-one, from an apparent heart attack. As a young man he'd visited Beijing with the Dalai Lama. Later, at the age of twenty-six and following the Chinese invasion, he underwent public humiliation and imprisonment. After his 'rehabilitation', over many years, he was released, and in 1989 he was allowed to return to Tashilhunpo to officiate at the reinterment of the bones of the previous Panchen Lamas, which had been disturbed during the Chinese destruction of the monastery in 1959. In somewhat questionable circumstances he died five days after delivering a speech highly critical of the Chinese.

In keeping with tradition, enough time had to pass to allow for the Panchen Lama's reincarnation to be born and subsequently recognised. This happened in 1995, when six-year-old Gedhun Choekyi Nyima was discovered in a place called Lhari in the north-east of the so-called 'Tibet Autonomous Region' of China. His selection was confirmed on 14 May 1995 by the Dalai Lama. On 17 May the young boy and his family were spirited away by the Chinese authorities and have not been seen or heard from since – now well over twenty years. Six months later the Chinese stated that they had found a young boy in Lhari called Gyaltsen Norbu and he was duly installed as the eleventh Panchen Lama. He lived in Beijing and made only infrequent appearances there as a young monk.

The Dalai Lama and the Panchen Lama are referred to as the sun and moon of Tibetan Buddhism. Traditionally they must mutually recognise each other's reincarnations, so there is clearly potential for control by the Chinese when the current Dalai Lama dies.

On that day in 2006 at Tashilhunpo I was watching the sixteen-year-old puppet Panchen Lama, Gyaltsen Norbu, making one of his first public outings in his official capacity. I was concerned about his possible reception. I thought there might be some public protest or jeering, until I realised that a large proportion of the crowd around me, those in the dark Western-style business suits, were the 'heavies' of the Chinese police.

I said to our guide, 'But this is the fake Panchen Lama!'

'Yes,' he replied. 'He is the Chinese Panchen Lama.'

'But what do the people think? They must disapprove of him.'

Sonam said, 'He is in a difficult situation. They feel compassion for him.'

I felt a little humbled. This was a basic lesson in Buddhism. Of course one should feel sorry for him. But karma is inherent in all these issues, and it may be that his appointment might even work for the long-term good of Buddhism in Tibet. In spite of what the authorities told them to believe, the Tibetan people would never accept that this was the real Panchen Lama, but they also would never wish this incumbent any personal harm.

A few days later, as we entered the valley leading to the North Face of Everest, we turned a corner and there was the Rongbuk Monastery. Founded in 1902 and sitting at an altitude of 4980 metres (16,340 feet) this was a fully functioning entity when the early climbing expeditions met the head lama in the 1920s. It was destroyed by the Chinese in 1974 but rebuilding started in the 1980s. I was pleased to see the prayer flags flying and monks and nuns busy bringing in the small harvest. Base Camp was a couple of hours' walk further up the valley, with Everest gleaming white in the afternoon sun, still 20 kilometres away but massive and always drawing the eye. It was pleasurable beyond description to be able to identify features known from the climbing tales. The Yellow Band, the First, Second and Third Steps, the Norton Couloir, the Hornbein Couloir, the Pinnacles, the North-East Ridge. We camped on the same small area of grass below the terminal moraine that Bruce, Norton, Somervell, Finch, Mallory and Irvine had occupied back in the 1920s as their base camp.

The day before we started trekking higher, one of the monks from Rongbuk came up to our camp and performed a *puja*, a prayer ritual and blessing for safety and success on the mountain. We stacked our climbing gear around a *chorten* made of rocks from the rubble on the glacier. Offerings were placed on the makeshift altar – water, rice and even some beer. The monk chanted for a good ten minutes before we were asked to bow three times then throw a handful of *tsampa*, barley flour, into the air, liberally covering each other.

Despite the lama's best efforts, our walk up the East Rongbuk Glacier and attempt to climb the 7000-metre-high Lhakpa Ri was sadly curtailed by bad weather.

*

I returned to the Rongbuk the following year, in September 2007, and this time my cousin Phil joined me. We were heading up to Advanced Base

Camp with a plan to climb Lhakpa Ri, the peak opposite Everest that is 7045 metres (23,113 feet) high. Chinese plans were even further advanced for the Olympics due to take place in Beijing the following August. We paid another visit to Drepung and Sera and the Potala and Jokhang. All along the tourist route from Lhasa to Everest Base Camp the show was being finely tuned and polished so that visitors would see Tibet at its 'best'.

Phil and I took the opportunity to go 'off-piste' when our group spent a night at old Shegar, the site of the famous 'Shegar Dzong' (Tibetan: *Shel-khar* – White Crystal Mountain). The fortifications and monastery buildings winding up the steep rocky mountain and reaching to its summit were a highlight of photographs taken by the Everest expeditions of 1920, '22 and '24. The black and white photographs, some then hand coloured, showed the whitewashed buildings of the monastery, established in 1266, and home to 300 monks. In the 1960s, during the so-called 'cultural revolution' the People's Liberation Army turned their guns on it, and it was completely destroyed.

Phil and I walked through the town and started to climb up through the ruins. We were met by a young monk who encouraged us to enter what was left of the *gompa*. A substantial courtyard was festooned with hundreds of prayer flags but the building itself was looking tired. The prayer wheels were all dirty, the paint coming off after many thousands of rotations. The pair of curtains hanging over the main door of the *gompa* was so filthy it was hard to recognise the symbols embroidered on them. The left-side curtain was barely hanging on its top corners. Inside, a couple of light bulbs were faintly burning. There were no butter lamps lit. There were none of the usual butter carvings (*torma*), or offerings of food, drink or money on the altar. All the way down the right side of the *gompa* the roof was unrepaired and gaping a metre wide. This monastery was not on the itinerary for Olympic visitors and was being ignored, to continue its inexorable decay.

The road up to Base Camp was much improved and the Rongbuk community was apparently thriving, as the monks and nuns were once again bringing in the meagre harvest from the tiny fields around the monastery. The prayer flags adorned the white *chorten* with Everest's North Face as its backdrop. However, the Chinese preparations had seen fit to include building a large blockhouse for the Chinese police and army at Base Camp, right next to the traditional grassy campsite.

Our climb up the East Rongbuk Glacier was as beautiful as before, with the massive ice pinnacles, known as *penitentes*, and the ever-dominating North Face of Everest. We had a fall of fresh snow and at our Advanced Base Camp campsite were enveloped in a cloud of powder snow in the tail end of a massive avalanche off the northern flanks of Changtse. Yet again, conditions wouldn't allow us to get up Lhakpa Ri. After two nights at Advanced Base Camp (6400 metres; 21,000 feet) we retraced our steps down to the lower Base Camp and embarked on the road trip along the new highway to Kathmandu.

In 2008, a year later and just before the Olympics began, I was dismayed to read that it was only four weeks after our visit to Drepung in the autumn of the previous year that some of the monks had taken part in a protest. They were whitewashing the walls of the Dalai Lama's old residence at Drepung but it was on the exact day that His Holiness was being awarded the Congressional Gold Medal in Washington. The paint job was interpreted as showing support for the Dalai Lama, and several monks were arrested. Then, a few months later, on 10 March 2008, it was the forty-ninth anniversary of the Tibetan uprising in 1959. That was the occasion when the Dalai Lama fled to India and there was much civil unrest and thousands killed by the People's Liberation Army in Lhasa. On this anniversary in 2008, three hundred monks from Drepung tried to march into Lhasa in a peaceful protest. This was simply too provocative so close to the showcase Olympic Games. Things got out of control. It was said at least twenty-two people died. Many were arrested. Forty-two of the monks were sentenced to between two and fifteen years' imprisonment and Drepung Monastery was essentially closed down for several months.

6
TIBET ONCE MORE

2010 saw cousin Phil and myself join my friend Joe Bonington's trek to Tilicho Lake in Nepal. This was to celebrate the fiftieth anniversary of Joe's father's first ascent of Annapurna II (7937 metres; 26,040 feet). Indeed, Joe's father, Chris Bonington, was trekking with us at a sprightly seventy-five years of age.

Chris was an excellent raconteur and loved regaling us with stories of his expeditions. His memory of the Annapurna II ascent in 1960 was very clear and at their old expedition Base Camp he told us of his arrival at that very spot fifty years earlier: 'And when we got to Manang the people from there made it absolutely clear to us that Gurung porters were not welcome and something really nasty would happen to them if they were there for another twenty-four hours. They, the Gurung, were Bhotias. At Manang there was not a single piece of Western clothing. They were all dressed in their Tibetan boots and animal skins. They very rarely washed. The women did but the men didn't. And then on the approach we came from Manang. We came up the other side of the river and made a crossing a bit higher up, as it was March and this place would have been under deep snow. But our lady porters carried all the way up to Advanced Base for us. I have a photo of a long line of the women, in their Tibetan boots, in knee-deep snow, going up that ridge there,' he said, pointing just above us. 'And something one of you said reminded me that one of the women had a baby at her breast sleeping and she, for the money, was taking a double load, so she was carrying about fifty kilograms.'

We had followed the trail of the Annapurna Circuit, and when we got to the old town of Manang Phil and I went off exploring. Manang appeared to have an old half and a new half. In the middle of town was the *gompa*, and we could hear chanting from within. We went to the entrance and a full ceremony was underway. Two rows of monks in their red robes faced each other and there was a caterwauling of noise, voices, the sound of drums and trumpets, pouring out between the highly decorated doors. The air was smoky with burning incense, the smell pungent and rich. We stood, spellbound, until a monk smiled at us and beckoned us inside. He came over grinning and, in excellent English, explained that he was the abbot and that this was the second day of funeral ceremonies for a venerable old monk who'd just died, and would we like a cup of butter tea? We stayed for almost an hour absorbing the atmosphere and took photographs and spoke to some of those involved. It was a special moment, which we savoured, to be involved in something as vibrant and mysterious as that ceremony. This part of Nepal, along with Mustang and Dolpo further west, was almost purely Tibetan Buddhist in its customs and religion and had been for centuries.

*

In 2011 I continued my personal journey through Himalayan Buddhism by trekking in Bhutan. I'd heard of their concept of measuring 'Gross National Happiness' and the new young fifth king seemed keen to induce the right sort of modernisation in his country. Joe Bonington had organised another trek and he was more than happy to have a doctor along, just in case. Chris was also on this trip, and it was marvellous to have this iconic and compelling storyteller to regale us with tales of mountaineering derring-do over our dhal in the evenings. The team flew from Kathmandu to Paro and the trek took us north, just to the east of Mount Chomolhari. This was beautiful countryside, the mountains not as high or austere as further west, but still snow-covered and spectacular. The trek was not short of Buddhist clarity for me, and especially so when we desperately needed help. One of our trekkers, a delightful Canadian lady called Mary Thomas, was going a bit slowly during the morning of day four of the trek. We'd reached about 3800 metres and stopped for lunch in a narrow valley just above the tree line. After lunch, which was a snack and hot drink carried on the friendly 'tea horse', Joe and I decided we'd hang back and keep an eye on Mary. Her friend Carolyn Bridgman and Tenzin, one of our porters, accompanied us as the main party went on ahead. In the early afternoon we'd only gone a few hundred metres when it was clear that all was not well.

'How you doing, Mary?' I asked.

'Oh. I'm so tired. I can hardly keep my eyes open.'

'Don't worry. Just take your time. We're with you,' said Joe.

Mary then staggered a little, so Tenzin helped support her. She took a few more steps and vomited up her lunch. She was walking no further. We laid her down on some of our gear by the side of the trail.

'We need help, Joe. Better let the guides up front know, and they should bring back the medical kit,' I said.

Joe and Tenzin set off running to catch up with the others. I checked Mary's pulse and blood pressure and watched her breathing and pupil size. I was realising that she had developed a life-threatening high-altitude cerebral oedema. About forty-five minutes after she had initially collapsed, Joe was back, out of breath, saying that the medical equipment and Sonam, our head guide, were on their way. She was, by now, more deeply unconscious.

I said, 'Joe. She's got cerebral oedema. Grab her arm round here. You're my tourniquet.'

I found a vein and injected some Dexamethasone, a potent steroid drug. I also administered some anti-emetic drug to help discourage further vomiting.

The sun slipped below the mountains and the temperature quickly started to drop. We were quite exposed at almost 4000 metres, and I thought Mary may well die. Suddenly, out of the near darkness, a man and a young girl miraculously appeared with a flask of tea and some biscuits. The girl had a small baby on her back. More people arrived. Our Bhutanese guide, Sonam, had spoken to the headman of a nearby village and help had been despatched. The local families, yak herders and nomads, helped us carry our patient a short way uphill into a family's hut, where we could all shelter. Despite the drugs Mary threw up down the back of our rescuer. I was able to give her more medication and we put her into the inflatable pressure chamber, a Gamow bag, that we carried for exactly this type of emergency. Joe, Sonam, Tenzin and I took turns pumping the foot pump all night to marginally improve the air pressure for her. A poignant moment during that long night was when Carolyn sat by her comatose friend – incarcerated as Mary was in the red vinyl cylinder – and, in the hope that she might hear and appreciate the dark humour, read out loud 'The Cremation of Sam McGee'. The poem includes the apt lines:

> It's the cursèd cold, and it's got right hold till I'm
> chilled clean through to the bone.
> Yet 'tain't being dead—it's my awful dread of the
> icy grave that pains;
> So I want you to swear that, foul or fair, you'll
> cremate my last remains.

and:

> The Northern Lights have seen queer sights
> But the queerest they ever did see
> Was that night on the marge of Lake Lebarge
> I cremated Sam McGee.

But the words of Robert W. Service were destined to be in no way prophetic, for by next morning Mary was awake, albeit pale and weak and still unable to walk. The local terrain was such that carrying her out was also impossible. The Indian Army, contacted by satellite phone, was able to pick her up by helicopter the next day, and she was flown to hospital in the capital city of Thimphu.

For two nights we had been sheltered by a young Bhutanese family and they gave what little they had to help us. This was again a rather humbling situation. We were immensely grateful, and we made sure that when we left we were generous with our thanks and donations of food and money. However, the best 'thank you' to them was when Mary, who'd so nearly succumbed to the altitude, and her friend Carolyn, made sure that as soon as possible afterwards they were given a new wood-burning stove via an organisation called the Himalayan Stove Project. Their leaky old stove, brought over from Tibet, had constantly filled their single-room abode with dense acrid smoke and fumes, enough to make everyone cough and become red-eyed.

We were reunited with a fully recovered Mary at the end of our trek, at a town near Thimphu, and later we all spent a splendid day climbing up to the famous Taktsang Monastery, 'Tiger's Nest', perched high on the cliffs above Paro, an iconic and justifiably famous Buddhist site.

Then, early in 2012, it was time to visit Tibet once more. This third trip of mine into Tibet was another attempt at climbing Lhakpa Ri, and with a climb up to the North Col of Everest itself thrown in. This time our group of three, a British father and son and myself, planned to drive up to Base Camp and tag onto a group led by Canadian climber Chris Szymiec. Chris's group was composed of four British climbers and a group of four young Swedes in their late twenties, all attempting to summit Everest.

After a couple of days in Kathmandu organising the paperwork, it was time for 'the off'. A minibus was to take us and our guide, Mingma Gyabu Sherpa, up to the Chinese border at the 'Friendship Bridge'. Mingma was a twenty-three-year-old sherpa who was only slightly higher than my shoulder, and I'm only 170 centimetres. Yet, Mingma had already climbed Everest and was now heading up there for his second time. (Known also as Mingma David Sherpa, he would later become well known as the deputy to Nirmal Purja, Nims Dai, when they and their team of sherpas climbed all fourteen of the 8000-metre peaks in record time, Mingma becoming the youngest person to do so.)

We left after breakfast from Hotel Manaslu, and it was good to be on our way at last. Five minutes later, just around the corner, we pulled into the open block of land opposite the Malla Hotel. We sat there for a while and after about forty minutes a car pulled up and more passengers climbed aboard our minibus. Two were Nepalese guides and the others, their two climbing clients. One was a huge man from Mongolia who spoke no English but, we were told, was a well-known professional wrestler in his home country. The other was clearly a European fellow, who looked about forty. As soon as the bus pulled away, he came and sat next to me and introduced himself.

'Hello, my name is Kwan.'

It sounded unlikely, so I repeated, 'Kwan?'

'No,' he said. 'Khu-wan.'

'Spell it?'

'J-U-A-N.'

'Ah, Whaan.'

'Yes, Kwan.'

And so we began our conversation. Juan Jose 'Polo' Carbayo was from Spain and was also a doctor. He'd been working in the Canary Islands and planned to climb Everest. Juan was absolutely charming. His English was very good. He had greying hair, a ready smile and more than a passing resemblance to actor George Clooney. Over the next few days we had long conversations and even developed plans to trek or climb in New Zealand in the near future.

The trail took us from the Nepalese border at 2300 metres (7545 feet), across the Friendship Bridge with its expressionless Chinese border guards, up to the Tibetan town of Zhangmu. We were confronted there by customs officials who rifled through our luggage. My medical kit, with its serious drugs, needles and syringes, was completely ignored. My handful of books was examined. My *Lonely Planet Guide to Tibet* was singled out. Free of all 'provocative' photographs, the official simply turned to 'D' in the index, saw 'Dalai Lama', showed his colleague and threw the book in a bin. 'Not allowed,' he said by way of explanation. We were permitted to carry on and were driven to a town called Nyalam (3750 metres; 12,300 feet). We had time to do a training walk during an acclimatisation day next day and got our first views of the snow-covered Himalaya. We were all doing well, and Juan and his Mongolian co-traveller were clearly Everest fit.

The next stop was at a caravanserai-style building in the town of Tingri. We were now getting close. Most of the pre-war expeditions to Everest had stayed here. The town has unparalleled views of Cho Oyu and, from a hill on the edge of the settlement, the first glimpse of Everest itself.

The final day's drive got us to the start of the Rongbuk Valley. As the truck turned the corner of the narrow gorge leading into Rongbuk that April 2012, it was clear that things had changed. Almost four years after the Beijing Olympics, the Rongbuk Monastery was completely silent. There were no prayer flags flying and no monks to be seen. The Olympic posturing was over.

We drove right up to the small village of tents spread out on the glacial moraine that composed the base camp for that season's climbing parties. Chris Szymiec was in the mess tent with the rest of his group, who were a week ahead of us. They were all struggling to adapt their oxygen masks so the expiratory valves wouldn't freeze up. The expedition *sirdar*, or chief guide, was a tough-looking sherpa with a moustache called Dorje Khatri. Dorje was a cousin of our guide Mingma and he very much took over looking after us. Dorje was charming. His English was good, and nothing was too much trouble. He was always on the move and appeared to have limitless energy. He smiled a lot.

Juan and his small group were in a different part of Base Camp, but we occasionally had tea together in our mess tent. Over a few days everyone slowly acclimatised and gradually headed up to the Advanced Base Camp (ABC) at 6400 metres (21,000 feet).

The East Rongbuk Glacier was free of loose snow and the way up to Lhakpa Ri was sheer blue ice and rock. No one was going up there. The other prize, of reaching 7000 metres on the North Col, was in sight. Dorje took us from ABC up towards the col on a day walk to its base. The going was slow, and at a place called Crampon Point we donned our crampons and continued towards the base of the giant 1000-foot wall of ice that led up to the col. The teams of sherpas carrying loads were ant-like on the pure white face. It was a memorably beautiful day. We reached the base of the ice wall at 6700 metres (22,000 feet) and, feeling good, looked forward to the climb up the next day.

On our return to our tents a message had come through. A storm was coming. Everyone was to leave next morning for Base Camp. The climb was over. Mingma volunteered to stay in ABC while the rest of us headed down.

I was able to give Juan a wave goodbye and, accompanied by Dorje Khatri, I headed back down to Base Camp.

The journey home from Everest involved a drive to Lhasa and a flight back to Kathmandu. I'd been to Lhasa on two previous occasions and was smitten by the place. The Chinese seem intent on building brutalist concrete monstrosities everywhere but to see the Potala Palace rising imposingly above the modern squalor is deeply moving. The Jokhang Temple is awe-inspiring in a different, more spiritual, way. To circumambulate the Barkhor is both a pleasure and a privilege, as well as huge entertainment. The people in their costumes from all over Tibet mingle with Chinese tourists and a few Europeans and stare at each other as though viewing aliens. I'm sure we Westerners were the outstandingly strange, weirdly dressed people attracting the longest gazes.

The Barkhor pilgrim circuit was busy as ever, but the police and army presence was disturbingly enormous. Up until that time there had been almost one hundred self-immolations. Young Tibetans would douse themselves in fuel and burn themselves to death in protest at Chinese rule. That could not be allowed to happen around the Jokhang. Rooftops were full of observers with telescopes, cameras and guns. Squads of troops were waiting, ready, one or two streets behind the Barkhor. Besides their guns and clubs, the patrolling groups of military were carrying brooms, blankets and fire extinguishers. They marched anti-clockwise, counter to the general flow of the pilgrim crowd, in squads of five or six, and would break up any group of more than three young men. I was able to sneak a few photos of the oppression with a view to sending them on to the outside world.

On my return to Australia I followed the Everest news avidly. Summits were expected, as usual, around 20 May, and naturally I wanted to see how my friends were doing on the main climb. Word filtered through on the internet. Chris and two of the Englishmen had summitted. Of my four Swedish friends, Jesper, Thomas and Lars had stopped at the second step, but Alex had reached the top. Then came news of a death. I read on expecting the worst and there was Juan's name:

> A Spanish mountaineer, Juan José Polo Carbayo, died at the weekend as he was descending the Tibetan side of Everest after conquering the highest summit in the world. 'Extreme exhaustion was the most likely cause of death', said Hari Parjauli of the Nepal-based company Himalayan Guides, that organised the expedition, adding that 43-year-old Carbayo died on Saturday after becoming detached from the rest of the group that made it to the top.

Chris Szymiec had seen his body high on the mountain and had the unenviable task of clearing out his tent and sending his belongings back to his family.

Juan's corpse was left at about 8300 metres, where it will remain. I was filled with sadness at the news and reminisced how we had planned a climbing trip to New Zealand.

*

My winter trip to Ladakh in 2013, when we'd seen the snow leopard tracks, involved walking about 100 kilometres each way along the ice of the frozen Zanskar River. It was the winter highway for the locals, and we met many families travelling both directions between Leh and the Zanskar region. Invariably a meeting involved smiles and reciprocal shouts of *julley*, the Ladakhi greeting, or *namaste* – and even the occasional *tashi delek*. The turn around point of our trip into the Zanskar region was Padum, where we could visit Karsha Gompa. We first saw this floating ethereally above the river, whose valley was filled with mist. The buildings nestling higher and higher into the snow-covered mountainside. As we walked up the steep alleys of the monastery, an amplified mantra, 'Om Mane Padme Hum', was belting out of a loudspeaker system. As usual the monks were friendly and keen to chat. One of the older monks explained that they were doing a non-stop recitation 'Om Mane Padme Hum' until they reached one million repetitions. They had been going for some six weeks and were close to 900,000. The end was in sight, with much good karma assured for all those involved.

The life for the people of Ladakh was stable and relatively secure. Being part of India, they lived in a democracy, with reasonable access to education and health care. Their religious freedom was respected. Not so just over the border in Tibet.

In spite of the common level of knowledge of the predicament and suffering of the Tibetans in the 'Tibet Autonomous Region', I was taken aback, indeed shocked, at seeing it firsthand. The customs and religion, even the language, of native Tibetans are severely restricted in their own homeland. The Chinese are fond of telling the world (in the words of their foreign ministry, 2007) that 'Since its peaceful liberation in 1951, Tibet has undergone profound social changes, including democratic reform, and opening up, and has achieved remarkable social and economic progress.' They say they delivered the Tibetan people from serfdom and slavery under 'the Dalai clique'.

My clear view is that the world of the 1950s was different and more simple, in every conceivable way, in every country worldwide. After all, we are talking about a time more than sixty years ago. Most nations have made massive progress in the last sixty-five years, without having been invaded or 'liberated'. The young Dalai Lama was someone who was keen to engage with the modern world and was already indicating his plans to lift Tibet into a more progressive era. Communications with India, the United Kingdom and beyond were his first step. Then China, quite simply, invaded and vanquished much of Tibet's culture and society. Some people asked the Dalai Lama if it was acceptable, in light of the Chinese occupation, for Western tourists to go to Tibet, and he replied, 'Go to Tibet and see many places, as much as you can; then tell the world.'

I'd seen modern-day Tibet. It was China. I'd also seen Nepal, Bhutan and Ladakh. These were places grounded in the current era of internet and communications, yet they retained their historical identity and religious freedoms and continue to develop. Would Tibet now be like these enclaves of Tibetan Buddhist culture if it had been allowed to develop at its own pace?

It was my hope that Dolpo would show me another aspect of how things might have been in Tibet. Every group of people, wherever they are in the world, will naturally seek progress and undergo change. For most of us in the West that is an ever-accelerating process. Would Dolpo be mired in history as a stagnant backwater, or would the monks be rushing around talking into their iPhones like people in India?

More selfishly, would I see a snow leopard? By way of insurance, I took with me a stuffed toy baby snow leopard I'd purchased from the Snow Leopard Trust. That way I'd be guaranteed to have a snow leopard in at least some of my photographs!

It was time to journey into Dolpo.

7
DOLPO

In the beginning there was a great ocean covering the land of Tibet. According to myth the gods sent wind and dust to create the land. In another version, they cut channels through the mountains and the sea drained away, leaving the Tibetan plateau.

The origin of the Tibetan people themselves is described in a document known as the 'Mani Kabum', which is attributed to King Songtsen Gampo. The story is of a *rakshasi*, or ogress. The male *rakshasa* was a hideous flesh-eating monster but the *rakshasi* was beautiful and used her feminine guile to get her way. A monkey ventured into the land of Tibet and the ogress tempted him into marriage. In different versions of the story, the monkey, known as Pha Trelgen, 'Father Old Monkey', was a manifestation of Avalokiteshvara, or Chenrezig, the god of compassion. The ogress was a manifestation of the goddess Tara, or Jetsun Dolma. Their marriage took place at Tsetang in the Yarlung Valley south-east of Lhasa. Even now there is a cave there which is said to be the birthplace of the Tibetan people. The ogress gave birth to six offspring, who became the founders of the main six groups or tribes of Tibetans.

I suspect that Tibetans are rather pleased with the modern scientific findings that the Tibetan plateau was once, back in Cretaceous times, deep below the Tethys Sea, resulting in the fossilised clam shells we can currently find high on Everest. They must also be happy that Darwin himself agreed with them, in his theory of evolution, that we all came from 'monkeys'.

Modern science has now gone a long way towards describing the true nature of how the Tibetan plateau and the Himalaya were populated. Since the complete mapping of the human genome was fulfilled in 2003, it has been possible to study the genetic differences between groups and individuals. It would seem that there were people living on the Tibetan plateau 30,000 years ago and these are genetically similar to the present-day Sherpa population. At the average altitude of the Tibetan plateau, the amount of available oxygen level, its 'partial pressure', is only 60 per cent of the sea level value. Over the last 3000 to 4000 years, there has been an assimilation of Han Chinese migrating from lower altitudes, and over generations the positive mutations, which are adaptations to high-altitude living, have been incorporated across the whole Tibetan population. This process is known as 'selective enrichment' and has resulted in a higher survival rate of newborns at high altitude, as well as a better metabolic response to low oxygen levels and an absence of chronic mountain sickness. Indeed, some thirty or more genetic variations with a beneficial effect for living at high altitude have been shown to have arisen in the last 4000 years. This was faster than scientists had previously thought possible and led the usually conservative scientific community to make the joke that the Tibetans are clearly 'highly evolved'!

Early historical documents from Tibet refer to an ancient culture in the kingdom of Zhangzhung (Shang Shung), which lay in the western and north-western part of the plateau. Certainly, neolithic and iron-age artefacts have been found in the Chang Tang and the far west of Tibet. The capital city of Zhangzhung was said to be near Mount Kailash. To the citizens of this area is attributed the rise of the Bon religion, with its story of an ancient Buddha-like character called Tonpa Shenrab Miwoche, the founder of Bon, who visited some 18,000 years ago from the mystical land of Shambala.

In the Yarlung Valley of Tibet, south of what is now Lhasa, a culture arose led by a series of kings, starting with Nyatri Tsenpo about 127 BCE. The land became known as Bod, the name by which Tibetans know Tibet. The thirty-second king in the line was born in 617 CE and was the famous Songtsen Gampo. At the age of thirteen he ascended the throne and sought to forge alliances with Nepal and China by marrying a princess from each. He established a new capital of Bod in Rasa, later known as Lhasa. A fortress was built on the red hill which later became the Potala. He established the Ramoche and Jokhang temples to house the statues of Buddha brought to Tibet by his princesses. Songtsen Gampo had plans for Tibet. Besides introducing Buddhism, he decreed that there should be a form of script developed for scholars to utilise. He was also expansionist and was most likely responsible for the conquest of the more westerly Zhangzhung.

It was at this juncture, in the late seventh and eighth centuries, that Bon and Buddhism met and confronted each other in the western Himalayan region. The Indian version of Buddhism, now long gone even from India, was able to incorporate many of the shamanistic and animistic aspects of Bon, with the resultant pantheon of deities we see in Tibetan Mahayana Buddhism. The Vajrayana, or Tantric, version of Buddhism was imported to Tibet around 760 CE, when the Guru Rinpoche, Padmasambhava, was invited to establish the Nyingma tradition by the thirty-eighth king, Trisong Detsen.

It is postulated that when the conquest of Zhangzhung took place, and its populace incorporated into a greater Tibet, many of its people fled to the south and into the hidden valleys of the Himalaya. These became enclaves of tradition and especially of the Bon religion. These isolated valleys later gave rise to the Tibetan stories of *beyuls*, as advocated by Padmasambhava – 'in the future when there will be warfare, strife, and difficult circumstances in the world, good people and dharma practitioners should travel to "Beyuls" or hidden valleys situated south of the Tibetan Himalayan range for refuge'. Dolpo, because of its geographical isolation, is such an enclave and it's around this time, the eighth century, that there was the first mention of Dolpo in the Tibetan records.

The Heart of the World: A Journey to Tibet's Lost Paradise was written by Ian Baker and published in 2004. It describes his many journeys in the 1980s and '90s to little-explored regions of far eastern Tibet, where the Yarlung-Tsangpo River, having flowed from Mount Kailash and past Lhasa, undertakes an enormous curve north and then radically south to plummet through an unknown, untravelled gorge to emerge 3300 metres (11,000 feet) lower, as the Brahmaputra River in Assam. Tibetan legend has it that in this gorge is the entrance to the most important of the *beyuls*, Beyul Pemako, the 'Hidden Land Arrayed like a Lotus'. Padmasambhava described it as the greatest of all the hidden lands, a 'celestial realm on earth'.

The Yarlung dynasty ended in the 840s with the death of the king Langdarma at the hands of the monk Lhalung Palgyi Dorje. Langdarma was anti-Buddhist and pro-Bon and had aggressively suppressed Buddhists in his kingdom. Palgyi Dorje famously shot the king with an arrow, fleeing on a white horse coloured black with charcoal. By swimming through a river and reversing his black cloak, he was transformed into a white-cloaked rider on his now white horse and evaded his pursuers.

In the ensuing power vacuum and during the tenth century, the kingdom of Guge arose in far western Tibet. It extended as far as Kailash to the east and Zanskar to its south. It is almost certainly the case that Dolpo was subservient to Guge. We have only known about the kingdom of Guge since the 1930s due to the efforts of Professor Giuseppe Tucci, an Italian who studied the ruins and frescoes of western Tibet. Tucci was born in Macerata, Italy, on 5 June 1894. He was a natural linguist and 'knew' Sanskrit, Hebrew and Iranian by the age of twelve. After he played his part in the First World War he travelled as much as possible to India, Tibet and Nepal. His special interest was Buddhist texts which had been translated from the original Sanskrit into Tibetan. This had occurred at the instigation of Songtsen Gampo who, around 650 AD, having decreed the need for a Tibetan script, had sent his minister Thonmi Sambota to India to study the art of writing and to introduce a specifically Tibetan style of lettering. This allowed Tibet to record its own history in its own language and script as well as translate some scriptures from Sanskrit. Many of the Sanskrit documents have been lost and all that remains are the translations in Tibetan, which made them unique and the reason why Tucci was so intrigued. According to Snellgrove, Tucci was also one of the first Europeans to enter the Dolpo region, having travelled from the Kali Gandaki to Tsharka, Tarap, Sandul then Tibrikot.

The end of Guge came when control was wrested by the Ladhakis, who in turn were displaced by the forces of the Tibetan fifth Dalai Lama in 1679–80 but before this, in the fourteenth century, Dolpo had turned to its east and paid its dues to the kingdom of Lo, now known as Mustang.

After many years of obeisance to Lo-Manthang, Dolpo had another change in its overlord. In 1768 the kingdom of Nepal was established and this incorporated the old kingdom of Mustang and thus its dependent Dolpo. Nepal became a closed country and nothing was heard of Dolpo for almost 200 years.

Snellgrove's book *Buddhist Himalaya* had as its subtitle *Travels and Studies in Quest of the Origins and Nature of Tibetan Religion*, and it was based on his journeys in Nepal in 1953 and 1954. However, he had spent virtually all his efforts to the east of Kathmandu and he was especially keen to undertake a long investigation of western Nepal, beginning from Nepalgunj and following a long circuitous route, close to the border with Tibet, to return to Kathmandu. This second journey took place in 1956 and was documented in the book *Himalayan Pilgrimage.*

One of the tasks he set himself was to visit the Buddhist centres of each place en route and by talking with the lamas, looking at the frescoes and *thangkas* and reading the sacred texts to ascertain to which branch or sect of Tibetan Buddhism the monastery owed its allegiance.

By the start of the first century CE Buddhism in India was well established but as it spread two distinct approaches developed. Theravada spread south and to this day, in places like Sri Lanka, the emphasis is upon personal enlightenment by meditation and study. As Buddhism spread into central Asia it developed as Mahayana Buddhism, with more importance placed on the Bodhisattva concept, the idea of continual rebirth and teaching for the benefit of all living beings. This 'greater vehicle' spread throughout China and Japan and incorporated elements of Taoism and Confucianism and ultimately led to Zen Buddhism. Sometime around 500 CE another change began when northern Indian Buddhism started to incorporate elements of tantra, or ritual practice, as a means of achieving enlightenment. This variant of Buddhist practice became known as Vajrayana or the 'Thunderbolt vehicle'.

When Songtsen Gampo (617–650 CE approx.) married his two princesses in the early seventh century he was attempting to introduce Buddhism into Tibet as a unifying religion. Princess Wengchen from China brought as a gift the 'Jowo Sakayamuni' statue, for which the Jokhang Temple was built in central Lhasa. Bhrikuti Devi from Nepal also brought a Buddha statue, the Jowo Mikyo Dorje, and this artefact was ensconced in the Ramoche Temple, also in Lhasa. Buddhism in Tibet was consolidated by the later king Trisong Detsen (740–798 CE), who established Samye Monastery around 779 CE and began the process of having Sanskrit scriptures transcribed into Tibetan. He also invited the great teacher Padmasambhava, the Lotus Born, to help quell the Tibetan demons, and there are many tales of his battles across the Himalaya. This early Tibetan school of Buddhism was called the Nyingma and its adherents the Nyingma-pa. This first effort to introduce

Buddhism to Tibet was overturned by Langdarma, whose suppression led to a 150-year hiatus. The Tibetan rule of the Yarlung dynasty collapsed in 842 CE. The second diffusion of Buddhism into Tibet began with the return of monks from Kham in Tibet and the invitation of the kingdom of Guge to Atisha (982–1054 CE), who continued the Nyingma traditions as well as starting the Kadampa school.

In 1073 the Gorum temple was started at Sakya and the name became associated with the Sakyapa whose sect became well established throughout central and eastern Tibet.

Later, the great teacher Marpa (1122–93 CE) from Lhodrak near Bhutan and his disciple Milarepa (1040–1123) established the Kagyu sect, with centres such as Drigung, Taklung and Pelpung. One of the four major subsects is the Karma Kagyu school, whose head is the Karmapa. The Kagyupa, Sakyapa and Nyingmapa are sometimes referred to as the 'red hats'. Only much later, with the rise of the teacher Tsongkhapa (1357–1409 CE), did the Gelug school begin, drawing upon and incorporating the principles of both the Sakya and Kadam traditions. The Gelugpa established the monasteries at Drepung, in 1416, and Sera in 1419, both on the outskirts of Lhasa. It was not until 1578 that Altan Khan, the Mongolian leader, proclaimed Sonyam Gyatso (1543–1588 CE) to be the Dalai Lama, the 'Ocean of Wisdom'. He was also declared as the third reincarnation in a line stretching from Gedun Drupa (1391–1474) through Gendun Gyatso (1475–1542).

The great monastery of Tashilhunpo at Shigatse was founded in 1447 but it was not until the mid-1600s that the fifth Dalai Lama named his tutor, Lobsang Chokyi Gyalsten (1570–1662), as the 'Panchen Lama' or 'Great Scholar'. He was also announced to be the fourth in his lineage and given Tashilhunpo as the seat of his power. Since that time the recognition of Dalai and Panchen Lamas has been co-dependent, each new incarnation of one leader requiring the assent and blessing of the current other. Sitting as the spiritual leader of the Gelugpa is the Dalai Lama, and the Gelug school is often referred to as the 'yellow hats'.

Snellgrove was eager to continue his exploration of the Buddhist Himalaya. He'd heard of Shey Gompa but had no idea to which Buddhist tradition it owed its allegiance or even if he could reach this remote place across the high snowy passes. It wasn't until he began his expedition north of the Bheri that he and the modern world even heard the word 'Dolpo'.

Trekking north from Nepalgunj near the border with India he had the intention of visiting Shey Gompa (SI: Sya Gompa) and then heading as far north as possible before turning east towards the Kali Gandaki. He was especially keen to visit some of the Bon monasteries he'd heard about but never seen. Having reached Ringmo on the edge of Lake Phoksumdo, he and his companions were about to start on the daunting crossing of the 5000-metre-high Kang La. He wrote that he was 'even more curious to know what kind of monastery Shey Gompa would prove to be. Of Dolpo as a cultural unit we had as yet no idea, for at this time even the name "Dolpo" was unknown to us.'

Sometime later, after they had travelled north of Shey, Snellgrove had an astounding and revelatory conversation. They had met, and were invited to stay with, the local headman of the village of Saldang, one Nyima Tschering. Tschering was born in Namdo in Tibet and, although denying being a headman, he had much influence in the area having married a local woman from Saldang. Initially Tschering was a little dismissive of these strange foreign visitors but when it became clear that Snellgrove not only spoke fluent Tibetan but was deeply interested in the Buddhist religion then he relaxed and became welcoming.

Snellgrove started by asking Nyima Tshering about Saldang, the area where he lived:

> It was during this conversation that we heard the name 'Dolpo' for the first time and learned that it referred to the whole region bounded on the west by the great watershed which we had crossed above Phoksumdo and on the south by the Dhaulagiri massif. To the north-west beyond Phopa it is separated by several days of difficult travel from the nearest villages of the Mugu Karnali. To the south-east beyond Tsharka (SI: Chharkabhot) it is likewise separated by bare mountains from the Kali Gandaki. To the north and the north-east it is bounded by the great Tibetan plain, which these people refer to simply as the 'north' (*byang*).

For the first time a modern Westerner heard the name that the locals had called this land for many centuries. Snellgrove's interest had been massively stirred:

> We pressed our questions about Dolpo as a unit and were told that it consisted of four districts, Namgung, Panzang, Tarap and Tsharbung. We told Nyima Tshering that the area was marked on our maps as Danbhansar and Chharkabhot. He accepted the latter name, pronouncing it, as we had already learned, as Tsharka without the suffix *-bhot*, but correcting the first one to Dastapla, interpreted as meaning 'ten townships'. These were the names that the 'Nepalese' had given to the country. As I sat in the dim light peering at the map, this strange land where we now found ourselves, gradually gained in coherence.

A picture of an important region with its own distinctive and unique history and culture, albeit massively influenced by its Tibetan lineage, was becoming clear. Snellgrove was to travel widely in these valleys reaching over 4000 metres altitude in the Himalaya. The nature of that rugged terrain, the valleys with their interconnecting high passes, meant that when it became our turn to traverse Upper Dolpo the geography of those same passes and valleys dictated that we had to closely follow the original route taken by Snellgrove.

Like many others in the Western world, I had been much impressed by the movie *Himalaya. L'Enfance d'un chef* by French film-maker Eric Valli. This was released in 1999 and known as *Caravan* in many parts of the world. It is a spectacular wide-screen epic of the yak-herding folk of Dolpo and the cultural issues of generational power shifts. It had taken months to film and used mainly local people as the actors. It was accompanied by a hauntingly evocative soundtrack by Bruno Coulais. The film showed the cycle of life and death, the daily work of yak herding and the struggle to exist in this inhospitable environment so high up in the Himalayan mountain valleys. The scenes in the villages and monasteries seemed medieval. One scene, shot on the narrow path above Phoksumdo Lake, was all loose stones and with a falling yak was quite terrifying. The movie was nominated for an Oscar in 2000. It put Dolpo slap bang in the public eye after centuries of being virtually unknown. However, hopes that it would attract funding, investment and tourism, and hence greater prosperity, for the region have largely been unfulfilled. I looked forward to seeing in real life the scenery featured in the movie, as there was quite obviously nowhere else on the planet like this intriguing land of Dolpo.

There was one other source of information on this ancient region that I'd only recently come across. Kenneth Bauer, an American, had published a book in 2004 called *High Frontiers*. In the introduction he claimed the book was 'a case study of change'. He'd lived in Nepal for several years and first visited Dolpo in 1995. Having been awarded a Fulbright scholarship, he was able to head off in late 1996 to over-winter in the village of Tinje in the Panzang Valley. He stayed with the family of Tenzin Norbu Lama, who was the Nepalese artist who had painted the frescoes for some of the interior scenes in the movie *Himalaya* and whose family home was Tholung Monastery above Tinje. In the spring he travelled south and followed the return of the Dolpo-pa who'd been away for the winter. Over the period 1996 to 2001 he gathered information and he was able to detail how the traditional agro-pastoralist lifestyle, with its seasonal planting, harvesting and travel to suitable grazing, had been dramatically curtailed since 1960 when the Chinese closed the border. During the time he was researching and writing there were also problems within Nepal because of the Maoist insurgency and Dolpo was not left unscathed. One chapter of *High Frontiers* was entitled 'A Tsampa Western', implying that the movie *Himalaya* was like a 'spaghetti western' set in a land of tsampa rather than pasta. In it, Bauer considered some of the implications of the movie's effect on the local people and their situation. Much had been anticipated in light of raising Dolpo's profile but, apart from a handful of people, the overall benefit seems to have been negligible.

And so it was, full of expectation, that I set off on my own journey to Dolpo arriving in the Himalaya on the tenth day of the third month of the Tibetan Wood Horse Year, 2041 – 9 May 2014 on the Gregorian calendar. Would I find a land fighting a losing battle against modernisation or would I be entering one of Guru Rinpoche's fabled and long lost *beyuls*?

8
IN KATHMANDU

I was to be met at Tribhuvan International Airport, Kathmandu, by a representative and driver from The Mountain Company. In the usual throng of porters and taxi drivers outside the arrivals building, the line of people holding up placards was out front. I immediately spotted my name and I was soon shaking hands with a tall man who said, in a superbly refined English accent, 'Hello, my name is Tootsie.'

'Tootsie?' I said a little incredulously.

'Tulsi,' he corrected me and I soon learned that this was the excellent fellow Tulsi Gyawali, who was to be 'our man in Kathmandu'. We had the usual entertaining drive through the city to the Hotel Tibet. It was good to be back.

Kathmandu almost beggars description. It is a spectacular morass of people, traffic, colour, smells, goods for sale, food stalls and cows, especially in the middle of the roads! Kathmandu is a Hindu town made of those bright red local bricks. The airport is the last oasis of calm before one enters the eddies and currents of swirling humanity filling the narrow streets.

Hotel Tibet is in the suburb of Lazimpat, and as soon as possible I dropped my bags then walked into Thamel to the Northfield Cafe. I got there about 1.00 p.m. and was pleasantly surprised to bump straight into Ade Summers, who was already ensconced at a table. I felt quite good in spite of only two hours' sleep, so had no hesitation in ordering a beer. We were joined by Tom, a friend of Ade's from 'Everest Rocks', a charity musical event held a few years earlier. Tom was just back from Base Camp, where he had been making the movie film sequences he was working on for the new Hollywood *Everest* movie. This was destined to be a mega-star blockbuster about the fateful storm in 1996 when eight climbers died, including Rob Hall and Scott Fisher, the expedition leaders.

One of my work colleagues, John Taske, had been on the climb with Rob Hall's group and had barely survived. Tom had to pack up and leave his work at Base Camp when, on 18 April 2014, three weeks before, a massive icefall had killed sixteen sherpas who were setting the route for the climbing season on Everest. It was, up to that time, the deadliest single incident on Everest. I'd seen it on the news at home and followed the rescue bid almost in real time. I had scanned the names of the dead with trepidation. First on the list I recognised was my friend Dorje Khatri from my last Tibet trip in 2012. This fine individual had been snuffed out in an instant with fifteen of his fellow sherpas. Communication from modern-day Everest Base Camp being what it is, I was able, with a sense of unreality, to watch Dorje's body being dug out from the hard-packed snow. The corpses of all the dead were flown out by helicopter and Dorje was cremated a few days later back in Kathmandu.

Ade and I had a lot to talk about, and despite recent tragedies it felt marvellous to be back in Kathmandu, talking mountains, beer in hand and a trek about to begin. After an hour or so my daughter Nicola and her friend Bec Moroney turned up. Old school friends, they were both now qualified nurses aged twenty-six and based in Brisbane. They'd been in Kathmandu for forty-eight hours and were having a great time. The two of them were about to leave on their first Himalayan trek to Everest Base Camp. Time indeed for another beer.

All Nicola and Bec had seen so far was Thamel and Durbar Square, so mid-afternoon the three of us jumped into a taxi to visit Boudhanath and its Great Stupa. I had a slightly ulterior motive, in that I was keen to visit the art gallery of Tenzin Norbu Lama. I'd been in touch with him by email before leaving Australia and knew that he was overseas exhibiting his artwork. However, I was keen to see his work and maybe meet his son, who was in charge of the gallery. We couldn't find it, so we did a couple of clockwise circuits of the *stupa*, joining the throng and taking photographs. Nicola and Bec loved the place, as it really is a spectacular and beautiful monument. The whole area is a Tibetan microcosm, and the mood is lively and friendly. It was quite a warm afternoon, so we had lassi and *momos* at a rooftop restaurant. We sat almost level with the giant painted eyes staring out in the four cardinal directions from the upper structure of the *stupa*, the afternoon sun gleaming on the gold-leaf-covered top. The plan for the evening was that Ade and I would meet up with some of the others who were to be trekking with us and who were already in town. Nicola and Bec were invited.

The venue was to be the K-too Steakhouse. We were joined by Ade and the 'Three Amigos'. This was the nickname given to the group of two men and a woman who had trekked with Ade several times before. They had all taken relatively early retirement from their jobs and frequently travelled the world together. They had chosen to stay, not with the rest of us at Hotel Tibet, which they didn't like, but round the corner at the recently renovated Shankar Hotel. It was a pleasant evening. I didn't get much of a chance to talk to Duncan and Susan, but Colin sat opposite me. A bespectacled, small man he seemed a little dour, even negative. When I asked if he'd read *The Snow Leopard*, I seemed to have touched a nerve. 'It's a terrible book,' he said. 'Hey, Duncan, Susan. *The Snow Leopard*. It's a terrible book, isn't it?' And they both nodded their agreement. He was strongly of the opinion that it was self-indulgent, and he felt sorry for the young son Matthiessen had left behind in the States. Nicola and Bec thought that Duncan and Susan seemed like a nice couple. In fact, they weren't a couple and the 'Three Amigos' were exactly that, three friends. Colin was an Australian who'd lived in England for twenty years or more and had worked in the financial world. Duncan was a rather well spoken, if slightly effete, man who lived in central London and had been involved in publishing. Susan was a retired psychiatrist who'd never really practised psychiatry but had worked in the arena of public health or welfare. I never found out exactly what she did. She was a dour woman from the north of England and spoke very little. As I walked the girls back to their hotel Nicola said to me, 'The couple seemed okay, but I'm not sure about Colin. You know how you said that there's usually one dickhead on every trek? Well, I think it might be him.' It gave me a warm inner glow to think that I'd brought up such a discerning and perceptive young lady.

10 MAY 2014

I woke suddenly in the darkness of the early hours clueless as to where I was. Jet lag had struck!

I got up at 6.00 a.m. for a leisurely breakfast, then the day rapidly escalated to being a rather busy one. There was the serious business of last-minute shopping and then packing for 'the off'. I walked over to the girls' hotel in Thamel to see them before their day of touring Kathmandu and the valley. We arranged a rendezvous for the evening. I had a long coffee break at the Northfield Cafe waiting for Pilgrims bookshop to open. The original iconic bookshop, next door to the Northfield, had burned to the ground in a disastrous fire in May 2013 exactly one year earlier. It had now been re-established about 200 metres down the same street. I bought several books at Pilgrims; it's a veritable treasure trove of obscure and out-of-print books, with especially huge collections on the subjects of mountaineering, the Himalaya and Buddhism.

Back at the Hotel Tibet, which was growing on me by the hour, Ade and I were having a good catch-up coffee on the fifth-floor rooftop bar, the Yeti Bar and Terrace. We were joined about midday by Harry Jones, the next of our group to show up. Harry turned out to be a charming, pleasant and completely bald Welshman from Anglesey. He told us he'd already been in Nepal for a few days seeing his in-laws, as he had married a Nepalese girl who used to work at the Shankar Hotel. It transpired that Harry and I were to be sharing hotel rooms and a tent for the duration of the trip. I was rather pleased, as he was an instantly likeable fellow.

In the early evening it was time for 'the briefing', the traditional pre-trek chat from the leader. The Three Amigos came over from the Shankar and we gathered upstairs in the Yeti Bar. This time we were joined by the next member of the expedition, Philippe Beck from France. Philippe ran his own business in Paris and was quite simply a huge individual, tall and rotund, 'Obelixian' one might say, with a seemingly poor command of the English language. Not a problem; this was simply an opportunity to inflict my schoolboy French on everyone. We were all given a map of Dolpo, but at 18.30 I had to give my apologies and set off for Thamel to meet up with Nicola and Bec. They'd been tourists all day and were loaded up with shopping as we went to the New Orleans bar for dinner. The live music was in full swing as we indulged in a few cocktails and a light meal. We adjourned later to Sam's Bar for a nightcap of several more margaritas. Sam's is an iconic Kathmandu bar and the rendezvous spot for many people fortunate to be returning to 'the 'du' and needing to meet up with friends. The walls are liberally festooned with graffiti-style writings and scribbles – quotations, witticisms and obscenities from customers, usually those lacking in sobriety. One of the better efforts was: 'World Religion Simplified':

Taoism – Shit happens.
Confucianism – Confucius says 'shit happens'.
Buddhism – If shit happens it isn't really shit.
Zen – What is the sound of shit happening?
Hinduism – This shit happened before.
Islam – If shit happens, it is the will of Allah.
Protestantism – Let shit happen to someone else.
Catholicism – If shit happens you deserve it.
Judaism – Why does shit always happen to us?
Rastafarianism – Let's smoke this shit.

We enjoyed this piece of graffiti in particular and got the photograph, but it prompted Bec to ask me 'are you a Buddhist?' My brain, lubricated by several margaritas, enabled me to give her my three-minute version of Buddhism. I explained that I wasn't Buddhist in a religious sense, but I understood and loved the principles and philosophy. I liked the fact that it encouraged self-reliance, non-violence and compassion. That the Buddha had recognised that we all experience ageing, sickness and ultimately death but once this was understood there could be a complete emphasis on enjoying the good times of one's own life while being compassionate towards others and their suffering. The Buddha was also so on the ball that he said 'don't take my word for it, work it out for yourselves'. The concept that everything is impermanent necessitated living one's life to the full and enjoying and appreciating 'the moment'. I said, 'It's important not to dwell on the past or to worry about the future. You have to enjoy the moment and it doesn't get any better than this. Being here in Sam's in Kathmandu, with you two girls, and having another margarita. Cheers.'

And so we toasted our time in Kathmandu, for in the morning we were going our separate ways, the girls to Lukla, the Khumbu and Everest, and myself to Pokhara then on to Dolpo.

Nicola promised she would leave me a message on their return from the trek at a particular spot among the graffiti on the walls at Sam's, to let me know she'd got back safely.

9
JUPHAL TO DUNAI

11 MAY

We left the Hotel Tibet at a most civilised 9.30 for the 11.00 flight to Pokhara. It was a clear morning and it looked as if all the Lukla flights had got away earlier. I hoped Nicola and Bec would have an enjoyable trek. Parental concern never ends, it seems.

By the time our plane took off the cloud was building up, and disappointingly we had no view of the mountains. I sat next to a German man of about forty who was on the last leg of a long journey from Stuttgart. He was overweight, exhausted and garrulous. He looked wrecked. He insisted on telling me that his reason for travelling to Pokhara was to have 'rejuvenation therapy'. 'I did it once before,' he said, 'and it took ten years off me.' He now thought it was time for a rerun. Apparently the process involved six hours a day of massage with Ayurvedic oils for seventeen days. The first thing he did on landing was to hurry to the edge of the tarmac to light up a cigarette.

We were met at the airport and taken to the Hotel Landmark on Pokhara's Lakeside Drive. This was my first time in Pokhara, Nepal's second-largest city. It was surprisingly warm and clammy, at 31°C. I went into the first bookshop I saw and bought a copy of *The Ascent of Rum Doodle* by W.E. Bowman for 200 rupees, about $2.50. I also picked up a newly published trekking guide to Dolpo, by Sian Pritchard-Jones and Bob Gibbons, and several strings of prayer flags.

Pokhara turned out to be a most pleasant town situated by the side of the lake, the Phewa Tal. An afternoon beer sitting at the street-front of the hotel allowed Ade, Harry and myself to be entertained by an endless procession of locals, sellers, beggars and tourists. We got word that the final member of our group, Alasdair Lawrence, had shown up and was sitting in the lobby. We were naturally keen to eyeball our latest travelling companion and shot over to say hello. He turned out to be a tall, solid-looking 'Aussie bloke' with a shaved head who'd just returned from a climb of Mera Peak. This trekking peak up the Khumbu stands at 6476 metres (21,246 feet) so our new friend Alasdair was fully acclimatised already. He told us that he travelled a lot and spent his time between London and Sydney but this hiatus in Nepal was part of his return to Australia on a more permanent basis. He seemed to be a little taciturn, the laconic type of rugged Aussie fellow.

In the evening we had a brief group meeting, then adjourned next door to the Moondance restaurant. Here I had another beer and a few of us had an excellent wild boar stew. This dish was certainly as good as the boar stew I'd had in Florence, where it is proclaimed the national dish. This Nepalese version was much referred to and discussed on many occasions a couple of weeks into the trek, when thoughts of tasty and exotic food had become an almost dominant aspect of daytime imaginings. The ubiquitous dhal bhat, a lentil and rice staple, does start to pall after a week or two.

12 MAY

Juphal (2475 metres; 8120 feet)
to Dunai (2160 metres; 7086 feet)
12 kilometres

In the cold, dark early hours next morning a disagreeably unwelcome alarm at 5.45 a.m. had us starting on the next leg of the journey. There were to be ten of us plus three crew on the twenty-seater de Havilland DHC-6 Twin Otter aircraft. We'd been joined on the flight by our *sirdar* – now officially termed 'guide' in the 'newspeak' of political correctness – whose name was Chandra Bahadur Rai, and a deputy guide, Bishwo Rai, both incredibly youthful. The noise of our small aircraft meant that we couldn't chat to them until after we'd landed. We also couldn't see the mountains on take-off from Pokhara because of the haze, but after being up in the air for about a quarter of an hour I got a glimpse of Dhaulagiri off to our right. Then, suddenly, we were completely above the cloud and for the first time I could see the true scale of these enormous mountains. We were level with Dhaulagiri and just behind us was the whole Annapurna massif, the two separated by the deep valley of the Kali Gandaki River. The sheer size was spectacular and they were a pristine glittering white in the early morning sun. The huge pyramid of Dhaulagiri is the seventh-highest mountain in the world and is 8167 metres (26,794 feet) high. Its giant neighbour, Annapurna, is tenth-highest, at 8091 metres (26,545 feet). Two of the fourteen 'Eight Thousanders' out of one aeroplane window!

The flight was just under an hour and we had a surprisingly smooth touch-down on the dirt landing strip at Juphal. We spent about an hour in the small town and had tea while the porters divided up the loads. Our porters had left Kathmandu days earlier and had a long bus ride to Pokhara then a four-day walk from there to meet us. On a large blue tarpaulin the edible essentials for the trek were laid out. Three hundred eggs in a stack of cartons. Packets of noodles. Tins of beans and sardines. Biscuits, teabags, sugar, pasta, rice. There was a vast amount, and all of it to be carried on the backs of our porters. This was also the first time we'd had a chance to talk with our guides. Chandra Bahadur Rai was an experienced guide in his early thirties. Ade had trekked with him before and said to me, 'Maybe other guides for climbing but for trekking Chandra's the best.' Bishwo, pronounced 'Bee-shoo', was in his late twenties and also highly experienced. Both spoke excellent English and could also speak Hindi and some Tibetan.

The first step of our journey was with Bishwo leading the way down a steep track and through the village of Dhagmara, which clung to the steep hillside surrounded by a mosaic of newly planted terraced fields. Below us and stretching many kilometres into the distance was the deep valley of the Bheri River. There was a school just below the airport, the Dolpo Educational English School, and many uniformed and smiling children gave us a shout of '*Namaste*' and a wave. They looked remarkably clean and smart in their long grey pants, bright red jumpers and striped ties. This was a Hindu settlement and a lot of the buildings had primitive looking carvings on the roof. These were shamanistic figures called *dhauiliya* or *dok-pa* and were looked on as protectors, most likely predating even Hinduism. Matthiessen said of them, 'Brutal human effigies in wood protect the low stonehuts.' I'd read of a local mountain spirit called Masta but wasn't sure if he was respected this far up the valley. It seems that traditionally these figurines were there to attract the attentions of the bad spirits and demons, thus leaving the human inhabitants of the house alone. The fields around Dhagmara could be counted in their hundreds, as they were narrow terraces only a few metres wide and up to about 20 metres long. Most were bright green or a pale yellow from the early crops of wheat and barley. One outstanding feature was the lack of weed control; there was quite literally a subsidiary crop of marijuana growing at the edges of most of the plots as well as along the irrigation ditches and even in the middle of the trail we were walking along. The dense patches of weed were a rich green and luxuriant and clearly of the finest quality.

From the outset Ade was walking poorly. He'd twisted his back towards the end of his previous trek and it was clear he had sciatic pain. He told us to just go on ahead and he'd catch up but, being only the first day of walking, I was seriously concerned that he may have to pull out.

About four hours of walking took us from Juphal (2475 metres; 8120 feet) down to Dunai (2160 metres; 7086 feet). We quickly dropped down to the fast-flowing river and after 4 kilometres reached a place called Kalagauda, which was a tiny hamlet of five or six houses, but here there was a painted tin-plate sign proclaiming 'Kalagauda. 2070 m. Great Himalaya Trail. Lower Dolpa Circuit'. It also told us that it was a mere '5.75 km. 1 hr. 20 min.' to Dunai. The Great Himalaya Trail is a network of trails stretching the length of the Himalaya, from Nanga Parbat in the Karakoram in the west to Namche Barwa in Tibet at its eastern end. It's over 4500 kilometres long and we were seeing a tiny fraction of it.

At the edge of Dunai was a pair of *chortens*, one of them with a gateway through it. This type of *chorten*, usually the entrance to a village, is known by the locals as a *ka-ni chorten*. This one was clearly old and was a true entrance *chorten* with a large opening to walk through. It was about 6 metres high and built in three, increasingly smaller, square layers. Each step was protected by a roof of slate and the whole surmounted by a white hemisphere topped by a shining gold-coloured finial. A pair of plaster discs with a relief carving decorated each side of the mid-layer. The north-facing wall displayed a pair of garudas, the mythical bird, with a dharma wheel between. The opposite side, facing south, carried discs with a horse on each. An ornate *kalachakra* emblem sat between. The east side bore a pair of elephants and the west a pair of peacocks. The mantra 'Om Mani Padme Hum' was repeated several times on the wooden lintel above the doorway. Inside the *chorten*, the ceiling, which was well protected from the elements, was immaculately painted with a series of nine mandalas. The walls just below the ceiling were adorned with metre-high friezes of the four supreme manifestations of the Buddha, with their vast entourage of gods and demigods. This particular edifice was a superb example of many similar structures, of varying ages, that we were to encounter over the following weeks.

Harry stopped in the shade of the *chorten* to talk to a couple of local women who had with them a small child. As Harry's wife is from Nepal he had a smattering of Nepali, enough to hold a simple conversation. Indeed, his ability to recite a few nursery rhymes in Nepali meant that he was much in demand to entertain inquisitive local children throughout the trek. Another twenty minutes brought us into Dunai itself, often called 'Dunai bazaar' as it is a single, narrow paved road following the riverbank, with dozens of shops and stalls lining each side selling all manner of clothes, shoes, cooking utensils, rice and hot chai. It was buzzing with activity and overwhelming in colour and aromas. We arrived at our campsite, in the large back garden of a teahouse named The Blue Sheep, at the far end of the main street. This was the end of the road, quite literally, for motorised vehicles. At our garden campsite the bright orange Mountain Hardware tents were just being erected and we were given lemon tea then lunch, followed by more tea. This was essential as the afternoon was hot and our walk had been sweat inducing. Adequate hydration at high altitudes cannot be emphasised enough.

Ade was well behind and I hadn't seen him for a couple of hours so I went out to look for him. He wasn't too far away in the main street but was still limping badly. He'd been buying painkillers at the pharmacy in town. I suggested he take three Panadeine, tablets containing both paracetamol and codeine, but he said he'd be alright and would take them that evening to try to get a good sleep.

In the afternoon I went off to climb up to a *gompa*, which we could see clearly on the opposite bank of the river. It was a short way back into town to the new suspension bridge then a brief climb up a narrow trail. Just over the bridge was a high walled compound topped with barbed wire, and with a gun turret on each corner. The local jail. On 25 September 2000, a group of up to 1000 Maoist guerrillas attacked Dunai just after midnight. Various government centres were assaulted and destroyed, including the office of the Chief District Officer, the Police Headquarters, the Land Revenue Office. The Nepal Bank Limited was captured and 60 million rupees, about US$5.5 million in cash stolen. The jail was attacked with grenades and pipe bombs and seventeen prisoners set free. The battle of Dunai continued through the night and by 6.30 a.m. fourteen policemen were dead and forty injured. On this day in 2014 the jail was a scene of tranquillity: there was only the noise of hammering as the prisoners were hard at work on new buildings.

A few more minutes and I was at the collection of buildings higher up the trail, which was a school and monastery complex. The *gompa* was closed but about half a kilometre beyond, and even higher up the hill, was another *stupa* next to some other buildings. This turned out to be a Bon school. Harry had also decided to climb up after me and we met at the school. The *stupa* was above the school buildings and up a staircase and when we saw that the decoration included the Bon reverse swastika symbol we made a point of walking the correct, anticlockwise, Bon way around it. From the school we could see the whole of the compact town of Dunai on the opposite side of the Bheri. Extending above the town there was an incredible zigzag path leading high up and disappearing into a gully filled with trees. This was the only route in and out of a small settlement at least 700 metres above Dunai. Each day the schoolchildren would have to scramble down and inevitably climb all that way back up after lessons. Like many other Himalayan villages and hamlets, for the old and infirm this would, at some time, become an impossible journey.

Harry and I dropped down to the river past a few houses. One of them had a handsome dog sleeping on the flat roof next to a rather striking two-faced *dok-pa* wooden effigy; a doubly well-protected household. We carried on down to the riverbank and saw some kids using an old rope pulley bridge. Without thinking twice we jumped in and let the local boys pull us across as we swayed wildly, the brown torrent only a metre or two below us. Harry gave the lads a few rupees for their trouble.

We were back at the campsite in time for afternoon tea and had plenty of opportunity to get ourselves organised in the tent. Harry and I were to be sharing for the duration, but we'd both done this trekking thing before and getting settled into the tent each evening and also the morning packing-up proved to be painless exercises.

That night I couldn't read *Rum Doodle* because of all the flies attracted to my head-torch. Still, some sleep was required. We'd only walked about 12 kilometres on this first day and it was virtually all downhill. The next morning we were to start going up!

10
TO THE BLUE LAKE

13 MAY

Dunai (2160 metres; 7086 feet)
to Chhepka (2672 metres; 8766 feet)
14.6 kilometres

We were woken with 'bed tea' at 6.00 a.m. It was more of a reawakening, in actuality. It had been a dodgy night's sleep due to the incessant barking of the village dogs. Across the Himalaya the dogs appear to lie around peacefully sleeping all day in the weak heat of the sun, then they spend their waking hours, during the long dark night, howling and baying at imaginary foes or each other. The local people seem to be immune to the noise and are invariably well rested by next day, unlike we visitors. I always use earplugs but they are not entirely 'dog-noise-cancelling'.

We packed up our gear from within the tent easily and quickly. Harry would prove to be a tent-mate of the first order. Breakfast allowed us our initial taste of the filter coffee which we'd been promised, and it was of the finest quality. This was already turning out to be a superb trip. We set off at about quarter to eight wandering down the already busy and vibrant main street of Dunai. Halfway through the town we saw and spoke to Thinle Lhondup, the old fellow who played the village chief in the *Himalaya* movie. He was clearly doing a little business transaction and said he'd be at his home in Saldang in a week or so and he would see us there. He was exactly as he appeared in the movie and as he spoke I realised that he had simply played himself in the film.

Once we left the main street of Dunai we would not be setting foot on a conventional road again until the outskirts of Jomsom, some 250 kilometres distant. We crossed the suspension bridge, turned left and headed on the narrow trail west along the Bheri to its junction with the Suli Gad, about 2 kilometres downstream. The Suli Gad is the main outlet from Phoksumdo Lake and once it joins the Bheri the combined stream joins the Karnali River then flows, ultimately, into the Ganges. The Suli Gad was a torrent of clear glacial water as opposed to the muddy brown of the Bheri.

Heading north we passed through a gateway proclaiming 'Welcome to Shey Phoksundo National Park & Buffer Zone'. The more common spelling is 'Phoksumdo'. We stopped at the park HQ in Sulighat to register our permits. The park was established in 1984 at the instigation of people like George Schaller, to protect the wildlife. It is Nepal's largest such area, covering 3555 square kilometres. We were now entering the restricted area of Dolpo. The permits were numbered and our group's permits ended at number ninety. So far this year only ninety trekkers had entered the region and the monsoon rains would be arriving in a few weeks! The fact that each permit was over US$700 may well have been a contributing factor to the low numbers of visitors.

We tramped on alongside the river, gradually gaining height. The trail was good and it was easy and pleasant walking. Just after the park entrance we passed through groves of silk trees (*Albizia julibrissin*) covered in the wispy pink tufts of their delicate flowers. By mid-morning the rain began. By the time we reached Kannin, our lunch stop, I was soaked. Our meal was on the verandah of a traditional old building and I had to rug up, as it was getting cold. In the village many of the houses and the bridges displayed the shamanistic *dok-pa* carvings.

We crossed several bridges back and forth across the stream and the going was steadily upwards, and hard in places. An hour after lunch we came into a village of about fifteen houses, all of them open and completely deserted. This was Raktang, apparently a place where nomadic herders would return from the summer high pasture and spend their winter. This type of seasonal settlement was known as a *doksa*.

The rain intensified, and during our last two hours of walking it was torrential.

We passed a police checkpoint after a steep climb up through trees where the clammy air was filled with a damp, musty, pine aroma, a true petrichor, but it was another hour to our destination of Chepka. Harry and I arrived at the same time along with our cook Saila and our second deputy guide Gopal Lama.

We took shelter on the verandah of a 'hotel', the Hotel Jhharana, in whose garden we were to camp. No tents or porters were to be seen. Chepka was a cluster of four or five stone houses separated by a narrow lane a couple of metres wide, which was by now flowing freely with muddy water. It was getting cold. It was off with the Sam's Bar t-shirt which Nicola and her friend Bec had bought me. I dried myself on a handkerchief and donned an Icebreaker merino top, fleece jacket, hat and gloves. Time to break open the first of a limited supply of Cherry Ripe chocolate bars; glacé cherries with coconut and a dark chocolate outer. Why are they only available in Australia?

Gradually the rest of the group and porters rolled in completely drenched. It was only now that I realised what a large caravan we were. There were eight of us, including Ade as leader. Chandra, our guide, had two deputy guides in Bishwo and Gopal. Saila, the head cook, had his staff of four kitchen boys. There were also seventeen porters who'd travelled from Kathmandu. At Dunai we'd picked up a local guide, Narendra, and a couple of local porters. That made thirty-six of us walking the trail, plus a pony-boy and his six horses that were coming as far as Shey. This was an expedition of imperial proportions.

Soon our mess tent was erected and it was enormous. A huge monstrosity of bright blue vinyl. It must have been about 4 metres by 7 metres. Although it was vast it was not at all cosy. Duncan when he arrived was in a bad mood as he'd taken a wrong turn before the police checkpost and walked for an extra half an hour in the wrong direction. He came in, soaked, after everyone else except Philippe who was clearly destined to bring up the rear at all times.

Dinner comprised mushroom soup, garlic mash, cauliflower and roast chicken pieces and it was hot, tasty and filling: just what was needed. I was always surprised at the calibre of the meals that the kitchen staff could cook up on a couple of gas burners. We were fortunate in having Saila as our head cook. Every day he would walk past us, travelling light with just his umbrella in hand, closely followed by the team of four kitchen boys, running in single file, singing or chanting, with the pots and pans clanking in the baskets on their backs. They'd try and get to camp early to quite literally 'put the kettle on' but their stops were frequent, hence the need for their bursts of jogging to keep up with Saila's constant and measured pace.

Before bed at just after 8.00 p.m., Ade gave us his talk on hypoxia and the dangers of high altitude. I tried to reinforce the message that no one is immune. Even Edmund Hillary fell victim to cerebral oedema in 1981. He was on an American expedition to climb the Kangshung face of Everest and was sixty-two years old at the time. When Mary collapsed with cerebral oedema on our Bhutan trek she was at only 3900 metres. This, and the more common pulmonary oedema, could strike anywhere and at any age once we were over 3000 metres. It was important that we look out for each other and spot any signs such as staggering, slurred speech, coughing, the blue tinge of cyanosis or sometimes even a sudden falling silent. However, I got the impression that my words fell on deaf ears with this experienced bunch of trekkers.

14 MAY

Chhepka (2672 metres; 8766 feet)
to Tapriza (3115 metres; 10,219 feet)
12.6 kilometres

A restorative night's sleep was had as the rain had stopped. Things were still sodden and damp and my Sam's t-shirt had, not surprisingly, been liberated from the washing line never to be seen again. Hot coffee and breakfast were just what was required before we set off at 8.00 a.m. It was good to get moving along a narrow path by the river. In places it was steep climbing, and we crossed the river back and forth several times on the distinctive stone and wood cantilevered bridges. Of this stretch of river Matthiessen said, 'I wonder if anywhere on earth there is a river more beautiful than the upper Suli Gad in early autumn.' This was, of course, the Nepalese spring, but the same sentiment could be applied.

We reached a place called Rechi for our lunch stop. There were only a few houses, but they were noticeably more Tibetan in style than lower down the valley. The tea shops here were run by Dolpo-pa from Ringmo. A woman was sitting on the ground weaving a strip of cloth in the traditional Tibetan style on a so-called 'backstrap' loom. A young girl was washing her hair in a yellow plastic bucket of cold water. We ate lunch sitting in the bright but barely warm sun and, as we were almost out of the tree line, could see snow-covered peaks to the south back in the direction of Dunai. Always a heart-warming spectacle.

An easy and pleasant one and a half hour's walk after lunch brought us to a series of buildings just before Amchi Hospital. This was Tapriza Secondary School, a school with its own *gompa*. Two long double-storey structures stood either side of the central playground. Schoolrooms were on the ground floor and dormitories upstairs. At the north end of the playground stood the *gompa*. This institution has been funded since 1998 by the Tapriza NGO Switzerland. It is named after Tapriza (Tibetan: *Ta-pi-hri-tsa*), a Bon teacher in the eighth century from a nomadic family in Zhangzhung. He attained illumination and practised at a holy place called Senge Tap near Mount Kailash. The school was a place where 200 children were boarders coming from villages all over lower Dolpo. For one year the school had been able to produce enough electricity from solar power to run several laptop computers, a copier, a printer and a television.

Alasdair and I went straight up to the *gompa* and spoke to some of the kids, who were having a break for drinks. 'What your name?', 'Where from?' the boys shouted out. 'I'm Big Al from 'Straylia,' responded my friend. English was very much on the curriculum here. The *gompa* inside the school grounds was unpainted and there were no outward signs to show that this was a Bon institution. Prayer flags flew on poles adding a bit of gaiety to this already vibrant place and a noticeboard carried photographs of the pupils who had been most successful in examinations over recent years.

The tents were being erected in a level, broad field just below the school and we settled in to enjoy what was left of the day. The kitchen and mess tents were up. The afternoon sun was warm and the porters were lying on the grass enjoying being unburdened. The half dozen ponies grazed in clear contentment. All was right with the world.

I was attempting to read E.M. Forster's *A Room With a View*. It seemed totally alien and somewhat inappropriate to be indulging in a tale of nineteenth-century Florence and 'English manners' in the middle of the Himalaya, but nevertheless a pleasant read. It was some months later, when I was reading Wade Davis's book *Into the Silence: The Great War, Mallory and the Conquest of Everest* that I learned that one of the main characters in *Room With a View*, George Emerson, was based upon Mallory himself. At Cambridge, both Mallory and Foster were members of a secret society known as the Apostles.

15 MAY

Tapriza (3115 metres; 10,219 feet)
to Ringmo (3648 metres; 11,968 feet)
5.6 kilometres

We set off in glorious morning sunshine and walked around the school then over a bridge shaded by the trees of the riverbank. A mere fifteen minutes of leisurely walking delivered us to Amchi Hospital, where the clinic was simply one building in a place advertising itself on a large yellow sign as 'Welcome to Chunuwar (3134m). Available services Lodge, Food & Beverages, Campsite, Garden, Vegetable, TeleCom'.

The *amchi* tradition has existed for thousands of years. It is based on the herbs and natural products of the Himalaya and Tibet. Its practitioners study for many years to attain mastery of the Four Medical Treatises, the Gyud Shi. Diagnoses are made by consideration of the pulse and the three humours of bile, wind and phlegm. Treatments are made under four main banners: diet, behaviour modification, herbal medicines and physical therapy. The latter includes bloodletting, cauterisation and moxibustion. Potential unpleasantness and scepticism notwithstanding, Ade's back had been so bad that he was keen to seek some treatment from the *amchi*. However, he was to be disappointed, as the clinic was closed and, not for the first time, the *yarsa gumba*, the 'caterpillar fungus' (of which more later) hunting season was blamed. Chunuwar was a nice little settlement with only a few houses, but it could boast a splendid flowering group of Himalayan strawberry trees (*Cornus capitata*), a type of dogwood, covered in thousands of pale pink blossoms. The *chortens* here carried the Bon symbol of the anti clockwise swastika.

We had a steady climb up to the winter village, or *doksa*, at Palam (3397 metres; 11,145 feet). A few nomads had also stopped here and tagged their tent onto one of the empty houses. We had a short break as we were now in brilliant sunshine and as we were just above the tree line we had a perfect view of the snow-clad peaks in every direction. David Snellgrove had overnighted here in 1956 after he had made a visit to the village of Pungmo a little further west.

Another kilometre brought us to the start of the real climb. We could see the high point ahead at the top of a ridge. Many zigzags along a steep, rough and loose path brought us to that point; however, it simply led us round a corner with a view of even more steep zigzags and an even higher point ahead. This climbed up to another ridge where some of the porters were resting. Narendra, our local guide, didn't want to stop and pointed to an even higher ridge with prayer flags and a pergola/rotunda on top. Eventually we got there and I downed a most necessary and welcome litre of water and a chocolate bar.

The breathtaking surprise was that this was the spot where we got the first, and possibly best, view of the Phoksumdo waterfall. At a drop of over 200 metres this is Nepal's highest waterfall and it is spectacular in its power and noise as it jets out over a series of four or five cascades. We were by now well above the tree line and had clear views across the valley to the mountains in the east. A short climb up the loose rocky track of another 50 metres gained us a cairn covered in prayer flags and from here we glimpsed the lake. A small triangle of an intense blue luminescence glowing through the trees less than 2 kilometres away. We were within reach of Phoksumdo.

As Thoreau said, 'A lake is a landscape's most beautiful and expressive feature. It is Earth's eye; looking into which the beholder measures the depth of his own nature.' So, were we observing nature or was nature watching us?

11
RINGMO

From the day's high point where we'd had our first glimpse of the lake there was a gentle 2-kilometre walk downhill on a wide trail through trees which brought us, after half an hour, to Ringmo – a height gain of 400 metres for the day.

At the edge of the village were several ancient *chortens* painted in cream and ochre colours. The main entrance *kani chorten* had a wooden platform high up supported at each corner by wooden posts. This was a pattern I had seen infrequently on my travels. In Manang, just north of Annapurna, there had been a similar form, but with a smooth plastered surface and painted a bright white. The *chortens* in Ringmo had a much more rustic finish, rough plaster and wood with the red and cream colour applied seemingly haphazardly. Nevertheless, the overall effect was imposing and pleasing. There were scattered dwellings numbering thirty or so. In the centre of the village one of the larger buildings was a store with a limited selection of beer, biscuits and noodles. About 100 metres beyond the houses we came to our campsite on the edge of the lake. There was a clear view to our left of the trail we must soon follow. It was the precarious track, set into the face of the massive cliff, 'the Demon's Path' spectacularly featured, with plummeting yak, in the *Himalaya* movie.

How to describe the colour of the lake? 'Pure' is the first word which springs to mind. It is also profoundly 'blue'. It wasn't simply a reflection of the blue sky. It was lighter than that, in the nature of glacial waters worldwide, and it had a uniformity which may have hinted at the immense depth of the lake. The clarity was evidenced by the rocks visible near the water's edge fading rapidly into a deeper blueness. The brightness and depth of colour of lapis lazuli is probably closer to the mark. Turquoise, which adorns many of the Dolpo ladies, is probably a bit too pale and greenish to be the definitive colour of the lake. Alasdair told me that after the trip when friends saw his photographs a couple of them asked why he'd photoshopped the colours and, of course, he hadn't. Even Peter Matthiessen had trouble describing this most imposing body of water. He said, 'Its translucent blue-green colour must reflect a white sand on the lake floor far below,' and then he relied on another commentator. He carried on: 'Truly it is a lake without impurities, like the dust-free mirror of Buddhist symbolism which "although it offers an endless procession of pictures, is uniform and colourless, unchanging, yet not apart from the pictures it reveals"', a snippet from *The Tantric Mysticism of Tibet* by John Blofeld. Maybe it can just be said that the lake was an amazing and unique 'Phoksumdo blue' and, 'mirror-like, reflects the emotions and passion of the observer'. Though it may evade explicit description, this expanse of exquisite blueness makes one's spirit soar.

As we had lunch and then got the tents sorted out, some light rain began. This turned to sleet by the time we had afternoon tea, during which Ade announced that he had some news about our intended route. The Kang La (5350 metres; 17,552 feet) was blocked by snow! The Three Amigos were visibly disappointed. They had attempted this route and been turned back by snow two years earlier and that's why they were attempting this Dolpo trek for a second time. 'Fortunately,' Ade explained, 'there are a couple of alternatives.' We braced ourselves.

Alternative Route One would take us off-piste up another valley and over an apparently unnamed pass.

'Eleven groups have gone over that way this week and not come back,' said Ade and was greeted with cries of 'That doesn't sound very good'.

'Okay,' said Ade, 'they haven't been forced to return then.'

Equally positive news was that only that morning someone had travelled this route and arrived in Ringmo from Shey. This was seriously good news after all.

Alternative Route Two would take us past the lake and then north-east to Saldang, missing out Shey Gompa. This was the way that George Schaller had returned to Ringmo from Saldang after Matthiessen had left and where he'd glimpsed a snow leopard just north of the lake.

The rain continued and it was relaxing just staying in the cosiness of the tent until dinner. Once again Saila's eclectic menu hit the spot and was consumed with gusto.

In a couple of days we would give Alternative Route One our best shot and make for Shey Gompa. First we had an acclimatisation day to look around Ringmo.

16 MAY

Rest day, Phoksumdo

The day was clear and the lake, total eye candy.

After breakfast, Colin and Duncan collected their packed lunch and set off for a day's walking up a ridge to the east of Ringmo. This was to be their modus operandi, whereby they didn't take rest days but went as high as they could. The rest of us were happy to rest, recuperate and absorb as much of the local culture as we were able, be it monasteries, local shops or just talking to the people as they worked their fields and tended the animals.

At 10.00 a.m. a few of us set off to the Bon Gompa, about twenty minutes' walk away on its own promontory at the south-east corner of the lake. The Tibetan name for Ringmo is 'Tsho' and the name of the monastery Thasung Tsholing Gompa. The surface of the lake insisted on remaining its unbelievable blue and the eye was constantly attracted to it, so one had to remain vigilant and work hard to look at the trail so as not to stumble. Then, instantly it was eyes back to the stunning aquatic vista. The purity of this water is obvious. No boats ply its surface, no fish swim below. At its edge there is no sign of weed or algae. Understandably, this lake has always demanded respect and been revered. Snellgrove walked this path in 1956 and said, 'The water is edged with silver birch and the gleaming whiteness of the branches against the unearthly blue of the water is one of the most blissful things that I have known.' I couldn't help but agree wholeheartedly. Among the ancient juniper trees higher up the bank a large and crumbling *chorten*, with a smaller companion, marked the boundary of the monastic land.

The main track leading up to the monastery proper had, on its left, a row of eleven *chortens* in various stages of decay. Matthiessen had reported that although the inhabitants of Ringmo were in the main Buddhist, one of them said to him, 'I am Buddhist, but I walk around the prayer stones the wrong way.' Many carved *mani* stones were scattered on and around these rocky *chortens*. I was especially familiar with the mantra 'Om Mani Padme Hum' in all its manifestations – carved, painted, embroidered. These stones were different. Instead of being a series of six Tibetan symbols making up the mantra – 'Om – Ma – Ni – Pad – Me – Hum' – these inscriptions were longer. They carried the Bon mantra 'Om Matri Muye Sale Du' and this is made up of eight symbols – 'Om – Ma –Tri – Mu – Ye – Sa – Le – Du' – only the first two being the same as the Buddhist inscriptions. I think that David Snellgrove gave the best interpretation of 'Om Mani Padme Hum' as being 'O thou of the jewelled lotus', the mantra of Avalokiteshvara, Chenrezig of Tibet. However, he had trouble translating the Bon mantra. He says 'Om' is the ancient Indian mystic symbol. 'Matri Muye' meant nothing to him. He was told that this was the language of Zhangzhung but dismissed this information as 'this language is largely a pretence'. 'Sa Le Du' is a Tibetan phrase and can be translated as 'in clarity unite'.

Walking past the row of slowly deteriorating *chortens* brought us to the main group of ancient buildings but there was only one monk at the monastery when we arrived. The other monk, the one with the key, had been conducting a *puja* the evening before to bless the new hydroelectric system that was being installed in Ringmo. He hadn't yet returned and there was speculation that the celebration may well have gone on until the early hours. At the time of Snellgrove's visit there were only two monks here but also twelve laymen, some of whom were married and 'who interest themselves more or less in the religious life'. One of the two monks came from the Tibetan province of Kham. He was a charming man whose incredibly long hair was wound up on his head into an impressive top-knot. Snellgrove said, 'He manifested no surprise at meeting travellers like us and no wondering curiosity at our tents and equipment. He just met us on equal terms as fellow-beings.' He had lived at Ringmo for twenty-seven years and the following day while visiting Snellgrove's camp, he related the myth of the origin of Phoksumdo Lake. There was a village many years before where the lake now is. A demoness was fleeing from 'The Lotus

Born' – Padmasambhava or Guru Rinpoche – who was in the process of transforming Tibet into a Buddhist country. To the locals living in the village the demoness gave a lump of turquoise as a bribe to stop them telling Lotus Born that she had passed that way. However, the more powerful Padmasambhava turned the turquoise into a pile of dung and the villagers were so incensed at what they took to be the trickery of the demoness that they revealed where she was hiding. She exacted her own revenge by causing the flood which inundated the village and that is now the lake.

Dolpo Amchi Namgyal Rinpoche, a well-educated monk practising traditional medicine in present day Dho Tarap, tells a slightly different tale in his book *Dolpo. The Hidden Land.* Around 700 CE the Red-Handed Demoness was active and powerful in Tibet. When Padmasambhava arrived there at the invitation of King Trisong Detsen he used his powers to kill her, but upon dying she gave being to three new demonesses who fled into Dolpo. The eldest went towards Tarap and gave a yak herder a large turquoise as a bribe not to give away her destination. When the Lotus Born spoke to the yak herder he pulled out the turquoise, which instantly turned into a snake. He destroyed the snake and, knowing he was on the right path, carried on to Tarap. In the meantime the demoness had used soil from India to dam the river, thus filling the valley with water. Guru Rinpoche used his sword to cut a gorge, now known as the Kyezig La, draining the water before he went on to kill the demoness. The second of the siblings fled to the Phoksumdo area, where she filled the valley with water. Padmasambhava made short work of despatching the witch and then created the outlet for part of the lake to drain away via the waterfall. The third demoness went to a place called Tidru in the lower valleys, where she was soon found and quickly destroyed and the Great Man, having rid Dolpo of the three sorceresses, erected *chortens* there now known as 'The Three Containers'.

In 1956 Snellgrove was disappointed that the monastery buildings at Ringmo were in such a state of disrepair, one of the main buildings actually in danger of falling down. Seventeen years later George Schaller was able to report that one of the two monks had died and the other men had moved away. The monastery was locked up and in an even more dilapidated condition.

The monk who was there on the day of our visit was happy to chat while sunning himself but, sadly, unable to let us in to the *gompa*. Like Matthiessen, we were disappointed that we couldn't see inside. Snellgrove had described the interior frescoes and statues in eminently precise detail, so it really was a pity to miss out on a viewing. We had to be content with seeing the quite splendid set of front doors with a pair of fierce white dragons and, at the top, a small figure of Shenrab, the Bon deity. I had a good scramble around the main buildings and got the photographs I needed. From the slopes above the monastery there was a remarkable view of the dozen old and crumbling ochre-painted *chortens* along the trail, with the endlessly hypnotic blue of the lake behind. Looking west across the water was the towering peak and sheer bulk of the Kanjiroba Himal, brilliant white with snow and a sharp pyramidal peak reaching up to 6612 metres (21,692 feet).

I headed back through Ringmo to find out how the installation of a new hydroelectric system was going. In the centre of the village the largest *chorten* was a walk-in *chorten* with a single doorway but this was blocked off and the edifice apparently undergoing renovation. This 250-year-old structure is known as the Kalsang Ombar and was built by the great master Treton Namkha Gyaltsen from Pugmo. Indeed, it is one of four built by him to create a giant geographical mandala along with the others in Pugmo, Dho-Tarap and Parla. Snellgrove waxed lyrical about this particular Ringmo *chorten* and the superlative paintings inside. He considered the ceiling with its nine mandala panels to be the finest painting he'd seen on his travels and was convinced that there was no one around who could recreate anything like it. It was thus a bit disappointing that the whole thing was closed. I carried on past the Kalsang Ombar and looked down the bank of the river, occupied by a couple of dozen people, to the site of the hydroelectric construction, which was a hive of frenetic activity.

Alasdair had spoken to the leader, a fellow called Peter Werth, the evening before and got the story. Six men from North America were working on behalf of an NGO called Himalayan Currents, which is 'dedicated to solving energy and water problems throughout the Himalaya region'. They had installed a water pump at the Tapriza school and a combined wind and solar tower at the school in Saldang. A group of them had brought the mechanics of a turbine, the blades, lifting mechanism and bearings as well as the electrical generator itself, in bits from America and had spent a couple of weeks attempting to install it. The main job had been to construct a channel from rocks in the shallow river about 200 metres downstream from where it left the lake. Across the channel was a beam and that would allow the turbine blades to be rotated in and out of the water for maintenance. By damming the stream to one side the water would flow through the channel, turn the blades and produce an estimated 5 kilowatts of electricity for Ringmo. A whole series of poles around the village carried the wire to all the houses in readiness for the great switch-on. The 5-kilowatt output would be enough to provide a light bulb or recharge a battery for each house, but not much more. I spoke to one of the fellows, a Canadian, who was helping install it. They were having a lot of trouble with a rock obstructing the blades and quite a few people were in the icy water trying to fix it. Many of the villagers sat on the bank watching the show. Some were building a fire to warm the workers once they got out of the stream. Philippe took off his shoes to paddle across the knee-deep shallows to see how it was going. This gave the locals, both young and old, a brilliant opportunity to pelt stones around him to give him a soaking. Hilarious fun for them, and me, and Philippe bore it with a smile and a display of true Gallic sangfroid. The team had been struggling for almost an hour and the people in the water were getting dangerously cold and the watching crowd a little bored. At last there was a shout of 'all clear' and the turbine blade was lowered into the gushing water. It instantly started turning at about 60 per cent of its working speed. By the end of the afternoon the flow of water had been increased and the electricity was heading, day and night, into Ringmo.

Just before lunch the mess tent blew over! All vastly exciting, especially as I was in it at the time, but Chandra and the boys as we called them, using the term in its familiar rather than derogatory sense, had it standing again in a few minutes with plenty more rocks securing its edges. Duncan and Colin were still away up a ridge, Harry was meditating by the lake and building stone cairns and Susan was in her tent. Alasdair and I decided to go for a walk along the left bank of the river and climb up through a forest to get a view of the waterfall from its eastern side. It was a most excellent viewpoint and the cataract seemed twice as big from this aspect as we could see directly onto its lower cascades. We could also see our route up from Amchi Hospital of the day before, with its tortuous, narrow and impressively steep track to the pergola. As we returned, at the edge of the village, a family was out ploughing their small fields. The pair of dark brown *dzo*, the yak-cattle hybrid, was led by one of the men as they pulled a simple 'T' piece of wood.

At the end was a wooden ploughshare tipped by a short piece of metal. The ground was a dry and dusty powder full of rocks. As the team went by a couple of women with picks turned out and threw to one side the larger stones. The family gave us a wave and a '*Tashi delek*' as we went by and paused to smile, suitably briefly, for our photos before the intense work of ploughing went on.

Back at camp it was the usual 3.30 p.m. afternoon tea time. Colin rolled in exactly on time but of Duncan, there was no sign. Apparently, not long after he and Colin set off with their packed lunches after breakfast, they'd split up! I was incredulous. Travelling alone in the mountains is courting disaster. Colin hadn't seen him since 9.30 that morning. Colin had gone up the ridge but Duncan had, for some reason, taken off up a valley. There was still no sign of him at 16.30 so, as he was now an hour overdue, Bishwo was sent off to find him. Another hour went by and Colin and Susan were starting to get quite upset. 'He may have sprained an ankle,' said one. 'He might have pulled his back,' bemoaned the other. I was thinking he might well be in very dire straits. A serious injury to him would put the dampeners on the rest of the trip. However, he rolled in unscathed at 18.00, just as it was getting dark, saying to Ade, 'Sorry. I miscalculated.' And that was it. No further explanation was forthcoming, but he was physically intact. Ade was fuming but was really unable to say anything.

Dinner was a quiet affair as the Three Amigos seemed, justifiably, subdued. After dinner, once the rest of us started talking about climbing and our own adventures, the three of them, now relieved and thinking they were no longer 'in the dog house', started their own near hysterical conversation and just about drowned us out. Hysteria may well have been in the air that evening, for in the morning we all knew we faced the daunting obstacle of the Demon's Path.

12
CATERPILLAR FUNGUS

In May 2012, I was in Lhasa following the trek up to Advanced Base Camp on the north side of Everest. The shops and market stalls around the Barkhor sell everything from beads and Buddhas to prayer flags, paintings and yak butter. There were skins and tails from a variety of animals, some endangered. I was relieved not to see any snow leopard pelts. It was, however, still possible to buy a decorated human skull or a flute made from a human femur. The traditional musical instrument is known as a *kangling*; quite literally 'leg' (*kang*) 'flute' (*ling*). When Ekai Kamaguchi travelled into Tibet in 1900, he passed along a remote Dolpo valley and wrote, 'At some places the thawing snow had revealed the bleached remains of human beings, probably frozen to death. The curious thing was that the skull and leg bones were missing from every one of the skeletons I came across. It was explained to me that the Tibetans manufactured certain utensils, used for ritualistic purposes, from these portions of human bones; and that it was their practice to appropriate them whenever they came upon the remains of luckless wanderers.'

After my second or third *kora*, a circumambulation of the pilgrim's way, around the Jokhang I spotted a traditional medicine shop at the eastern end of the Barkhor. I went in and found that the proprietor spoke a little English. I explained that I was a doctor and was interested in seeing the caterpillar fungus if he had any. I'd only recently heard about this 'traditional medicine' and had seen a documentary on the strange life cycle of a fungus living on a dead caterpillar, called *Cordyseps sinensis*. My new friend produced, from under the counter, a glass-fronted box about 10 x 15 centimetres. Inside were exactly twelve desiccated caterpillars with dark brown curled twigs coming out of their heads. Each was 7 or 8 centimetres long. I asked the price and he told me it was 40,000 yuan. The exchange rate at the time was 6.5 yuan to the Australian dollar, so that meant about $6100 for the dozen, over $500 each. They weigh in at around half a gram each so the going rate for the caterpillar fungus was $1000 per gram. Gold was trading at $54.30 per gram. The little dry worms in front of me weren't just worth their weight in gold, they were going for twenty times that.

In March 2013 the *Want China Times*, an English language newspaper based in Taiwan, carried an article entitled 'Prices of caterpillar fungus surge out of control'. The prices over the years had risen from $19 per kilogram in 1982 to $482 in 1993. In the 1990s much was made of 'medical research' hinting at some efficacy for the powdered cordyseps, and the prices really began to take off. By 2003 the price, as quoted by the Shanghai-based *First Financial Daily*, was $2571 per kilogram and by 2012 had reached $142,680 per kilogram. This made my Lhasa cordyseps seem somewhat overpriced at $1,000,000 per kilogram. I guessed that I was being quoted the Western tourist price of ten times the local going rate.

Ian Baker, in *The Heart of the World*, tells of his first retreat in meditative pursuit of understanding the Tibetan notion of the hidden lands, the *beyuls*. In 1986 he trekked to the north-east of Kathmandu and at the behest of an old lama called Chatral Rinpoche he was to spend over a month alone in a cave. He says, 'I had brought a month's supply of mung beans and brown rice, as well as carrots, onions and spinach. To fortify my diet, I'd bought a bag of yartsagunbu (*cordyseps sinensis*), a high-altitude caterpillar fungus favoured by the Chinese Olympic team, from a Tibetan trader in Kathmandu.' He didn't say how many were in the bag or how much they cost but it must have been an ample supply. He stayed in his cave for a week longer than he anticipated and said 'My food supplies had dwindled and I lived on little more than lemon water and sautéed yartsagunbu'.

So, what is so special about the caterpillar fungus?

Traditional Chinese medicine has long relied upon herbal and animal-based concoctions. The basic list of plant extracts, animal parts and minerals runs into the many hundreds and the various combinations probably represent over 100,000 medicinal recipes. Consequently there are such esoteric items in their pharmacopoeia as human placenta, fungi of every variety, animal parts such as horn and gallstones, insects such as scorpion and centipede, leech, human pubic hair and quite literally snake oil. More disturbing to Western sensitivities is the use of tiger penis and rhinoceros horn. It must therefore come as no surprise that when an organism was discovered that was half animal half plant it had unique and remarkable qualities attributed to it.

The use of this phenomenal creature/plant dates to at least the fifteenth century, when it was mentioned in a Tibetan medical text by Zurkhar Nyamnyi Dorje (1439–75) and it was called by its Tibetan name – *yartsa gunbu*, or 'winter worm, summer grass'. In Nepali this is rendered as *yarsa gumba* or *yarsha gumba.*

The scientific name was originally *Cordyseps sinensis*, *Cordyseps* being a genus of over 400 species. However, genetic studies have shown that the particular species present in the Tibetan fungus is unrelated to the 400 or so others, and in 2007 the more correct nomenclature of *Ophiocordyseps sinensis* in the family *Ophiocordycipitaceae* was applied.

Modern chemical analyses have revealed a potentially active compound which has been named 'cordycepin' and about which many claims have been made. It is said to have a suppressant effect on the immune system, so possibly anti-inflammatory. However, there is still no scientific proof of efficacy.

The peculiarity of the *yarsa gumba* hinges on its bizarre life cycle. In Tibet and the high Himalaya the *Ophiocordyseps'* victim, the ghost moth, lives at an altitude between 4000 and 5000 metres and lays its eggs in the high pastures. In the late summer the larvae of the ghost moth (genus *Thitarodes* of the family *Hepialidae*) develop from the eggs and move underground to feed on the roots of various plants. As they grow and pass through the increasingly larger stages known as 'instars' they ingest the spores of the *Ophiocordyseps sinensis*. The larvae move to a position a centimetre or two below the surface of the ground, head end up, in preparation for the change to a pupa and the metamorphosis into the moth in the spring. However, the infected caterpillar, lying dormant over the winter, is totally taken over and consumed by the hyphae of the fungus. In the spring a brownish shoot, with a blunt cap, begins to emerge from the head end of the carcass of the caterpillar. It pokes its way just a few centimetres above the ground. The cap, like all mushrooms, produces more spores to then infect the next generation of insects.

In his book *Entangled Life*, scholar and fungus expert Merlin Sheldrake describes some other varieties of *Ophiocordyseps* that can infect and apparently control the behaviour of insects. He calls them 'zombie fungi'. One in particular, *Ophiocordyseps unilateralis*, infects the normally earthbound carpenter ant and compels it to climb up a plant stalk and in its death throes clamp on by its jaws. Mycelia then grow out and bind its legs to the plant. Sometime later the tiny mushrooms emerge from the ant's moribund head to spread the spores to 'take over' the next ant.

The incredible increase in value of the *yarsa gumba* has meant that the financial incentive to leave one's village and journey many kilometres to dig for caterpillar fungus is huge. This has led to an annual exodus. Whole families leave their home town or village and head off to higher altitudes for the collecting season. Until 2001 the collection was illegal, but the Nepalese government, sensing an easy profit, started charging a fee. One effect of this migration is that during May and June, when the fields should be ploughed and crops planted for the short growing season, there are not enough workers available. Fields are underprepared and untended. At best it may be the old people and children doing the work. Dolpo provides as much as 50 per cent of the annual *yarsa gumba* harvest and the rich pickings mean their traditional agricultural work is sorely neglected.

And the reason for recounting this tale of complex biology and sociology? We were there in Dolpo at the absolute height of the short digging season. People were still travelling to the high pastures from their remote villages, and we saw plenty of evidence of the upheaval: quiet villages, closed schools and whole families on the trails. If we came across any locked-up house, monastery or school our guides or the locals would simply shake their heads and mumble, sagely, 'Ah, *yarsa gumba*.'

During our short time in Inner Dolpo we came across many individuals and families heading up the trails to the high pasture. Villages were silent and near deserted, with few men and only small numbers of the old and the children.

I was to learn more disturbing facts about the societal and environmental upheaval wrought by this modern pharmacological goldrush upon my return to Australia.

13
THE DEMON'S PATH

17 MAY

Ringmo (3648 metres; 11,968 feet)
to Phoksumdo Khola (3712 metres; 12,178 feet)
via high point approximately 4000 metres (13,123 feet)
9.1 kilometres

A clear blue sky and a frosty morning. The camp was packed up, breakfast eaten and we were off at 8.00 and without hesitation onto the 'Demon's Path'. In the movie *Himalaya* this was the way Thinle led his caravan by way of a shortcut. George Schaller had looked across at this quasi-aerial path from the lakeside and remarked to Peter Matthiessen, 'That's not something you'd want to do every day.'

We were at the start of the path merely fifteen minutes after leaving our campsite. The trail began at water level, then, only a metre wide, it ascended to follow the cliff about 20 to 30 metres above the lake and gradually got a little higher, to 50 metres or so above the blue water. This was where the yak plummeted off the precipice so spectacularly in the movie.

It was mesmerising to be in such a surreal setting, which required the taking of two or three steps then a hasty glance at the view, then more steps, head nodding down, then up and round. You didn't want to miss the view, but you couldn't afford a single misplaced step. In places the trail was suspended on logs wedged into cracks in the cliff face. Two hundred metres brought us to a left turn, from where the narrower path contoured round a small bay while keeping us suspended 40 to 50 metres above the pristine blue lake surface. Matthiessen said of this section of the trail: 'One horrid stretch, lacking the smallest handhold in the wall, round a windy point of cliff that is one hundred feet or more above the rocks at lake edge, and this I navigate on hands and knees, arriving a lifetime later.' Snellgrove simply says, 'The track climbs round the western side of the Phoksumdo Lake, keeping close under the cliffs that tower above. Where it can go no further one must trust oneself to a slender gangway of silver birch suspended on pegs driven into crevices in the rock.' For me this section of our route was one of the highlights of the whole trip.

After an hour of pure exhilaration, the track led us down into a grove of trees at the bottom of a canyon carved by the outflow from a glacier on the southern edge of Kanjiroba. Beyond, the trail climbed up a series of ridges to reach a high point around 4000 metres. We could look down on the lake from our viewpoint 400 metres above this vivid monochrome Himalayan loch and back to the Bon monastery and Ringmo, from whence we'd come. It was hard going but an absolute pleasure. This was idyllic trekking, the stuff of dreams. After a short break it was all downhill towards the north end of the lake. On a particularly steep and rocky stretch we were overtaken by a yak herder in a bit of a hurry, driving a group of eight or nine young black yaks. They stormed past us gambolling, snorting and prancing in a cloud of dust, cavorting and clearly enjoying themselves.

The trail to the top end of the lake descended through a long stretch of mainly silver birch trees and we had lunch about midday, sitting on a tarpaulin on the lake shore. I happily nodded off quite easily on the grass after lunch with a rock as a pillow. This was heavenly. It was also the site of Matthiessen's 'Silver Birch Camp', where he and Schaller enjoyed talking about snow leopards beside a blazing log fire and expressing trepidation about the high pass they had to cross before reaching Shey. We shared those same anxieties.

After our break there followed a two-hour walk up the long flat valley of the Phoksumdo Khola to our next campsite. All the while we were negotiating our way below the massive face of Kanjiroba Himal (6612 metres; 21,692 feet) towering over us on our left-hand side. Just before reaching camp we heard, then saw, a couple of small avalanches plummeting off the hanging glaciers. I was reminded of the character Binder's description of the magnificent north face of Rum Doodle in the book *The Ascent of Rum Doodle*: 'The North Wall is a sheer glass-like face of ice broken only by rock, snowfields, ice-pinnacles, crevasses, bergschrunds, ridges, gulleys, scree, chimneys, cracks, slabs, gendarmes, Dames Anglaises, needles, strata, gneiss and gabbro.'

It was now becoming clear what the usual trekking order was. Everyone on these trips walks at their own pace and one of the pleasures of trekking is to be able to vary your speed. You can go slower in beautiful surroundings, faster if the weather is about to change, necessarily slowly uphill, and always with time to stop, look around, get a photograph or have a chat. Usually a group will spread itself out over quite a long distance and just regroup at lunch stops and campsites. We always had Chandra, or one of the two deputy guides, Bishwo or Gopal, out front leading. Then Alasdair, Colin, Duncan, Harry and myself, regularly swapping the order. Susan would be some distance behind, then Philippe way back. Ade liked to move up and down and would hover around the middle of the group to be in touch with everyone. Now his back was much better, he had no trouble taking the lead when necessary. Everyone has their own style of walking. I like to use a pair of trekking poles and get into a steady rhythm. Alasdair would use them on steep downhill stretches to take some strain off the knees. Harry wasn't keen on poles and neither was Colin. Duncan, however, always carried two poles; he utilised the right one but the other seemed to be used for waving around and potentially stabbing the person behind if they got too close. Ade and Chandra used a single pole.

As we wandered up the valley the going was easy as it was so flat. At one point a couple of locals trotted by on their ponies. They were colourful characters, their animals handsome and decked out in bright trappings and decorated blankets. The second of the pair spoke English and said, 'You go Shey?' When we said 'yes', he said, 'No problem. Pass open,' so we knew we'd be able to cross. The campsite in the valley was in a clearing with a primitive *chorten* built on a large boulder. The tents were soon up with tea at 16.00 then into the massive mess tent. Again, another pleasure of trekking is to be able to sit in the mess tent and chat over tea and biscuits. Chandra and Bishwo had a daily chess match and both claimed to be ahead in their long-term series of battles. Most of us would bring books and diaries and we'd swap notes about the day's events. It was fascinating to compare Matthiessen's 'Snow Leopard' trek and Snellgrove's progress in *Himalayan Pilgrimage* with our own journey. This day's walk for Snellgrove had been decidedly boggy as all the log bridges were down and the river higher following the spring thaw. Snellgrove had been here at the beginning of May, so we were travelling about two weeks later in the season than him.

Dinner was most welcome, then it was early to bed. We'd been up to 4000 metres this day but were basically back down to lake level. Tomorrow was going to be a long way up but, even then, still short of the pass leading to Shey.

18 MAY

Phoksumdo Khola (3712 metres; 12,178 feet)
to High Camp (4731 metres; 15,521 feet)
8.6 kilometres

Another beautiful clear and cold morning. The boys had a fire going and in the still air the smoke hung over the camp smelling richly of conifer. Kanjiroba towered, gleaming, above us, the cloud of the previous evening completely dispersed.

The gentle walk continued along the valley, slowly rising. This was the way, directly north, to the Kang La. But that was not to be our route. We came to our turn-off up a particularly narrow gorge immediately on our right heading due east. This was the way into 'alternative one', which was to lead up to the valley we had to traverse to reach the pass. At the base of this chasm was a clump of pussy willow, *Salix caprea*, each tree covered in furry grey catkins. Beyond lay a cleft in the mountain with a torrential stream pouring over massive rocks, a steep cataract of one waterfall after another.

It was a strenuous morning of climbing boulders and crisscrossing the torrent. The trail itself was invisible in places but the only way was up. There were large patches of old grey ice in spots the sun never reached in this deep forbidding gorge. We'd soon left all trees behind. At around 4200 metres (13,799 feet) we stopped for lunch in a slightly wider part of the valley where we could lounge in the sun. I was amazed to see half a dozen of the porters suddenly dash onto the opposite bank of the stream and swarm up the hillside where they spent a happy but unproductive half hour searching for *yarsa gumba*. Later, when we'd reached around 4500 metres, the going became extremely laborious. Harry and I were the least acclimatised and we lagged a bit behind the leaders, although still ahead of Susan and Philippe.

At last, in the late afternoon, we reached our high campsite at the top of the valley, at 4700 metres. It was apparently at the head of the valley, with a 20-metre-high frozen waterfall behind us, and the trail winding up to the skyline was about 100 metres above that and some half a kilometre away. We were at the same height as the famous 'Snowfields Camp' mentioned in *The Snow Leopard* and which Matthiessen found intensely lonely and uncomfortable. I thought our position was reasonably sheltered and I loved the view back to the Kanjirobas but I must confess to feeling a bit angry with Ade, as we had gone from 3700 metres to 4700 metres in one day, three times the recommended ascent rate. It wasn't his choice of course. There was no other way of doing this and in fact everyone was feeling just plain tired. I understood the importance of drinking a lot of water so walked off to the base of a small ice field to gather a couple of litres of meltwater. The walk, about 100 metres there then back, took over twenty minutes due to the limiting effects of high altitude.

I made sure I drank my two litres of water and spent the next hour taking plenty of photos. There was no real point in erecting the mess tent, so we had dinner served in our tents. Tomato soup and noodles was all I felt like as my appetite was suppressed. I was otherwise well: no headache and my breathing was fine at rest. I went to sleep fully expecting someone to get sick during the night.

19 MAY

High Camp (4731 metres; 15,521 feet)
to Shey Gompa (4388 metres; 14,396 feet)
via pass at 5315 metres (17,437 feet)
9.1 kilometres

Next morning was intensely cold but I'd had a good few hours' sleep and felt ready for the challenge of the pass. Bed tea was at 5.00, the sun not quite risen, so we had time to reach the pass while the ground was still frozen. The others were all mercifully well and after quickly packing up to get warm we were off at 6.00. Leaving the frozen waterfall to our left we had an hour's hard slog to reach the point on the skyline we had seen from our camp. Here we simply entered another higher valley, which opened up to an impressive vista of massive snowfields in all directions. We followed the stream for a half hour, then, crossing it, we turned north and had a remarkably long climb up loose scree which reminded me of the volcanic ash of Mount Ngauruhoe in New Zealand. However, this stuff we were struggling up was made of small and wet fragments of slate. Halfway up this slope we got word that one of the porters was unwell. He was a small man about forty years old and a bit of a smoker. I'd noticed him coughing incessantly, and Ade and I thought it best to send him back down to Ringmo.

The going was tediously slow as we passed the 5000-metre mark. Harry and I hit our 'VO2 max'. We could breathe as much as possible and walk as slowly as possible but we'd reached a limit. One or two breaths per step and a rest every few metres was all we could manage. We were nowhere near sufficiently acclimatised to be attempting this height with any confidence. Alasdair and Ade had been much higher in the last couple of weeks. Duncan and Colin had some recent altitude trips behind them. Susan was a fair way behind even Harry and myself and, as usual, Philippe was fighting a rear-guard action at a pace all of his own. Still, speed was of absolutely no consequence. It was a gorgeous day in the mountains, so even though it was hard work there was a certain masochistic pleasure to be had in simply being there. Living in that particular moment was a privilege and there was nowhere else on Earth I'd rather have been.

Onwards, ever upwards, and after a long four-hour plod we reached a pass which we later found out was called Nagdalo La, with a superb view across Dolpo and into Tibet. Behind us was the long ice-fluted face of Kanjiroba. Ahead a thick ridge of snow led to a north-facing snowfield, at the end of which we could see the lake and valley described in Matthiessen's book as being between the Kang La and Shey. The lake, completely frozen over, was Matthiessen's 'Black Pond', where he camped after his crossing of the Kang La. The steep-sided valley ahead of us drew the eye past the waves and layers of mountains to the far horizon where there stood a spectacular peak made of brown rock and glacier clad, standing higher than all the surrounding mountains and resembling in shape the Matterhorn in the Alps. Gopal was next to me.

'Hey, Gopal. What's the name of that big mountain over there?' I said, pointing directly at it.

Gopal shrugged. 'Sorry. I have no idea.'

I turned to Chandra, who'd been this way before, but he was also unaware of its name. I resolved to find out about it on our return. It turned out to be Danphe Sail (6103 metres; 20,022 feet), sitting just on the border with Tibet and about 45 kilometres from where we stood. It was still unclimbed, most likely because of its remoteness. The Matterhorn itself stands at 4478 metres (14,691 feet), more than 1.5 kilometres lower.

The boys had hacked a path through the lip of the snow ridge and were trying to get the horses down. Three went but the other three refused and nothing would entice or force them. Eventually the pony boy and his charges were paid off and they headed back to Ringmo. I think that secretly he was quite pleased to be heading back, but it meant that we had six horse loads of gear that would need transportation to Shey somehow.

Ade gave us the height of the pass from his GPS. It was 5315 metres, the same as the Kang La. We'd ascended 1700 metres in thirty-six hours but now, thankfully, it was time to start going down.

Everyone else had crampons or 'yak-trax', but Chandra and Bishwo didn't, so I was happy following their example, knowing that I could trust my boots. It was an easy 100-metre traverse across to a point where the next obvious way was straight down with an inelegant 100-metre glissade on our backsides. Wheeeeh! It was great fun and I was soon followed by Alasdair and Harry. After the sheer discomfort of the ascent, going downhill was joyful and breathing was easy. At the bottom a pile was made of the gear which the horses had been carrying. Much of it had been rolled down the slope. Some of the porters were to come back the next day for it. We marched on down to the valley leading to Shey Gompa.

We approached the 'Black Pond', leaving it to our left and continued downstream. The river in this valley, Matthiessen's 'Black River', was the Hubalung Khola, which flows north to join the Sephu Khola at Shey, the two merging to form the Tartang Khola and continuing to flow north. The distance was deceptive. Another large flat snowfield had to be crossed. I stepped off the rocks onto the snow and disappeared in it up to my chest. We were all spread out at this stage and there was no one else around. I kicked my way out and took a more promising path across the slushy snow. After another pair of large boggy snowfields, largely managed on my backside, the trail joined a reasonable track which followed the river. I'd seen some buildings way down the valley and as I got closer some *mani* walls appeared at the trailside. This was on the Crystal Mountain *kora*, the pilgrims' circuit of the holy mountain. One interesting feature that I'd never seen before was the occasional *mani* stone carved in the form of a six-spoked wheel or six-petalled flower. The tip of each point bore one of the classic symbols of the Om-Ma-Ni-Pad-Me-Hum mantra. These *mani* stones are called *mani dhokhor* and seem peculiar to Dolpo. The going on the trail was now quite good but it wasn't until well after 2.00 p.m., eight and a half hours after leaving high camp, that we reached Shey. Six water-driven prayer wheels, their streams supplied by a conduit from the river, led the way to an old bridge and, looking up, there was Shey Gompa sitting high on the opposite riverbank. Its main buildings and *chortens* glowed warmly in the afternoon sun in their ochre and cream livery. This was a welcome sight. We had arrived at the Crystal Monastery.

14
UNDER CRYSTAL MOUNTAIN

After the long walk down from the Nagdalo, La Shey was a welcome sight, and I crossed the wood-and-stone bridge to finally reach the Crystal Monastery. Our tents were being erected on an area of grass just to the left as I faced the ancient *chortens* and the imposing red *gompa*. There was no mess tent, as it was still lying in the snow at the foot of the pass awaiting collection the next day, so tea was a blissful picnic on the grass. Behind our campsite, where the slope started to climb steeply up to a ridge, the ground was peppered with prodigious holes up to half a metre wide and there we saw, standing almost upright, a huge marmot. The Himalayan marmot is a large chocolate-brown animal almost a metre long with yellow patches on its face and chest. This creature wasn't shy but would quickly disappear into its underground warren if anyone approached it.

We had arrived safely at Shey Gompa. The sun shone, the valley was quiet to the ears and all around was a visual feast for the eyes. There was an overwhelming sense of peace and tranquillity. Dinner that night was served in our tents.

It had been a long day, and an early night was much needed.

20 MAY

Rest day at Shey, walk up to Tsakhang Gompa

A thousand years ago the great lama Drutob Senge Yeshe was sent from

Tibet to teach the residents of Dolpo, the Dolpo-pa. He found them to be a wild group of people who worshipped a fierce mountain spirit. He went to a cave near Shey where he meditated and gained enlightenment. Riding a flying snow lion, Drutob Senge Yeshe did battle with the spirit of the mountain, who unleashed a horde of snake monsters. The snow lion reproduced itself 108 times and the earth spirit was vanquished and transformed into a 'thundering mountain of purest crystal'.

> I flew through the sky on a snow lion
> And there, among the clouds, I performed miracles.
> But not even the greatest of celestial feats
> Can equal once rounding on foot this Crystal Mountain.
> —Drutob Senge Yeshe

This was the tale recounted by American scholar Joel Ziskin, who travelled to Dolpo in the mid-1970s and published his account in *National Geographic* in 1977. He'd journeyed to Dolpo to try to ascertain what evidence might remain of the early contact between Bon and Buddhism. He was intrigued by the stories of ancient spirit battles and the continuing influence and practice of shamanism. A monk at Shungtsher (termed 'Shangsher' by Ziskin) told him of Crystal Mountain but said that the expert was an old hermit called Tulku Tsewang at Tragyam Gompa. When they arrived there the reclusive Tsewang was on a year-long retreat, but they were able to send him a note. His reply, sent to them on a chalkboard, was: 'It is good that you have questions. Look around you. The answer is there. We shall meet after Shey.' This referred to the upcoming annual festival held at the Crystal Monastery. Besides the annual ceremonies, every twelfth year in the dragon year of the calendar, there is a great festival at Shey which is held for a week following the full moon of the seventh month of the Tibetan calendar. It is believed that a *kora*, or circuit, of Crystal Mountain in the dragon year is as good as performing a *kora* in all eleven of the other years put together. The last major festival was in 2012.

Back in the 1970s, Ziskin and his companion, Oga, journeyed to Shey and arrived the day before the full moon and joined the crowd of the faithful gathering for the festivities. They were introduced to a weathered old nomad who had done over a hundred *koras* of Crystal Mountain. He produced for them, from within his patched woollen coat, a crumbling manuscript telling the legend of Shey and even containing poems said to have been written by Drutob Senge Yeshe himself. It recited the story of the 108 snow lions and the transformation of the earth spirit into the mountain of purest crystal, finishing with 'A white conch shell fell from the sky and the yogi rose on his lion and pierced a hole in Shey's summit. Rainbows arced across the heavens.' Ziskin concluded that in the end Buddhism didn't so much crush the old beliefs as simply absorb them.

The next day Ziskin joined the throng of pilgrims and completed the *kora* himself, and then it was time for him to begin his long journey back to Kathmandu. They returned east to Namgung and the Tragyam Gompa. The old hermit, Tulku Tsewang, had emerged from his retreat and was sitting crosslegged in his *gomtri*, the square wooden meditator's crib. They asked him about the significance of Crystal Mountain. Was it a pillar of the world, as the old men said, or was it a symbol of transcendence as the monk at Shungtsher had told them? 'There are many paths along the way,' the Tulku answered. 'The yogi understood that the true nature of existence is impermanence. To a flea, a man might seem immortal. The people of Dolpo think of their mountain as indestructible. But is it? The stars have seen many such mountains come and go.'

That the Crystal Mountain *kora* is ancient and well-trodden is indisputable. Even coming from Japan Kawaguchi knew of it and was keen to perform the circumambulation. In his book he doesn't call it by the name Shey, or even Crystal Mountain. Upon saying goodbye to his companion he says:

> I turned to my guide, and told him that he could now go back, as I intended to make a lonely pilgrimage to Khambuthang, the Sacred Peach Valley, by myself. Nothing could have given him more astonishment than this intimation, for he had all along been under the impression that he was to accompany me back to Malba. He stoutly opposed my venturing on such a perilous expedition, which nobody, he said, but a living Buddha, or Bodhisattva would dare to undertake.

Kawaguchi does not discuss this side trip in his account but the map at the end of the book shows a distinct circular path north of 'Thorpo' or 'Tsaka', his versions of Tsharka, and south of the Tibetan border.

Back on our own journey I'd slept poorly due to a blocked nose. A bit of nasal congestion is common at high altitude, along with snoring and breathing through the mouth and the irregular 'Cheyne-Stokes' respiration; all up, a recipe for a rotten night's sleep. Shey sits at 4160 metres (13,648 feet) so no surprise really. Bed tea was at 7.00 a.m. and it was an absolutely beautiful morning. Harry and I sat outside on a mound where the grass was as short and smooth as a putting green due to the grazing of sheep and goats. There, joined by the others, we indulged in a scrumptious picnic breakfast. That morning's plan was to walk the 3 kilometres up to the spectacularly situated Shey Tsakhang Gompa.

Near our tents, next to the stone kitchen building, a man in a red-and-grey tracksuit and his son were sitting. They were joined by a rather rotund middle-aged man. This was Lama Tsondru, a Tibetan Rinpoche living at Shey. I got my small stuffed-toy snow leopard out of the backpack and I took it over to get a photo with the little boy, who, it turned out, was called Dorje. The Rinpoche was quite happy to have his photograph taken with the toy animal too. Harry came over and dug into his supply of inflatable balloons he'd brought for the kids. The little boy seemed pleased but a bit less so when, a few minutes later, the Rinpoche waddled off in the direction of the main *gompa* with a bright green balloon wobbling behind him. Fortunately Harry had a large supply and young Dorje was happy to receive a couple of balloons of his own.

Dorje's tracksuited father turned out to be one of the five lamas living at Shey. His name was Phurpa Tinley and he and his son were to be our guides. Young Dorje was a happy little boy dressed in a bright red jacket with an intricate yellow design, fluffy cuffs and collar of fur and a green trim down the front. His grey tracksuit pants and Chinese 'trainers' required only his black-and-red beanie to top off the ensemble. He picked the purple heads of the Himalayan primula (*Primula denticulata*), which were popping up all over the valley, and tucked one each side of his hat. He skipped along easily as we laboured in the thin air. His father told us, via Chandra, that soon the boy would be sent to Kathmandu to train as a monk. He was six years old.

Our walk to Tsakhang took about one and a half hours. We dropped down to the river and over the old narrow bridge but turned right before the water-driven prayer wheels and headed north. Just before the trail started its steep upward climb there was a final *mani* wall. Perched on the end of it was a magnificent bleached yak skull sporting a splendid pair of horns. The trail was a well-trodden one, as it was the final section of the Crystal Mountain *kora*. As well as the newly sprouting primula along the trail there were patches of a delicate lilac flower, the Himalayan gentian (*Gentiana ornata*). As we made our slow progress uphill, we found ourselves several times climbing up to a scarily high *chorten* on a ridge and turning a corner to see the next even loftier high point. Across a final gorge we could see the monastery buildings set, apparently flush, into the cliff face. Matthiessen and Schaller came this way to count the blue sheep. The first time Matthiessen visited the *gompa* two monks sat outside. One, mending his boots, looked to be about twenty and the other older monk was tanning a goat hide with a mix of brains and rancid butter. This older man he described as 'a handsome cripple' dressed in rags. They merely nodded to Matthiessen but said nothing. About ten days later, just before he left Crystal Mountain, Matthiessen made a second visit to Tsakhang to pay his respects to the Lama of Shey, who he was told was in retreat there. On his arrival the young aspirant monk, or *trapa*, was again outside. His name was Takla and he was twenty-two years old. They could hear the lama himself chanting inside the main *gompa* building and he soon joined them on the sunny ledge. Karma Tupjuk was fifty-two and came from Muktinath in Manang, north of Annapurna. When he was eight, he'd been recognised as a tulku, the reincarnation of the previous Lama of Shey. Now, after many years of emulating the hermit-like existence of his predecessor in the Kagyu lineage, the great Milarepa, he was permanently confined to Tsakhang by legs deformed with arthritis. He walked on crutches and could just manage to climb the log stairway of the *gompa*. Matthiessen described the 'old' monk as 'an imposing man with the long hawk nose and carved cheekbones of a Plains Indian'. His skin was 'reddish-copper', teeth white, hair tied up in a braid and he was clothed in an old leather jacket. A wolf skin hung in the doorway which he would wrap himself in at night. Matthiessen had a long conversation with this venerable man of Shey who, he said, kept looking at Crystal Mountain with a smile upon his face.

On this day of our visit, looking up the final slope to Tsakhang, I saw a pale cream-coloured building where guests were accommodated and, just past it, the slightly larger bright ochre *gompa* building with its decorations and prayer flags. I couldn't stop taking photographs. Beyond the Tsakhang complex a thin trail traversed the steep cliff towards a much smaller *gompa*, a single-roomed cell with a *chorten* about half a kilometre away. This was the Dolma-Jang, the Green Tara, and a true hermitage style *gompa* for retreats. It has a walled-up cave behind it which is said to be the original place where Drutob Senge Yeshe meditated before his battle with the mountain demon. The Lama of Shey told Matthiessen that only a year before his visit a group of wandering Kham-pa had stolen a fine statue of the goddess from the cave and this explained why the locals were suspicious and wary of their new visitors that year.

Crystal Mountain itself was the dominant feature high to the south-west and this was arguably the best view of it. Near a small bridge just before the final 100-metre climb up to the *gompa* the lama stopped me and, with his son Dorje pointing to the ground, showed me a large ammonite fossil about 15 centimetres across embedded, with fragments of others, in the rocks we were walking on. It was strange indeed to be there, so high that breathing was still an effort, and to think that everything around us, including Crystal Mountain itself, was once submerged in the darkness of the deep Tethys Sea. We reached the *gompa* buildings and looked around the outside. This was the monastery in the movie *Himalaya* that Thinle approached on horseback in order to see his lama son and try to persuade him to help lead the caravan. In the movie the interior, with its frescoes, was filmed elsewhere. In reality the main doorway opened onto a wooden staircase which led up to a small open area which, in its turn, opened onto the temple and living area. A log ladder, the one mentioned by Matthiessen, led up to the roof which had at its back the cliff face streaked with its rich earthy colours of beige, ochre and a dark grey like a giant watercolour backdrop. The ceremonial banners were perched on the corners and beyond them the unobstructed view of Crystal Mountain. Its upper third was covered with snow but a steely grey rock pyramid was its summit. I never saw any sign of the quartz crystalline rocks said to give the Holy Mountain its name.

On exploring the dark interior of the *gompa* we saw the main prayer room, the kitchen and the lama's bedroom. The prayer room was about 5 by 4 metres and hugely ornate. The walls were painted a deep red and decorated with large versions of the 'eight auspicious symbols'. This was in turn overhung with *thangkas* and banners which were fixed to the ceiling beams. There were several prominent photographs of the Dalai Lama. Shelves at each end stored the dozens of prayer books. There was a metre-high statue of Tara and, in front, a slightly smaller Sakyamuni Buddha statue. Flowers and peacock feathers in jars were either side of the main altar. There were butter lamps, bells, conch shells, trumpets and a well decorated drum within easy banging distance of the lama's seat. The kitchen, by stark contrast, was spartan and grey. A butter tea churn hung on one wall and there was a central small iron fireplace. Along one wall was basic wooden shelving with a series of Chinese 'thermos' flasks, vases and cups. A shelf along another wall had plenty of kettles and cooking pots.

Our lama friend, Phurpa Tinley, started a fire in the stove in the kitchen. He used his bare hands to crumble up the discs of dried yak dung to fuel the iron stove. 'You like tea?' he asked us as he crumbled a brick of tea into the pot with his unwashed hands. Naturally the trio declined tea instantly! I reckoned that the boiling water would kill any bugs so, like Harry and Alasdair, said 'yes'. The tea was good and served in glasses without yak milk.

We sat around and asked Phurpa Tinley questions with Chandra translating. Colin said 'I've got a million questions for him' and asked about three but we were all able to ask him various things. It turned out that the lama was thirty-five years old. He became a monk aged nine and had been taught at Tsakhang by the previous lama (possibly the younger one Matthiessen met). He was quite happy that his son, Dorje, was soon to go off to Kathmandu to train as a monk as well. On a shelf in the kitchen area of the *gompa* were a few books. One of them was Snellgrove's *Himalayan Pilgrimage*. It was an old copy and had clearly been scribbled in by children. It turned out that Snellgrove himself hadn't actually visited Tsakhang as he'd heard the lama was in retreat and didn't want to disturb him.

We headed back to camp for a late lunch. Some of the porters had returned from retrieving our gear from the snowfield this side of the pass. Lunch was picnic style on the grassy knoll but the mess tent was now back after three days and in the afternoon I sat in there and caught up with my diary. One of the pleasures of trekking is having the time to simply sit and think or chat with fellow trekkers and our guides and porters. Harry and I swapped notes about our visit to Tsakhang. It turned out that we both had a similar depth of interest in Buddhism. For Harry the thing he'd been most looking forward to on this trip was seeing Shey and spending a period of contemplation there. It was thus even more appreciated that Adc and Chandra thought we should spend one of our spare days here to even better rest and soak up the atmosphere.

Alasdair came into the tent and joined in the conversation.

'So how long have you been in Australia, Bill?' he asked.

'I got there at the end of 1990,' I said, 'and settled in pretty much from the first beer.'

'Whereabouts in the UK did you come from?'

'I was born in Newcastle upon Tyne and went to school there but went off to London for university.'

'I know about Newcastle,' Al said. 'My dad's an engineer and he lived there for a couple of years. He thought it was a great place.'

'Oh really? Where did he work?'

'A company called Parsons in Byker.'

Parsons was an engineering firm started by Sir Charles Parsons who'd developed a marine turbine for the navy in the 1880s.

'Amazing. My dad worked there too. He was just on the "shop floor" but he was there for years,' I said. 'And my uncle too. He was an electrical engineer and worked there until he retired.'

That was my uncle John, cousin Phil's dad.

What a small world, as the cliché goes, but in Buddhist terms this was just another example of how everyone and everything is in some way interconnected.

21 MAY

Second rest day at Shey

It was another uncomfortable and restless night as we were at 4300 metres and still acclimatising.

I was out of the tent at 6.30 a.m. and watched the sunrise over this incredible place. I had tea at 7.00 a.m., then a welcome breakfast at 8.00 a.m. with a jump-start coffee. As we were enjoying breakfast Chandra told us that he'd just breakfasted with 'Caravan Hero' Thinle, over at the *gompa* where the old man had spent last night. Thinle had come the same way as us, but his horse had been injured crossing onto the ice. He was unable to ride it and was blaming our pony boy, whom he'd met as he made his way back to Ringmo, for telling him the pass was good to cross. Chandra said he'd sent a message with Thinle to our local guide Narendra telling him we were spending an extra night at Shey. Narendra and some of the porters had already gone ahead to our next stop at Namgung.

Colin and Duncan once again decided not to linger and were planning a climb up the ridge directly east of camp. Alasdair thought he'd tag along, so they collected packed lunches and left after breakfast with strict instructions from Ade to be back in time for tea at 3.30 p.m.

It was at this point we had a demonstration by Philippe of his unique shaving technique. Standing midfield in a pair of his voluminous baggy shorts he posed with the small aluminium bowl of hot water on a rock, about to perform his ablutions. He'd taken pride in shaving each day and wasn't at all put off by the lack of a mirror. The result was a certain inequality in the level of hair on each side of his head. From one side he looked somewhat normal, from the other, with the hair a good inch above his ear, he was like a caricature of a Norman warrior lifted from the Bayeux Tapestry.

Mid-morning we went over to see Shey Gompa itself, or 'Shelri Sumdho Monastery' as the sign above the door to the *gompa* proclaimed, *sumdho* or *sumdo* being the Tibetan for a confluence of two rivers. This monastic centre had been established approximately 800 years ago by Tensin Radsin, and his reincarnate lineage still presides there. Chandra had arranged for the keeper of the keys to meet us in front of the main *gompa* entrance. Naturally we approached it by walking in a clockwise direction around the whole complex. What struck me immediately was that the large retaining wall didn't enclose a field for crops but was a vast arena of *mani* stones. This area was at least 30 by 40 metres and completely filled to a depth of up to a metre with thousands and thousands of *mani* stones. They were of every size, type of stone and quality of finish but they were most definitely the accumulated result of hundreds of years of masons' efforts. Our circumambulation brought us past a row of three *chortens* then round the back of the main *gompa* and a smaller two-storey dwelling next to it, both painted the usual dull ochre colour. The smaller residence had a tiny wooden door and three small windows in the upper storey. A pole with prayer flags protruded from each corner of the house. I think this was the house that Schaller spent the night in when he first arrived at Shey, before they set up camp near one of the houses further up the hill. There was no formal courtyard in front of the *gompa* itself, just a large open space with unobstructed views across to Crystal Mountain. A pair of 2-metre-high *chortens*, each surmounted by a pole bearing prayer flags, marked the limits of this open piazza. One of them bore a splendid set of animal horns almost a metre across. I initially thought they belonged to *bharal*, or blue sheep, but they seemed too big. In *Stones of Silence*, George Schaller, when talking to the Lama of Shey at Tsakhang, said, 'I query him about Tibetan argali, about whether this large sheep occurs here, for at the base of the flagpole in front of the monastery is a weathered skull.' This same set of horns was still perched there all these years later.

On each corner of the *gompa* there was a ceremonial 'Victory Banner'. These were quite unique in being black yak hair bound with white canvas strips and surmounted by a stylised skull with red eyes and a large red grinning mouth. A blue trident, or *trisul*, stuck out at the top. There was a notable absence of the traditional 'wheel of dharma and two deer' sculpture so common above the entrance of many *gompas*. It was also noticeable that, apart from the water-driven ones on the other side of the river, there were no prayer wheels anywhere around the complex nor any fireplace outside for burning incense or juniper. Once the outer doors were unlocked, we were in a verandah-style area with some older frescoes. Either side of the inner door were the 'Four Great Kings', the traditional guardians of the cardinal points. These images, highly stylised and formulaic, can be seen in the entrance vestibule of most Tibetan Buddhist temples. To the left were Guardian King of the South, blue-faced Phakyepo, carrying a sword, and Yulkhorsung, white-faced and playing the lute, the Guardian King of the East. To the right, yellow-faced Namthose held a victory banner as the Guardian of the North and then the red-faced Chenmizang, Guardian of the West, held a small *chorten* and a snake. On the end walls of this area were a painting of the Buddha in the deer park and, on the opposite end, a wheel of life depiction. The door itself was covered with a fabric wall hanging showing the Eight Auspicious Symbols in an intricate pattern. Passing through this entrance brought us into a further decorated vestibule, before a second set of doors leading into the main Assembly Hall, which was about 10 metres square. It was classically traditional in its internal layout, with quite modern, bright paintings on the inside walls. The head lama's chair was towards the back on the right, with his prayer books, cymbals and a conch shell on a platform in front. Several drums were suspended from the ceiling along with many brocades and *thangkas*. All the religious books were stored high up on shelves near a skylight. The back wall was tiered and filled with more than a dozen Buddha statues, most draped with *katas*, the silk scarves that people give as offerings. There were many pictures of deities and monks, lots of small *torma* (butter sculptures) and plenty of monetary donations and bowls for gifts of food and drink. There was even a fluffy toy rabbit.

Peter Matthiessen spent three weeks camped next to the monastery and it was locked the whole time he was there. He was hugely disappointed that he never saw the inside. A couple of days after he left Shey the key somehow materialised and George Schaller, having bartered the price of admission down from 100 rupees to five, was allowed to enter on the eve of his own departure. He reported that it was rather dingy but there were painted wall hangings, old swords and ancient muskets.

David Snellgrove had also found it difficult to gain entry but in 1956 he returned from Saldang to witness the annual festival held in the fifth Tibetan month at the time of the full moon, or mid-June our calendar. In *Himalayan Pilgrimage* he didn't give much detail concerning the interior of the *gompa* but he talked a lot about the three-day religious ceremony. He'd always looked forward to seeing Shey, because up until then he hadn't visited a Kagyu monastery. He knew this to be nominally a Karma Kagyu centre as there was a large painting of the Karmapa, leader of the sect, on the back wall. However, from the ceremonies he subsequently witnessed it was clear that there was a large overlap with Nyingma tradition. I looked closely at the altar of the *gompa* to see if I could spot a human skull goblet. Snellgrove mentioned this artefact at least twice as being an integral part of the three-day ceremony, but it was clearly locked away between each annual event. There was already the soft toy placed, by way of an offering, on the altar. I didn't think it was inappropriate for my toy snow leopard to be photographed on the abbot's chair apparently observing the ceremonial conch shell trumpet. I was able to capture most of the brightly coloured frescoes, clearly executed since Snellgrove's visit, adorning the side and back walls. This was not as large and richly decorated as some monasteries, but Shey was clearly a centre of special significance for the people of Dolpo.

After making a donation of our own we left and continued the circuit back towards our campsite, which led us past the two especially large reliquary *chortens*, both locked. The horse motifs on the side facing the path told us that we were passing to the south. We had a lazy afternoon. I stretched my legs by climbing up to the group of three small houses 50 metres or so above our campsite. From this vantage point there was a splendid panoramic view from the Kang La to the south, down onto Shey Gompa, across to Crystal Mountain and north towards Tsakang and the Dolma-Jang hermitage beyond that. Harry had already spent a little time up there when I joined him. He was loving this place and had a look of utter contentment on his face the entire time we were at Shey. As part of my exploration and acquisition of knowledge about Buddhism I'd made attempts at learning to meditate. I could concentrate on the breathing and send away unwanted thoughts for short periods, and I also found it a useful technique for relaxing. I could feel my heart rate settle. In times of external stress, common in my work, I could maintain calm. Here at Shey no effort was required to be in the moment.

On his visit, Matthiessen had sought out a special place on a rock ledge just above the *gompa*. He was a Zen adherent and believed there was merit in sitting for hours in contemplation. He wrote, 'I have a meditation place on Somdo mountain, a broken rock outcrop like an altar set into the hillside ... I arrange a crude rock seat as a lookout on the world, set out binoculars in case wild creatures should happen into view, then cross my legs and regulate my breath, until I scarcely breathe at all.'

I didn't forget to breathe while Harry and I sat quietly above Shey and the two of us shared a tranquil and special half hour of simply 'being there' in the presence of the Crystal Mountain.

Colin, Duncan and Alasdair had a long day of it but were back for afternoon tea, and by dinner it was intensely cold and time to get the down jacket out. By now I'd finished *A Room with a View* and was more than happy browsing through *Himalayan Pilgrimage* and the Dolpo guidebooks. Harry was slowly rereading *The Snow Leopard* and we'd swap notes about what had been said in the past about the places we were now living in and enjoying.

In direct contradistinction to our chosen reading material Philippe turned up in the mess tent with a new paperback in his hand, instantly recognisable by its cover; *Cinquantes Nuances de Grey*, as it was titled in his French version.

'Hey, Philippe, how come you're reading that?' I challenged.

'Ah. My girlfriend. She says I must read thees,' he said, rolling his eyes.

15
TO NAMGUNG

22 MAY

Shey Gompa (4388 metres; 14,396 feet)
to Namgung (4419 metres; 14,498 feet)
via the Sela La (5117 metres; 16,788 feet)
10.2 kilometres

My birthday! 22 May, same date as Peter Matthiessen.

After bed tea I went off for my morning sojourn in the toilet tent. As I emerged Ade yelled out 'Happy Birthday!' so everyone in Shey could hear. Damn! They knew. I'd been hoping to keep it quiet.

There were general birthday wishes from everyone over breakfast, but sadly it was now time to leave the Crystal Monastery after a most tranquil couple of days. What could be better than to wake up on one's birthday at Shey Gompa with a clear sky and the prospect of a stroll through that most otherworldly landscape? We were off to Namgung and at eight on that spectacularly beautiful morning we began our gentle walk up the Sephu Khola, Matthiessen's 'White River', heading east away from Shey. There was no sign of birdlife or *bharal*, so I reasoned there was little chance of there being a snow leopard in the vicinity. However, my hopes were buoyed by the knowledge that Chandra had spoken to a traveller who had seen a snow leopard only two days earlier, in the very valley where we were walking.

The climb was gradual and the valley initially quite wide and open. It was a cloudless, bright day without a breath of wind. But this was high in the Himalaya and the air temperature still hovered around zero.

Ade and I were walking and talking together when I heard, right behind us, some appalling coughing and the raucous clearing of a throat, then the crescendo launch of viscous phlegm through the air.

'Sounds like another one of the boys has a bad chest,' I said.

'No. It's the same little guy,' Ade replied. 'He refused to go back down to Dunai, so Chandra said he could carry a half load and he's going all the way.'

Holy hell! He was seriously unwell. I hoped we wouldn't end up overseeing his demise. There was absolutely no medical help around for at least 50 kilometres. I resolved to keep a much closer eye on him.

We passed several families travelling in the opposite direction on their way to visit Shey. On the opposing riverbank was a smart-looking but deserted hamlet of six or seven houses, probably a *doksa*. The valley closed in and deepened and steadily turned north with a frozen waterfall at its head. The effort required seemed a little easier than a few days previously, so the acclimatisation process was clearly going well. Clambering over the rocks around the waterfall led us into the flat valley beyond where we stopped for lunch. Our lama friend from Tsakhang, Phurpa Tinley, was there as he was making a visit to Namgung and Saldang. We offered him some food and he was happy to spend some time chatting to Chandra and the porters.

After lunch there was a zigzag climb up to a ridge and a gentle track to the Sela La (5117 metres; 16,788 feet). This was immensely enjoyable walking. We'd climbed over 600 metres from Shey and everyone was feeling good. The cairn at the pass had many prayer flags and Ade helped me fasten a string of them in memory of Dorje Khatri, my friend who'd been killed in the Everest avalanche of 18 April. He was a gentle, strong man, a natural and compassionate leader to whom nothing was too much trouble. He possessed true 'Buddha nature'.

It was a long and spectacular walk down to Namgung, beginning with a gentle traverse across terrain reminiscent of the North Yorkshire moors except we were still at 5000 metres. Snellgrove compared it to a hike in the Cairngorms, and so it was, apart from the views of the Tibetan plateau and mountains not 30 kilometres away. The trail was well marked and level. The grass was dry and brown then, after a short time, we had increasingly better views into Tibet and across the valley hiding Namgung. We passed herds of goats and then realised that it was one great diffuse herd under the care of a single goatherd, a woman in her twenties who was in deep conversation with our Tsakhang lama friend as we passed. Soon the scattered buildings of Namgung deep in the narrow valley of the Namgung Khola came into view way below us. Set into the cliff face hundreds of metres below on the other side of the valley was the old *gompa* which we thought must have been destroyed in an earthquake so decrepit was its appearance. A zigzag trail down a canyon led us to river level and we were left with a tricky crossing, boulder to slippery boulder, to arrive at our campsite adjacent to some ancient-looking *chortens* half a kilometre upstream of the main monastery complex.

It took a while for our gear to roll in. Some locals came looking for medicine and Ade and Chandra did a mini clinic with me looking on. An old man with red inflamed eyes needed some eye drops and a young boy with a cough was given a couple of paracetamol tablets.

We watched some serious goat herding on the opposite riverbank, the way we'd come down. The female goatherd we'd seen earlier managed to round up over a hundred goats in apparently effortless fashion as she moved quickly back and forth across the whole steep hillside to head off wayward groups. It was an impressive performance of an ancient skill.

The main *gompa* at Namgung was a steep 500-metre stroll down the valley. Duncan and Colin had gone straight there on arrival and returned saying it was worth a look, so Harry, Alasdair, Chandra and I walked down there in about fifteen minutes. The river was to our right and we could see, as we got closer, that a narrow gully came down through the cliff from the left and where the gully joined the river there was a sufficiently flat area to build the *gompa*. Beyond the red-painted building we could see the ruined monastery buildings a little higher set back into the cliff. We kept bearing left and clockwise into the gully to get around a row of twelve *chortens*. This led to a small group of stone, fortress-like houses and then a narrow entrance courtyard in front of the main *gompa* building. Space here was limited. Above the door our friend Phurpa Tinley, the Tsakhang Lama, was installing the shiny new dharma wheel on a spike between the two deer facing it from each side.

A young man in his twenties had the key and welcomed us to the *gompa*. It transpired that he was the incumbent lama and he spoke extremely good English. His name was Dolpo Maniwa Rinpoche (also, Dungse Ogyen Gyaltsen). He'd been to school in Mysore and had even taught in Malaysia.

His father, Lama Chosang Rinpoche, was the chief lama of Namgung. His younger brother was the boy who'd been up to our camp seeking some pills for his head cold. The brother had looked to be about nine years old and was soon to begin his monastic training as he was already a recognised reincarnate, Tulku Tenzin Lhundrub. Young Tenzin helped show us around the *gompa* and was happily banging the ceremonial drum for us. Our new lama friend, Dolpo Maniwa Rinpoche, was eager to tell us about the place. The old monastery wasn't destroyed in an earthquake but simply fell down due to poor building and age. This new *gompa* was about thirty years old but had been robbed several times and many of Namgung's oldest and most treasured statues and *thangkas* were gone. The lama and his brother were more than happy for us to take photographs and while the youngster continued banging the ceremonial drum the lama posed in one of the elaborate pieces of ceremonial headgear, fur rimmed, covered in demons' eyes and fire and topped with a skull. He was also happy to display for us some of the ancient and faded *thangkas* still in the monastery's possession.

The day was wearing on and in the shadow of this deep valley it suddenly became intensely cold. As we were leaving we were asked to look at the wife of the old man with the inflamed eyes. The old man turned out to be the uncle of Dolpo Maniwa Rinpoche and was himself a lama, Lama Tinley Rinpoche. He and his wife lived in one of the square stone fortress-type houses we'd passed on the way in. His wife was called Palzom and she looked to be in her seventies. She had a problem with painful legs and displayed her limbs for us up to the knees. The joints were red and swollen and clearly immobile from arthritis. Her tibia bones on both legs were curved and thin because of osteoporosis. Chandra had joined us and had his 'pain-relieving' spray in his backpack. This was simply an aerosol which had a soothing and cooling effect and could be useful in relieving muscle spasm. We gave her a few paracetamol as well, but it was sad to see this and to understand that this was just the way of life for many in Dolpo. At some point there is an end to mobility and that means staying where you are until death. This pleasant old lady would never leave Namgung again, but like the old Lama of Tsakhang who Matthiessen had met in 1973 there was a pragmatic, almost joyous, acceptance of her lot in life, even in the face of suffering.

When Snellgrove first came to Namgung in 1956 the current *gompa* hadn't yet been built and the old monastery built into the cliff face was even then quite rundown. He described its main temple room as being, like Shey, a Kagyu-pa monastery of the Karma-pa sect. Above the main temple was a smaller temple chamber with *thangkas* and Tibetan printed texts. Apparently, at that time, there was no lama and the monastery was being looked after by two brothers. Some 400 metres downstream lay a smaller more recently built temple which had been constructed about eleven years before at the instigation and expense of the Lama of Shang, who hailed from Tibet. This was Tragyam Gompa where Joel Ziskin would later meet the hermit Tulku Tsewang. Snellgrove ended up meeting the illustrious and renowned Lama of Shang soon after leaving Dolpo in 1956. They met briefly at Kagbeni and then, a few weeks later, at the village of Pisang north of Annapurna. The Precious Lama was impressed that Snellgrove could read and converse so well in Tibetan. When Snellgrove returned to Dolpo in 1961 he met the Lama of Shang for a second time at Tragyam Gompa in Namgung. However, the lama had died three years before in 1959 in Bawa in Tibet! One of the Dolpo villagers, assisted by two nomads, had crossed into Tibet and retrieved his mummified corpse. The mummy was then installed in full regalia in the meditation position in the main temple at Tragyum Gompa. Snellgrove said, 'As we had once known this lama as a friend and helper we went up to Namgung to pay him our respects. The face and hands were not improved by the gilt that covered them and the smell was not very pleasant.'

Corneille Jeste also met the lama's mummy in 1961, when on pilgrimage with his storytelling friend Karma. In his book *Tales of the Turquoise* he devoted a whole chapter to the story of the 'Mummy of the Lama of Shang'. He told of his life and death and the mummification process using salt to pack the body with during transport. Salt which was subsequently used as a medicine because of its miraculous healing powers. When they spent the night at Tragyam, which Jeste calls 'Trakyem', the pair bedded down in the temple with their heads pointed towards the altar as a sign of respect for the mummy perched there. Karma felt obliged to recite a tale about the *rolang*, the corpses that walk, but there was no mention of any smell.

Much later, after my return to Australia, I was able to contact the Namgung Lama, Dolpo Maniwa Rinpoche, who had internet access while staying in Kathmandu. He was able to answer many questions about the Namgung Monastery complex and his own teaching program. I asked him about Tulku Tsewang and the Lama of Shang and in answer to my question

'What happened to the body of the Lama of Shang?' he replied, 'Sorry, whose body? Lama of Shang. I didn't understand that.' When I explained that it was the man who had made the building of Tragyam possible he said:

> Yes. This is right. But Shangpa Rinpoche and Tulku Tseyang is not Dolpo man. They from Tibet. But they have many devotee from Dolpo and Mustang. After (his body was brought to Namgung), devotee did fire *puja* near Shey Tsakhang Gumba. Body burning in fire. Haha. Sorry my English not good. Now don't have that body.

So the venerable mummy of the Lama of Shang had not finished its travels after Snellgrove and Jeste had met it. He was taken for a final cremation ceremony over to Tsakhang, beneath the gaze of Crystal Mountain itself.

That evening, in our vast mess tent, dinner was served, then, surprise, surprise, a birthday cake with four candles. I was also given a birthday card from Tulsi back in Kathmandu. The cake was iced and in bright red writing said 'Happy Birthday Bill'. This was fabulous. Saila and his kitchen staff had excelled themselves. It is a remarkably special skill to be able to bake a real and delectable cake in a tent, on a gas burner and at almost 4.5 kilometres altitude. I relished the moment.

16

CARAVAN HERO

23 MAY

Namgung (4419 metres; 14,498 feet)
to Saldang (3850 metres; 12,631 feet)
to Dora Sumdo (3701 metres; 12,142 feet)
16.5 kilometres

The trail from our camp at Namgung led straight uphill above and behind the *gompa*. As we came to the gully we had to traverse around it with clear views down to the monastery complex about 100 metres below. The only other houses in Namgung, four or five of them, were across the river among a handful of narrow bare fields and the occasional *chorten*. There was a steady climb for an hour or more, the trail veering from east to north until we eventually came to a flag-topped cairn on a ridge with the by now ubiquitous incredible views into Tibet. In the middle distance was an impressive pair of rocky twin peaks, while to their left, on the horizon, Danphe Sail soared at a distance of about 35 kilometres.

There was now a long traverse along an easy trail, giving us another afternoon of superb hill walking at 4000 metres. We passed a herd of seventy or more goats being tended by a group of shy young girls about ten years of age. Another young girl, a basket on her back and leading a fully laden horse, passed us heading towards Namgung. She flashed a broad smile as we wished each other '*Tashi delek*'. Not long after a whole family passed us. They had three overburdened horses, the first being led by the young son of the family in a red Chinese tracksuit. The father carried an infant on his back. Behind him his wife wore a traditional *chuba*, the Tibetan woollen skirt, and she sported turquoise and coral earrings, the whole ensemble set off with a bright red tracksuit top. The old lady bringing up the rear, who may have only been around fifty, was moving slowly. She wore a knitted jumper and had a bright red folded shawl precariously balanced on her head to keep the sun off. These five looked and sounded exhausted as we exchanged '*Namaste*' and '*Tashi delek*'. Chandra said they were heading up for the *yarsa gomba* season, but we had no idea how far they had already travelled.

We started down towards Saldang which we could see was fairly spread out along the valley below to our right. A garish red roof was next to the school. In one corner of the schoolyard was the 'power tower' installed by Peter Werth's team, a combined wind and solar electricity supply for the school. We stayed high and headed for a large house above Saldang which belonged to Thinle, 'Caravan Hero'. There was a large eroded gully to cross just before but we had a clear view across to Thinle's house with its series of outhouses then well-manicured fields with a row of six *chortens* marking the boundaries of his land. More *chortens* were scattered in among the fields. His family, four women and a man with a red headscarf, were out ploughing. The single white horse was pulling a simple wooden plough. As we entered the farm a massive brown and buff mastiff reared up, barking, restrained by a suitably robust chain. Thinle's grandchildren were pretty cute and keen to hold Harry's hand as they walked past the hound. Saila had set up a kitchen in one of the outhouses and we had lunch on the roof; sardines, *chapati*, salad and cheese in the glorious warm sunshine. A pair of Himalayan griffons soared just over our heads before settling, looking unfeasibly large, on the trail we'd just passed along. A few minutes later they were disturbed and took once more to the air as Philippe came down the trail his standard half hour behind.

Thinle himself was not to be seen as he was said to be elsewhere in Saldang. We were sorry to have missed this famous character. His son invited us to look around their house, so, clambering past a giant pile of dried yak dung, the winter's fuel supply, we climbed the stairs to the upper level. There was Thinle's bedroll in a corner on the floor. Just beyond was the kitchen where the family were now gathered after their morning of ploughing. Thinle's son poured generous cups of yak butter tea while his wife made *chapati* on the hot plate.

After lunch the plan was to walk out via a high, more scenic, route while the porters took the easier path along the Nangkhong Khola. We'd only gone 20 or 30 metres up the hill before we heard the strangely familiar tones of Thinle, 'Caravan Hero', himself, yelling at us that we were going the wrong way. We slipped back down the slope and Chandra started talking to him. I pulled out my toy snow leopard and introduced the two of them for the photo opportunity; Thinle was happy to smile and pose for us. The old man had sore knees, so Chandra offered to use our pain-relieving spray on his swollen joints.

After this photo opportunity we said our goodbyes and, now on the correct trail, we set off through indescribably beautiful high country with limitless views of the brown Tibetan plateau and distant snowy peaks. We were heading north under a clear deep-blue sky with no wind and the river inaudible and hidden deep in its gorge off to our right. The warbling of the native songbirds, the occasional bleating goat and the sound of our own footsteps accompanied us as we walked quite literally beyond *The Snow Leopard*. For it was at this geographical point that Peter Matthiessen turned south and started his long journey back to his children in the States. He'd spent his last night in Saldang in the home of a friend of Jang-bu, one of his companions. The party sat and drank *chang*, the local beer, as the sun went down. Matthiessen said that on that evening he sat there 'peaceful as a Buddha' enjoying the company of his friends Jang-bu, Dawa, Gyaltsen and Tukten, the Tulku, with whom he'd shared his time at Shey. As they left next morning heading for Namdo, the village south of Saldang up the valley of the Nangkhong, he drew a good comparison between Saldang and Ringmo. Both, he said, were at roughly the same altitude, but Ringmo was a Himalayan village just within the tree line, whereas Saldang was an occupant of the vast treeless desert of the Tibetan plateau.

After an hour or so we arrived at a *chorten* and were met by two young women with ponies heading the opposite way, on their way towards Saldang. They turned out to be teachers at the local school, and they spoke superb English. They were heading off on leave as the school had just been closed for the start of the *yarsa gomba* season. A couple of hundred metres beyond the *chorten* was the school itself, the Karang Gangjong Rikshung Primary School, on the edge of the visually stunning village of Karang. This settlement was distributed across a massive natural amphitheatre set high above the Nangkhong River. Some of the extensive terraced fields were just turning green with the shoots of new crops. The traditional stone and mud-daub square dwellings sported prayer flags and were spread thinly around the valley. A basic undecorated old *gompa* and ancient *chortens* took central position. The newer *gompa* was at the top end of the village and so we sadly missed visiting it. We entered the school grounds and had a chat with the teachers and kicked a ball around with a few of the kids who'd been left behind because their families were too distant.

On we marched into Karang. From within, the village seemed even more beautiful: sprawling, unspoilt and positively medieval. No antennae, motors, noisy radios. Just the sound of the breeze, the horses and the occasional birds. This was a true paradise. The villagers were friendly and would briefly, with scant interest, look up from their work and say '*Namaste*' or '*Tashi delek*'. The children kept a safe distance from we strangers but still smiled and waved as we passed by. We had to walk down through the village, past the old *gompa*, then drop all the way down into a deep gully only to climb up through the settlement on the other side called Marang. Climbing past a group of three *chortens* we regained the ridge and continued our high and spectacular route northwards.

17

DORA SUMDO, THE MAGIC OF CONFLUENCE

We started our long descent towards the river by traversing a dusty brown landscape; the air was dry and the sky brilliant and clear. We were still at around 4000 metres altitude. As we dropped closer to the river the ground became dramatically more eroded so that the trail wound back and forth through a bare rocky moonscape, along ridges of loose soil, connected by precarious log and boulder bridges. Still at about 300 or more metres above the river we started passing rows of square *chortens*. They were two-and sometimes three-storeyed and painted white with a band of blue-grey above a band of ochre colour at the top of each level. I hadn't seen that type before. Three hours after leaving Karang we were on a trail about 50 metres above the Nangkhong, which was a swift flowing, silt-laden river following wide curves along its level rocky bed. About 1 kilometre ahead we could see that the gorge was wider and on the opposite bank there were some of the usual red-ochre and white *chortens*. Another river valley joined the one we were in. This was the place known as Dora Sumdo. It was here that the north-flowing Nangkhong River joined the larger westward-flowing Panzang, eventually to become the Karnali.

There is a belief that a *sumdo* is a place of special significance. The Tibetan spelling of Dora Sumdo is *rDo-ra gSum-mdo*. *gSum-mdo* means 'lower valley of three waters' as the confluence is of two rivers and the resulting stream becomes a third. *Shel Sumdo*, or 'crystal confluence', is a name the locals have for Shey.

Hermann Hesse, in his Buddhist novel *Siddhartha*, alluded to the mystical and symbolic nature of flowing waters:

> the river is everywhere at once, at the source and at the mouth, at the waterfall, at the ferry, at the rapids, in the sea, in the mountains, everywhere at once, and that there is only the present time for it, not the shadow of the past, not the shadow of the future.

Just before the junction of the two rivers a narrow rickety old wooden bridge crossed the Nangkhong to a small grassy area in front of a row of large *chortens*. These were built and maintained by the lamas of Yangtsher in the fifteenth century. There was a low modern stone building that Saila had occupied as his kitchen, the tents were going up and the tea and biscuits were soon forthcoming. It had become windy and clouds of dust were flying. Lying in the tent I was able to look out directly on the junction of these two rivers and west towards a sinking sun filling the wider valley with a bright yellow glow. Just visible, over 1 kilometre down the valley and several hundred metres above the left bank of the Panzang was the monastery of Shungtsher, originally a Sakyapa foundation but now Nyingmapa.

Quite unexpectedly a group of a dozen black yaks ambled past on the stony riverbed next to the stream. They were driven by a red-jacketed Dolpo-pa on a pure white horse. Pleasant sounds accompanied the vision. Over the rushing noise of the water there was a gentle clip of hooves and jangling of the yak bells. The occasional snort of the animals, with the herder shouting '*dzo*' and whistling to encourage the herd. This was a timeless and tranquil scene conducive to a deep sense of calm.

It started to become cold, and the down jackets were donned before dinner. The next day we were to visit the oldest remaining monastery in Dolpo.

24 MAY

Dora Sumdo (3701 metres; 12,142 feet)
to Muri (4136 metres; 13,569 feet)
12.5 kilometres

I was woken at 5.30 a.m. with the sound of sleet falling on the tent. By the time we'd consumed an excellent breakfast the sleet had stopped and the cloud was breaking up. Our group now turned east, after travelling north for many days, and we started off up the Panzang. The view into the valley was dramatic with low clouds and filtered pale light highlighting the silhouettes of many *chortens* and old buildings. A walk of only 200 to 300 metres brought us to the bridge across the river. On this, the left bank, just before the bridge were two old *kani chortens* with beautifully painted, but deteriorating, ceilings and walls depicting mandalas and the pantheon of deities.

Over the bridge and a few hundred metres further upstream we started a steep ascent towards a row of ten *chortens* high above us on the skyline, all the same height and with white prayer flags mounted on top. As we approached this isolated row of artefacts it was clear that this was the way to a higher *gompa*, the Margom Yangtsher retreat, which we could see another 500 metres up the mountain. The main Yangtsher Monastery was level with us a similar distance away up the valley, but we were separated from it by a deep dry canyon, 'the Devil's Ravine'. We had no choice but to take the loose trail down into it and haul ourselves up the other side. We emerged slightly above the main *gompa* buildings, some 100 metres away. There was a long white wall and some single-storey buildings with many *chortens* around and within the complex. Chandra had gone ahead to find a key but apparently all the monks were away chasing the caterpillar fungus so, once again, we were to be denied entry. I walked towards the main building across the bright white chalky ground. A line of prayer wheels was set into the main wall, and I was inclined to give them a spin. As I got closer it was clear that something was awry. The half-dozen recesses in the wall now contained only seven or eight wheels where there was space for twenty or more. Those that remained were all broken. They were wooden cylinders hung on wooden spindles never to turn again. Nothing remained of any external decoration. All were open to the elements, exposing the tightly rolled paper inside with the repetitions of thousands of prayers and mantras. Nothing could fix these old devices and yet I was hesitant to pillage the remains in some forlorn attempt to preserve a piece of their history. They abide there still, slowly and inexorably deteriorating as another example of impermanence.

A doorway in the wall led to an open area and the main entrance *chorten* to the inner monastery courtyard. This *kani chorten* appeared to be quite new and was most certainly recently decorated inside. The ceiling was divided into nine bright mandalas and around the four walls were the protective deities and their cohorts of other heavenly beings, all rather well executed. The main courtyard beyond was about 40 by 20 metres, and several doors opened off it into the temples, all sadly locked. Alasdair and I shinned over a wall and were able to explore the enclosed area filled with old *chortens* and row upon row of *mani* walls. Snellgrove had described this ancient place, with its three major temples, in enormous detail, so it was even more frustrating that we couldn't see inside. He determined from the various paintings and statues inside that this was originally a Sakyapa foundation but the temple in main use was clearly Nyingmapa. The ceremony he witnessed there in 1961 was essentially the same as he'd seen at Shey in 1956 and there'd been ceremonial masked dancing in the main courtyard. He determined, from the old documents he read in the *gompa*, that the monastery buildings were 600 to 700 years old, but some say that the consecration occurred almost 1000 years ago. The name Yang-tsher, from the Tibetan *gYas-mtsher*, means 'right-sided settlement' but its religious name is 'Island of Enlightenment'.

During his over-winter stay in 1960–61, David Snellgrove was in Saldang and was browsing through the small collection of books in the private temple of his friend, the headman, Nyima Tschering. He was rather pleased to come across some old manuscripts which were biographies of some eminent Dolpo lamas. By making enquiries he was able to assemble and copy the biographies of four old lamas which told much about the history and daily life of the Dolpo-pa. The validity of the stories was remarkable because they had been written while the subjects were still alive or by their disciples soon after their deaths. Snellgrove published the account of his journey and the translations of the lives of the lamas as 'Four Lamas of Dolpo'. By necessity, but rather quaintly, he stuck to literal translations of the lamas' names.

The first lama lived from 1456 to 1521. His name was *bSod-nams blo-gros*, which translates to 'Merit Intellect'. Lama Merit Intellect was from Lo and was encouraged to enter Dolpo in 1480 by his own teacher, who suggested it was a good place for solitary meditation. Buddhism was already established in Dolpo, with several small monasteries, but Merit Intellect is credited with founding Margom and Thakar monasteries, with only Margom now remaining in its lofty position above Yangtsher.

Merit Intellect's successor and biographer was *Chos-skyabs dpal-bzang*, translatable as 'Religious Protector Glorious and Good', who lived from 1476 to 1565. He is credited with establishing Yangtsher Monastery, as the community had quickly outgrown Margom. When Snellgrove was at Yangtsher in 1961 the incumbent was the seventeenth in succession from Religious Protector Glorious and Good.

The third lama, *dPal-ldan blos-gros*, is 'Glorious Intellect' and he lived from 1467 to 1536. He was a disciple of Merit Intellect but preferring a life of meditation he established himself in a monastery at Hrap above the village of Tsa in the upper Nangkhong Valley.

The fourth biography was that of the ninth incumbent Yangtsher Lama, *bSod-nams dbang-phyug* or 'Lord of Merit', who lived from 1660 to 1731.

All four biographies give an insight into the daily rituals and tribulations of medieval Dolpo. There are stories of ceremonies, sickness, death. Of the building of new temples and of visits by, and to, important neighbours. All in all a window into Dolpo history which, before Snellgrove's endeavours, was a total unknown.

It was good to have been able to wander around this remote and extremely old religious settlement. In many ways it gave an indication of solidity and continuity of a community which is still of immense local importance. Walking a short distance took us through the village of Nyisal, which is essentially the support town for the monastic settlement. It sits on a slope of loose ground which has been eroded over the years and the place is divided by gullies which entailed much climbing down and up the other side on thin tracks. From the confluence of rivers at Dora Sumdo to the southern end of Nyisal is a distance of only 3 kilometres and in that short distance I was able to count over ninety *chortens* of every conceivable size, age and condition.

After a couple of hours' walking, the river valley had become narrow and steep. High above Nyisal we came across another family on the move. The middle-aged man was accompanied by two teenage girls and a much younger girl. They were travelling with little luggage, were poorly clad and seemed rather subdued and unhappy. Usually we managed to raise a greeting and a smile but these unfortunates seemed quite miserable and didn't want to converse. Even the offer of chocolate didn't seem to help.

We had a short stop for lunch after which the walk became gradually easier, simply following the river and steadily climbing higher. We turned north-east up the valley of the Muri Khola. A necessary detour, but this was a most pleasant and gentle walk. Around 15.30 we came to a *chorten* and could see our campsite in a terraced field, just beyond, on the outskirts of the tiny village of Muri.

As the tents went up the weather turned and it was suddenly cold with wind and light snow. We hastily reached for our down jackets. We were at 4136 metres (13,570 feet) so that day we had gained about 400 metres.

18
ALONG THE PANZANG

25 MAY

Muri (4136 metres; 13,569 feet)
to campsite above Shimen (4227 metres; 13,868 feet)
via the Muri La (5073 metres; 16,643 feet)
7.57 kilometres

We left camp before 8.00 a.m. and within a few minutes were on the edge of the small, pretty village of Muri. Most of the villagers seemed to be out in the fields already and Chandra asked one of them the way. He merely pointed directly uphill, and the slog began.

We were having to take this detour over the Muri La because the Panzang River was impassable between Nisal and Shimen. This way we could drop down from the Muri La into a side valley and rejoin the Panzang at Shimen itself, a mere 7 kilometres upstream. Snellgrove maintained that there were villagers living less than 10 kilometres apart who had never visited the other village their whole lives.

From the outset the going was hard as we left Muri. Covering the hillside in every direction were clumps of rock-like plants, large round growths which on close examination were covered in small white to pink flowers. These were *Androsace muscoidea* and the Alpine Garden Society says:

> it has globular, silky-woolly winter rosettes 8–15mm across, pinkish-mauve to lilac with a yellow or orange eye which ages red, in umbels of three to eight on stems up to 6cm in height. Kashmir, Nepal, south-western Tibet, westwards to the Hindu Kush, mainly above 3000 m, on stony slopes in the drier regions.

Well, 'stony slopes in the drier regions' was very much the clime.

The zigzag trail quickly gained height and the views became increasingly impressive. After half an hour we startled a group of twenty or more bharal that stood directly ahead of us on the trail. They were motionless and merely stared for a few minutes until, moving at our snail's pace, we eventually got too close and, as one, they took off across the hillside to our right. George Schaller would have relished such a sight.

As we gained the first ridge there was a small cairn and we could look south to see the whole face of Kanjiroba. We had walked many kilometres since camping directly below that colossal, icy massif a week before. As the day went on we could see the weather darkening in that direction. Being the end of May the monsoon was approaching but we were well within the rain shadow of the Dhaulagiri massif.

The path continued steeply up to a sheltered gorge, which was entered after a scramble over a rocky slope. I was relieved to see the leaders had stopped for a break when, a couple of minutes later, Harry appeared over the rocks with a beatific smile of utter contentment on his face. He was loving this journey. After a ten-minute rest and snack there was a gentler climb across a small snowfield up to the pass itself at 5073 metres. This was Snellgrove's 'Mo Pass' and gave us a marvellous view to the east and south-east. The weather was sunny and calm on the pass. There was much discussion as to whether or not Dhaulagiri could be seen. We should have been able to make it out but there was cloud to the south-east as well as to the south past Kanjiroba. Could Dhaulagiri be hidden?

The wind suddenly picked up and it was time to start our descent. This was a sharply steep and treacherous rocky trail which was dusty and hard work. By 13.30 we were down in the valley of the Chanpyang Khola, a tributary of the Panzang. Our campsite was a level place in mid-valley a few kilometres above Shimen.

Our tent was the first one up, so Harry and I were in there just as the snow started falling. About 14.30 the kitchen tent was up and running so we had hot juice and noodle soup. By teatime the snow was getting heavy. I spent the afternoon rugged up in the tent reading *Himalayan Pilgrimage* and catching up on the diary.

By dinner time the snow was 'all about'. Saila and the boys excelled themselves despite the conditions and only two burners to work with. The meal was a delicious tomato and aloo soup with the potato skins thin and roasted and floating like seaweed in miso soup. Talk about living the dream.

26 MAY

Shimen (4227 metres; 13,868 feet)
to Tinje (4153 metres; 13,625 feet)
18.2 kilometres

By morning the snow was gone. We set off about 7.45 a.m. with an easy downhill walk through this dramatic deep rocky valley to the outskirts of Shimen. Our first sight of the town was the *gompa* perched on a ridge of rock jutting out from the cliff face on the left side of the gorge. We climbed up to this small temple above the town and there, surrounded by a group of old *chortens*, we had a view of the dozens of terraced fields below us which had only recently been planted and were just showing a fine new growth of bright green. We dropped down to skirt the upper edges of the village and head back up the Panzang Valley. The houses of the village were liberally spread out among the many well-kept fields. A scattering of willow trees made this place less austere than many of the others we'd passed through. Snellgrove also came this way and liked the place a lot. He said, 'I realised that Shimen was the most pleasant of Dolpo villages just because of its many trees.' The reason for the apparently abundant fertility was an ingenious irrigation system. Starting at the top of the village, from the same valley we'd descended, a stream had been channelled along a gentle slope and retained by a built-up wall less than a metre high. By simply moving stones the water could be directed off into other channels running downhill into groups of fields, or even individual fields. We left the village by walking along the narrow embankment containing the upper stream.

A short way into the valley we passed, leaving it to our right of course, the 'world's longest *mani* wall'. It was about 300 metres long and associated with a dozen or so *chortens*, but there were gaps and I think other places have laid claim to be the longest. In the cliff above was a row of *chortens* in front of a series of shallow, partially walled in, caves. This was a small retreat-type monastery and clearly currently unused.

The Panzang Valley became narrower and deeper. Ahead of us loomed a large barrier of solid rock 100 metres high. The river flowed through a deep gash between it and the cliff opposite. The trail, by necessity, had to bear off left and follow a small steep stream bed upwards to circle behind the rock barrier. When we were halfway up we were surprised by a group of trekkers coming the other way. There were seven or eight Europeans, and Chandra and some of the others stopped to talk to them. I nodded a brief '*Namaste*' and carried on, feeling, unreasonably, that these other tourists were in some way intruding upon my oasis of serenity. It turned out that they were a group of Swedes and were trekking a lower Dolpo circuit, having come from Dho Tarap.

As we climbed out of the lesser valley we emerged into an open, flat grassy area, a true 'alp', called Mendo and used by nomad families to graze their goats. There was a *drogpa* family there in their white summer tent and a herd of about seventy of the tiniest and most incredibly cute goats I'd ever seen. They bleated incessantly and skipped around the place trying to find their mothers. The *drogpa* children waved and yelled at us but seemingly didn't want to get too close. The other side of this idyllic meadow brought us to a narrow path that led down to rejoin the Panzang.

Within a few minutes Pu Gompa appeared on the opposite bank. A small monastery with a whitewashed enclosing wall and plenty of faded prayer flags. Just beyond the walls were a few *chortens*, and there was a quaint cantilevered wooden bridge across the Panzang leading to it. Ade had trained as an engineer and would wax lyrical about these bridges and their elegant and solid principled design and execution.

Carrying on along the gradually opening valley, just before we reached the village of Phalma we had a clear view of the rest of this valley and at the end a spectacular mountain. This was another Shangri-la moment. A remote valley with *chortens*, *mani* carvings and a majestic 'Karakal-like' peak 'serenely poised', as Conway would have it. This mountain was dark-blue-grey rock in stepped sheer cliffs leading up to a pyramidal summit, the whole thing streaked with lines of pure white snow. Wispy high-altitude clouds above it lent an even more ethereal air. This was Kula Ri (6060 metres; 19,881 feet), and the sacred mountain of Panzang. Like Crystal Mountain it has a *kora*, a merit-earning circumambulation, and this was described by Corneille Jest, who performed this trek with his storytelling friend Karma in 1961. Phalma was a tiny hamlet and in no way our end point for the day.

Past the few houses we crossed a stream and left via a large white *kani chorten*. A level and broad track crossed the floor of a wide green valley and after 2 kilometres brought us to the edge of Tinje, a much larger village. As with most places the name is subject to variation depending upon who is saying it or, with even more variation, spelling it. Snellgrove called the place 'Ting-khyu'. The Survey of India had it marked on maps as 'Tingjegaon', the 'gaon' just meaning village. Apparently the derivation was from the Tibetan *ting*, written as *gting*, meaning a 'deep place' and *khyu*, 'run' or 'flow'. This place was completely Tibetan in appearance and also remarkable for being entirely treeless. We spotted two or three Chinese motorbikes, one without wheels, parked outside some larger houses. We theorised, probably correctly, that these might be used for a little illicit trade with the Chinese, as the border was only about 10 kilometres away. Tibet and the Chinese could be the only source of fuel for these machines.

There were some powerfully handsome-looking yaks in the small enclosures of the Tinje homesteads. One man was grooming a splendid animal with a long dark coat, and its ears and horns were decorated with blue and red tassels. A little further along and we came upon a house with an open yard and when we peered over the wall there was a fresh yak hide, bloody side up, a vivid wet crimson sheet, drying in the sun. A few metres away, the old lady of the household sat next to the butchered remains of the large animal, apparently waiting for the villagers to come and buy her wares now the word was out that there was fresh meat to be had. Saila clearly didn't hesitate: that evening we dined on yak.

We passed through the centre of the village and then took off across the well-kept fields, following the tortuous paths on the retaining mounds of earth between the plots. Many people were in the fields tending the soil, planting and rounding up animals. We were largely ignored and dropping down to, then through, a large *kani chorten* and over a bridge we came to our campsite on a grassy island in the river. This had been a long walk and after a clean-up and donning warm gear the mashed potato and yak burger slipped down a treat.

Narendra and two of the porters from Dunai were leaving us next morning as they had another Upper Dolpo trek to join. After dinner we said our goodbyes and, as is the custom, gave them their tips. The ever-pleasant and smiling Narendra, being a local guide from Dunai, had been responsible for getting us over the alternative pass and successfully down to Shey.

We returned to the tent after dinner under a clear starlit sky. The northern hemisphere constellations still appeared a little strange to me.

Sleep came easily, and there was to be a most welcome rest day here in treeless Tinje the next day.

19
THE MAN WITH THREE THUMBS

27 MAY

Rest Day Tinje
Visit to Trolung Gompa

We had a marvellous breakfast to begin our rest day at Tinje – coffee, semolina with plum jam, cheese and onion omelette, and pancakes. Food was becoming a regular topic of interest and discussion. One of the physiological compensations that the body makes to high altitude is four-fold production of a hormone called leptin, which is an appetite suppressant. Generally the appetite is diminished at great height but other metabolic and hormonal changes require that the body takes in as much energy as possible. The compromise of small frequent amounts of tasty food fits the bill. Saila was doing a great job but that didn't stop us dreaming of that wild boar stew back in Pokhara or frequent thoughts of chocolate, fish and chips or sushi or anything that was a little different from dhal bhat.

Colin and Duncan planned to head off up a ridge to the east of camp. I never did determine quite why they seemed to spurn the cultural side of the trip to go walking uphill every single day. Each to their own. For Harry and me, the plan was to walk to Trolung Monastery 2 kilometres out of Tinje. This was the home of Norbu Tenzin Lama, the artist now based in Kathmandu. We'd heard that there was a *thangka* painting school there and it was where Norbu's father and many generations before him had been renowned artists. The story goes that when Dolpo was subservient to Lo-Manthang the dues were paid by sending Dolpo-pa down to the Kali Gandaki to carve *mani* stones and, in the case of Norbu's ancestors, to paint the frescoes in the monasteries of their overlords. Many of their paintings were now old and undergoing restoration.

About 9.30 a.m. Harry and I set off for Trolung Gompa. Trolung, sometimes spelled as 'Drölung', was so-called from the Tibetan *sgrol-lung dgon-pa*, meaning 'place of salvation'. We walked through the eastern part of Tinje and turned into the valley of the Polte Khola, which flows down from the Tibetan border a mere 20 kilometres straight ahead. The track went past the old fort, one of few in this part of the world but testament to the fact that this has always been frontier territory. The fort was a square-based structure of three storeys which looked quite formidable. Snellgrove made camp near the fort in 1956 and said it was close to the house of the Headman of Tinje. From there we had a slow climb up past a series of *mani* walls. It was harder going than it looked and it was a poor trail, but Harry and I stopped frequently just to admire the view and have a chat. We could see the fresh hoof prints of a horse and knew that someone had gone ahead of us to the monastery that morning. The *gompa* was never in view as it was always just over a ridge and couldn't be seen until we were almost on top of it. The stops for breath were every few minutes, and after almost an hour of climbing Tinje village seemed a lot more distant beneath us than the half kilometre we knew we had gained above it. Across the valley, on the ridge above the campsite, we could see Colin and Duncan moving slowly at about the same height as ourselves.

The photo opportunities were endless, with a great shot everywhere one looked, especially south towards the sacred mountain of Kula. This really was a special mountain. It had a markedly distinctive shape, with several vertical cliff faces. There was little snow on it, which gave it a more rugged appearance. It stood alone and dominated the valleys around it, reminding me once again of the mountain Karakal in James Hilton's *Lost Horizon*.

Then, just over the trail above us appeared the top of a *chorten* about 100 metres away. We'd arrived. As usual it seemed appropriate to circle the whole complex in a clockwise fashion. Passing several *chortens* and a ruined and collapsing building we could see the low entrance to the *gompa*. We made our tentative way past a chained mastiff, but he didn't stir. This must have been one of the few contented hounds in the Himalaya, but a cynic might say he was preparing for a busy night of barking and howling.

We stooped under a small doorway and entered the *gompa*, climbing up a narrow, dark staircase which brought us into a small courtyard about 5 metres square. 'Hello, *tashi delek*!' we shouted several times. Suddenly there were people. A man of about thirty appeared wearing a red woollen hat. We learned that he was the lama and named Nyima Dondup. Behind him was someone we took to be a younger lama who looked to be about twenty and was named Rigzin. He spoke a little English. There were also about five young boys. These were students of Nyima Dondup. An older thin man in his fifties hovered in the background. This was Norbu.

On the wall of the courtyard, under a sheltering eave, I spotted a photo of the artist Tenzin Norbu Lama. He was the artist who did the paintings in the movie *Himalaya*. He had the gallery in Kathmandu I'd tried to find, and I'd been in touch with him by email before I left Australia. I pointed at the photograph and said, 'Ah, Tenzin Norbu Lama' and the boys in the *gompa* grinned, liking that I recognised him and knew who he was.

We were invited into the main temple area, which was small but beautifully adorned with plenty of old paintings and artefacts. Quite a few of the statues appeared to be portraits rather than the standard stylised figures. There were shelves with many small Buddha figurines, as well as grotesque masks, drums and the black ceremonial dance hats similar to those that our friend, the Namgung Lama, had shown us.

The kids enjoyed having their photos taken and seeing the results. We left a monetary offering on the altar. Once they realised the size of the donation we were asked if we'd like some tea, and flasks of real yak butter tea were produced. It was excellent and I had two cups. I asked Rigzin, the young lama, to take a photo of Harry and myself in the courtyard enjoying our 'cuppa'. I was then able to get more photos of the Trolung 'team' with my toy snow leopard. Just as we were leaving I noticed that the older man, Norbu, had an extra thumb on his right hand. He was completely at ease when I commented on it. There was much laughter and more photographs. Harry was incredulous but quite understood when I said that this was a common abnormality but in our world we remove them soon after birth so they are rarely seen. We said our goodbyes and it was a nice, quick, easy-breathing walk back down the hill to camp, where we arrived soon after 12.00 p.m. Colin and Duncan arrived about the same time.

Later, upon reading Snellgrove's book, it turned out that he'd had a similar experience when he'd visited Trolung. He'd also been welcomed in the same small courtyard. He met the old lama, who was looked after by his niece. The niece's husband was the local artist who had painted the walls of the *gompa* and I assume that he was the father of Tenzin Norbu Lama. Snellgrove stated that the *gompa* was 'manifestly Nyingma-pa' judging by the paintings and trappings.

Just before lunch the mess tent collapsed with me inside. There was only the gentlest of breezes, but it was quite broken this time. The boys propped it up but it appeared to be terminal. After lunch Harry, Alasdair and I went for a walk around Tinje, but it was desperately quiet. Harry stopped to talk to some of the local children, who always enjoyed his Nepalese nursery rhymes. It seemed that one of the main jobs the kids had to do was collect water. There was a pipe at the upper end of the village and a crystal-clear stream of water ran out continuously to be collected in a huge variety of plastic or metal containers, which the tiny children especially struggled to get back to the houses. We were approached by a woman in her twenties who, without hesitation, pointed to her right ear. It was horrendously infected. The whole canal and most of her earlobe were inflamed and weeping. The left ear was similarly affected, and the poor woman must have been in great pain. It was most likely that her eardrum was involved and she was heading for permanent deafness. The chronic infection needed a prolonged course of antibiotics, but all I could do was send her over to the campsite where Chandra gave her a short course of penicillin and some ear drops.

We decided to head back but had a short stop at a house where three men were on the roof making the walls a little higher. The method they were utilising was to use plenty of flat stones with a thick layer of mud between. The mud came from a hole dug in the ground just outside the house, where a man was waiting for two young girls to keep the supply of water coming from the spring. He mixed it with the dirt then loaded up the basket of another girl, who was about fourteen. She then had to lift the obviously heavy load with the forehead strap and stagger round the house to a ladder on the other side. It was the men's job to carry the rocks up to the roof. They all seemed rather good-natured about their hard labour and didn't mind us stopping for a chat.

After afternoon tea our tent was invaded by some of the local kids. Harry had a supply of mints and balloons to dish out and the word had gone round. They were great fun and particularly enjoyed looking at the photos we'd taken around the village. They recognised all the people up at the *gompa* and there was much giggling at their own portraits.

Dinner was peppered yak meatballs, *momos* and peaches. Not common items on too many menus but it was a major hit here in Tinje. Philippe was sitting quietly up one end of the table, engrossed in his book. The occasional guffaw emanated from his corner of the tent. After twenty minutes Philippe looked up with a big grin on his face, 'You know, there are some very good bits in this book,' then it was eyes down and straight back into his world of bondage.

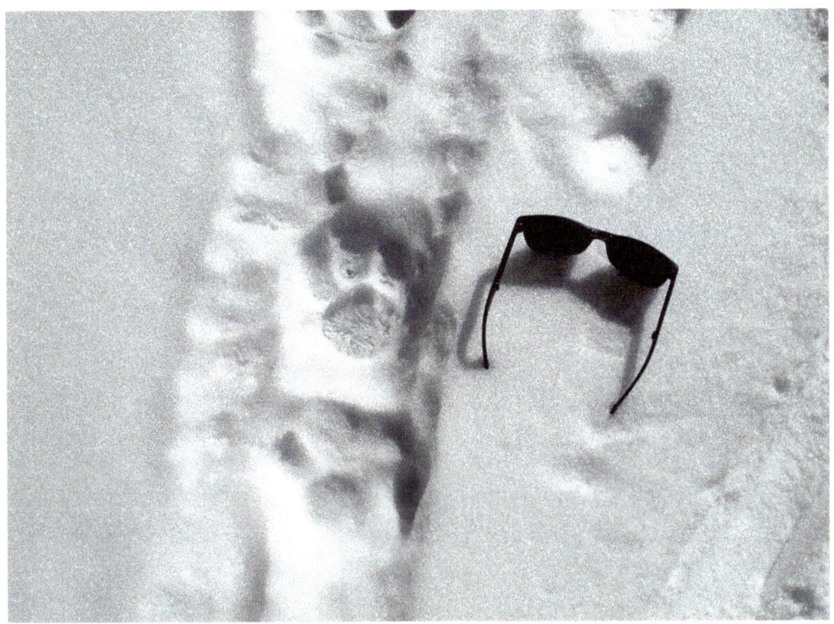

Footprints and dragged tail marks of the snow leopard in the Ladakhi snow, winter 2013

Ade on the Chadar ice while Mr Hat and Phil wait

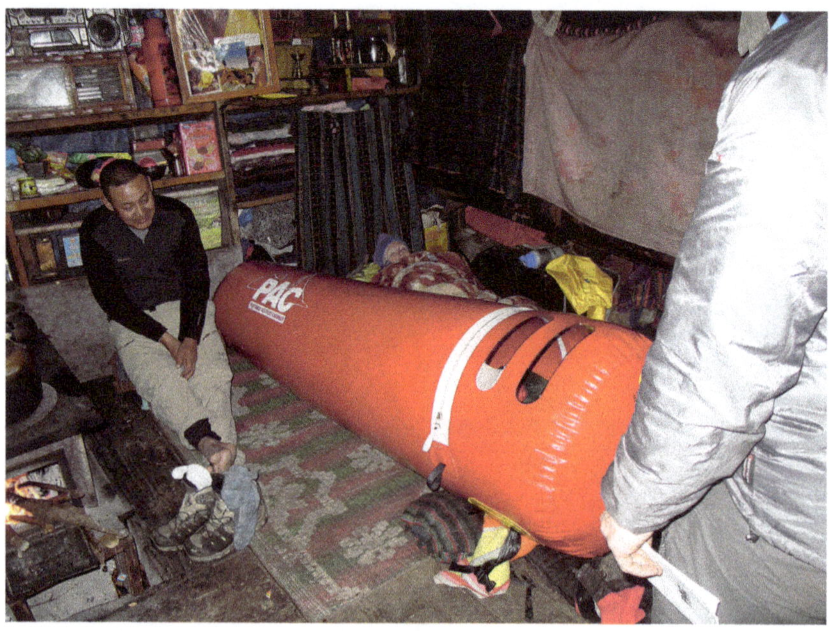

Mary in the Gamow bag with Carolyn next to her – Sonam, Joe and I took turns on the foot pump

Mary is helped into an Indian army helicopter

Dorje Khatri and me, just below the North Col of Everest with Lhakpa Ri behind us

Caterpillar fungus (*Ophiocordyseps sinensis*) known as *yarsa gumba*

'The water is edged with silver birch and the gleaming whiteness of the branches against the unearthly blue of the water is one of the most blissful things that I have known.' —Snellgrove

The Demon's Path above Phoksumdo Lake

With Thinle Lhondup at his house in Saldang

Phurpa Tinley, Dorje and Lama Karma Tsondru Rinpoche at Shey

Shey Gompa

Our base camp at 5353 metres, in front of the snow dome of Danphe Sail, 6103 metres

The main street of Kattike the day after the earthquake

Outdoor clinic at Meghre in the district of Ramechhap

Chhiring Bhotia and Ian Wall at a checkpoint on our way to the blue lake of Phoksumdo

Payza Pelzang, Tsering Norboo and Jigmet Dadul on the ice at the confluence of the Zanskar River and the Indus, Ladakh

20
TO TSHARKA

28 MAY

Tinje (4153 metres; 13,625 feet)
to Rapka (4508 metres; 14,790 feet)
17.4 kilometres

I had a poor night's sleep; I was woken at 4.00 by Cheyne-Stokes breathing and couldn't really get back to sleep. This is the irregular breathing common at high altitude but which generally improves with acclimatisation. The breaths reach a crescendo then diminish over the next couple of cycles before the breathing stops for fifteen or twenty or thirty seconds. Then there is a small breath or two followed by a massive intake of air enough to wake yourself up. It's not dangerous but certainly has nuisance value. Interestingly, the drug acetazolamide, trade name Diamox, stops it completely, but I don't usually take it, preferring to keep it in reserve.

We left our idyll at Tinje by climbing about 30 metres up a hill behind the campsite, and this brought us directly onto the end of the old 'CIA runway'. There were still markers made of small boulders set into triangular and L-shaped patterns in the turf. The fairly flat area of short grass stretched 1 kilometre directly down the valley towards Kula. It seemed that everyone referred to this as 'the CIA runway': it had been constructed on the orders of the CIA but was never used. In the early 1960s the Americans funded and trained a paramilitary force of over 4000 Tibetans to run insurgencies across the border. Operation 'Shadow Circus' ran between 1961 and 1974 and was based mainly in Mustang. Other 'war camps' existed and there was one near Tinje. In the early '60s a Swiss engineer was sent to arrange construction of the simple airstrip. In *High Frontiers* Kenneth Bauer says that his host family in Tinje said of the Swiss gentleman that 'He had a nice radio and a good revolver'.

As we headed south it seemed as if there was a continual stream of people with yaks and ponies leaving Tinje and heading in the same direction as us. We thought they were either moving up to higher pastures or off to hunt for *yarsa gumba*. When I looked back, I could see Philippe standing head and shoulders above, and completely surrounded by, a family of eight *drogpa* further surrounded by their many *dri* and half a dozen horses. Tinje looked picturesque on the hillside behind. Many of the groups of travellers crossed over to the left bank of the Panzang after a couple of kilometres, and we followed a parallel course for the next few hours. That route on the other side of the Panzang led further east and over a pass to the Central Dolpo town and major monastic settlement of Dho Tarap.

There were several nomad families camped on both riverbanks, most of them in classic black yak-hair tents.

Soon after our lunch stop, where we consumed a packed lunch, we came across a family of goat-herding *drogpa* who were happy to talk and let us photograph the milking of their animals. The goats were tied by a rope around the horns, which was then wrapped round the horns of a goat facing the opposite way. The next goat was brought in and tied the opposite way to the previous goat so that the result was two ranks of animals facing each other, all tethered, head-to-head, by the horns – twenty or more goats in each rank. The old lady of the family then went around and by bending herself almost double she quickly milked each one. Nearby there was a square enclosure of piled-up rocks, with about thirty tiny bleating baby goats. The goat nursery.

Soon after, the valley divided in two and we took the more southerly branch and started following the Kehein Khola.

The afternoon was a long steady stroll along the gradually widening valley to a high camp at 4500 metres. The weather was calm and sunny and decidedly pleasant. Our tents went up in a crescent formation; to one side was the mess tent, which had been repaired by being much shortened and as a result it was a little cosier.

29 MAY

Rapka (4508 metres; 14,790 feet)
to Tsharka (4321 metres; 14,176 feet)
20.8 kilometres

We woke to find that 5 centimetres of snow had fallen overnight. It was still snowing, and our tent, 'number ten', was seriously leaking, with water flowing in both sides. Luckily our gear and sleeping bags were untouched.

Breakfast on that frigid morning was essential, but as we broke camp the snow was lessening and after about an hour of walking alongside the river we were able to shed a couple of layers of clothing.

We came to the place where we had to cross the river. There was no bridge. The porters busied themselves with throwing rocks into the stream to create stepping stones. Chandra and Ade were about 100 metres downstream, looking at crossing there. I was sure I could see my way over. I danced my way from stone to stone to be first across and, with a loud gloating cheer, did a victory pirouette on the last rock. One final step to the riverbank via an unexpectedly muddy rock and I was suddenly lying on my right side in a few inches of bone-chilling icy water. My camera had a bit of a dunking too. I climbed out to the resounding jeers of my porter friends. But there, unbelievably, directly in front of me, about 10 metres away, was a smoking yak-dung fire. Serendipitous indeed. It had been left burning overnight by a trio of locals that we'd travelled with the previous day and who were on the caterpillar fungus hunt. They'd gone ahead of us and had camped at this exact spot the previous evening. Their smouldering, smoky and smelly fire was more than welcome. Alasdair had wet feet and legs after his crossing so joined me in drying off.

We continued a long steady march up the valley and were well over 4700 metres so feeling the lassitude of high-altitude walking. It was strange weather, with dark skies and snow all around. We arrived at a false summit, marked by a small cairn, and we could see the real pass an unsettlingly long way off, about another 2 kilometres uphill.

Eventually we arrived at the Mo La (5030 metres; 16,502 feet) and it was uncomfortably windy. We didn't linger at the top but dropped down over the ridge to get some shelter.

We then started on the three-hour journey down to Tsharka, the way being disrupted regularly by a whole series of deep gullies that we had to climb deep into, then slog our way out of up the opposite side. Tsharka itself was unseen, hidden, as it was, deep in the valley of the Bharbung Khola, which flowed west to eventually pass through Dunai as the Bheri. We came, at last, to a crumbling old *chorten*, the first of a series. Then finally we gained the walkthrough entrance *kani chorten* and the incredible, medieval-looking town of Tsharka was just beyond. Snellgrove had done this last couple of hours in the dark, helping one of his exhausted porters down. When he first entered the walls of this unique place he felt as if it were an ancient fortress. He spent a few days there. He later said of Tsharka, 'Perhaps because of the first strange night, Tsharka never lost its charm for me, although it was the filthiest village I have ever lived in.'

The entrance *chorten* had some badly deteriorated paintings on the ceiling inside. It was situated well above and a couple of hundred metres before the edge of town. Down below us to our right was the large modern monastery, and across the river we could see the ruins of the Bon Sarchhen Gompa, with several *drogpa* tents in the enclosure.

On the outer edge of town, having passed a row of *chortens* of varying age and decrepitude we approached a second, more modern, *kani chorten* and, passing through this were rewarded by a much better display of paintings, nine mandalas on the ceiling and various Buddhas around the walls. Nevertheless, there were signs that even these decorations were beginning to decay.

We entered the town and it really was fortress-like, with a distinct medieval feel. Some of the rock-and-mud houses resembled turrets and were separated only by narrow alleyways. We walked down through the muddy lanes of the old town and out via the south gate. This was where, at the beginning of the movie *Himalaya*, the inhabitants of the town poured out to meet the returning yaks bearing the body of Thinle's son. A new bridge over a side stream brought us to a small cluster of relatively new buildings. We settled into some chairs in the sunshine in front of the Karnali Hotel while the boys put up our tents in the grounds of the Dhaulagiri Yak Hotel directly opposite. It wasn't a 'hotel' in the Western sense; up here hotels were traditional local houses where the main room could be used, for a small fee, to get warm, eat and then sleep on the benches around the perimeter.

As the sun went down we moved into the main room of the Karnali Hotel, where the standard yak-dung stove was burning, the smell distinctive but not unpleasant. Smoke was leaking out and filling the room, as always. The large matriarchal hotel owner and her daughter spent their whole time boiling water and cooking rice and noodles for their slow but steady stream of customers.

The daughter, in her twenties, spoke superb English. Her name was Tsewang Wangmo and she had trained as a teacher in Kathmandu. She beamed a stunning smile as she let me take some photos of her preparing the yak-butter tea in a large wooden churn. Tsewang was dressed in the traditional Tibetan garb of a striped *chuba* over a lilac embroidered dress. Her hair was in a long braid and she sported several necklaces and bracelets of silver bearing chunks of coral and turquoise. She told us that the hotel was closed in winter, when the whole family went back to Kathmandu. She had sisters living there permanently. Her plan was to get a job teaching in a government run school as there was a generous pension scheme allowing retirement at the age of forty-five.

Having dumped tent 'number ten' because of its sieve-like quality, Harry and I took occupancy of our new tent, number five, but it arrived with the last of the porters and we didn't get our gear into it until well after 19.00.

We had dinner in the delightfully typical Tibetan room at the Karnali. A woman asked me to look at the tooth of her daughter, who was about ten. I got my torch and peered into the child's mouth. One of her molars had an enormous cavity in it but it was a first tooth and due to be lost anyway. The child wasn't distressed and the pair seemed happy with a dose of paracetamol. It again reinforced the fact that there was absolutely no basic health care in Dolpo. I made a mental note to find out, on my return, what facilities there may actually be and if there was any way to help.

Saila and the boys didn't let us down with dinner. We were warm and well fed, and it was great to be there in the iconic village of Tsharka with some free time to explore the next day.

21
TSHARKA: A DAY IN THE PAST

30 MAY

Rest day at Tsharka

We breakfasted sitting in the sun outside the Karnali 'hotel'. It was gloriously warm in that sheltered spot under perfectly clear skies. Colin and Duncan again opted for a packed lunch and went off on another of their walks up a hill above the town. Alasdair and I considered that our time in Tsharka was an opportunity too good to miss: to be able to look around this ancient town, which we'd first seen in the opening sequence of the legendary *Himalaya* movie. In that spectacular scene yaks tore down the hill in a cloud of dust carrying Thinle's dead son to the gate of the village. The women, children and old men came rushing out to see what was amiss. And now we were at the same spot, so off we went exploring.

One of the houses at the end of the village had a group of people loading up a horse, which was resplendent with the usual trappings of a Tibetan rug as a horse blanket and tufted red trim on the bridle. A young man was off on a trip, this being the height of *yarsa gomba* season. We stopped briefly to say '*Tashi delek*' and watched the mother of the family smearing the horse's ears with butter, followed by a generous smudge of the stuff on the animal's forehead: a local ritual to bless the journey.

A hundred metres upstream of the town the village women were doing their washing in the river. About a dozen of the local ladies were perched on the large pale-grey boulders of the river and rubbing, stamping and beating their laundry items. Some were up to their knees in the icy water and treading on everything from blankets to blouses, *chubas* to large rugs and horse blankets. A few metres up the riverbank was a constructed rectangle of boulders piled over a metre high and about 10 metres wide and 15 metres long. This was steadily covered by the cold wet washing and acted as an efficient clothes dryer. The breeze circulated between the rocks and under the drying clothes. The sun was intense enough, even in the chill air, to warm the stones, so they acted as a heat sink. I wondered how people back in the UK and Australia might enjoy this natural, environmentally friendly and efficient set-up. They would certainly miss their push-button whitegoods.

We wandered over to the old part of town less than 100 metres on the other side of our campsite. Walking up the earth ramp got us level with the first little side street, which we dived into. This pleasant old place was entirely constructed of brown stones held together with a loose muddy mortar. Most doorways had a carved or painted inscription in stone fixed over the lintel. We peered into the yards and greeted the locals with a loud '*Tashi delek*'. Generally they stared back at us as if we were strange beings from another world.

We returned to the campsite and Alasdair was keen to buy some jewellery from the owner of the hotel. Her schoolteacher daughter Tsewang, who spoke excellent English, wasn't at home but elaborate miming and broad smiles conveyed the gist on both sides in the bargaining. Alasdair managed to buy the coral and turquoise necklace quite literally from around the lady's neck. She knew she was on to a winner now, so she brought out some other items wrapped in a handkerchief-sized cloth, mainly turquoise and coral beads. Among the cluster of loose stones there were a few *dzi* stones. I'd been on the lookout for a good specimen of this ancient type of bead or amulet. Their origin is steeped in mystery, but examples of these stones have existed in families for hundreds of years. The Tibetan name is *dzi* or *gzi*, pronounced 'zee', and they are said to confer good luck, ward off evil and protect the bearer from physical harm. There are many stories and legends suggesting where they came from, but my favourite is that they once adorned the demigods in heaven in ancient times. When they became worn or tarnished they were discarded down upon the earth. That is why no one has ever found a stone in perfect condition. The dzi stones are a type of agate and usually have distinctive markings by way of dark lines and circles, or eyes. The more eyes, the more valuable. Reinhold Messner often wears one that he bought in Tingri, Tibet, in 1981. They can cost many thousands of dollars. From our friendly landlady in this ancient village, I bought an excellent, clearly modern, stone with three eyes, along with two coral beads, for R.10,000 – about $120. A bargain, and it will always remind me of a heavenly and relaxing day in Tsharka.

Alasdair was keen to keep on bartering, as he wanted to buy a piece of turquoise from our new supplier with the intention of giving it as a gift to a close friend back in Australia. Our landlady jeweller had several reasonable-sized pieces and Alasdair got himself a bargain in a lump about the size of a small hen's egg. Corneille Jest, in his *Tales of the Turquoise*, gave some insight into the types and value of this semi-precious stone. In Tibetan culture the turquoise is much revered as a precious item and, because it can be susceptible to destruction and decay, it also possesses a 'spiritual' quality. The Tibetan word for turquoise is *yü* and that for the life force or spirit is *la*, so *la-yü* translates as 'vital spirit turquoise' and it is a common theme in folk tales and legends. The wearing of turquoise helps guard a person's life force. The turquoise, like people, will live and ultimately die. The efficacy of protection is related to quality and there are three main types. Yü-trugse are the colour of the heavens, a pale, whitish blue. Yü-trugkar are blue and white. The most valuable are the yü-trugmar, which have veins of red and black and are said to come from lakes. The beautiful piece that Alasdair had just purchased was heavily marked with black veins: a fine yü-trugmar.

After lunch Alasdair, Harry and I walked about 1 kilometre upstream to the new bridge then back down the other side to visit the Bon *gompa*. It was, as when Snellgrove visited it, a ruin. There were several tents of a nomadic goat-herding *drogpa* family in the grounds. There were no men around, so we assumed they were off '*yarsa gumba*-ing'. There were a few children and several young women who were driving the goats uphill. Two older women were simply wandering around the camp. One carried a child and was spinning a prayer wheel in the usual clockwise direction of a Buddhist, so she was clearly not a Bon adherent. The other old woman approached Alasdair and did an elaborate mime that clearly conveyed that she had problems with her joints and her eyes, but we were unable to help and could only shake our heads saying 'sorry'.

The main part of the *gompa* was locked and no shaft of light penetrated so absolutely nothing could be seen on peeping through a crack in the doors. Snellgrove reported that in 1956 there was nothing of great interest in this main temple. He was, however, intrigued by a smaller temple which was unique in displaying a Buddhist fresco on one wall and a Bon fresco on the opposite one. Sadly, even then, this smaller temple was decaying and on the day we visited it the decay seemed terminal, the frescoes were barely recognisable and only the borders remained, in faded pastel shades of red, green and blue paint.

Snellgrove also spoke of his visit to Dolpo in 1960. Upon his arrival at the home of Nyima Tschering in Saldang he was told that there had been some issues of unrest in the region. Only two months earlier a raiding party of Khampa warriors, who were at that time based in Mustang to fight the Chinese, rode up to Tsharka and stole over a hundred yaks to feed themselves. With the border to the north closed and this threat to the east, it was at this time, around 1960, that the Dolpo-pa began taking their yaks and goats south for the winter.

We dropped down to the river as we'd seen two young girls crossing directly back to the main village through the shallows. By wading knee-deep across the boulder-bottomed river we had a cold but quite exhilarating return to camp in time for tea. Duncan and Colin had arrived back from their hike and, as was usual when the two of them were away, we'd seen next to nothing of Susan who always kept very much to herself. Philippe was clearly a man of infinite capacity for rest and had enjoyed his day.

Dinner that evening was consumed in the smoky warmth of the hotel living room. A perfect rest day.

Next day we were heading off once again, into some exceedingly remote valleys and trekking parallel to the Tibetan border.

31 MAY

Tsharka (4321 metres; 14,176 feet)
to Norbulung (4772 metres; 15,656 feet)
15 kilometres

After an efficient breaking of camp and breakfast in the sun outside our favourite Tsharkan hotel we set off upriver, past the long *mani* walls to the bridge then, having crossed over, followed the river south, gradually getting higher. It was another perfect day with few other people on the trail.

After an hour or so we turned into a side valley, to be confronted by a drop to a long suspension bridge with a daunting rocky climb of over 100 metres up the other side. After a short rest, and a chocolate bar, we did the climb. It was treacherously loose underfoot and quite exposed in places, but the view opened up and we felt on top of the world. The trail continued across a high meadow before rejoining the river and reverting to a rugged up and down pathway in the valley.

We dropped down to a wide flat area near the river, where we had lunch. A chill breeze had picked up but that didn't stop me from nodding off on the ground with my backpack as a pillow. The day had been dusty and as I woke up I coughed up a plug of mucus with a streak of blood. The perils of high-altitude trekking.

After lunch the walk was surprisingly level and easygoing, and then the river gorge started widening into a vast alpine meadow. A few yaks were grazing higher up on the hillside facing us across the river.

Norbulung was a beautiful campsite. We were on a wide grassy plateau which was full of the holes caused by the burrow-building efforts of marmots. About a kilometre away on the opposite riverbank were a couple of nomad tents with ponies and goats milling around.

The rest of the afternoon was spent settling into the tent after the easy 15-kilometre stroll we'd just enjoyed. That evening there was no wind and no cloud. There was a sliver of new moon hanging sickle-like just above the mountains. A brilliantly clear Jupiter was close to it and a vivid red Mars directly overhead. Once again, all was right with the world of Dolpo.

22

OVER THE JUNGBEN LA

1 JUNE

Norbulung (4772 metres; 15,656 feet)
to Niswas La (5120 metres; 16,798 feet)
to Jungben La (5561 metres; 18,244 feet)
to River Camp (5133 metres; 16,840 feet)
13.9 kilometres

After observing the beauty of the previous evening's sunset I fell into a deep slumber, only to be suddenly woken a couple of times by our nomad neighbours from across the river trotting their horses right past our tents. They were paying a visit to our porters. The raucous noise of bells and many horses' hooves about a metre from our heads startled us abruptly out of sleep.

Bed tea arrived, along with another beautifully still and sunny morning. We set off at a gentle stroll up the valley. About an hour and a half brought us to a much-narrowed part of the river requiring more of a climb. It wasn't difficult to reach the cairn marking the Niwar Pass at 5120 metres (16,798 feet). However, from our new vantage point we could now see the Jungben La at 5550 metres and still about 2 kilometres away across a broad vast plain with the Sandachhe Himal directly ahead. This was the same valley where, in 1900, Kamaguchi had stumbled across the skeletons of dead travellers emerging from the melting snow but missing their skulls and thigh bones.

It took another hour to reach the real start of the ascent and there was a choice of trails up to the pass 400 metres above us.

Once on the tracks, what had appeared to be a straightforward trek turned into a steep prolonged endurance test. I took a breath for each step and counted to a hundred. Then did it over and over again just to keep moving. Reinhold Messner said of his solo Everest climb, 'Every breath up there was an ordeal and still I took it as a gift.' At a mere 5500 metres breathing wasn't quite such an ordeal but our movement uphill was pitifully slow.

About two thirds of the way up, and about half an hour from the pass, it started to snow. It was light at first, but within minutes we lost the view of the surrounding mountains. I pulled on my outer waterproof but my legs still had a single layer. Another twenty minutes brought Ade and myself to the top. By this time the snow was heavy and visibility was about 20 metres. Chandra, Colin and Alasdair were already at the top but it was getting quite cold. Ade hung some prayer flags off the cairn but it really was time to go down the other side as quickly as we could.

Chandra led the way rapidly down the steep zigzagging path on wet loose rubble. We got down the 400 metres or so to our campsite by the river, the Lhanimar Khola. The lead porters were huddled there under their plastic sheets. After a short time the other porters began to arrive and fortunately our new tent, number five, was the first to go up. The fact it wasn't leaking was a definite plus and once our wet gear was stashed down the sides it was comfortable. Time to get dried off, don the merino leggings and climb into the sleeping bag to enjoy the sheer luxury of the air mattress. Ade and Chandra were naturally a little concerned about Susan and Philippe, but Gopal had been assigned to bring up the rear and the three arrived, cold but safe, about half an hour after the rest of us.

Hot juice came around once Saila's kitchen was up and running, with tea and a snack following at 15.30. I got my 1-litre aluminium water container filled up with boiling water to act as a hot water bottle and retired to my warm tent. We were expecting a cold night. The snow had stopped and there was a clear sky. We were still at 5100 metres and this was our highest camp. The down jacket was required over the sleeping bag as an extra layer of insulation.

2 JUNE

River Camp (5133 metres; 16,840 feet)
to Sangda (3770 metres; 12,368 feet)
12.1 kilometres

Harry, as usual, slept like the proverbial log, and we both enjoyed the novelty of a dry tent. When we woke the river was partially frozen but the weather was perfectly clear and straight down the valley was the pyramidal snow-covered peak of Tashikang, standing at 6386 metres (20,951 feet). We hadn't been able to see it the previous day because of the snow but it was quite simply a stunningly beautiful sight.

We set off on a level trail along the river valley, and after traversing the hillside for less than an hour there was a short rise to a cairn on an unnamed pass. The view from here was undeniably astounding. We were used to vistas gradually opening up as we reached a pass or climbed a hill. This one was an instantaneous eyeful as soon as the track reached the cairn. We'd been deprived of the view from the Jungben La the day before, so this, especially given the cold, clear, sunny morning, was even more special.

We were looking down a deep gorge of a valley which led directly east into the even more massive Kali Gandaki Gorge. I could see the Thorung La across the Kali Gandaki, and way below us were the tiny villages of Ghok and our destination of Sangda, still seven hours away. Towering over the other side of the valley above Sangda were the glacier-clad peaks of Tashikang then Tsartse (6343 metres; 20,810 feet), with the giant ridge of the Lumbuk Danda ranging further eastwards. In 1900, when the Japanese monk Kawaguchi came up this valley, he described the trail as 'a treacherous slope which yearly claimed, as I was told, a pilgrim or two as victims to its sand avalanches'.

At the cairn Chandra helped me hang some prayer flags. This time they were for my father, who was Buddhist without even knowing it. He'd died in 1990 after a long battle with heart disease. I started taking some photos of his prayer flags and realised fully, not for the first time, how much I still missed him, twenty-five years after his death. Om Mani Padme Hum.

We started our descent. It was scarily steep in places and seemingly unending. It was loose slate scree and extremely tortuous. Snellgrove came down this way in 1954 and said of it, 'One may certainly describe it as an interesting descent ... One makes one's way delicately across precipitous scree slopes threatened by rocks that hang out from the crags above.' We gradually got down, over about an hour and a half, to an area of several acres of relatively level ground covered with ancient juniper trees. It was still another hour beyond and down to get to the river Keha Lungpa, where we had a picnic lunch just across a new suspension bridge. Several of us could feel the strain in the knees, and Ade's back wasn't too good.

After lunch a direct climb uphill of over 100 metres brought us to the trail which we'd seen so clearly from high up on the pass and which was a long traverse across a cliff face leading into Sangda several more kilometres down the valley.

At one point we had an excessively steep descent into a gully which dished out knee strain to the point of limping. There was an easy river crossing at the bottom then the usual climb out the other side. Thankfully, another kilometre further on, we crossed the final gorge just above a waterfall. An easy trail wound round the hillside and suddenly there was a *chorten* of a markedly different design from the usual Dolpo type. We had entered the southern part of Mustang.

Just past the *chorten* the village of Sangda came into full view. It sat in the centre of an extensive array of terraced fields in various states of cultivation and appeared to be somehow mysteriously suspended above the massive canyon below. In one of the fields, just beneath the main group of houses, we could see some of our tents had been erected.

Kawaguchi said, 'Sanda is a literally snowbound little village, open to communication from the rest of the world only during the three summer months, and that through the precarious mountain path I had come over.' Snellgrove called the place P'a-ling and said of it, 'The people spoke a form of Tibetan very close to that of Tsharka and were friendly enough. The village stands on the right bank of the Keha Lungpa and consists of about twenty-five houses. It is also known as Sangdak (SI: Sangdãh) meaning "Pure and Clean" but this is properly the name of an abandoned village which can be seen on the far bank. Also on that side but higher up are their winter quarters, of which the proper name is Gok, but the term Gün-sa, which just means "winter-place" is also used.' Even though Kagbeni was a much more accessible place, the people of Sangda maintained closer social and religious ties with the lamas and the Dolpo-pa of Tsharka and Tarap.

Our campsite was splendid, with views back to the pass we'd descended from that morning. Towering over the village were the snow-and glacier-covered peaks of Tashikang and its more easterly companion Tsartse, seemingly just above our heads.

After dinner we received a visit from an American trekker and his Belgian friend. They were walking the Great Himalaya Trail from east to west and had started near Kangchenjunga only a few weeks earlier. They were keen to hear about conditions over the passes. They were carrying all their own gear and buying food on the way. We guessed that they had lean times ahead crossing Dolpo and never quite worked out if they had actually bothered with permits.

The best climb of the day was into the sleeping bag, once again knowing that the next day was a rest day to simply enjoy being in this tranquil place.

23
SANGDA

3 JUNE

Sangda. Rest day.

After a blissful eight hours of sleep I was awake and out of the tent at 6.00 a.m. and took my bed tea in the glorious sunshine enjoying the grandeur of this spectacular place. In the early hours I thought I'd heard a gurgling of flowing water and, sure enough, the villagers had used the irrigation system we'd seen in places like Karang and Shimen where a stream could be diverted to flood a field or group of fields. The narrow plot near us, about 8 metres by 20, was now a pool of water like a rice paddy. Many of the locals were already out working in the fields. There was a ploughing of several of the fields going on with a couple of pairs of the *dzo*, yak and cattle cross breeds, pulling the standard wooden 'T' bar plough.

At breakfast Ade announced that this morning's coffee was the last. This was met with general moans of despair, but we knew that we only had to put up with such an intolerable situation for another couple of days. It reminded me of George Schaller's story of his stay at Shey soon after Peter Matthiessen had left. Schaller wrote that over several days he noted that whether the cook served tea or coffee it always tasted the same, to the point where he felt obliged to say something. The cook replied that the sherpas want coffee but the Sahib wants tea so 'Half and half, sah'.

Colin and Duncan again requested a packed lunch and were off on their wanderings up a ridge south towards Tashikang. Ade and Harry did some washing at the ground-pipes which were spouting icy water at the edge of the village. I happily wandered round this tiny place which, like many of the Dolpo villages, was entirely without electricity or any sign of communications. I sat outside in a chair at the campsite catching up with the diary and scanning the trail up towards the pass for any sign of activity. Yesterday there had been many groups of ponies and yaks heading up to the *yarsa gumba* hunt. I saw no movement and no sign either of our American visitor and his companion. Across the valley and a long way below us was the deserted village that Snellgrove thought was the original 'Pure and Clean' Sangda. When he and Corneille Jeste had travelled up to Sangda from Jomsom in 1960 they camped here to acclimatise and wait for a yak convoy into Dolpo but the weather became a serious issue. It was much later in the year, in September, and the residents of Sangda were bringing in the harvest of wheat. On 2 and 3 October it rained incessantly and the field in which they were camped became flooded. The whole party was struck down by heavy colds and high temperatures and they were feeling desperately unwell. They moved into one of the houses where Snellgrove occupied a dungeon-like outhouse. The rain fell as snow higher up on the pass but the way they'd come up to Sangda was also blocked. They were stuck in the village for days to come. They used the courtyard of the largest house, the 'hotel'. Rain and sleet continued, and news arrived that one of the houses had collapsed. It was a heap of rubble and the now exposed wall of the adjacent house looked next to go. They returned to the courtyard just in time to hear a sudden crash as the courtyard wall of the hotel collapsed. The whole place was running with water and they were seriously concerned that much of the village would slip into the depths. It took until 7 October before the storm passed and they couldn't help but feel that the villagers thought them somehow to blame. When the time came to leave the party moved across to Gün-sa for the night, and as Snellgrove remained feverish, he rode a yak up towards the pass taking five hours to get to their camp by the river. They still had to ascend to the Jungben La which Snellgrove called the 'Kyi-tse La'. Next day they struggled through deep snow and even the yaks couldn't get through and a retreat to Gün-sa, Ghok, was undertaken.

After lunch Harry, Chandra and I went up to the 'shop'. This was the 'hotel' where Snellgrove had camped and which still carried a sign saying

'Sangtak Guest-House'. The shop was a corner of the main room in this large house and there was a poor supply of goods; a few soft drinks, some biscuits and packets of noodles. The woman of the house was there with two children, a little girl of about eighteen months and a boy of three with obvious cerebral palsy. She told us, via Chandra, that the girl was her daughter and the little boy was her sister's child. The sister was out working in the fields. The unfortunate child had a severe squint, an incessant cough and snotty nose and he was tied by a short length of rope to a post so he couldn't fall into the fire. I said to Harry that he would most likely develop a serious chest infection in the foreseeable future and would certainly have a short life. We agreed that the family would most likely be thoroughly pragmatic, take the Buddhist view and pray for a better rebirth for the poor little fellow.

We had a lazy afternoon. The wind picked up and there was dust everywhere. It was too hot in our small tent and the best place was the mess tent. Susan wasn't seen all day. Duncan and Colin returned in the early afternoon and Colin said at tea, almost in passing, that he'd seen a snow leopard. This was astounding news. He'd had a brief sighting of the animal about 200 metres above him on the ridge. He didn't sound particularly excited by the sighting and I teased him by asking if it wasn't just a hornless spotty goat. He snapped that I was just being jealous, which I have to admit was true, and nothing more was ever said on the subject. Harry and I agreed that if we'd seen even a glimpse of the elusive cat we would probably have carried on like it was all our Christmases at once.

At dinner Ade, rather sombrely, reminded us that the adventure was not yet over and the following day was likely to be one of the toughest yet.

24

TO THE KALI GANDAKI

4 JUNE

Sangda (3770 metres; 12,368 feet)
to Bhima Lhojung La (4450 metres; 14,599 feet)
to Dhagarjung (3153 metres; 10,344 feet)
17.8 kilometres

Up at 5.00 to a nice calm, sunny, no-coffee morning. The locals were already up and had begun ploughing the small field near us, the one they had flooded the previous day and which had now drained completely and was once again dry. As usual they used the pair of *dzo*, yak-cow hybrids, with the wooden plough, a man out front leading the animals and a second guiding the plough-share. Two women with pick-like tools seemed to be removing stones and tossing them to one side.

The start of our day's walk was a steep 400-metre climb directly uphill behind the village. This was seriously hard work. I put my head down and, taking one breath for every step, counted my steps to 100. Then repeated the process. I kept on without stopping to 500. I looked around. The village was a bit smaller below us. All the time we'd been in Sangda I'd been conscious of an otherworldly sensation of being suspended between earth and sky. The narrow strip on which the village was perched was above a deep and massive gash in the land, so deep that we couldn't see the river. Yet we were so high that we seemed an integral part of the snowy peaks and the deep azure sky. Now the village looked so small the feeling of near flight increased. Still there was the need to get the head down again, to walk and to do more counting. This time to 600. This brought me to just below a cairn on a ridge. Here were quite incredible views in all directions. The trail ahead could be seen traversing round a giant natural amphitheatre below the snow slopes of Tsartse. Some of the narrow pathway in front looked quite exposed with steep cliffs directly underfoot.

After walking around this section of trail we came to another cairn on the next ridge which revealed the next massive valley to be traversed. Each loop gave us a little height gain.

Another couple of ridges brought us to a cairn where we stopped for lunch. This was the high point of the day, the Bhima Lhojung La at 4450 metres (14,599 feet), 700 metres above Sangda, our starting point. From this high spot we now had the clearest view yet across the Kali Gandaki Valley to the Thorung La.

A rapid drop in height after lunch and a gradual turn south brought us to a large *chorten* with a view of the summit of Annapurna and the Nilgiris framed in prayer flags. Only the summit of Annapurna could be seen behind the foreground Nilgiris and from this viewpoint it had a curvature that resembled the Sydney Opera House and which was the very slope that Herzog and Lachenal struggled up in 1950.

We could look across the valley to the towns of Muktinath and Kagbeni. For the first time in over three weeks we could see roads and occasional trucks and cars, albeit as small moving dots many kilometres away.

More descent brought us to a steep drop into a canyon with a more gradual climb out the other side which led up to a new dirt road. A road after all this time! We followed the uniquely flat wide trail uphill for about another kilometre towards yet another large *chorten* on a ridge. Alasdair was waiting for us there. Surely the edge of our destination village? But no, from there we could look down on the extensive fields and buildings of Dhagarjung, our real destination, at least another 3 kilometres away. Alasdair observed, 'It looks like a metropolis down there. They've got "skyscrapers" of three storeys!' And so it seemed when the tallest buildings we'd seen in the previous 250 kilometres had been *chortens*.

From this point on the wind was directly in our faces. This was the infamous afternoon gale which blows up the Kali Gandaki Valley every day and limits the flights into and out of Jomsom. Our eyes filled constantly with dust and streaming with tears we made our way downhill, over the next hour, into the centre of the village. Here we were guided to our campsite in the enclosed grounds of a 'hotel'. We settled into its traditional Tibetan style dining room for some hot lemon juice.

It had been a nine-hour walk and everyone was a little weary, but it had been a great day. Tea and biscuits, reduced by the journey to crumbs, in the late afternoon then, at dinner, Ade announced that there were now two ways to Jomsom next morning. The old way, over a pass with a steep descent directly into Jomsom, or down to the river, across a new suspension bridge and along the road. An easy choice. As Harry said, 'I came to see Upper Dolpo, not Upper Jomsom.'

5 JUNE

Dhagarjung to Jomsom
10.6 kilometres

It was a disturbed night's sleep, with dogs barking and a cockerel crowing, but we needed an early start to avoid the wind which would be a certainty later in the morning.

After breakfast Ade, Bishwo, Alasdair, Harry and I set off down to the river. Colin, Duncan, Susan and Philippe, along with Gopal, were heading over the top.

Almost an hour brought us to the small village of Rangling, just before the suspension bridge. As we entered the village a motorbike went by carrying three people. The one on the back was a young monk with his red robes flying in the breeze. This was the first vehicle we'd seen in over three weeks and the sound of its engine seemed strange and inappropriate to our ears. Soon after, the first of several aeroplanes flew directly overhead on their way to Jomsom Airport.

The bridge was a new and long suspension design well over 100 metres in length. Once across it was only two hours into Jomsom itself along the new road. This road carried a constant stream of taxis full of Hindu pilgrims up to Muktinath, one of the holiest of Hindu sites, dedicated to the god Vishnu. The popular destination for Hindus of Mount Kailash has become much restricted by the Chinese in recent years, so the number of tourist pilgrims to Muktinath has massively increased. The new road was thus quite busy, but being a simple gravel road it had already been carved up by streams of water and the heavy trucks.

The long main street of Jomsom runs parallel to the airport runway and we sauntered its full length knowing that these were the very last few minutes of the trek. The final hotel at the furthest edge of town was ours, the Hotel Dhaulagiri. Ade, Alasdair, Harry and I had no hesitation about tucking into a second breakfast of fried eggs on toast. We settled into our rooms and then I prepared for lunch by having an exquisite first beer. I'd been looking forward to it for a couple of weeks. I wandered up the main street, the only street, and managed to get an email off to my wife, Paula. Then Harry and I popped in to the 'German Bakery' for coffee and delicious apple and chocolate crumble.

In the evening we had our final meal and the traditional end-of-trek presentation to our guides and porters. This was a fun occasion, where we thanked them and gave them their tips. They had been a great crowd. Always cheerful and helpful. We were hugely indebted to them as the trek would not have been possible without their support and goodwill. The chronicles of Snellgrove and Schaller and Matthiessen were scattered with anecdotes of intransigent and surly porters causing delay and angst. Not so with our journey. Chandra, with his deputies Bishwo and Gopal, had run a smooth and happy operation. To wind up the evening there was a raffle of unwanted gear donated by us, the clients. The usual fare was made up of items such as trekking poles, t-shirts, water bottles, unused batteries, socks and so on. Chandra got exceedingly lucky that night by inheriting a pair of Philippe's voluminous brown pantaloons. There was, to finish, another of Saila's special cakes, with 'Happy Endings' written on it, and all washed down by more beers. I was especially glad to see that our porter friend with the appalling chest infection had staggered on through and was now urgently self-medicating with the local *raksi*, a drink rather like Japanese sake. Then suddenly the party was, sadly, over.

6 JUNE

Return to Kathmandu

An unwelcome early call at 4.30 a.m. for our 5.30 a.m. flight. We'd been told the night before that the luggage allowance had been reduced to 15 kilos. This was impossible as we had a month's worth of gear each. The solution was that we each put stuff, mainly dirty washing, into bags to go back on the bus with the porters who were being driven back to Kathmandu. Our non-essentials would get back to us next day.

We had a light breakfast then a stroll down to the airport terminal, literally 100 metres away. Most of the porters were a little hungover. As we boarded the plane all our porter friends stood in the hotel garden waving us goodbye. It was only a half-hour flight to Pokhara but again there was no view of Dhaulagiri.

In Pokhara we had a couple of hours to kill. Alasdair had to pick up some luggage from the hotel, so he, Harry, Philippe and I jumped in a taxi and headed off into town for a proper breakfast at the Moondance restaurant.

After the short flight back to Kathmandu Tulsi picked us up and we were back at Hotel Tibet in no time. Saturday traffic is easygoing in Kathmandu. The rest of the day was spent meeting friends and shopping in Thamel. At Sam's I found my daughter Nicola's message written in a felt-tip pen above the main staircase: 'Happy B'day Bill Crozier 2014. EBC Rocks! Love you. xo'. She and Bec had made it to Everest Base Camp and back to Kathmandu and hadn't forgotten to leave a message for me on the wall at Sam's.

25
THE DOLPO MOMENT

7 JUNE

Kathmandu

I took morning tea in the lobby of the Hotel Tibet with Ian Wall and his wife, Sarita. They ran a small trekking company called Off the Wall Treks, and they'd made all the arrangements for the treks I'd done with Joe Bonington to Tilicho Lake and to Bhutan. They were both well and it was good to catch up.

Mid-morning Harry, Alasdair and I jumped into a taxi and went over to Boudhanath to check out some Tibetan handmade yak wool rugs and to try and find Tenzin Norbu Lama's art gallery. We had a relaxing, laidback lunch of *momos* and sandwiches on the rooftop of the Paradise restaurant, gazing back at the giant eyes of the Great Stupa.

Following lunch we had no trouble finding Tenzin's gallery. He wasn't there that day but the young manager, Phurba, was looking after the place. Phurba is Tenzin's son and his English was good. He was interested when we told him we'd just returned from Dolpo and seen his old family home in Tinje. I'd already transferred my photographs onto my iPad so I was able to show him the pictures I'd taken at Trolung Gompa. He recognised all the people we met there – the lama and his young pupils. I said, 'Do you know the man with the extra thumb?' and he said, 'Yes ... Me!' holding up his own double thumb. It turned out that the man at Trolung was his uncle and this was a bit of a family trait.

The paintings in the gallery were superb, just like the murals in the movie, but, sadly, a bit out of my price range.

After a beer in the Hotel Tibet's Yeti Bar in the evening we wandered over to the K-too restaurant in Thamel for a farewell dinner. The Amigos were already there as they were still staying at the Shankar rather than Hotel Tibet. I had the best ever satay chicken, pepper steak and fried apple *momos*, a brilliant meal after the relative austerity of trekking fare. Philippe was in good form, churning out his delightfully garbled English. Harry was up on cloud nine, still hardly able to believe he'd been to Dolpo. Alasdair's booming laugh came easily and frequently. It was party time. Colin and Susan didn't say a word all evening. Duncan was quite relaxed and joined in the celebration. Then it was time for a final drink in Sam's Bar. Colin and Susan jumped into taxis outside K-too and with a mumbled goodbye and a brief handshake they were off. Duncan at least said a proper goodbye.

Alasdair and I agreed that a couple of other trekkers would have altered the whole group dynamic for the better. At one point in the trek I'd written in my diary 'the "Three Amigos" form an opinionated clique and are very ready to criticise yet apparently have little to offer'. Harry, by now assuming guru status in my eyes, rather more pragmatically said, 'If they hadn't have come as a group there wouldn't have been enough of us for the trip to have run.' He was right. At least they made the numbers up and the rest of us were able to have our Dolpo moment.

And so we trekkers returned to what passes for *real life* for each of us. But I could not let go of Dolpo. Modern communication and the availability of information led me to some interesting new discoveries.

I found out that David Snellgrove was alive and well, now in his nineties and living in Italy. He was even active on Facebook, and he was able to see and 'like' some of the photographs I'd taken.

Ken Bauer was also on Facebook, and we were able to swap notes about recent events. He gave me the link to his update on Dolpo with his thoughts on the issues forced upon the Dolpo-pa by the annual *yarsa gomba* collection stampede.

I was even able to talk to my new friend, the lama from Namgung. He made the annual journey back to Kathmandu for winter and was teaching in a monastery near the Great Stupa at Boudha. He was able to give me a lot of insight into recent events and life in the modern version of Dolpo.

However, a lot remained unchanged in this remote Himalayan enclave. David Snellgrove summed it up when he said, of his second visit there:

> I realised now that after a whole winter of isolation in Dolpo I had not learned to accept its normal terms of life. It seemed absurd to be there in the summer when all the tracks and passes were open, and yet to be cut off from news of the outside world. At the same time it was extraordinary, even wonderful, to reflect that here was one part of the world where conditions of life still continued not only as they had been in Dolpo a thousand years before perhaps, but also much as they had been everywhere else in the world until a hundred years ago. Maybe one gains in historical perspective by living even a short while in just such circumstances oneself.

I hope that I have gained a little historical perspective myself. It is always the case that when I return home after a trip to the Himalaya I appreciate greatly those things we take so much for granted in Western society. Even something as innocuous as being able to turn on the tap and drink what comes out without worrying about catching diseases thrills me for weeks.

In *High Frontiers* Kenneth Bauer states unequivocally that his book is 'a case study of change', and he documents well what has happened in Dolpo, particularly since 1959 and up to his sojourn there in 1996.

I was hoping, on my journey through Dolpo, to see some version of old Tibet hanging on, unchanged, in the twenty-first century. I'd seen the current version of Tibet in China and how rapidly change was happening there. In Bhutan, with its constitutional monarchy, I had a sense of what may have become in Tibet had it not been occupied. If we assume that the young fourteenth Dalai Lama would have engaged with the West and embraced technology, then a modern Tibet, unsullied by the People's Liberation Army, may well have become a progressive and developing nation. In Ladakh the people live in the democracy that is India, and there I saw how modern transport and communications could integrate seamlessly with a large and traditional monastic community. No doubt my expectations were coloured by repeated readings of *The Snow Leopard* and many, many viewings of *Himalaya: L'enfance d'un chef*, but I went with an open mind. I hoped to see an 'olde worlde' society with the modern accoutrements of schools and hospitals. The reality was both better and worse than my selfish desires for observing a vestigial medieval society.

Like people all over the Himalaya, the Dolpo-pa try to retain their traditions and values but change is inexorable and inevitable. Of course one of the main Buddhist concepts is that of impermanence. Change, whether slow or radical, will always be accommodated and accepted. The question is how they deal with change and 'progress'. Throughout their history, the people of Dolpo have had little power to determine their own future. They are caught in the country of Nepal, a democracy, where they are a minority group of different ethnicity and religion from most of Nepal. To the north their traditional grazing grounds and trading partners have been off limits since 1960. The poor agriculture and harsh winters mean a more frequent annual exodus to Kathmandu or lower valleys. The young people of Dolpo get a taste for education, city living, modern technology, fun and games. Very few of them want to return to a lifestyle quagmired in centuries past.

In mid-July 2014, a mere four weeks after my return, I came across a disturbing video and article posted online by the Asian Human Rights Commission (AHRC). They told the story of an incident in the village of Dho (Dho Tarap) on 3 June, the exact same day we were having a tranquil rest day at Sangda. The result was two people dead and about fifty injured.

Apparently a group of so-called Buffer Zone Management Committee (BZMC) officials, along with thirty-five armed police from Dunai, confronted two groups of locals. There had been disagreement over the collection of fees or royalties from the harvesting of *yarsa gumba*. It seems the scale of royalty fees for locals, district and non-district, had more than tripled from the previous year from NR1000 to NR3000 for gatherers from outside the district and from NR150 to NR500 for locals. On top of this the hunters were expected to walk the three or four days down to Dunai to pay the fees in person. There was also the threat to open up the high meadows to more people, even though no funds had ever been ploughed back into maintaining the resource.

On 2 June receipt books and NR800,000 were confiscated with no attention paid to the other concerns of the local community members. On the morning of 3 June the local committee demanded the return of the receipt books and the money. On their arrival that afternoon the police were immediately hostile and quickly resorted to violence. Around three dozen rubber bullets were fired at the villagers and a baton charge led to severe beatings. A house-to-house search rounded up all the men of the village and the leaders were taken into custody. Women and the elderly were also beaten as the thirty or so houses were searched. A thirty-year-old was found unconscious outside the village next morning and soon after died of his injuries. The police said he'd fallen off a cliff. A forty-seven-year-old man was severely injured and flown to Kathmandu by helicopter. He died in hospital there. The villagers bore the cost of medical expenses and the helicopter. The report also told of a raid on the village of Tsharka, with more beatings and three people arrested.

Ken Bauer wrote an update of *High Frontiers*, an essay published in the *Tibet Journal* entitled 'High Frontiers: Dolpo revisited'. In it he published the result of interviews with fifteen Dolpo-pa traders and farmers about their current practices and changes they'd endured in recent years. One section was headed 'The rise of caterpillar fungus and the new economy of Dolpo'. He concludes that the current *yarsa gumba* trade props up the economy of Dolpo and means that the people return annually. However, in the longer term the urbanisation of the young will result in fewer subsequent generations having the desire to return to a life of seasonal subsistence farming in a neglected region with poor health and educational infrastructure.

The sense of irreversible change happening right now in Dolpo could still not taint what was, for me, a feast for the senses. I enjoyed the whole Dolpo experience and made new friends. I promised myself I'd return.

And what about the snow leopard? Lucky I took my own little toy version as we were unlikely to ever see one. Our young assistant guides, Bishwo and Gopal, had been walking the Himalaya for ten years apiece and had never seen one.

I thought that the final words on my trip to Dolpo should be left to Peter Matthiessen. He died on 5 April 2014 from leukaemia, only a month before we began our trip to Dolpo. He was survived by his third wife Maria, son Luke and daughter Sara from his marriage to Patsy, and son Alex and daughter Rue from his marriage to Deborah. Back in 1973 Matthiessen visited the Lama of Crystal Monastery, who was on retreat at the cliff-hanging *gompa* at Tsakhang. The lama had gone on retreat there eight years previously and ill-health and leg problems had meant he'd been confined to Tsakhang and knew he was unlikely to ever leave. When Matthiessen asked if he was happy, the lama merely waved his arms in the direction of the sky and Crystal Mountain and said, 'Of course I'm happy here! It's wonderful! Especially when I have no choice!' Peter felt as if he'd 'been struck in the chest' at the purity and simplicity of the almost Zen sentiment. He walked back to Shey contemplating the essence of this place and the time he'd been privileged to spend there.

'Butter tea and wind pictures, the Crystal Mountain, and blue sheep dancing on the snow – it's quite enough.

'Have you seen the snow leopard?

'No! Isn't that wonderful?'

2015

DOLPO POSTPONED

26
GOING ROUND AGAIN

I knew early on that the second trip to Dolpo would be radically different from the one taken the previous year.

Five weeks before 'the off' I received an email from Roland Hunter, who ran The Mountain Company. Juphal Airport was to be closed throughout April and May so work could be done on the runway. This meant that we now had to fly from Kathmandu to Nepalgunj on the Indian border. From there we could take a smaller single-engine Cessna aircraft to a runway at a village called Masinechour, several hours' walk to the west of Juphal, and hence a much further walk along the Bheri to reach Dunai. This was actually an interesting proposition. Nepalgunj had a reputation for being more 'Indian' than 'Nepalese' and was also David Snellgrove's starting point for his initial foray into Dolpo. The Bheri Valley would be a most pleasant and level walk for a first day of trekking.

Snellgrove was not enamoured of Nepalgunj. He had to spend three days there in 1956 garnering supplies for the seven-month trek ahead. He still needed 'such items as sugar and soap, paraffin and methylated spirit, pots and pans, an umbrella, tins of milk and packets of tea, supplies of rice and flour'. He also encountered some 'problems of porterage' and he identified precisely the philosophical differences between the sahibs and the 'coolies'. 'I assumed that I would be paying them a high wage for travel on our terms, namely stopping and camping where we pleased, whereas they were carrying the goods of some helpless stranger who parted readily with his money and would be quite content to come along with them at their pleasure.'

Saturday, 25 April, was Anzac Day in Australia. This highly revered public holiday was even more special in 2015 as it was the 100-year anniversary of the landing of Australian and New Zealand troops at Gallipoli. At home in Brisbane it was a lazy day with a Sunday feel about it: a training walk, coffee and sitting at the internet. I should have been sorting my gear for Nepal, as it was, by then, less than two weeks to 'the off'. About 4.30 in the afternoon there was a Facebook post from Roland Hunter, who was already in Nepal, saying 'Earthquake in KTM. I am ok'. I immediately looked at some of the news networks. The first report I saw said 'Earthquake in Kathmandu. Two dead' but over the next hour increasingly worrying reports started coming in. It was a 7.8 on the Richter scale with the epicentre between Pokhara and Kathmandu.

It was the biggest earthquake since the one that had devastated Kathmandu in 1934 over eighty years previously. Photographs were being uploaded on Facebook and Twitter. The 60-metre-high Bhimsen or Dharahara tower had completely collapsed. Many visitors had been inside at the time. Durbar Square buildings, many of them hundreds of years old, had been completely flattened. There were numerous deaths. The tally kept increasing. Then came news that an avalanche had been triggered by the earthquake at Everest Base Camp. That there were many killed there and even more missing.

Over the next day the bad news kept escalating. The number of official dead kept rising through the hundreds and into the thousands, yet the outlying towns and villages had not even been assessed as all communications were down.

Gradually friends reported online that they were safe. Tulsi was camping out in his garden. Ian Wall and his wife Sarita were fine, but Sarita had a great-aunt who was missing. (Her village was destroyed and her whereabouts unknown; she was feared dead. Three weeks later she turned up in Kathmandu having walked into the next valley wearing only flip-flops on her feet and had been able to hitch a ride on a scooter.) Ian posted on Facebook soon after the initial shock describing what it was like:

> A real knee wobbler ... lot of damage in town but house here ok but lots of broken glass etc. Old historic buildings down and at least one

road out. Just had another big wobble ... wonder when we can get back in house.

A little later he posted:

We are all ok and the house is good ... aftershocks ... been a few big ones but not as big as the main one ... beginning to get dark now ... camping in the garden tonight! Sadly many killed in the town, airport closed and things all very subdued as you would expect ... helicopters flying ... hospitals at capacity and Gov. called a state of emergency asking for foreign support. Durbar Square Ktm. virtually flattened – all temples and other historic buildings. The big old minaret in the middle of town by Ratna Park collapsed ... being a Saturday it was packed with a reported 400 people, few had any chance to escape. Reported as being the biggest quake here with the main tremor going on for what seemed like many minutes. The only way I can really describe is that it felt like being on a bouncy castle with a herd of elephants running across the other end of the water-bed ... literally took me and the others off our feet. Impossible to stand up in the garden. Big avalanche on Everest Base Camp ... Pumori ... not sure of the exact details, also Camp 2 I believe was hit with avalanches going down into the Cwm.

Ade Summers was on the western side of Dolpo and was unaware there'd been an earthquake, but his family in Wales heard on television that he was missing. He eventually got a message through that he was safe and on the bus from Jomsom back to Kathmandu.

On the Monday morning Roland wrote from Kathmandu:

Hi all, as I am sure you heard in the news yesterday there was a large earthquake in Nepal causing huge amounts of damage to buildings and with fatalities reported throughout the country. Luckily all of TMC [The Mountain Company] groups are fine and accounted for. At the moment it is too early to say whether we can run your Upper Dolpo trek as planned therefore I will be in touch in a few days to let you know our decision once I have more information. Clearly we need to take advice from the government authorities to determine whether they

> will allow us to proceed or not. Also we need to consider whether it is appropriate to come to Nepal during a natural disaster requiring international aid. By the way I spoke to Ade [leader for Dolpo] this afternoon and he is fine making his way back to Kathmandu from Jomsom. I will assess the situation further and when I have more information I will be in touch again with an update on the feasibility of organising Upper Dolpo this year.

Of course, our Dolpo trek was cancelled. Most foreign governments had issued travel advisory warnings about going to Nepal. But I had flights booked and a whole month off from my medical practice. I should at least go and see what I could do to help. If I couldn't help medically, I could certainly put up tents, build shelters and carry food.

I was determined to go.

*

My Thai Airways flight entered the Kathmandu Valley on the morning of 7 May. It was cloudy and the mountains were hidden from view. Looking out of the plane window the first sign of damage I spotted was seeing the usually tall and prominent brickworks chimneys now decimated. As we landed it was no surprise to see that the airport resembled something out of a Vietnam War movie. Massive cargo planes, piles of equipment on the tarmac and dozens of helicopters coming and going.

The drive to my hotel in Thamel revealed scattered areas of damage. Plenty of walls had fallen over. An entrance archway to one of the old palaces had collapsed. There were gaps in the street where houses had stood. Some streets were blocked off and all the open spaces played host to new villages made of tents and bright blue or orange tarpaulins.

I met old friends that afternoon at the Northfield Cafe. Everyone had a tale to tell of where they were and what they'd been doing when the 7.8 earthquake had hit. Most were out of Kathmandu and somewhat shocked on their return. Ade turned up at 15.00. It was marvellous to see him looking so well, and we were soon joined by Roland. Ade surprised me by telling me that my old *ami* Philippe was in town and in a little while he joined us. It was incredibly good to see him. He'd been on a trek around Dhaulagiri and the only indication they'd had of the earthquake was a distant avalanche on the slopes of Dhaulagiri itself.

That evening in Sam's Bar the crowd gathered once again. Ade was flying out next morning. We were joined by several others, including Roland and his fiancée, Helen. A pleasant American girl called Amy had lived in Kathmandu for several years. She freely admitted that most people were on edge or even traumatised. Everyone was having trouble sleeping. The aftershocks were frequent and caused everyone to stop what they were doing in trepidation.

We all agreed that the timing of the earthquake had been fortuitous. Saturday is the 'day of rest' in Nepal and a day when the children aren't at school and offices are empty. Had the earthquake struck on any other day the death toll would have been many times greater, with schoolchildren and workers killed in their tens of thousands as the buildings fell upon them.

Next morning I went walkabout to see the damage for myself. As I entered Durbar Square I was stunned. The destruction of the old wood and brick temples was almost total. The remaining buildings displayed massive cracks and were mostly beyond repair. Already the clear-up had started and bricks were being piled up. Vendors had their fruit and vegetables spread out on the ground as they'd always done. Life was going on. I caught a glimpse, in the distance, of Swayamabunath, the Monkey Temple, on its hilltop across the valley. The collapsed south tower was conspicuous by its absence. I walked back to the top end of Thamel to the 'tank', the deep, brick-lined spring where people did their washing, and which was just round the back of the Malla Hotel. The formerly massive hole in the ground was now filled with the rubble of a hotel which had collapsed into it. Seventeen people had perished there. I was aghast.

I took a taxi over to Boudhanath to meet my lama friend from Namgung Monastery in Dolpo, the Dolpo Maniwa Rinpoche, Dungse Ogyen Gyaltsen. We strolled around the giant *stupa*. All the prayer flags were down and large cracks were obvious in the upper gold structure above the painted 'Buddha eyes'. A lot of the white plaster casing had fallen off the main hemispherical body of the *stupa*.

Back in Thamel there were many groups of rescue personnel walking round in their bright, clean uniforms. Plenty of 'L.A. Rescue Department', and lots of European and Japanese teams, all buying souvenirs, as they were about to leave; the basic rescue work was done.

It was good to meet up with Ian Wall that evening in the Northfield Cafe. 'So, Crozier. What are you doing here?' was his greeting. I explained that I had the time off work and my flight had been booked so I thought I might be of some use.

He gave me a rundown on the current situation. He had now been living in Kathmandu for fifteen years. His wife, Sarita, a Nepalese nurse, was well but her mother had been visiting her family in their village called Gumpathang in Sindhupalchowk, to the north-east of Kathmandu, when the quake hit. She wasn't heard from for several days, until she'd managed to walk out, hitch a ride on a motorbike and then a bus back to Kathmandu. Her village had been essentially destroyed. Gumpathang was a remote place near the Tibetan border and help was not getting there anytime soon. Ian was resolved to make a trip with a jeep full of rice, tarpaulins, sleeping bags and tents as soon as he could. I offered to go as medical back-up. Sarita's sister, Gita, who was a student aged twenty, would be coming as a translator and medical assistant. We faced a four-hour drive then a six-hour walk to get there, but we were prepared for longer.

27
SINDHUPALCHOWK

TUESDAY, 12 MAY

We left Kathmandu on the morning of 12 May. In the four-wheel drive were Ian, Sarita's sister Gita and three of Sarita and Gita's uncles, who came from Gumpathang. We drove out of the Kathmandu Valley past a badly damaged Bhaktapur and many reduced brickworks chimneys before heading north up the Araniko Highway towards the Tibetan border. The solid rim of the Kathmandu Valley seemed to have been protective in some way, as there were fewer destroyed buildings up on the ridges. The road led down to the town of Dolalghat, where the wide shallow Indrawati River was joined by the more vigorous and fast flowing Sun Khosi. We knew that the main road was blocked just beyond Bharibise to the north, but shortly before there we turned off north-west into the valley of the Bhote Khosi.

As soon as we entered the wide valley we could see that there was much more destruction here. The smaller villages had houses mainly made of rocks simply stacked up, with mud slapped in the gaps. The roof was then positioned on top of the piles of rocks. Everything had fallen over in the quake. Bright tarpaulins gave an indication of where people were trying to exist next to the ruins of their homes. Animals still had to be looked after and the crops tended and there was nowhere else to go. As we drove into the small town of Jalbire, a truck was offloading sacks of potatoes to the waiting crowd. The police told us that the jeep wasn't allowed to go any further, but a local farmer had a truck and he might help. Sure enough, for a sizeable fee, he was prepared to take us further up the road. Our load was transferred and we all piled into the back.

The road was a rock and mud track just wide enough for one vehicle. It was slow progress lurching from side to side and with much stopping and starting. We picked up a couple from Gumpathang that one of the uncles spotted walking along the trail. The Tamang woman had a broken left arm in a full plaster-of-Paris cast and had been facing an eight-hour walk back to what was left of her home. She lay, in obvious pain, on some of the bags of rice and was thrown around for the next hour.

We'd often see the villagers from Gumpathang heading down the valley as they made their way to collect any supplies they could. Everyone waved and smiled when they recognised Gita's uncles in the back of our truck. We'd occasionally stop for a chat and catch up on news about the situation higher up the valley. We found out that the road was blocked not much further ahead.

Just before midday we stopped at a stretch of deep viscous mud that the truck driver wasn't prepared to attempt. It was time to walk. There were quite a lot of villagers on the trail who were happy to do an about-turn now that they had rice and tarpaulins. In less than twenty minutes all the bags and supplies were being carried on people's backs and shoulders as they continued their journey uphill.

A few hundred metres' walk brought us to a wide shallow river that was easy to cross and a bit of a meeting place. Plenty of locals were washing and socialising there. The day was by now extremely hot and humid and walking slowly gave me time to simply observe. Across the narrow valley the terraces were green with new crops of potatoes and corn, but every single house was a pile of rubble. Orange tarpaulins marked the new living quarters. Our trail followed the contours of the valley, gradually gaining height. No house or shop had remained intact but the local people, peering out of the ruins, still smiled and said '*Namaste*' as we passed.

We came across an open area where a helicopter load of rice had been dropped. A hundred or more villagers were there, and the police were allocating a sack of rice per family according to a list they had. It was all very orderly. Not for the first time it struck me that there was civil order, and no disorder. This was not like the stories I'd heard coming out of Haiti or, indeed, following Hurricane Katrina in New Orleans.

It was an extremely hot day and I stopped at a spring-water pipe to fill up my water bottles. Ian and Gita walked on ahead. I added a couple of water purifying tablets to my bottle and plodded on. It was getting close to 1.00 p.m. and within a few minutes I came around a gentle bend and ahead of me was the single wrecked street of a village called Kattike. This place looked like it had been badly hit. Buildings on both sides of the street were cracked, leaning and essentially ruined.

I took out my camera to record another heartbreaking scene.

I pressed the shutter button.

The world changed.

Gravity performed a mad and random pirouette.

It was an explosion with no noise.

Did I move or was it the ground beneath?

A wall 10 metres in front of me fell over.

Now there was noise and the air was filled with dust and screams.

Boulders as big as the sacks of rice fell all around me.

Across the valley a massive landslide plummeted down towards the river.

The street had disappeared in a huge cloud of dust and still screams rang out. Ian and Gita were somewhere in the maelstrom. I dropped my backpack and ran up the street. People were emerging, coughing, dusting themselves off.

Most people were frozen to the spot and their fear was palpable.

I spotted Ian. He was standing just outside a shattered building and he was moving. He was wiping down his dust-covered face and arms. 'Are you okay?' I asked. 'Yes. I'm alright' was all he could say between coughs. Gita was nearby, visibly upset but safe.

I looked into the remains of the nearest house. 'Is there anyone inside?' I asked but no one knew. I went from door to door shouting, 'Hello!' No replies.

A squad of soldiers materialised within the dust cloud. They had shovels and pickaxes. They came running down the hill along with some French paramedics. They had an encampment just up the slopes. We spent a few minutes looking in some of the houses. Then there was a call for help up the hill. Someone mentioned a head injury. I only saw minor cuts and bruises.

Suddenly the word was to move up to the terraces. I heard Ian, about 30 metres up the slope, shout, 'Bill! Bill! Get up here! Get out of the street!' The aftershocks would be coming.

The whole village was gathering on the narrow terraces of farmland above Kattike. We didn't have to wait long. Twenty minutes after the first shock came a second massive jolt. The crowd was mainly on its knees. There were screams and howls of despair and primeval fear. People clung onto each other. Nowhere felt safe.

More shocks followed.

An official report I found later stated:

> A major earthquake occurred in Nepal on 12 May 2015 at 12:50 pm local time (7:05 am UTC) with a moment magnitude of 7.3, 18 km (11 mi) southeast of Kodari. The epicentre was on the border of Dolakha and Sindhupalchowk, two districts of Nepal. This earthquake occurred on the same fault line as the larger magnitude 7.8 earthquake of 25 April, but further east than the original quake. As such, it is considered to be an aftershock of the 25 April quake. It struck at a depth of 18.5 kilometres (11.5 mi). Shaking was felt in northern parts of India including Bihar, Uttar Pradesh and West Bengal. Tremors were felt as far as about 2400 kilometres away from the epicentre in Chennai.

We had been right on top of the epicentre. The immediate aftershocks that we felt over the first hour were reported as being 6.4, 6.2 and 5.8.

The hot, still afternoon in Kattike wore on. People needed water and to get something to eat. Slowly the crowd dispersed towards their tarpaulin shelters, already established on the terraces after the first big quake.

Gita had been gone for a little while and suddenly came up the hill with a beer in each hand for Ian and me. This had the appearance of a modern-day miracle and a most welcome one. Mama, the mother of Sarita and Gita, had a sister who'd moved down the valley from Gumpathang to Kattike to run a guesthouse a few years earlier. Hers was the large pink edifice whose remains we could see directly before us in the main street. It was leaning and beyond repair. 'Aunty', as she was known, now had a tarpaulin shelter with a stove and she was carrying on her business as best she could. She knew that we were there and made sure we were sent some refreshment. I've rarely enjoyed a beer more.

Ian and I put up our tent. It was brand new and an Asian style with space for ten people. It was home for Ian, Gita, me and any of the cousins who wanted to pile in. As the day moved into twilight we were invited down the terraces to Aunty's shelter.

Up the valley a snow-clad peak raised its head above the clouds. It glowed a delicate pink as it caught the rays of the setting sun. This was Phurbi Chyachu standing at 6637 metres (21,774 feet) on the border with Tibet, and its ethereal beauty was a simple reminder that our human travails were of minor significance. My friends and I were alive and safe for the time being.

So, just after 18.00, we went down several terrace levels to the 'sheds', the temporary shelters where the villagers had set up camp. All living, cooking and sleeping was done under the blue and orange tarpaulins held up by makeshift wooden frames. Here Aunty gave us another beer and an excellent meal of curry, rice, dhal and potatoes. The potatoes were boiled and the plateful was served with a saucer of salt and chilli flakes to dip them into. They were the 'ambrosia' to the 'nectar' of the local beer, but Aunty couldn't believe I was eating the 'dirty' skin and tried to take my plate away so she could peel them. I laughed and asked Gita to tell her that the skin was the best bit.

There was another minor jolt during dinner. People instantly stopped eating and talking. They sat motionless, waiting with bated breath. Then, as a minute went by, life slowly started up again.

Afterwards it was time to retire up the hill to the tent, to settle in and catch up with diary writing. This had been a long and challenging day.

Sleep came easily, with only a couple of interruptions in the early hours as the earth itself shuddered to remind us all of our human frailty.

WEDNESDAY, 13 MAY

I woke at daybreak and was out of the tent before 7.00. It was clear we were going nowhere today. I drank some water and had a chocolate bar for breakfast.

I decided to take a walk down what remained of the main street to get some photographs. I made my way down the terraces past where the villagers, under their tarpaulin shelters, were cooking breakfast and trying to make order of their remaining worldly possessions. Worried expressions were on most faces but those to whom I said '*Namaste*' raised a smile. One extremely pretty Tamang girl, who looked about eighteen, carried her baby up from the communal water supply with a fixed look of terror etched on her face. She had clearly been crying non-stop.

The main street of Kattike was about 200 metres long with buildings on both sides. Not a single building remained undamaged. Many were completely collapsed or the remaining walls were leaning at improbable angles. The street was blocked along most of its way. I carefully climbed over the rubble of timber and stones. At one point I came across a young girl sitting in the middle of what had been the road with a tub of filthy-looking water, scrubbing the family pots and cooking utensils. She didn't even glance at me as I passed by.

One of Sarita and Gita's uncles had gone straight up to Gumpathang the previous afternoon. Late in the morning he returned to Kattike and, somewhat improbably, was now wearing a rather elegant tailored Western three-piece suit. The way was extremely dangerous, he said, because of the landslides, and there weren't many people left in the remains of the village. Most of the people had been heading down the valley for rice the previous day. Two of the uncles and their wives were again to set off for Gumpathang but were only prepared to carry sleeping mats and sleeping bags. Anything else was too heavy.

We had an early lunch of rice and potatoes under Aunty's tarpaulin, washed down with a rather bitter but refreshing *chang*, the ubiquitous Himalayan home-brew beer made from barley, millet or rice. On a small flat area below Aunty's terrace a group of nine or ten young girls had gathered and they had a battery-powered tape recorder with Nepali music blaring out. These kids, between about seven and twelve years old, were like any other group of girls around the world. Some were showing off and others more reserved. One or two were the leaders and all were getting into it, until one of them, to loud moans, decided to switch tunes. Then the wriggling and gyrating and giggling would start up again with the next song.

The rumour went around from some village sage that there would be another large earthquake between 13.00 and 14.00. Soon after 12.00 the whole village started gathering on the terraces up the slope near our tent. Most sat under trees for the shade as it was another sweltering day. There had been one or two small tremors in the morning. Two o'clock came and went and the rumoured quake didn't materialise. The crowd dispersed with the unspoken sentiment that it was much better to be safe than sorry.

We were joined in the afternoon by a cousin of Gita and Sarita called Dorje. He'd been in Gumpathang for several days with a Thai photographer called Pong. They planned to leave Kattike next morning in a four-wheel drive. We were welcome to join them. Later that evening, after boiled potatoes at Aunty's, Pong told us that we actually had a six-hour walk to begin with, so an early night was required.

THURSDAY, 14 MAY

Aunty woke us at 5.00 to say that some tea was ready down at their shelter. I packed up in my routine way, then went down for the sweet, spicy milky chai. It was a pleasant morning, but the sun wasn't yet up when we set off at 6.00.

The crew was Ian, Gita, her cousin Dorje, Pong and three of the Lama family cousins. A few of the villagers came along to help carry our gear. We were accompanied for the first two hours by a cute little black-and-white dog, who eventually got hungry and turned back to the village for his scraps.

The walk was pleasant enough, only a bit of uphill. It was soon clear that the second earthquake had again severely disrupted the land and everything on it. There were many landslides and massive boulders blocking the road that hadn't been there two days before. The road was impassable except on foot. In places cracks almost half a metre wide had appeared across the muddy trail.

We stopped at the edge of Jalbire, the village where we'd picked up the truck and which we'd driven through on the 12th. No traffic could now get through that place. The devastation was complete, and the street filled with debris. Just beyond Jalbire we had to climb steeply uphill about 100 metres to avoid a large landslip that had carried away the road. At the top of the hill was a village of about fifteen houses, all completely wrecked. At the edge of the village were the remains of the school. There had been two buildings, both destroyed, one of them pancaked flat: another example of how fortunate the timing of the first quake had been, as there would have been few surviving children in the flattened building had it been a school day.

We carried on for several more kilometres, Ian and I just chatting. It was ridiculously hot but we drank plenty. After about 6 kilometres we arrived at a village called Naubise, where Dorje had negotiated a ride in a ute to Kathmandu for NR20,000. Extortionate but worth it.

We had to take a different route out of the main valley by climbing up to the local capital of Chautara and then down to Dolalghat. We passed dozens of villages, all of them devastated beyond redemption. The people were just milling around salvaging what they could.

After about three hours we stopped for lunch of two boiled eggs and a beer. That was the fare I thought least likely to be contaminated. We got talking to a couple of relief workers, a German and a Croatian, who were engineers. Their organisation was planning to be in Nepal for the next two years to help rebuild.

At last we drove into Kathmandu. There seemed to be a bit more damage but it was quite scattered. I was dropped off at the edge of Thamel and walked round the corner to my base, the Backyard Hotel. I fired up the internet. I learned that the quake had been a 7.3. I had underestimated how big this news would inevitably be; it had immediately ricocheted around the world. Naturally everyone we knew was frantic because we'd been completely isolated and hadn't been heard from in almost three days. Just before we started the drive back from Naubise, Ian got a phone signal and spoke to Sarita. She'd been on the internet and Joe Bonington in Sydney had phoned my wife, Paula, to let her know that we were all unharmed. I later spoke to a much-relieved Paula, who appeared to think that the earthquake had happened because we'd only recently made our wills. 'I knew something would happen because we'd written them,' she said, only half jokingly.

I had a welcome shower and got some photos posted on Facebook. There was an overwhelming response from family and friends around the world.

Thamel was remarkably quiet. Many Nepalis had gone off to their home villages to help out. I went off to Roadhouse to eat but it was closed. Fire & Ice was also closed. There was a squad of American doctors and nurses, about twenty of them, wandering around Thamel in operating scrubs, which struck me as entirely inappropriate out in the streets. I resisted the temptation to say anything to them. I ended up in that old safe haven, the Northfield, and had a Nepali thali which was outstanding, with an Everest beer of course.

It was time to think of the next relief journey. My heart was heavy and I knew that there was still much to be done.

28
KATHMANDU TO RAMECHHAP

FRIDAY, 15 MAY

Thamel remained quiet as many businesses had closed. The workers from the restaurants and souvenir shops were still heading back to their villages to help family and friends and there were no tourists anyway. Central Kathmandu had become a mere shadow of its usual madhouse self. The teeming throngs of people and motorbikes had simply evaporated.

I was still able to buy a new filter and lens cap for my camera, which I'd cracked in a stumble in Kattike. Pilgrims bookshop remained open and I enjoyed browsing, chatting to the owners and, as always, buying several books.

It was round to the Northfield late afternoon to meet up with Ian and Sarita. We were soon joined by another couple, friends of theirs, who were introduced as Sian and Bob. It took me a few minutes to work out that they were Sian Pritchard-Jones and Bob Gibbons, who'd written the guidebook to Dolpo that had been so useful the previous year. I told them how much I enjoyed their book and we had a great chat about Dolpo and our recent adventures. Ian and I were planning to leave next day, so it was back to the hotel to pack. Soon after eight I went up to an unusually quiet Sam's for a couple of Everest beers. It was most pleasant just sitting alone, reflecting, sipping and letting the time slip by.

SATURDAY, 16 MAY

I got a taxi over to Ian's and arrived before 7.00 a.m. We were planning to take supplies to Sarita's father's village of Meghre in the district of Ramechhap to the east of Kathmandu. Inevitably the truck was delayed to the extent that we weren't going anywhere that day. We started working on plan B, the helicopter option. We'd been 'reliably informed' that the roads were blocked to our destination.

In preparation for a possible flight we packed and weighed all the bags and gear. Thirty bags of rice at 20 kilograms each, tarpaulins, sleeping mats, sleeping bags and a tent.

We had a welcome snack lunch then Ian and I went off to town. We parked in the grounds of the Malla Hotel in an effort to find one of the porters whose house had been destroyed. Ian knew him well and heard that he, his wife and two small children were sleeping under a canopied statue in a park near the Malla. That's where we found them, lying on the marble structure with only one blanket between them. Many others had tents and tarpaulins but this family had nothing, so they were more than pleased when Ian was able to give them a tarpaulin and a couple of sleeping bags. They could at least join those camping on the grass of the park.

Then off to the MAF office, the Mission Aviation Fellowship, a helicopter charity. This was a Christian organisation that provides subsidised flights for remote supply and rescue. They were warmly welcoming. We spoke to an American girl who told us the basic deal. They subsidise 70, 80 or 90 per cent of the cost, starting at $1800 an hour. Thus Meghre would be, at three hours round trip, $5400 dollars, or $540 at 10 per cent. However, we'd need three helicopters, so getting on for $1600. However, the boss, a solid, bullet-headed Swiss who'd spent fourteen years in Afghanistan, said 'Sorry. No go' as Ian was a private company and not an NGO or charity. So it was now on to plan C and we drove back to Ian's house.

We were just having a coffee when, at twenty past five, the whole house shook with a significant earthquake. Everyone in the neighbourhood ran out of their houses screaming. Babu, Sarita's son, shot down the stairs and out of the front door along with the two dogs. It was all over in a few seconds. Ian and I were up on the third floor of his house, so we had little choice but to stop our conversation until the tremor stopped then carry on with our coffee.

We got news via 'Papa', Sarita's father, that the truck would be arriving in the morning and there was an alternative route into Ramechhap. I was to stay the night at Ian's and so it was time for a beer while Sarita cooked a delicious meal. Over dinner we discussed my holiday. I thought that after this aid trip to Meghre it would be nice to spend my birthday at Lumbini, Buddha's birthplace. Then over to Tibet for a week. Sarita said she would sort it out. Dinner was excellent. A home-cooked beef curry with saag and dhal. I slept comfortably on the lounge floor.

SUNDAY, 17 MAY

Amazingly the truck arrived early. I was up at 6.00 a.m. and it was already half loaded. I joined in and by a quarter to eight we were on the road again, this time heading east to the district of Ramechhap. Papa owned a bit of land in Meghre and many of his relatives had been affected by the earthquake. He was keen for us to get there to help. However, he spoke not a single word of English so all our communication over the next few days was to be third hand at best.

Ian and I were in the back of the open truck, on top of the rice, with the truck driver's 'mate'. Gita and Papa were in front in the cab. We stopped out near the airport to pick up one of the women from the village of Meghre who was getting back to her family.

Time passed slowly. It was hot and dusty perched on our pile of supplies. We stopped for a lunch of boiled eggs, then, within minutes of setting off, a tyre blew. I was resigned to a long stay in the middle of nowhere, but it only took the boys about twenty minutes to change the wheel. I was quietly impressed.

On we went. We stopped at various checkpoints. The road was good, having been built by the Japanese in recent years. This was the Dhulikhel Sindhuli Bhittamod Highway. We left the main highway once we'd entered the district of Ramechhap and started the long, slow climb up to Meghre. The weather began to cloud over and with an hour still to go it started to rain. I donned wet weather gear and we sat under a tarpaulin. We arrived at the village above Meghre soon after 18.00, a journey of over ten hours. The rain was torrential so we went into a teahouse and imbibed some excellent hot sweet tea. Papa was in some conference with a group of locals.

The rain stopped and Ian, Gita and I decided to walk down to Meghre so we would have time to put up the tent before dark. Ian said it was about ten or fifteen minutes all downhill. My backpack and luggage weighed 25 kilograms between them. The dirt track went on and on. Six kilometres and well over an hour later we got to the family home. 'It was a bit further than I remember,' said Ian unapologetically.

By now we realised that, really, quite little damage had been done in the area compared to Sindhupalchowk and we felt like we'd been to some degree conned into bringing so much stuff. I felt bad when I thought of the poor people in Kattike and how little they had.

I decided to sleep in the remains of Nana's house. When Papa arrived, after dark, he ordered Gita, his daughter, to sleep under a tarpaulin with the rest of the family. He tried to persuade Ian to do the same. I was happy indoors so spread a tarp, opened up my gear and made ready for bed. It had been a long day.

MONDAY, 18 MAY

I was woken early by a lot of local noise: goats, birds, people. We were brought tea at 6.00 a.m. by Gita's cousins and it was a beautiful sunny day. Ian had already been for a quick walk around the place. Papa turned up, with his incomprehensible and poor English, and told us that the truck was coming down at 10.00 a.m. then heading back to Kathmandu the next day.

We walked around the village, with a stop for tea at one of the tarpaulin shelters. Even though there appeared to be minimal damage there was no doubt that many of the houses were cracked and unsafe. More to the point, the people themselves felt threatened and scared to sleep in the hazardous structures. Most families had chosen to build tarpaulin-covered shelters in their gardens or on the farm terraces and felt safer existing outdoors. A couple of years previously, with Ian and Sarita's help, most of the houses had been supplied with the modern efficient cooking stoves provided by The Himalayan Stove Project. This was the same organisation that had been used to arrange for a new fireplace for the family in Bhutan who'd sheltered us for two nights when our trekking companion, Mary, became sick with cerebral oedema. Indeed Sarita now featured on the organisation's website as their poster girl, next to one of the stoves. These gadgets were so light and portable that at the time of the quake they could be lifted up and rapidly carried outside. All the families had rescued their stoves and they were now in use, all in a row, outside the wooden-framed tarpaulin shelters.

Back on Nana's verandah Ian said, 'I think that goat's trying to have a baby,' and sure enough, less than 10 metres from us, a nanny was squeezing out a glistening black sac with its newborn inside. Within five minutes it was over, and the new mother was licking her baby and encouraging it to stand. In less than ten minutes it was suckling at her bloated teats. The poignancy wasn't wasted upon us. Amid so much tragedy and destruction the cycle of birth, life and death was never-ending. I felt happy for the goat.

About 10.30 a.m. we heard the truck coming down the hill and we went off to the waiting crowd. Papa and Ian started distributing the rice and tarpaulins. Gita, whose English is usually good, announced that they were 'giving out the rice and trampolines' until I explained the difference. She and I went off to one side of the throng to begin our health clinic.

There were no acute or new injuries so a chair was placed in the middle of the crowd and the 'patients' took turns jostling for position. Once in the hot seat the patient would rub their head or belly or a joint to indicate where their problem was. There were many complaining of 'headache, dizziness and belly pain'. Plenty of joint pain. One man had a dangerously high blood pressure of 185/110. There was a young man with severe tonsillitis and large lymph nodes in his neck. Gita did a marvellous job of marshalling the customers and translating for me. She even had some eminently sensible suggestions as to what they may have wrong with them. We finished about 13.30 after seeing more than fifty people.

We got word that the truck was apparently leaving at 7.00 a.m. next day but we had to get back up the hill with our many bags. For some reason the driver didn't want to come back down the hill.

We had a lazy afternoon on the small stomped-dirt verandah at Nana's house. Then Papa started getting pushy about going up the hill to his brother-in-law's house for dinner. Ian and I were rather looking forward to our merely-eighteen-months-out-of-date 'instant' shepherd's pie. We dug in our heels and enjoyed the army MRE ('Meals Ready to Eat'). Then at 19.00, having been promised *raksi,* we made the half-hour walk up the hill to Uncle's. Food was served even though we'd already eaten. While waiting for our *raksi*, Uncle rather proudly demonstrated how to pluck a large crane fly out of the air, pull the wings off and eat the body fresh. This was not classically Buddhist although the house decoration certainly indicated that was his belief. However, the *raksi* was excellent and two mugs of it did the trick. We rolled down the hill and were fast asleep soon after 10.00 p.m.

TUESDAY, 19 MAY

I was woken abruptly at 4.40 a.m. by another strong earthquake. The whole house shook for half a minute. I learned later that it was a 4.4. I rolled over and went back to sleep, but it was an early call just after 6.00 as it transpired that we had to walk up the damn hill. Some of the cousins helped with the bags. My blue bag and the drugs went up by motorbike. So, carrying my 14-kilogram backpack I made the 6 kilometres, all uphill, in one hour. I stopped briefly to take some photos of the wreck of a school. This picturesque building was single storey, built around three sides of a square, with a large and ancient looking *chorten* in the middle. Several walls had fallen over and the place was clearly unusable.

I got to the truck at 7.50 a.m. Papa rolled up the hill almost an hour later and ambled off to a tea shop for tea with his friends. He stuck to his own agenda but a little verbal encouragement from me, despite his lack of English, got him quickly into the truck so we could set off.

We had fellow travellers in the back. Two Tamang women and their three girls, a fellow with a badly scarred face from old burns, and the truck driver's mate, who blessed himself every time we passed a Buddhist shrine.

The journey was pleasant and faster than the outward leg. We left just after 9.00 and I was back at the hotel in Thamel at 16.50, so just under eight hours. I posted some photos on Facebook, then it was off to Sam's for beer and popcorn and to write my diary. It was uncannily quiet both in Sam's and in Thamel in general.

WEDNESDAY, 20 MAY

A day in Kathmandu to regroup. I went off to Shona's, a Kathmandu institution where climbers and trekkers would drop in for a chat with expat Mark, whose wife Shona gave her name to the tiny, dark store. I went to buy a couple of pairs of trekking pants. A fellow turned up asking about boots and I recognised him as Russell Brice, the New Zealand climber. I introduced myself and we had a few minutes' chat. He was heading off to K2 in Pakistan but not climbing himself. I wandered round Thamel a bit further afield than before. It was surprising how much damage there was with many buildings cracked and rendered uninhabitable.

Sarita had done a splendid job of arranging my travels for the next ten days. All I'd done was mention over dinner that I'd like a couple of days in Lumbini then a week in Lhasa and she'd fixed everything.

The day was another hot pre-monsoon one, so the beers were especially refreshing. We were joined by a fellow called David who was with a tall blonde woman from Manchester introduced as Melanie Barnett Southworth. She'd been about to attempt Everest when she was stopped by the avalanche. She was due to fly out in a couple of hours but with the stated intention of returning the next season for another go. David and I got on well, swapping notes about recent events. At one point in the evening he jumped up and said, 'I've got a present for you.' He returned a couple of minutes later with a copy of his book – *Penguins on Everest* by David Durkan – which he signed for me, and which turned out to be a highly entertaining read.

The evening ended over at the New Orleans, where an example of an emergency shelter had been erected made of corrugated sheet iron and costing only $100. It looked pretty sturdy but probably not even slightly warm when the temperatures plummeted.

Then it was back to the Backyard Hotel to pack, as I was off to Lumbini in the morning.

29
THE BIRTHPLACE OF THE BUDDHA

About 2500 years ago, on the Gangetic plain of northern India, the spouse of an important tribal leader went into labour. She was in the jungle, on her way to her father's village, when she gave birth to a son. The mother was the queen Maya Devi, wife of King Suddodhana of the Sakya, and she gave birth to the prince Siddhartha Gautama in a jungle clearing near a place called Lumbini. The young prince led a sheltered life but as a man he yearned for truth and knowledge. He left his family home and sought enlightenment. Siddhartha became the Sakyamuni Buddha, a focus for the influential and massive movement that is worldwide Buddhism. In the early years his message of compassion and pursuit of the Middle Way spread across India and beyond, and the places where he lived, taught and died became centres of pilgrimage. Large temples and memorials were built at those locations, including ones at Lumbini, his birthplace; Bodhgaya, where he found enlightenment; the Deer Park, where he first taught; and Kushinagara, where he died. In the first few hundreds of years after his *paranirvana* the pilgrims would come from as far away as Japan and Sri Lanka. Highly descriptive accounts were written of the places where the Buddha had spent his life.

Around the year 270 BCE a powerful king came to rule over an area of northern India called Magadha. This ruler was the emperor Ashoka (c. 304–232 BCE). He fought a great war in the south but was so mortified and appalled at his destruction of the neighbouring Kalingans that he foreswore violence and turned to Buddhism. He made devout pilgrimages to the thirty-two sites associated with the life of the Buddha and erected inscribed columns to mark some of the places on his progress.

Many years later pilgrims still travelled to pay respects at these old sites and in 401 CE a Chinese monk called Faxian (337–422 CE), with his companion Tao-chin, entered the region of the Maghadans and spent several years travelling. His diary gave much detail of places and distances between the various religious sites. Similarly, in 631 CE the Chinese Buddhist monk Xuanzang (602–664 CE) made a fifteen-year pilgrimage to the subcontinent and kept a detailed record of where he went and all he saw, much of it agreeing with the notes of Faxian from 200 years earlier.

Late in the first millennium a resurgence of Hinduism and the subsequent Muslim invasion of India in the early twelfth century tipped Buddhism into a major decline. The established religion, in the country of its origin, was effaced and never recovered. The temples and *stupas* of the great Buddhist complexes in northern India were no longer visited. They fell into decay, were consumed by the jungle and forgotten for hundreds of years.

With the British colonisation of India there was a rekindling of interest in the history of the area and scholars became adept at reading and translating the ancient Sanskrit and Pali scripts. In the late 1800s curiosity was stirred by brick ruins emerging as jungle was cleared near the Nepalese border. The Ashokan columns, mentioned by Faxian and Xuanzang, had been spotted by Europeans as early as the 1500s, when Thomas Coryat reported one which had been moved to Old Delhi. In the mid-1800s the archaeological survey of India was established under the leadership of Alexander Cunningham. In 1851 they discovered the Sanchi pillar at India's oldest stone complex, in Madhya Pradesh. More of Ashoka's pillars and carved proclamations came to light. In 1896 Nepalese scholars, assisted by Dr. Anton Führer, discovered the great stone pillar at Lumbini. King Ashoka had it erected after his visit to the old shrine in 249 BCE. The edict carved into it, in Brahmi and Pali script, read:

> King Piyadasi (Asoka), the beloved of the gods, in the twentieth year of his reign, himself made a royal visit. Sakyamuni Buddha was born here, therefore the (birth spot) marker stone was worshipped and a stone pillar

was erected. The Lord having been born here, the tax of the Lumbini village was tax reduced to the eight part (only).

Since then the archaeological work has moved on and many other nearby places identified which pertain to the life and teachings of the Buddha. Most recently a full excavation of the ancient temple beneath the more recent structures has been undertaken. Many layers have been revealed, dated and identified. The stone, said to be the actual rock that Maya Devi stood upon to give birth to the Buddha, has been uncovered at the exact centre of the ancient temple. A UNESCO excavation published findings in 2013 that gave carbon-dating data supporting a time of before 550 BC for a wooden structure postulated to be the earliest Buddhist shrine so far discovered.

It was to this sacred place in the Nepalese Terai that I was heading in order to celebrate my own birthday.

THURSDAY, 21 MAY

At 7.00 a.m. the airport was quiet with few passengers but already busy with helicopters and planes.

The Yeti Airlines flight took off at 8.40. Through the early morning mist I could make out the giant *stupa* of Boudhanath, but even more striking was the vast number of tents and tarpaulins colouring every area of spare ground between buildings with their vivid orange and blue. The people of Kathmandu, too frightened to remain in their cracked and unstable buildings, were camping out en masse. As the small plane gained height during its forty-minute flight west I had superb views of gleaming white Manaslu, Annapurna and Dhaulagiri out of the right side of the aircraft. We landed at Gautam Buddha Airport, where a two-storey open-plan building constituted the terminal. I retrieved my bags from the pile of luggage on the ground in the centre of the only room. The 15-kilometre drive to the Buddha Maya Garden Hotel near Lumbini was a fierce introduction to the heat of the Gangetic plain. It was over 40°C at mid-morning.

The Buddha Maya was a large modern hotel and when I went down for breakfast, just after 10.00, I realised that I was the only guest staying in the place.

About 14.00, despite the heat, I went off to the Sacred Garden to see the Maya Devi Temple and the Buddha's birthplace. The Ashoka column stood just outside the relatively modern building erected over the ancient ruins.

Near the temple was the 'birth pool', overlooked by a large, old, bodhi tree said to be from a cutting of the one at Bodhgaya. I selected a leaf to press and keep from this special place.

Then the searing heat overwhelmed me; I bought some bananas and headed back to the hotel for an air-conditioned quiet evening.

FRIDAY, 22 MAY

It was my birthday and I'd just had the best night's sleep I'd enjoyed in two weeks. Hoping for a slight early morning relief from the inevitable heat-wave I set off at 7.30 a.m. for the Sacred Garden.

I phoned my lovely wife Paula back in Australia while sitting just outside the gate of the Maya Devi Temple and told her where I was and what I was there to see.

U Thant, a devout Burmese Buddhist, was Secretary-General of the United Nations from 1961 to 1971. In April 1967 he visited Nepal and proposed the development of Lumbini into a major centre of pilgrimage for Buddhists from around the world. A committee was inevitably formed and in the 1970s a master plan was developed by Kenzo Tange, a Japanese architect. An area 5 miles by 5 miles was envisaged, with the central square mile encompassing the birth site, the Maya Devi Temple and the Sacred Pond. To the north of this was the Monastic Zone and a cultural village. Many nations began building monasteries and temples within the zone. In 1997 UNESCO granted the area World Heritage Status and the construction has since gone on apace.

About 200 metres north of the Maya Devi Temple stands a bizarrely incongruous 3.5-metre-tall shiny gold statue of an infant Buddha. The right hand is raised and the figure, made in Bangkok and presented by the people of Thailand, looks like a manga drawing, an anime Siddhartha. Just beyond the statue is a plinth with an 'eternal' flame and from there extends the canal, a shallow waterway 1.38 kilometres long and separating the east and west monastic zones. I took a steady, increasingly sweaty walk past the various buildings. In the end I spent three hours walking around looking at a host of modern buildings, in old style, adorned in a glittering variety of national architectural accoutrements. The Korean temple was three storeys high with upward-curved eaves on the roof. It had a cladding of bamboo scaffolding obscuring most of it, as it was being extensively renovated. The Vietnamese complex had green glazed roof tiles and ornate dragons on its gate. The Germans had built a low, red-roofed edifice with a massively out-of-proportion *chorten* on top. The Thai monastery was a beautiful and ornate construction of filigree-like intricacy, as though wrought with icing sugar. The Myanmar Golden Stupa is exactly that. An elegant gold-painted building gleaming in the hot afternoon sun. This whole area was a veritable Buddhist Disneyland.

Here and there were handpainted signs on tin sheets nailed to trees or tied to posts. In English they gave sage advice such as 'No one saves us but ourselves. No one can and no one may. We ourselves must walk the path. Buddha' and, more pertinently given the heat, 'The Buddhas do but tell the way, it is for you to swelter at the task'.

I got back to the hotel around 11.00, by which time the temperature had already climbed to over 40°C. I spent the rest of my birthday cocooned in the air-conditioning watching videos and keeping up with fluids.

SATURDAY, 23 MAY

I felt compelled to take one final trip to the Maya Devi Temple, the birthplace.

This time I went specifically to have a closer look at the nativity carving, which is a large and ancient tableau suspended on a wall above the birth-stone. It dates most likely to about 400 CE and is incredibly worn, so much so that the figures appear almost abstract. It is a classic scene of Maya Devi, arm raised to hold onto a tree, attendants around her and with the infant Siddhartha at her feet.

Then I went back to the hotel to kill time and escape the unbearable heat. Reports on television detailed how people in India were suffering in this fiery heatwave.

By mid-afternoon it was time to leave for the Gautam Buddha Airport. The plane left as scheduled but after half an hour among towering and oppressive cumulonimbus clouds, we were being thrown around too much and returned to Lumbini airport. None of the twenty or so passengers had any idea what was going on. We sat in the terminal in the stagnant 40°C heat with no air-conditioning for over an hour, then we were shepherded back onto the plane for take-off again just before 19.00. The night-time arrival in Kathmandu was delightful for the fresh storm-cleansed air being a mere 17°C. Ian was waiting for me and we went straight into Thamel to the Northfield, where I had my first beer in three days.

A couple of days later I saw a report of the Indian heatwave: 'Delhi hit a high of 45.5°C (113.9°F) on Monday by which time over 1,100 Indians had died from the heat in the previous week'.

SUNDAY, 24 MAY

I had a day in Kathmandu and at 9.00 a.m. I went off walking. I wanted to check out the state of Swayamabunath, the Monkey Temple. It was a good walk over there, about 3 kilometres. There was devastation the whole way: cracked buildings and monuments, and plenty of places had completely collapsed. Tarpaulins were the new decor all across the city.

I climbed up the long set of more than 300 steps, resplendent with the dozens of resident monkeys, but the way was blocked at the top. Demolition was already happening. On my way down again I was approached by four Nepali men in their twenties. I was wary, as commonly conversations are started as a way to sell something or extract money out of a tourist.

'Where you from?' their spokesman said.

'Australia,' I replied, in a reticent tone.

'Why are you here?'

I explained that I was a doctor and trying to help my Nepalese friends.

These four young men couldn't have been more charming. They'd come on their own initiative to help clean up the steps and the park around the temple. They were all studying business and English at college and were more than keen to try out their English on me. We chatted for a quarter of an hour or so, and as I left they thanked me in a most genuine and sincere way for coming to Nepal to help in its time of need. I felt humbled by their gratitude.

I took a taxi back to the Backyard Hotel to clean up and pack, for the next day I was off, once more, to Tibet.

Seeking my evening refreshment, I was stunned to find that Sam's Bar was closed until 10 June.

Ian and I had a meal at the Northfield before adjourning to Tom and Jerry's bar for an Everest beer. A couple of strong tremors wobbled our world once more as we drank our ales. Nepalese life continued to be on shaky ground.

30
LHASA ONCE MORE

MONDAY, 25 MAY

I had a breakfast of eggs and coffee at Tribhuvan International Airport and then the plane took off on time at 11.40. There were only about twenty people travelling to Lhasa that morning, on a jet big enough for 200. Flying north-east over the Himalaya provided tremendous views of Makalu, Lhotse, Everest and Cho Oyu, all in a line stretching west below us. Immediately after landing the officialdom was noticeable. My 'group visa' was checked. I was officially a group of one. Everyone's bags were searched for contraband books. I had three books in my suitcase and a ton of medical drugs. There was no interest in drugs and the book policeman, although unsmiling, was fairly happy with the *Life of Buddha* and *Lost Horizon*. He wasn't too sure about Kipling's *Kim*, as it had a drawing of a lama on the cover, but eventually he waved me on. Luckily the expensive and highly illegal copy of Lonely Planet's *Guide to Tibet*, that I'd picked up on a whim at Kathmandu airport, was in my backpack, which they didn't check.

I was met just past immigration by the man who was to be my Tibetan guide for the next week. I shall call him Norbu. He presented me with the traditional scarf, the *kata*, by way of greeting, and it was instantly clear that he spoke excellent English. We stopped near the airport to change money before the hour-long drive to Lhasa. The Lhasa Gonggar Airport sits at over 3500 metres (11,400 feet) in the wide valley of the Yarlung Tsangpo River, about 60 kilometres south-west of the city. Lhasa itself lies in the valley of the Kyi Chu, which is a more northerly tributary of the Yarlung Tsangpo. A tunnel connecting the two valleys reduces to one hour what was previously a two-hour drive into Lhasa.

This was my fourth time visiting the 'Forbidden City' and I had seen marked changes on each trip. The first new regulation I was confronted with on this visit was that every single car and bus had to stop on the outskirts of the city for ID cards and passports to be checked. There were many cameras, on overhead gantries and buildings, for car-number-plate and face-recognition surveillance.

I arrived at my hotel, a Tibetan family-run establishment, in the old Muslim quarter on the edge of the Barkhor itself. It was a nice traditional building, and as it was 3.5 kilometres above sea level it was breathtaking work to lug my 18-kilogram bag up the two flights of stairs. I got the wifi password from the front desk but later found out that over 1200 websites are blocked by the Chinese, including Google, YouTube and Facebook. I couldn't even send an email.

I went for a walk around the Barkhor. There were further evident changes since my last visit. All entry points to the pilgrim circuit were policed and all bags were x-rayed. There were still armed soldiers and police on corners and rooftops. Clusters of cameras were installed high up on many of the buildings. I was told that people no longer go to walk the *kora* because of these face-recognition cameras. Red flags were flying every 10 metres all the way round the Barkhor just above the shopfronts. The rather quaint store names had previously been displayed as large signs in Tibetan script, Chinese and English. All the English names had been expunged, causing a loss to the English language cornucopia of such remarkable phrases as 'Auspkious Yreasures Shop', 'Public Useful Carpet Shup', 'Treet Grottoes' and 'Saikang Auspicous Rabbit Shop'. All the mobile shopping stalls were gone, leaving the circuit looking more open and less crowded.

I did three leisurely *koras* of the Barkhor, taking plenty of photos. There were scarcely any Europeans around, so I attracted plenty of stares and smiles. Many people stopped me to check out my *dzi* stone, the one I'd bought in Tsharka the previous year.

I made a return visit to the Makye Ame restaurant, an old building standing at the south-east corner of the Barkhor. Now a restaurant, this building had been beloved of the debauched and promiscuous sixth Dalai Lama in the early 1700s. He would sit and watch the people going about the *kora* while planning his amorous adventures. I had a more sedate couple of Lhasa beers and some yak *momos*. It was still good to be back in town.

Lhasa is a special place. It has a style, presence and inherent mystery all its own. Over the centuries it had developed a mythical reputation which inspired people to travel there, often involving immense personal discomfort and hardship in their efforts to enter the 'Forbidden City'. The sheer geographical isolation of the high plateau and the desire of the Tibetans to keep out foreigners prevented most travellers from getting to the fabled town. In the early 1600s a series of Jesuit priests managed to get to Shigatse, then Lhasa, with official passports. In the 1700s a mission of Capuchin monks, a Catholic order, settled in Lhasa for twenty-five years before being expelled. In the 1800s the 'Great Game' was being played out across the Himalaya and the politicians became deeply interested in Tibet. The Tibetans themselves, encouraged by a weakened Chinese authority, began to look on the Russians and the British as clear threats. Their borders were firmly locked down. The British sent pundits to explore and spy, and a few individuals, such as the Swedish explorer Sven Hedin, did their best to enter the elusive capital city. One of the more successful adventurers was Ekai Kawaguchi, the Japanese monk, who slipped into Tibet via Dolpo in 1899, reached Lhasa and spent his 'Three Years in Tibet'.

These years during which Western adventurers launched themselves at the mysterious city of Lhasa, most frequently with horrendous outcomes, are documented in Peter Hopkirk's excellent book *Trespassers on the Roof of the World: The Race for Lhasa*. He tells the remarkable, hardly credible, stories of the British-backed pundits, the Russian colonel Nikolai Prejevalsky, the American William Woodville Rockhill, Frenchman Gabriel Bonvalot, and two British Army officers: Captain Hamilton Bower and Surgeon-Captain W.G. Thorold. All suffered enormous hardships only to be turned back by the vigilant Tibetans within days of reaching Lhasa.

The public was enormously entertained, if not horrified, by the book published in 1898 entitled *In the Forbidden Land*, about Henry Savage Landor's travels in Tibet. The tale spun by this colourful adventurer of his torture and the nightmarish privations suffered by himself and his two servants at the hands of his Tibetan captors was initially dismissed but ultimately backed up by medical examination and other documentation.

Hopkirk concludes that apart from Kawaguchi, who had the advantage of being a Buddhist Asian, the first Westerner to enter Lhasa did so as the head of an army during one of the empire's more controversial military expeditions. But such is the power and spiritual influence of the holy city that Francis Younghusband experienced an epiphany during his sojourn there and left Tibet a changed man.

Francis Edward Younghusband, who was born in 1863 in Murree, India, is described by his biographer, Patrick French, as 'the last great imperial adventurer'. In 1903 Lord Curzon, the Viceroy of India, had charged him to enter Tibet and fend off a perceived Russian threat. This was all part of the 'Great Game' played out across the Himalaya. His army consisted of a half company of sappers, eight companies of the 23rd Sikh pioneers, six companies of the 8th Gurkhas, a Maxim gun detachment and Royal Artillery squad with two ten-pounder guns, medical staff, surveyors, road builders and hundreds of 'coolies', making a total retinue of around 10,000 men. To help move this procession, 3000 ponies, 5000 yaks, 5000 bullocks, nearly 7000 mules and six camels were mobilised.

They left Darjeeling on 5 December 1903 and by the 12th struggled across the Jelap La at 4270 metres (14,009 feet) and entered Tibet. The road led north, and near the town of Guru tense negotiations with the Tibetan officials began. These became protracted. High-ranking lamas from Lhasa arrived and were adamant that there would be no deal. Things did not come to a head until 31 March 1904, when a battle ensued resulting in the slaughter of between 600 and 700 Tibetans, with only twelve wounded on the British side.

An advance was then made upon Gyantse, almost 100 kilometres to the north. Gyantse was, and still is, dominated by the magnificent Gyantse Dzong, a huge fortification. This was surrendered without a fight and Younghusband again settled in to await further negotiations. However, word of forces approaching from Lhasa led to a confrontation at the end of April, below the hanging glacier of the Karo La (5020 metres; 16,470 feet). It was clear that Lhasa was not prepared to talk, and on 5 July the reoccupied Gyantse Dzong was taken by force and the advance upon Lhasa begun. On 1 August 1904 the fabled city was, at last, seen by Major W.J. Ottley and the following day Younghusband rode with a friend to take a look, saying, with typical English understatement, 'Well, O'Connor. There it is at last.'

The *Times* correspondent Perceval Landon had been travelling with the expedition and regularly sent back dispatches. He subsequently wrote an account called 'The Opening of Tibet', which was a bestseller. He accurately described the squalor of Lhasa and the poverty of its inhabitants but, like all the other Westerners on the expedition, he was amazed by the Potala with its lofty red and white walls and its 1000 rooms. Edmund Candler, the correspondent for *The Daily Mail*, had lost a hand to a swordsman at the battle outside Guru. He nevertheless remained a Tibetophile and said of the Potala that it 'surpassed the greatest expectations. The golden domes shone in the sun like tongues of fire.' It was 'not a palace on a hill, but a hill that is also a palace'.

Younghusband was to find that the god-king, the thirteenth Dalai Lama, had fled at the urging of a Mongolian monk called Agvan Dorzhiev, a person who had caused much angst to the Indian Viceroy, Lord Curzon, as he was a Russian subject and was thought to be reporting to St. Petersburg. Younghusband was left to negotiate with a high-ranking Tibetan monk to whom the Dalai Lama had entrusted his seal of office, a man the Englishman called 'the Ti-Rimpoche'. Intense discussions began at once and the outcome was that after a few weeks, on 7 September, a document written in Tibetan, English and Chinese, the Lhasa Convention, was signed and received the Dalai Lama's seal in the Durbar Hall of the Potala Palace. Younghusband had his agreement and was able to leave Tibet.

On their last day in Lhasa the Ti-Rimpoche came bearing gifts. He and Younghusband had developed a degree of respect for each other, and the English colonel was presented with a small bronze statue of the Buddha. In his own account, *India and Tibet*, published in 1910, Younghusband takes up the tale:

> Before leaving on the following morning, the Ti-Rimpoche visited me, and presented each of us with an image of Buddha. He had also visited General Macdonald and given him a similar image. He was full of kindliness, and at that moment more nearly approached Kipling's Lama in 'Kim' than any other Tibetan I met. We were given to understand that the presentation by so high a Lama to those who were not Buddhists of an image of Buddha himself was no ordinary compliment. And as the reverend old Regent rose from his seat and put the present into my hand,

> he said with real impressiveness that he had none of the riches of this world, and could only offer me this simple image. Whenever he looked upon an image of Buddha he thought only of peace, and he hoped that when I looked on it I would think kindly of Tibet. I felt like taking a part in a religious ceremony as the kindly old man said these words: and I was glad that all political wranglings were over, and that now we could part as friends man with man....
>
> ...When I reached camp, I went off alone to the mountainside and gave myself up to all the emotions of this eventful time. My task was over and every anxiety was passed. The scenery was in sympathy with my feelings; the unclouded sky a heavenly blue; the mountains softly merging into violet; and, as I now looked towards that mysterious purply haze in which the sacred city was once more wrapped, I no longer had cause to dread the hatred it might hide. From it came only the echo of the Lama's words of peace. And with all the warmth still on me of that impressive farewell message, and bathed in the insinuating influences of the dreamy autumn evening, I was insensibly suffused with an almost intoxicating sense of elation and good-will. This exhilaration of the moment grew and grew until it thrilled through me with overpowering intensity. Never again could I think evil, or ever again be at enmity with any man. All nature and all humanity were bathed in a rosy glowing radiancy; and life for the future seemed nought but buoyancy and light.
>
> Such experiences are only too rare, and they but too soon become blurred in the actualities of daily intercourse and practical existence. Yet it is these few fleeting moments which are reality. In these only we see real life. The rest is ephemeral, the unsubstantial. And that single hour on leaving Lhasa was worth all the rest of a lifetime.

Tibet, Lhasa and Buddhism had exerted their inexplicable yet pleasurable and benign influence over the adventurer and warrior. The spiritual realisation dramatically changed the course of his life. When he died in 1942, at the age of seventy-nine, Sir Francis Younghusband's coffin was carried through the Dorset countryside bearing the bronze Buddha statue presented to him by his old lama friend thirty-eight years before.

TUESDAY, 26 MAY

I woke up in Lhasa, my nose stuffy because of the altitude. The day was to be spent in the city and Norbu was at the hotel at 8.30 a.m. We drove off to park near the Potala. There was a bit of a queue outside the main gate, but it was soon moving. Only a handful of the tourists were Europeans and there were many more Chinese tourists than I'd seen previously. Norbu said that the local guides call the Chinese tourists 'mosquitoes' because 'there are so many of them and they are very annoying'.

The *kora* around the Potala was especially busy. Apparently it was a noteworthy and auspicious day, one of a series, leading up to the Buddha's birthday. Norbu also mentioned the upcoming sixty-fourth anniversary of 'liberation'. I quickly corrected that to 'invasion' and he didn't disagree.

After yet another ID and passport check we started the climb up the Potala stairs, for these days the local guides were permitted to enter the palace. As long as the steep climb was done slowly the altitude could be tolerated. Some of the Chinese visitors were having a most uncomfortable time of it. The tour was excellent and I made a concerted effort to remember the sequence of the rooms. As usual, photos weren't permitted.

After the visit to the Potala we walked over to 'the New Mandala' restaurant discussing things like 'the seventeen-point agreement' and the movies *Seven Years in Tibet* and *Kundun* on the way. Norbu said that friends had wanted to send him a copy of *Kundun* but 'it is too dangerous'.

Following lunch we walked over to the Jokhang, the most revered temple in Tibet. It was busy as always. In the entrance courtyard there were hundreds of *torma*, the butter statues, as this was a special day. Guided groups were allowed to go past the long queue of pilgrims, most of whom were country people and nomads who had travelled long distances to pay homage. The interior was dark and fragrant, lit as it is by thousands of perpetually burning butter lamps. The floor was greasy and slippery from the years of spilled butter. Chapel after chapel was entered. The pilgrims gave their offerings of small denomination money and poured molten butter from their large Chinese flasks to top up the butter lamps. When I got to the Jowo statue, the sitting Buddha donated by the princess Wenchen in 641 CE before her marriage to King Songtsen Gampo, it was a great surprise to see it gleaming gold and naked. It had been stripped of all adornment – robes, head-dress, its hundreds of precious *dzi* stones, turquoise, emeralds and coral – and was having its annual layer of gold applied by a pair of monks. Perceval Landon, in 1904, had described this effigy as 'the most famous idol in the world'. Of his visit to the 'Jo-kang' he said, 'three of us were to become the first white men to look upon the great idol of Lhasa'. Upon entering the temple, 'The smell is abominable. The air is exhausted and charged with rancid vapours. Everything one touches drips with grease.' But then he saw the Jowo: 'The first sight of what is beyond question the most famous idol in the world is uncannily impressive.' He spends three pages describing the statue itself, its splendid decoration and its history. 'It is a Gautama as a pure and eager prince, without a thought for the morrow, or a care for today.'

In the afternoon I walked up to the new Barkhor Supermarket, about 1 kilometre from the Barkhor itself. The hundreds of mobile stalls which used to surround the Jokhang Temple had been moved to the large new building and coachloads of Chinese tourists were taken directly there to do their souvenir hunting. I had a quick look around and suffered a moment of possibly unprincipled disappointment that apparently there were no longer skulls or thigh bones to be bought. I called into a 'traditional medicine' shop where the three men drinking tea spoke little English. I asked, 'How much *yarsa gumba*?' while pointing at a pile of them. One of the men reached under the counter and pulled out a yellow plastic bag full of even more and put it on the scales. It was 465 grams. He displayed on the calculator 60,000 – about 130,000 yuan per kilogram, or $26,000. This was a bit less than I expected. In fact, in 2015 *The Kathmandu Post* was reporting a massive plummet in prices, from $30,000 per kilogram the previous year to around $15,000. At about A$30 each, this was remarkably cheap compared to the price I was quoted in 2012 of A$500 each. The expensive specimens I'd seen in previous years were of the finest quality, in an expensive shop and I, as a Western tourist, could be ripped off without any qualms. Buyers are quite discriminating about quality and size. Smaller specimens, with discolouration, were much cheaper. There had also been an exponential rise in price from the collectors in the mountains, who got less than A$10 a specimen, to the shippers, then dealers in Tibet and a final massive price hike at the outlets in large Chinese cities and Hong Kong. Nevertheless, the caterpillar fungus remained, on a weight alone basis, more expensive than gold, and the poor farmers of the Himalaya would persist in their annual hunt for the 'winter worm, summer grass'.

I took my evening meal in the New Mandala restaurant, just off the Barkhor, where I luxuriated in my fare of yak burger and chips with lemon tea served in a plastic Minnie Mouse mug. The next day was to be spent outside of Lhasa at a famous and ancient centre of learning.

31
THE LAMA WITH THE YELLOW HAT

Objectless compassion, Chenrezig,
Lord of stainless wisdom, Manjushri,
Conquering mara's horders, Vajrapani,
Crown jewel of the Sages of the Land of Snows, Tsongkhapa,
Losang Drakpa, at your feet, I pray.

The Migtsema, or Mantra of Tsongkhapa

Losang Tsongkhapa, the man from Tsongkha in Amdo, was born in 1347 and became a much-revered leader, scholar and teacher to whom is attributed the foundation of the Gelugpa sect of Tibetan Buddhism. It is said that both the Buddha and Guru Rinpoche prophesied his coming to Tibet. His birthplace is now marked by the well-known Kumbum Monastery in Amdo. Peter Fleming, the brother of Bond author Ian Fleming, visited Kumbum in 1935. He was undertaking a seven-month journey from Peking to Kashmir with his companion the Swiss journalist Ella 'Kini' Maillart. The narrative of this expedition was published in 1936 as *News from Tartary*. They had a tough time with Chinese bureaucracy and to fill in some imposed waiting at Sining, modern Xining, they arranged a side-trip to visit 'The Great Lamasery' of Kumbum. Fleming explained that Kumbum means 'a hundred thousand images' and tells the tale. Tsongkhapa was born close to the monastery site. When he was seven years old he had his head shaved and his mother threw the hair to the ground. In time it grew into a white sandalwood tree, the leaves of which each carried, miraculously, an image of the great teacher. A monastery was inevitably built at such an important place.

As a young monk Tsongkhapa settled in Lhasa and was influential in introducing a Middle Way monastic code based on the teachings of the third-century teacher Nagarjuna. By the age of fifty-two he was so well established in Tibetan society that he was able to get support and funding to refurbish and rejuvenate the Jokhang Temple and to establish the New Year festival, still celebrated, known as Monlam (Tibetan: *smon-lam chen-mo*). He was given the opportunity of establishing a new monastery near Lhasa and he chose a lofty position about 40 kilometres up the valley of the Kyi Chu. He called the new centre, which was established in 1409, Ganden (Tibetan: *dGa'-ldan*), after the pure land realm of Maitreya, the future Buddha. The new order he established was the 'Ganden Tradition' or the Ganden 'Lugs', and the Tibetan *dGa'-ldan lugs* was shortened to *Gelug*, with its adherents known as Gelugpa. Tsongkhapa and his followers adopted the yellow hat. Throughout Tibet and beyond there are statues and paintings of the yellow-capped sage, invariably flanked by his two most devoted followers: an easily recognisable trinity.

Within a short time the sect grew in size and Tsongkhapa was responsible for establishing Drepung Monastery in 1416 and Sera Monastery in 1419, the year he died.

I had visited Drepung and Sera on previous visits to Lhasa and it was time to make the journey further afield and visit Ganden.

WEDNESDAY, 27 MAY

Norbu was waiting out the back of the Flora hotel with his car at 9.00 and off we went. The road out of Lhasa to the east was being upgraded, so there was a lot of off-road track to drive on, crowded with massive trucks. As we followed the river and continued east it was clear that a huge amount of construction work was being done across the valley of the Kyi Chu. A vast new town of high-rise buildings was being fabricated.

After an hour of slow driving through the burgeoning, ugly megalopolis we turned south into a wide and tranquil-looking valley and started the long tortuous climb up to Ganden itself. Halfway up, the buildings of the monastery came into view. It was simply spectacular lying up near the skyline in its natural amphitheatre.

I'd read up on the history of Ganden and that it had been almost totally destroyed in the recent past. More than 2000 monks lived there in 1959. It was partially destroyed in the upheaval after the Chinese invasion and then in 1966, during the Cultural Revolution, it was shelled by the Red Guard. The elaborate tomb of Tsongkhapa was dismantled and his mummified body burned. Fortunately, the monk who was forced to burn the corpse was able to retrieve some of his skull and some ashes. These remains were hidden away and later installed in a new tomb which has arisen, along with most of the other buildings, in the massive rebuilding program that has been going on since the 1980s. The result is the splendid collection of red-and-white structures nestling in their eyrie high in the mountains. It has been home for many years to about 400 monks. In 1996, when a ban was placed on images of the Dalai Lama, there was a riot and at least two monks were killed when the PLA fired upon the rioters. After the protests in 2008, when the Dalai Lama was awarded the Congressional Gold Medal, it was felt that there had to be a permanent police and army presence to make the upstart monks behave, so unsurprisingly one of the new buildings is a large police garrison.

Norbu and I began by doing the *kora*, a clockwise circuit of the whole monastery complex following the ridge line above and behind the buildings. There were excellent views north up the valley of the Kyi Chu. Every 20 or 30 metres around the *kora* there was a marker stone indicating some significant rock formation or place where a saint had been, or simply an ancient carving in the cliff above. There was thus 'The place where Druk pa kunlek magically made his print' and 'The place where Tsongkhapa left his hat' and 'The three natural statues of the Buddha of infinite light', although they all looked rather well handcarved to me.

Halfway around we came to the cemetery, a sky burial site. I was intrigued and captivated. It was a slightly sloping stone platform about 3 metres square with drainage channels built in. I was surprised to see a large axe lying near one corner and then, nearby, a pile of knives and saws. I knew what I'd find if I mooched around and, sure enough, I started spotting bits of bone all over the place: fragments of skull, an ulna, a clavicle, but a surprising absence of small bones or teeth.

We had a bit of a climb to rejoin the *kora* but at its furthest end we came to Tsongkhapa's chapel painted a deep yellow colour. There was a small cave inside where the great man is said to have meditated for three years.

On to the main meeting hall, a vast room with ornate columns and bright hangings on ceiling and walls. Monks were in full chant with their daily prayers. The large central building, painted a dull red, contained the ornately rebuilt tomb of Tsongkhapa, with only the fragment of his skull within. Adjacent to this was the throne room with his old, cushioned throne in a glass case. On the way out Norbu asked the monk who was quietly guarding the place to give us a blessing. We were then both tapped gently on the head with a cloth bag, pillow-like, containing something soft. I later found out that the sack contained the yellow hat of Tsongkhapa himself and the soft shoes of the thirteenth Dalai Lama. How auspicious.

Throughout the complex there were many statues and painted murals of Tsongkhapa, recognisable by his bright yellow hat and almost always represented as flanked by his two principal disciples, Gyaltsab Dharma Rinchen and Khedrub Gelek Palsang. When Tsongkhapa died in 1419 at the age of sixty-two, these followers, each in turn, succeeded him as the leader known as the 'Ganden Tripa' (Tibetan: *dga-ldan khri-pa*). This position is unique in Tibetan Buddhism as it is a meritorious appointment held for a period of seven years. It is the Ganden Tripa who is the head of the Gelugpa sect and not the Dalai Lama himself, even though he is Gelugpa. The lineage is well documented and the current incumbent, Thubten Nyima Lungtok Tenzin Norbu, is the 102nd Ganden Tripa, who began his term of office in May 2009.

The eighty-sixth in the lineage was Lobsang Gyeltshen (Tibetan: *blo-bzang rgyal-mtshan*), who was born about 1840 and whose time as head of the Gelugpa was 1900 to 1907. This was the self-same gentleman that Younghusband described as one who 'more nearly approached Kipling's lama in *Kim* than any other Tibetan', his Ti-Rimpoche, who became his friend and gave him the bronze Buddha statue.

Norbu and I went back to the meeting hall to spend a most relaxing and meditative half-hour listening to the monks continue their chanting. One of the more senior monks led the chanting with a deep, gravelly and resonant tone.

We had a cup of sweet spicy tea and a *momo* in the canteen built for pilgrims before heading back to Lhasa, arriving about 15.00.

I couldn't resist another circuit or two of the Barkhor, as there were a few more hours of daylight. I must confess I derived a distinct distorted satisfaction from finding a stall, at an indoor market, which had six human craniums for sale. And that was after the sheer perverse pleasure of seeing, in an antique shop, a 'very rare *thangka* on human skin' for a mere 1.8 million yuan or $360,000. Lhasa was becoming an expensive destination.

As I sat at a rooftop restaurant on the Barkhor indulging in lemon tea and potato *momos*, a roof-laying ceremony was going on next door with the Potala as a backdrop. A group of about twenty-five young men and women stomped their way in a circle around the loose clay of a new flat roof, singing in unison and smashing down hard with weighted long-poled tamping tools. It was another timeless scene of work being done exactly as it had been for hundreds of years.

Then it was back to the Flora to repack: tomorrow I was off to Shigatse.

THURSDAY, 28 MAY

We'd arranged to leave at 9.00 a.m. I found that there was a whole eight-seater people mover just for me. Norbu was the guide and we had a driver, Pemba. Pemba spoke no English whatsoever, but he had a constant smile. We headed west out of Lhasa and the road was quite familiar. Since I'd last passed this way, only two years earlier, the highway had become paralleled by the now finished Shigatse railway line, an extension of the famous Xining to Lhasa rail link.

We had to stop at several checkpoints and then had to proceed to the next checkpoint in a specified time. This meant that speed was strictly controlled for tourist buses. One 80-kilometre stretch had to be done in no less than ninety minutes. Thus the 250-kilometre journey I estimated would take three and a half hours actually took six hours. The last 90 kilometres were painfully slow.

Norbu told me it was only the tourist buses so inflicted. Certainly trucks and local buses kept overtaking us. For the last 50 or so kilometres before Shigatse the Tsangpo River Valley was wide and open. The river followed huge meanders with the low brown hills beyond. The sky was vast and bright blue. The few clouds, floating high, were tiny puffs of brilliant white. This was the wide, open vista of Tibet of people's dreams and imaginations. Small villages of square houses beset with prayer flags were scattered on distant hillsides. There was the occasional *gompa*, painted red with shining gold decorations on the corners. Prayer flags were everywhere.

I checked into the Yak Hotel in the middle of modern Shigatse. Norbu then had to take my passport to get my 'Alien Permit' for the next stage of the journey.

At 16.15 we drove off to visit Tashilhunpo Monastery at the edge of the old town. It was a glorious day and quite busy with predominantly Tibetan pilgrims. The Saga Dawa festival was in full swing. It happens in the fourth month of the Tibetan calendar and is special because it contains the anniversaries of the Buddha's birth, enlightenment and *paranirvana*. The full moon, the fifteenth day, is especially significant and said to be the birthday of the Buddha. So Tashilhunpo was buzzing. The main courtyard was being repaved and there was an overpowering stink of sewage but the place still looked good.

As we passed a group of Tibetans Norbu translated a comment from one of them. 'Look. Even Westerners wear them,' said a mother to her young daughter pointing at the *dzi* stone around my neck.

The first chapel we came to was the one that contained the 26.5-metre-high statue of Maitreya. The next large building held the tomb of the tenth Panchen Lama, who had been persecuted by the Chinese and died suddenly in Shigatse in January 1989. His funerary *stupa* was huge and ornate. There was a sign saying the photography fee was 175 yuan, or $35, per chapel – so that attempt at state-sanctioned robbery was ignored and some surreptitious shots taken instead.

After the tour, at about 18.00, I adjourned to the Songtsen Restaurant in the main street for pickled radish and yak, apple lassi and a Lhasa beer. It was good to be back in this traditional Tibetan restaurant where I'd dined on several previous trips. It was a twenty-minute walk back to my hotel through the busy streets but an early night was required, for the next day we were to drive almost 150 kilometres west to visit the fortress-like monastery of the Sakyapa.

32

THE VALLEY OF THE PALE EARTH

The teaching and practice that is the essence of the Sakya tradition is called 'Lamdre (Lam/bras)' or 'The Path and its Fruit'. When the mind is obscured, it takes the form of Samsara and when the mind is freed of obstructions, it takes the form of Nirvana. The ultimate reality is that a person must strive to realise this fundamental inseparability through meditation.

His Holiness the Sakya Trizin

FRIDAY, 29 MAY

The Friendship Highway runs from Lhasa to Zhangmu on the Nepalese border. It is over 800 kilometres long and one of the more scary and spectacular road trips in the world. I'd been driven down it when it was still under construction. It was started in 1967 and only completed in the last few years. The earthquake had caused massive landslides on both sides of the border, and the road into Nepal was now closed for the foreseeable future. Zhangmu was said to be completely destroyed. However, the Friendship Highway is only the final western end of the China National Highway G318, which runs an astonishing 5746 kilometres from Shanghai to Zhangmu. At a place called Lhatse the highway turns southwards towards the towns of Tingri, Shegar and Nyalam near the Nepalese border. The westward-leading road, the G219, carries on another 1000 kilometres to Lake Manosarovar and that holiest of mountains Mount Kailash.

Before 9.00 a.m. we were heading west out of Shigatse. The road was once again familiar, as I'd been this way several times. The bare brown Tibetan hills had a splash of lilac on their lower slopes as a type of gorse was in bloom.

The valley of the Trum Chu, to which we were heading, lies about 25 kilometres south of the Friendship Highway and over 140 kilometres from Shigatse. From ancient times it was known for the colour of its soil or earth (*sa*) which is especially pale or grey (*kya*), thus giving the place the name of Sakya.

The Nyingmapa monk Khon Khonchog Gyalpo (1034–1102) established the monastery here in 1073. His son and grandsons continued its development and out of it emerged the new order of Tibetan Buddhism, the Sakyapa. The head of the order is known as the Sakya Trizin, Konchog Gyalpo being the first. During the thirteenth and fourteenth centuries the Trizins ruled Tibet under the auspices of the Mongol Yuan overlords. The buildings at Sakya have a Mongolian architectural influence, giving them a more fortress-like appearance than other Tibetan monasteries.

The usual petty traffic checkpoints meant the journey took three hours. At one of the enforced stops, where we simply had to wait so as not to exceed the time limit, I got out to stretch my legs. There were a couple of tea shops and plenty of truck drivers and travellers. I came across a large skinny dog who was skulking around trying to avoid people. I couldn't help noticing his right front leg was badly damaged and infected with a large raw and festering wound extending halfway up the limb. I hoped his end would be quick, reflecting that back in Australia he'd be put down as a stray. While I was being negative, Norbu went over to one of the tea shops and bought a packet of biscuits. He knelt in front of the poor hound and emptied the packet so the suffering animal could tuck in. I was profoundly moved by this simple lesson in compassion and have since reflected on the unspoken moment frequently.

Branching off the main highway into the valley of the Trum Chu we passed through the standard security checks and reached Sakya. The old village of Sakya is famed for its buildings being painted a grey colour and decorated with red and white vertical stripes.

The monastery was a vast fortress-like edifice in the same dark grey. It presented itself as a magnificent and secure citadel. Norbu and I approached the main gate through the massive walls, which I estimated to be about 10 metres high with towers at least 15 metres high on each corner and an equally high and imposing gatehouse. Just before the main gate was a large burner for juniper branch offerings and next to this a granite block with lettering carved in Tibetan, Chinese and English. It stated:

> SAKYA MONASTERY. Sakya monastery was founded in 1073 by Kon-Gonchok Gyalpo and extended in 1268 by Phagspa. It is the main monastery of Sakya sect in Tibetan Lamaism. There are a lot of cultural relics. Among them the most famous ones are; The Pattra, the rare large scripture book titled *Bodi Jaglungma*, the mandalas, chinaware and murals made during the Yuan dynasty. It was listed into a key preserved cultural relic unit of the Nation by the State Council in 1961. Erected 1993.

We walked through the opening in the impressively thick walls and could see the huge monastery building enclosed within. We entered the complex and were immediately in the main meeting room. It was vast. Columns made of whole tree trunks held up the structure. Trees that size have never grown on the Tibetan plateau; they must have been brought from far away. One was said to have been supplied by Kublai Khan himself, as was a famed conch shell. There were many magnificent statues. I invested in the 20-yuan fee to get some good photographs.

We came to a sign over a low door that said 'The Great Sutra Collection'. I thought little of it but dipped my head and passed through. I was confronted by an astounding sight. A vast library of books along a wall at least 10 metres high and 50 metres long. Shelf upon shelf of tightly packed books. Lonely Planet says simply: 'Sakya's famous library is accessible from this hall but hidden from sight and it is rarely opened up to tourists.' On checking my photos later I was able to estimate that the shelving was eight shelves high and fifty sections long, making 400 cubicles. Each contained on average thirty-six books – 14,400 in all. It was like the final scene in the warehouse at the end of *Raiders of the Lost Ark*, shelf after shelf of precious artefacts. Some of the books were sticking out a little and Norbu said that these had moved over the years with the not infrequent earth tremors. He also told me that the library was saved from the Chinese Red Guards during the Cultural Revolution when the tiny door was covered by piles of bags of rice as the Great Hall was stripped and used for storage. They had never discovered the treasures lurking within.

We explored some of the smaller chapels then went up onto the roof. It was possible to walk around the massive fortress walls and see across the valley to the original site of Sakya Monastery, which was undergoing restoration.

Lunch was at a local place and consisted of a few *momos* and sweet tea. I was now used to being the only Western face around and attracting plenty of stares, but this local diner was a delight, full of characters with weather-beaten faces and traditional Tibetan clothing. It was like stepping through a doorway into central Asian history.

There followed another painfully slow drive back to Shigatse. Norbu watched the banned movie *Kundun* on my iPad. When he had finished watching, he wordlessly, but with tears in his eyes, returned the iPad to me. For years any image of the Dalai Lama or even any mention of him has attracted severe penalties from the Chinese authorities. Yet the Tibetans still revere him and try to get all the news they can surreptitiously. To watch a whole biographical story, including its scenes of Tibetan persecution by China, was profoundly moving for Norbu.

We stopped briefly at the revamped '5,000 km from Beijing' distance marker and got back to Shigatse about 17.30. I went straight off to retrace the *kora* of Tashilhunpo one more time. From the main monastery gate, the start of the clockwise circumambulation involves a steep climb up the side of the monastery complex and along the back wall. The whole processional way is lined with hundreds of prayer wheels mounted at shoulder height. The truly devout make a point of touching and spinning every wheel. I overshot a bit and ended up close to the newly reconstructed *dzong*. The one which is like a mini Potala but was rebuilt within the last few years. It is merely a concrete shell filled with offices for the Chinese. I walked back through the old town to the main street then once more into Songtsen restaurant for a Lhasa beer. I was thoroughly enjoying my sojourn in old Tibet.

SATURDAY, 30 MAY

An early start meant avoiding some of the ridiculous speed restrictions so we were on the road to Gyantse at 7.50. It was a good fast run and we arrived at the picturesque old town a few minutes after 9.00.

The driver parked the van just outside the Pelkar Chode Monastery complex. There was a lot of activity, with a large number of pilgrims, and there was much renovation work being done. The famous Kumbum multi-layered *stupa* was enveloped in bamboo scaffolding and its upper floors and viewing platform closed. In the main *gompa* building the great hall was cleared of everything, all its hangings, bench seats and statuary, but the side chapels were still open. I had been looking forward to seeing one statue in particular. On my visit to Gyantse in 2007 our guide on that leg of the trip was an ex-monk who was no longer allowed to live in a monastic settlement. He pointed out one particular life-sized ceramic statue of a deity where the brown glaze on the face had run and formed a streak under the left eye, creating a line down the cheek. The Tibetans especially revered this statue, he told us, as they said it had shed a tear for what happened to Tibet in 1959 when the Dalai Lama left Tibet for exile.

Outside in the bright morning sun there were dozens of workers all over the roof, singing and hammering in unison.

Only the first two levels of the nine-storey Kumbum were open, but it was fun exploring and photographing the many dozens of exquisite statues in their small chapels. This 35-metre-high edifice has over seventy small chapels most decorated by murals dating back to the fourteenth century. Directly across the courtyard and towering over the old town was the giant fortress of Gyantse Dzong completing the illusion of having been transported back to medieval times.

We did a *kora* of the whole complex. There were several old ladies, spinning their prayer wheels and wearing white waistcoats with a sun or a moon symbol on the back. Norbu informed me that these were worn with pride as they signified that the wearers were over eighty years old.

Climbing back into the van we left Gyantse about 11.00. It was a pleasant drive with some more of the weird speed limit business slowing our progress. The road took us over a first pass, at more than 4000 metres, then up to a second pass where an impressive glacier comes right down to the road. This was the 5020-metre-high (16,470 feet) Karo La. There had been a battle fought here in 1904 as Younghusband advanced upon Lhasa. It was difficult enough walking around because of the altitude so fighting there must have been especially tough.

Soon after we were on a rough bit of track due to 'roadworks' when there was a large 'clunk' and obviously something was wrong. I reckoned the fuel supply had been damaged as the car would run for a while then simply slow and stall. A few minutes later it could be started. Repeat for the next few hours, a few hundred metres at a time. Better going downhill, obviously.

Eventually we got to the town of Nangartse on the edge of the blue Lake Yamdrok-tso. At the renowned 'Lhasa restaurant' I ate lunch, but afterwards came the laborious stop-start climb up to the Khamba-la (4794 metres; 15,728 feet). It was painful. Norbu and the driver would raise the bonnet at every stop and look and fiddle and nothing would change. Another couple of hundred metres and another stall. Once we got to the top it was a long steady roll downhill to the valley of the Tsangpo. Eventually, about 30 kilometres short of Lhasa we gave up and called to get a taxi. Instantly a fare-paying minibus stopped. One of Norbu's friends had recognised him by the side of the road. There were two seats left in the bus, so we jumped in, leaving our driver to sort out the van. We were back in Lhasa at 18.15 having undergone the standard compulsory identity and passport check.

SUNDAY, 31 MAY

It was time to leave Lhasa and Norbu was at the hotel at 8.30 for the one-hour drive to the airport. We got there only to discover that the flight had been cancelled. There wouldn't be one for two days. There was an American fellow and a group of seven Swiss who were all missing their connections back to Europe. Norbu and two other guides argued with the desk people. Suddenly there would be a flight the next day and they would put us up in a hotel back in Lhasa rather than at the airport. I was forced to have another day in Lhasa, which was no problem from my point of view. So Norbu and I drove back into Lhasa, with several more identity checks, to a modern hotel about 2 kilometres west of the old town. I had a spot of lunch then walked to Chagpo-ri, the hill which used to have the medical school on its summit and which was blown up by the Chinese. At the base of the hill I explored a large covered market selling fish and yak meat and rice, and from there it was only a matter of a few hundred metres to the start of the *kora* around the Potala. I slipped into the stream of pilgrims performing their steady clockwise circumambulation. The hand-held prayer wheels of all sizes were constantly spinning and the people were chatting, children playing. The costumes were from all over Tibet. One nomad was even taking his goat, suitably adorned with colourful beads and ribbons, on a leash to accompany his meritorious circuit. It was a hot day and people stopped for ice-creams or just to rest in the shade of the trees. On the north side of the Potala is a lake, and on a small island a tiny temple had been built. This was the Lukhang Temple, the temple of the Dragon King, built in the time of the sixth Dalai Lama. A narrow, elegantly arched, stone bridge led across to the island and the three-storey shrine. There was little inside but it is famous for its series of murals painted in the eighteenth century, documented by Ian Baker and Thomas Laird in *The Dalai Lama's Secret Temple: Tantric Wall Paintings from Tibet.*

I felt privileged indeed to have had the extra time in Lhasa and to be able to wander freely around the magnificent 'hill which is also a palace'.

MONDAY, 1 JUNE

The lunchtime flight from Lhasa to Kathmandu was memorable for its dazzling view of the mountains. Kanchenjunga was to the left of the plane and after only half an hour of flying there were Makalu, Lhotse and Everest below us to the right. All the details were clear: the South Col and the Geneva spur, the Kangshung face, the South Summit and the highest point in the world. Beyond them, Cho Oyu with its rounded dome of a peak. Then, because the visibility was so clear, in the distance could be seen the bulk of Annapurna and the distinctive shape of Dhaulagiri and just to their right Manaslu. Then as a complete bonus, standing alone on the Tibetan plateau to the north of the chain of Himalayan giants was Shishapangma. There are only fourteen mountains in the world over 8000 metres and on this flight I'd seen nine of them, eight of them in one gaze. It was extraordinary, visually stunning and a reminder, like looking at the night sky, of how vast nature is and how tiny and insignificant we humans are.

Nothing much had changed at Tribhuvan International Airport in the week I'd been away. All the military planes were gone but there were still large numbers of commercial cargo planes on the tarmac. Between the aircraft were palettes piled high with sacks of food and equipment. I hoped that this massive amount of relief was actually going to leave the airport at some point and get to where it was needed out in the countryside.

I settled once again into the Backyard Hotel, where the staff were more than helpful and incredibly friendly. They were interested in what I was up to and told me just to come and go as I pleased.

I bought two *thangkas* in a shop just round the corner from the hotel and then decamped to the Northfield for dinner with Ian and Sarita to debrief them on my latest Tibetan adventures.

I had six full days left to spend in Kathmandu and wanted to spend them as constructively as I could.

33

A WEEK IN KATHMANDU

TUESDAY, 2 JUNE

A barking dog woke me at 5.00. I dozed for a while then headed off for an early breakfast at a restaurant in Thamel called La Bella.

I took a taxi to Pashupatinath, the Hindu temple on the banks of the Bagmati River. This had been a busy place of late as it's one of the major cremation sites for Kathmandu. That morning about seven cremations were underway. The pungent smoke drifted over the whole complex. Families sat around patiently waiting for the various ceremonies to be performed, the nearest and dearest often wailing and sobbing as the eldest son circled the exposed corpse three times before applying his small flame to the pyre. I stayed for a long time just watching the rituals and the bereaved. A perfect time and place for contemplation. Maranasati is the Buddhist practice of meditating upon and being mindful of death. From Pashupatinath it's a few kilometres' walk over to Boudhanath. The day had become another hot one, and refreshment near the Great Stupa allowed me to see the scaffolding going up around the giant eyes. The whole square edifice with its gold spire and massive painted eyes would have to come down and be rebuilt on top of the giant hemisphere.

I'd decided that the week I had in Kathmandu should be put to good use. It was a time to meet up with people – 'networking' in the modern parlance – to decide on future plans and what I could, if possible, contribute to the rebuilding and the healing.

That evening I met up with my American friend Amy Prevatt at Roadhouse. We went on to the New Orleans, where we were joined by Claudia, a Dutch woman living in Scotland who'd arrived for a week to see what effort she could make to help a country she knew and loved. We were also met by an American guy called Jim who had already set up 100 corrugated iron shelters in Sindhupalchowk. He was a toilet construction expert so his skills in building basic shelters were more than valuable.

I was asked by an American ex-marine to look at his Polish girlfriend's dog bite. She had been attacked a few days before and now had angry-looking, infected teeth marks on her calf. The wound was large, red and swollen but the pus was freely draining. The Nepalese doctors had wanted to give her a general anaesthetic or an epidural to incise it. I reassured her that she certainly didn't need that and I dressed the wound and started her on antibiotics and painkillers.

Over the next few days I was able to explore the bookshops and gear shops and wander as-yet untravelled backstreets to observe more of the damage to buildings and decimation of people's everyday lives.

The Northfield had by now started doing some reconstruction of its own and had also run out of any Nepali beer. The situation was looking dire.

By mid-week the weather had turned and it was raining steadily. Not the monsoon yet but it was a lot cooler. I took a taxi to a meeting at the Cafe Soma opposite the Russian embassy in Baluwatar. Jo Chaffer, a trek leader, and a Nepalese fellow with the splendidly forthright name of Man were there discussing a future bike trek. Ian arrived a few minutes later and we had a good chat about the area immediately south of Dolpo. Ian and I went back into Thamel to check out some stores. We called in to the Nepali Mountain Federation and the Nepal International Clinic, where Ian knew many of the staff. We then stopped by KEEP, the Kathmandu Environmental Education Project, and after that the Porter Gear Depository, which rents quality equipment to the porters at low cost. These were interesting individuals and groups who were highly motivated to improve life in a post-quake Nepal.

The following morning I took a walk down to Durbar Square and along the famous Freak Street, its street sign bent by falling bricks. The clean-up was slowly progressing but the size of the rebuilding task ahead was clearly overwhelming for most people, who had little choice but to set up their stalls in the rubble and sleep under tarpaulins in the remains of their houses. Just below the Monkey Temple, at Swayamabhunath, a small field had been given over to the survivors, many of them now orphans, from the villages of Langtang. They were cramped and spent much of their time lining up at the water tankers for their meagre daily supply of water.

I arrived at the New Orleans late morning to meet up with Tulsi Gwyali for lunch. Naturally his business, organising travel and treks within Nepal, had been badly hit. It was good to get his perspective on the situation. Like most of the Nepalese I'd met Tulsi's response was a mixture of fatalism, pragmatism and, despite everything, an irrepressible optimism.

The remaining few days slipped by and I never tired of looking around Kathmandu and talking to people. It was clear that I had much to do in terms of spreading the word about the scale of the disaster and how much help would be required in the coming months. I'd expressed my concerns to all who would listen that the coming monsoon would seriously affect water supplies by washing contaminants from dead animals and people into the wells and springs. Dysentery and a multitude of gut infections would be inevitable. The wet weather and cramped living conditions would mean that chest infections and influenza would flourish. The young and the old and the infirm would be especially vulnerable. And then there was the winter. If decent shelters weren't built before October or November then the intense cold of winter, especially in the higher valleys near the Tibetan border, would carry off many, many more people.

On my final evening I went to K-too restaurant with Ian, Sarita, Gita and Babu. Thamel was, by now, desperately quiet, as tourists and locals had left town – and I too was on my way.

34
ANOTHER DOLPO MOMENT

I returned to Australia with much on my mind. My few weeks in Nepal and Tibet had been frantic and kaleidoscopic. Could I formulate any conclusions or derive any new direction?

I'd done a lot of travelling in the mountains, in the Himalaya in particular, and also in several less lofty Buddhist countries. What made me do it was a simple love of the outdoors and travel itself. I wasn't searching for anything in particular, but it found me anyway.

I was struck by love of a way of life. An attitude. A philosophy. A guide. A Buddhist way of viewing things that was fundamentally and markedly different to the consumer-driven, frenetic, competitive Western upbringing that had imbued my early life and medical training.

Discovering Dolpo through literature and then by trekking through its valleys and over its passes and staying in its villages, reinforced my understanding of it as a unique and legendary destination. I had been keen to go back, but the earthquake had stopped that. Another, somewhat different, journey had taken its place.

But to echo Matthiessen's response to not seeing a snow leopard ('No! Isn't it wonderful'), I could say, having had to cancel my trip to Dolpo in 2015, 'Did you see Dolpo? No. Isn't it wonderful!' For what I did see instead was still an important part of my personal journey and knowledge.

One of the books I'd picked up in Pilgrims was Peter Hopkirk's 1982 book *Trespassers on the Roof of the World*. It was a riveting read with classic tales of heroic adventure and misadventure. Towards the end of the book I read a few lines that gave me goosebumps. 'Speaking of the handful of radio operators stationed at listening posts in Tibet during the Second World War,' he wrote, 'in 1943 they were to find themselves caught up in one of the most bizarre gate-crashings of all. It came, without warning, from the sky.' He then recounted the story, published in 1965, as it had been told to William Boyd Sinclair, entitled 'Jump to the Land of God; The Adventures of a United States Air Force Crew in Tibet'.

In November 1943 a US Air Force C-87 cargo plane with a crew of five was flying 'the hump' from Kunming in China back to their base in Jorhat, India. A fierce storm developed and they were blown way off course. As they ran out of fuel they spotted the lights of a town far below and then came the time to bail out. They all landed safely and were reunited, after a cold night wrapped in parachutes, at the home of a friendly, but no doubt bewildered, Tibetan family. The plane had come down near the village of Tsetang, across the Tsangpo from Samye Monastery. They were guided to Lhasa and after a journey of almost two months made it back to their base at Jorhat. Their reception in Lhasa was less than friendly, as the local population had seen and heard the plane fly over and then crash. To place themselves higher than the Dalai Lama was unforgivable, and they had been lucky to escape the wrath of the crowd.

Apart from the amazing similarity to my father's old yarn I was stunned to read that the name of the pilot and crew leader was Lieutenant Robert E. Crozier. He was from Waco in Texas and clearly not directly related, but what a strange appellatory coincidence.

When I read the original account of Crozier and company's journey by Sinclair it turns out that the crew gave an interview to the BBC radio in India, so it is possible that Dad heard the story at some point in 1944. But surely he would have remembered the pilot having the same surname and told me about the coincidence?

So it was that my own interest and absorption in all things Buddhist and Himalayan seemed to have come full circle. Everything is connected. One of the eight auspicious symbols, the Endless Knot, represents the intricate interconnectedness of all things as well as the circular nature of phenomena, samsara.

I'd travelled a great deal in the Buddhist Himalaya. I'd seen incredible things, met remarkable, charming people and learned a lot, especially about myself.

Ian Baker's book, *The Heart of the World*, was graced with an introduction written by His Holiness the Dalai Lama. The great man had much to say on the subject of Guru Rinpoche's Hidden Lands, the *beyuls*.

> Pilgrims who travel to these wild and distant places often recount extraordinary experiences similar to those encountered by spiritual practitioners on the Buddhist path to Liberation.
> In the Buddhist tradition, the goal of pilgrimage is not so much to reach a particular destination as to awaken within oneself the qualities and energies of the sacred site, which ultimately lie within our own minds. Such places often have a power that we cannot easily describe or explain. When approached with an awareness of the emptiness and luminosity underlying all appearances, they can encourage us to expand our vision not only of ourselves, but of reality itself.

I'd had extraordinary experiences.

I was aware of the qualities and energies of places such as Dolpo as they existed simply as perceptions in my own mind.

My outlook and vision were enhanced such that my personal values and appreciation of the world around me, not just in Dolpo and the Himalaya but in my home country, were fundamentally altered. The rock-solid certainty of existence itself assumed a more indefinite, nebulous appearance. Was this Buddhism?

Life for everyone is, in actuality, precarious and short. I see this every day in my professional medical world. As the Buddha himself said:

> This existence of ours is as transient as autumn clouds. To watch the birth and death of beings is like looking at the movements of a dance. A lifetime is a flash of lightning in the sky. Rushing by, like a torrent down a steep mountain.

Perhaps, in Dolpo, I saw and passed through a *beyul*. But, like the evasive snow leopard, did I ever actually see and experience a *beyul*?

I had to return to Dolpo.

2016

DOLPO ONCE MORE

35
TO THE 'GUNJ

Nepalgunj, nowadays a busy border-crossing town of more than 70,000 people, was fulfilling all the lowly expectations I had of it. Our afternoon flight from Kathmandu was short and, once out of the Kathmandu Valley, quite dull as we descended over the flat Gangetic plain. 'Welcome to Nepalgunj' announced the large red letters above the small airport terminal building. The 'Gunj at last! As anticipated it was flat, dull, hazy, hot and humid.

We disembarked our plane to 37°C of scorching heat and were met by the two fellows who were to be our guides. Chhiring Bhotia was our chief guide. A solid, smiling fellow with quite good English who greeted each of us and shook our hands. The other guide, Wangchhu Sherpa, was also our cook. He was a small wiry man with a moustache. He'd recently been as high as the South Summit on Everest before he'd had to turn around and descend with his client. He also did the rounds, shaking our hands, and laughed as he said, 'I am Wangchhu. Say my name like "One Two" or "One Shoe".' This pair, who were to take charge of our lives for the foreseeable future, began by getting us onto a bus to the hotel.

We drove, not into the centre of Nepalgunj, thus missing its undoubted decrepit charms, but merely to its northern outskirts to the modern and still being constructed Siddhartha Hotel. This edifice boasted a swimming pool and quirkily intermittent electricity so light and air-conditioning were virtually strobe-like. The website of this 'three-star-rated' hotel was marvellous in its manipulation of written English, displaying such gems as: 'with its multi storied huge building established in large property provides the magnificence of accommodation, facilities cum services which reflects the excellence of the modern art of living in the spacious and luxurious hotel' and 'we at Hotel Siddhartha try to cherish every movements the travellers while their stay, whether short or long duration. We have maintained a respectful homogeneity of service and hospitality which comes straight from the heart. A retreat with us is sure to make you feel a home far away from the home'. So, secure in the knowledge that our movements were being cherished, we settled in for one night's stay before our flight next morning to Juphal and the mountains.

This expedition was to be much more than a trek. It had been over a year in the planning. Alasdair, from my previous trip to Dolpo, and I had spent a week in New Zealand at the end of 2014 attempting to climb Mount Aspiring. At 3033 metres (9950 feet) this is the second-highest mountain in the Land of the Long White Cloud. We got to within 100 metres of the summit but were forced back by falling blocks of ice on a warm day. Inspired by that trip and a desire to return to Dolpo, our minds kept going back to the mountain we'd seen on the Tibetan border: Danphe Sail. This beautiful, Matterhorn-like peak was apparently unclimbed and exerted an irresistible attraction to explore it more closely and, with luck, be the first to reach its summit.

I had liaised with Ian Wall in Nepal and told him of our plans. He became enthusiastic and using his contacts in Kathmandu was able to fill in many gaps in our knowledge of this quest. The first, and most significant fact was that the impressive 'pointy' peak actually stood about 1 kilometre inside Tibet. In front of it, to the south, was a lesser peak, which was only 200 metres lower but was rounded and glacier-covered. This was the mountain named as Danphe Sail and listed in the Nepalese directory of unclimbed peaks. The Nepal–China border ran over its summit and east–west across its flanks. Its taller, more impressive, companion was off limits for reasons of retaining our personal liberty away from a Chinese prison but this snowy mountain was still a credible and worthy target for our climbing aspirations.

Plans moved on apace. I visited Sydney, where Alasdair had co-opted an old friend of his, Alex Cramb, and together we pored over maps and peered into Google Earth as the trip started coming together. One item much discussed was food. Alasdair and I had both lost weight on previous

Himalayan trips and we were keen to 'up' the protein load. 'I'd like something a bit more substantial than Spam,' said Alasdair. 'I think that we'll get some yak but I might take some jerky,' I said. 'Really I'd like the occasional beef bourgignon,' said Al, 'but I might just take some protein powder and add it to the porridge.'

It would be pre-monsoon. Ian and Sarita would arrange the porters, transport and camping gear through their company, Off the Wall Trekking. We thought of an approach from Rara Lake in the west, but logistics dictated that the only realistic approach was our previous march from Dunai to Phoksumdo and Shey. We would then head north from Shey to the village of Bhijer and follow a remote valley up to the base of the mountain. Ian had never been that way before and we knew of no one else who had. This would be uniquely off-piste, and most of our information would again come from the chronicles of Snellgrove and Jeste. It was therefore with much sadness that I received a message early in 2016, via Facebook, saying 'Prof. Snellgrove sadly passed away this morning Friday 25 March 2016'. Born on 29 June 1920 he had died aged ninety-five at his home in Italy. We'd had a little communication via the internet and he was still interested in Dolpo to the end.

Our expedition grew to five people when an old university friend of Alex's, Michael Salmon, committed to joining us.

I arrived in Kathmandu on 7 May, a day ahead of the others. Ian met me at the airport and as usual the immediate exposure to the rowdiness, heat, noise and smells of Kathmandu was intoxicating. Leaving my bags in the lobby of the Hotel Tibet the two of us went straight up to the rooftop Yeti Bar for a Ghorka beer. Sarita joined us soon after and it was marvellous to see her again. Then, completely unexpectedly, Ade Summers turned up. Ade was leading the Mountain Company trek to Upper Dolpo and also staying at the hotel. There were to be twelve trekkers in his group and they would be one day ahead of us during the early stages of our journey. Our paths would certainly cross. The day was getting better by the minute and, inevitably, turned into a prolonged catch-up with all kinds of people in Sam's Bar in Thamel. Kathmandu was buzzing, as the climbing season was in full swing.

Next morning I went over to Boudhanath to see the progress on the Great Stupa. Because of the earthquake damage from the previous year all of the structure atop the giant hemisphere had been removed and a brand-new building with 'Buddha eyes' and parasol was being constructed. The new works were encased in a massive web of bamboo scaffolding. From the top down to the western side of the base led a huge ramp, again made of bamboo, about 5 metres wide. Down the centre of this ramp a pair of rails had been placed so that a trolley could be hauled up loaded with bricks. At the bottom volunteers would pile up the next load of red bricks and it would be manually dragged up to supply the dozen or so builders working up top. A true labour of love and dedication by all concerned.

Less than 1 kilometre from the *stupa*, towards central Kathmandu, were two large fields packed with hundreds of the tarpaulin-festooned tent dwellings of the earthquake displaced. Many people were still existing under the most basic of living conditions more than one year after the destructive tremors. The ineffectual Nepalese government had been unable to agree on any mechanism whereby the millions of dollars of promised aid could be distributed, so it simply wasn't. The people continued to suffer.

The rest of the team arrived that evening. Again, Ian met them at the airport and soon after 5.00 p.m. they rolled out of the van. Alasdair, the big man, out first, followed by Alex. Then Michael who I was meeting for the first time. He was a friendly-looking, dark-haired man carrying a bit of extra weight. Oh well, he'd soon be losing that.

We ate together in Thamel that evening but had only the following morning to get organised before the afternoon flight to Nepalgunj. So next morning, Alasdair having some business to attend to, saw Alex, Michael and myself off to see old Kathmandu.

Alex had been there twenty-five years earlier, so it was a treat for him to revisit. The three of us wandered down towards Durbar Square. It was good to see that all the rubble from the earthquake had been carted off, but the scale of the destruction was apparent by virtue of the missing temples and the cracks in those that remained.

At some stage Alex said to me, 'I ought to tell you, Bill, that this trip isn't just about trekking to the mountain and meditation. It'll be the twentieth anniversary of my wife's death on the 27th when we're up at the mountain.' She died within a few days of giving birth to their daughter. 'I'd like to get some prayer flags and hang them for her.' I said I'd be delighted to help, so we stocked up on several rolls of flags.

Heading back to the hotel we passed many climbing gear shops and I stopped at one of the better ones to get a couple of carabiners. A thought suddenly crossed my mind. Turning to Alex and Michael, I said, 'Have you guys got pee bottles?' They looked at each other, then back at me, and said, 'No. We'll just get out of the tent.' I believe they thought I was pulling their legs as it took a fair amount of persuasion and explanation to convince them to invest in a 1-litre, wide-necked leak-proof container each. It would save them many a cold and uncomfortable trip outside the tent at night simply to pee. Then it was back to Hotel Tibet for final packing and off to the domestic airport for the flight to the infamous travel hub of ill-repute, Nepalgunj.

The 'magnificence of accommodation' which was the Hotel Siddhartha in the 'Gunj served us well for the few hours we were there. A couple of Ghorka beers went down beautifully with my 'Rara chicken', but some of the contents of Alex's curry defied identification and were deemed too dubious to be edible.

A short, restless sleep courtesy of a pack of barking dogs and intermittent air-conditioning had us all gathering, before dawn, for the 'continental buffet' of boiled egg and coffee and a 5.30 ride to the airport.

Nepalgunj Airport was as nondescript first thing on the morning of our departure as it was on our arrival but there were one or two little artefacts for our edification. The small snack bar displayed its name proudly above its door as the 'Hello Airport Canteen'. Just round the corner at the departure gate was a large sheet hung on the wall with the exhortation 'To keep the environment fresh among in words is the secret of verbal cleanliness'. We could only speculate as to the excesses of vile language which must have necessitated this singular injunction.

As always there was a certain amount of waiting time. One of the locals started talking to Alex and within a few minutes they had a map out and were perusing it. The Nepali fellow worked in the Phoksumdo National Park and had just been to a snow leopard conservation conference. He pointed out some of the areas where there were known to be relatively large numbers of snow leopards and we were going close to one of those valleys. Good news indeed.

After the usual delay, we were boarding our small plane in the full knowledge that about half our bags of luggage would not be on the flight. This was insurmountable. The bags would be sent next day or the day after.

The thirty-five-minute flight to Juphal was soon engaging, as we met the mountains then flew in among the valleys before the abrupt white-knuckle landing on the stony landing strip high on the hillside. We jumped out. Cargo was unloaded and within minutes the plane had turned around and was airborne and heading back to the 'Gunj.

We looked to see which bags of ours had turned up.

Certainly no tents.

This could get interesting.

36

LOWER DOLPO ONCE MORE

TUESDAY, 10 MAY

Juphal (2475 metres; 8120 feet)
to Dunai (2160 metres; 7086 feet)
12 kilometres

Alex and Michael were much impressed by the quantity of dope growing on each side of the path through Dhagmara as we dropped down from the airstrip towards the Bheri Khola. In fact there had been a dry spell of several weeks so the current crop wasn't quite as extensive or lush as two years before. Similarly, the intended food crops were a bit less advanced so most of the fields remained dusty and brown. I was keeping an eye open for the *dhauiliya* or *dok-pa*, the primitive but attractive shamanistic carvings decorating the houses. I saw a few good examples and even an unusual one carved out of stone.

We'd had tea in the village while some of our porters organised those few bags of ours which had turned up and then set off towards Dunai with our carry-on luggage and whatever we were wearing on leaving Kathmandu. Inevitably the afternoon rain shower came to remind us that our wet weather gear was still in Nepalgunj, so it was just head down and march into Dunai. I had been hoping to shelter under the *kani chorten* but the road had been moved. Just as the rain stopped I realised that the *chorten* was about 50 metres above and away from the new path the road now took.

Ian and I wandered through the busy little town of Dunai Bazar together, and I recalled that this was where we'd first met Thinle Lhondup, the colourful local figure who'd starred in *Himalaya*. Sadly, on 24 April, just sixteen days earlier, Thinle had left Dunai on his horse heading for Chhepka and been killed in a fall. A passing mule pushed both horse and rider over a cliff. The horse died instantly and Thinle soon after. I'd first heard of the accident from a Facebook friend, Kim Bannister, who runs her own trekking company, Kamzang Journeys, and who was leading a Dolpo trek. On 26 April she'd posted: 'Thinle was riding a short way behind us on a dangerous trail when his horse was forced off the cliff by a nervous mule heading down the trail. He passed away at our campsite, amongst friends, including two other trekkers who have met him previously in Dolpo.' The splendid old character was seventy-two years old. 'Caravan Hero' was no more.

After a pleasant stroll through the town Ian and I reached the Blue Sheep hotel and campsite at the end of the road. Ade and his group had camped there the day before, but given our complete deficiency in the tent department we, of necessity, booked ourselves into some of the rooms.

The sun was now almost shining upon us. Michael, Alex and I went over the river to take in the view from the Buddhist *gompa* and the somewhat higher Bon *chorten* next to the Dolpo Bon Society school. The dark-red square building of the Buddhist *gompa* is the main temple of the Dolpo Central Monastery and is a new structure completed in 2005 and inaugurated in 2007. It is the seat of the Venerable Dolpopa Master, Khenpo Menlha Phuntsok, who was born in Tsharka but, in spite of its importance, it was firmly locked and I was once more disappointed not to see inside.

A new suspension bridge had replaced the 'pulley and cage' device that Harry and I had enjoyed so much two years earlier, but we took the longer route back over the older bridge and then through the town on our return. Michael entertained the locals as he tried in vain to buy a 'large' t-shirt: even their largest size would barely get over his shoulders.

A dinner of dhal bhat on the verandah was followed by a welcome early night in the unexpected comfort of a real bed.

WEDNESDAY, 11 MAY

Dunai (2160 metres; 7086 feet)
to Chhepka (2672 metres; 8766 feet)
14.6 kilometres

In true Himalayan fashion a dog barked all night but I dozed happily until 8.00. Then, at breakfast, came the welcome news that all the baggage had arrived at Juphal Airport. We set off jubilantly at 9.00, still wearing the same clothes and with only our carry-on baggage that we had departed Kathmandu with two days earlier. Stopping briefly in the bazaar to buy ourselves an umbrella each, we crossed the main suspension bridge and turned left to follow the right bank of the Bheri.

Two kilometres of idyllic walking downstream and we turned north into the valley of the Suligad. A couple of hundred metres up, we came to a sentry box with three soldiers armed to the teeth.

'Can I see your permits?'

'Yes, here they are.'

'But this is a photocopy. I must see the original.'

'The original is coming with our guide from Juphal.'

'Then you must wait until he arrives.'

All, of course, said in a most friendly Nepalese way.

After an hour the irrepressibly cheerful Chhiring turned up and the essential documents were produced. Saying goodbye to our new military friends, we hit the trail once more. The weather must have been dry lately because most plants – the dope, the barley, all the fields – were less advanced than two years previously and I was a little disappointed that the silk trees (*Albizia julibrissin*) had few flowers on them. We had, however, passed many low shrubs with dark green shiny foliage and covered in impressively attractive bright red flowers with clumps of yellow stamens which I later identified as *Punica granatum*, the pomegranate.

It was good to get moving and it was only about 1 kilometre up to the Phoksumdo National Park HQ, where we were required, once again, to show our permits. Ian took the paperwork into the main office only to come out nearly ten minutes later shouting out to us, 'Michael! You have to come in here. They want to see you.' Michael disappeared for a further ten minutes then came the next summons. 'Hey, Alex. You're next.' Alasdair and I were left hanging around so we made ourselves comfortable. This was clearly going to take some time. Michael came out eventually and said, 'Bill, do you have a camera battery? He wants to look at the photos.' What the hell was going on? What laws had been transgressed? Were we all going down for spying? Another fifteen minutes slipped by and Ian, Michael and Alex slowly reversed out of the office saying their goodbyes to whichever official had been applying the pressure.

'What was all that about?' I asked.

'You remember the guy that Alex was talking to at the airport in Nepalgunj?'

'Yeah. The one who told us about the snow leopards?'

'Yes. Well, he's the boss here. Michael took a photo of him and he just wanted a copy!'

When they'd first gone into the park office the dapper little wildlife enthusiast from the airport had been unrecognisable in his official capacity wearing a khaki uniform, spectacles and an even more unexpected addition, a large neck brace. It had taken the boys some time to work out that we weren't in trouble and their 'friend' was simply being courteous and filling in his morning socially.

So, after two hours of delay, we were on our way once more and could at last relax and enjoy the simple pleasures of trekking in the mountains.

The Suligad Valley, beloved of Peter Matthiessen, led us north and I have to confess that it was harder going than I remembered. The trail was never level but some of the climbs up through the trees, dropping back down to the river minutes later, were sweat-inducing and even though we were still only at 2500 metres I was forcing the water down. As I'd reminded the team, 'If you pee anything darker than a chardonnay you need to drink more.'

A leisurely lunch at Sangta of fried Spam and spaghetti was most welcome as the rain held off. The small hamlet of Sangta had a fine collection of *dok-pa*, but from here we were leaving behind the shamanistic lower valley and entering a community with a totally Tibetan influence. The simple figure carvings gave way to *mani* stones and prayer flags.

Chhepka, our destination, was much further than I remembered. Michael was having a bit of a slow time of it but doing the right thing by going at his own pace.

We crossed the river several times on the cantilevered bridges before starting the climb up through the pine forest. There had been many fires recently because of the dry period but some fires had been smouldering for weeks and when we looked at the opposite hillsides there were scattered plumes of smoke all the way along the valley. In places we were walking through ash and charred branches that had fallen from higher up the slope. There was even the sporadic, still glowing, tree stump.

I arrived at Chhepka at about half past five. It was dry and much nicer than on my previous visit, on which occasion it had been a swamp. The others rolled in and I could see for the first time our group of porters and our mules. We had, besides Chhiring and Wangchhu our guides, four porters hired from Dunai. Our guides hadn't met them before, but we reasoned it was cheaper than bringing men from Kathmandu. Three of the boys were to be 'kitchen boys' to help Wangchhu with cooking duties and setting up the kitchen tent. These were Jaya and Min Bahadur and Rajendra Bohora. The other fellow, Ramesh, was to be a more junior, general help. We then had two 'pony boys' looking after the fifteen animals that carried all our gear. Being 'city boys' we referred to these friendly animals variably, throughout the trip, as horses, ponies, donkeys, and sometimes their real name, 'mules'. All fifteen were in fact real mules, the sterile offspring of a male donkey and a female horse. They were well behaved, tough and never caused us any problems. Despite the biological classification of the beasts, for the duration of the trip their handlers, Punna and Sudip, were simply known as 'the pony boys'. Punna carried himself with a certain self-assurance and liked his fashion accoutrements: pink belt, cool sunglasses, jeans low on his hips. He did bear more than a slight resemblance to the American rapper Snoop Dogg, and we often referred to him as 'Snoop' from day one.

Once the others had arrived in Chepka it wasn't long before the tents were put up. The Dunai boys were new to the game and initially a little bemused by the long poles of modern tents. Chhiring exercised some tough love in a loud voice and they soon got the idea. We settled in. It was good to be reunited with all my gear, and even though it was a balmy evening it was pleasant to don an extra layer or two as we sat outside for dinner. Michael was exhausted and had gone straight to his tent having said, 'That was hard work. It's the toughest thing I've ever done.' The rest of us enjoyed a good meal which was preceded by, surprise, surprise, hot face towels. This was an initiative of Wangchhu's and something of a treat every evening. I'd never seen this level of indulgence on any other trek and Wangchhu was rapidly becoming a living treasure.

THURSDAY, 12 MAY

Chhepka (2672 metres; 8766 feet)
to Rechi (3027 metres; 9931 feet)
8.2 kilometres

I woke at 5.00 and it was raining heavily. It was still nice to be back in a tent. There's something fundamental and cosy about being cocooned in the nylon shell, snug in the warmth of feather and down gear. By the time we'd indulged in a breakfast including fresh coffee – from the steel cafetière bought specially for the trip – the rain had essentially stopped. We were packed and up and away by 8.00.

Once again I'd forgotten how much hard work some of the trail was.

I was ahead of the others and came to a place where the bridge had been burned out. It was being replaced but the temporary crossing was a single tree trunk. Ramesh, our junior porter, and one of the bridge workmen guided me over. I then waited to get photos of the others crossing but there were to be no wet feet. The mules arrived and got across in their own way by wading a little distance upstream. My bag was on the lead mule and I could only watch as it was half submerged. Luckily, experience had taught me that everything should be wrapped in plastic bags or, even better, waterproof stuff sacks. My sleeping bag mercifully remained dry.

At one point in the morning's walk there was a series of zigzags climbing over 200 metres above the river then soon dropping right back down. I kept going and, after crossing a new metal suspension bridge, came to our lunch stop of Rechi. This was where the buildings and the people's clothing were noticeably more Tibetan. I'd just slipped my boots off when it started to rain. The others arrived twenty minutes later. Michael was going increasingly slowly and getting more tired. The rain intensified.

Over lunch indoors Ian suggested that, as the rain was now torrential and we were only a few kilometres short of our planned campsite, we should stay put for the night then tomorrow head on to Tapriza, Amchi Hospital and Ringmo. What a great idea. We tucked into lunch with the prospect of a relaxing afternoon ahead. I retired to my tent to change my socks for the first time since Brisbane a full week before.

I caught up on writing my diary and started my third reading of *Into the Silence* by Wade Davies, his account of the 1920s Everest expeditions and the influence of the Great War on the climbers.

That evening after dinner, as we headed back to our tents, the eerie dull glow of several smouldering fires could be seen high on the black silhouettes of the mountainsides opposite us.

FRIDAY, 13 MAY

Rechi (3027 metres; 9931 feet)
to Ringmo (3648 metres; 11,968 feet)
10.5 kilometres

A good sleep. It was a beautiful sunny morning at Rechi and we enjoyed coffee and breakfast outside.

It was only about 2 kilometres up to Tapriza, where the school was situated. Alasdair and I had taken a good look around there on our previous visit. The school is sponsored by a Swiss NGO, Tapriza Organisation, and named after 'Tapihritsa', a great Bon teacher from Zhangzhung in the time of the Tibetan king Trisong Detsen: so about 760 CE. We didn't tarry at the school as classes were underway but just beyond the buildings there was a new suspension bridge across the river, now named the 'Phoksumdo Khola' and the trail continued to Amchi Hospital. Here we stopped to have a noticeably early lunch as there was nowhere else to stop and cook until we'd climbed up to Ringmo. No sign of diminished appetites so far.

In the afternoon the gentle trail led us up to the seasonal and currently deserted village of Polam (3397 metres; 11,145 feet) then the long climb began. I'd forgotten exactly how arduous it was. There were many zigzags on a rocky trail up to the ridge, a traverse around a steep narrow valley then more zigzags up to the next ridge. Then I could see the pergola and cairn at the top of the ascent.

I hit the proverbial wall. It was too little fuel or water or both or just a case of slow acclimatisation. I just plodded on, more and more slowly, and eventually reached the pergola overlooking the Phoksumdo waterfall. Ian and Alex were already there. I drank a litre of water and had some chocolate. It had become quite cold and windy. The dust was being blown around and it was time to put on warm and windproof layers as well as gloves. This was one of the best viewpoints for seeing Nepal's highest waterfall. Alex and Michael hadn't seen it before and were suitably impressed. I was feeling the cold so set off along and up the trail and within ten minutes reached the crest of the ridge. A string of prayer flags hung overhead. A wide sandy lane led gently down and was lined both sides with birch and pine. As I stepped under the prayer flags it was like passing through some strange aperture into a different world. I'd left a harsh cliff of rock and wind and cold and within a few steps it was calm, warmer and noiseless. I was forced to turn on my heels to check reality. Sure enough, less than 50 metres behind me there was nothing but a bare rocky slope dropping several hundred metres to the valley below. Alasdair was approaching and, contrasting my new situation, he was still being battered by wind and dust, his bright red jacket flapping in the breeze.

It was a pleasant downhill walk into Ringmo, with the five of us discussing 'what was the first album you bought?' In my case, *Every Picture Tells a Story* by Rod Stewart and the Faces in 1971.

We sauntered into the village soon after 2.00 p.m. On the edge of Ringmo we came across Ken, an American from Ade's party. We started having a chat and Chhiring joined in. I pointed out the electricity poles and mentioned the hydroelectric installation two years ago. Chhiring asked a local about it. It was not working and hadn't been for some time. He was told that the level of the lake had dropped because of the drought so there was no more electricity. (In fact the lake level hadn't dropped so other issues were at play.)

We came across Ade just before reaching the campsite. He said that his group was going over to the *gompa* at 17.00. They'd been promised the keys this time.

I wandered up to Ade's campsite to see if Saila, our cook from 2014, was there but he wasn't their cook this time. Ade invited me into their mess tent for coffee and we were joined by our old friend Chandra. It was remarkably good to see him and we talked about family, friends and trekking. They did mention that there was a local woman who had a broken arm but they thought she was being sorted out. I walked a little further down to our campsite near the edge of the lake, where I dug out the medical kit. I had a large blister on my left heel due to my change of socks. I should have stuck with my week-old pair.

We went over to the Thasung Tsholing Gompa at 17.00 with all of Ade's group but it came as no surprise when the lama didn't show. The people in Ade's party seemed rather dour and didn't even talk or smile much with each other. I took plenty of photographs from the *gompa*, as the blue lake was astoundingly beautiful at any time of the day and from the monastery the backdrop beyond the lake was the great ice barrier of Kanjiroba. The birch trees which had so impressed Snellgrove around the edge of the lake were outstandingly brilliant with their creamy white colour, and much of their bark was peeling off and hanging in sheets. This was a natural feature, but probably accelerated by the recent parched conditions.

It was good to look at the lake, organise the tent, watch the lake for a while, have tea, then spend some more time gazing at the lake. A superb dinner at 18.30. Hot face towels, of course. Thanks again, Wangchhu. Then a bit more lake gazing before bed at 20.00. It was a rest day tomorrow and I needed to spend some more time just looking at the beautiful Phoksumdo lake and chilling.

37
PLACE OF THE MENDRUB

In 1996 Marietta Kind, a Swiss anthropologist, made her third visit to the village of Tsho (Ringmo) to study the Bon religion. She was especially interested in an ancient ceremony and series of Bon rituals called 'Mendrub'. After close involvement with the organisation and execution of the entire Mendrub festival at the Thasung Tsholing Monastery she published her account in 2002, entitled simply *Mendrub* and subtitled *A Bonpo Ritual for the Benefit of all Living Beings and for the Empowerment of Medicine Performed in Tsho, Dolpo*. This was a marvellous tome in which she considered the history of Bon itself, as well as those who'd previously researched the religion. She also gave much detail on the people, buildings and history of the village of Ringmo. Then, in 2012, Marietta published her definitive account, based on her studies from 1990 to 2008: *The Bon Landscape of Dolpo: Pilgrimages, Monasteries, Biographies and the Emergence of Bon*. This was quite simply the mother lode: a vast amount of the information we needed concerning the rest of our journey was contained within. Of course David Snellgrove was an early contributor to the study of Bon when he translated manuscripts he was allowed to study at Samling Monastery and which he eventually published as *The Nine Ways of Bon*.

SATURDAY, 14 MAY

We took our coffee outside then breakfast while observing that lake. It was always mesmerising. Ade's crew were leaving at 8.00, and Ian and Ade had a chat about the best way over the Kang La to Shey and how long it should take, then their group was off on its way along the devil's pathway.

I walked a couple of hundred metres behind camp, skirting a scattered and bleached yak skeleton, up to the square *chorten*, sprouting prayer flags, on the hill behind Ringmo. This, Marietta Kind informs us, is the Yul Lha Jowo Chungsa, *yul lha* meaning 'local god'. It is extremely old and had evolved over time into a Buddhist monument. Each year a local family, to the exclusion of the other villagers, performs a ritual to encourage Jowo Chungsa to provide rain and a good harvest. There was certainly a good view of the whole settlement of Ringmo laid out below me. I dropped down to the centre of the village to the Kalsang Ombar. Still looking derelict since my last visit the large *chorten* now merely had a pole across the doorway which I could step over. The floor was covered in straw. I expected the interior decorations, about which Snellgrove had waxed lyrical, to be deteriorating but at first viewing they were indeed glorious. Then on closer examination, the ceiling of nine mandalas had had newly printed or painted laminated mandalas simply stuck over the older fading and damaged mandalas which Snellgrove had seen and photographed. It was a little disappointing but the wall paintings were rather good.

I returned to camp and decided to head off to the monastery once again as the light was perfect and the lake itself gleaming perfection. The silver birch with their shedding bark looked even more special in bright sunlight with the water sparkling in the background.

As I entered Thasung Tsholing, at the end of the row of eleven *chortens*, which I now knew were named 'the Eleven Lama Dungten', I spotted a Bon version of the *mani dhokor*, the circular *mani* stone carving, but this with the eight petals for each syllable of the Bon mantra rather than the six of the Buddhist equivalent.

The monastery was once again deserted so I simply sat on the steps leading up to the main doorway for twenty minutes or so of contemplation. Quite suddenly, after my enjoyable period of quiet, a small, skinny, elderly monk came noiselessly round the corner. He was surprised to see me. I said, 'Go into *gompa*?' while pointing at the door. He shook his head while miming the turning of a key. He moved on and I stayed on the temple steps for another five minutes.

I was walking past the row of *chortens* when I heard a shout, and I looked up to see the monk standing in front of one of the old buildings up the hill. He was beckoning me up to his house. It was, in fact, one of the old chapels, called Gyakar Gompa: Kham Gyeshu. I assume it was named after Kham Gyeshu, the lama Snellgrove had met in the 1950s, whose hair was piled up on his head and who Snellgrove thought the most interesting person in Ringmo: 'He was the first cultured Tibetan we had met on these travels, and his company pleased us immensely.'

I quickly went up the slope to the wooden-framed entrance of the building and the lama led me inside. The ground floor of the building was a storeroom full of wood. A carved log ladder led up to the next floor where there were two small rooms. The monk's bedroom was about 2 by 3 metres and his prayer room about 3 by 3. The prayer room was hung with *thangkas* and had a low table with his prayer books. I pointed at the main shrine and asked, 'Bon?' He nodded then gave a large smile as I recited 'Om Matri Muye Sale Du'. At the rear of the room were shelves with many small statues of Shenrab.

It was back to camp to relax for the rest of the day. It was hot, windy and dusty.

Alex and Michael returned from a trip up to the village.

Alex said, 'There's a woman up in the village with a broken arm.'

I said, 'Yes. I know all about her. A doctor in Ade's group saw her yesterday. She's meant to be going down to Dunai.'

Twenty minutes later Chhiring came into the mess tent and said, 'Woman with broken arm is here to see you.' Everyone moved out of the mess tent pretty quickly and I settled the poor woman into a chair. She clearly hadn't gone to Dunai but she had paid a visit to the local *amchi*, a practitioner of traditional Tibetan herbal and holistic medicine. I helped her take her right arm out of her shawl, which was being used as a sling, and gently laid the injured limb on our table. The local medicine man had parcelled it up with a brown, sticky herbal concoction wrapped in a sleeve of silver birch bark. Fortunately the potion didn't smell. It was clear on examination that both the ulna and radius were fractured. I could feel the bones grating. There was surprisingly little swelling and she was able to move and feel her fingers. The skin was intact, so it wasn't an open fracture with the risk of infection. I said to Chhiring, 'We need a splint.' There was nothing obvious around our camp so I walked the 100 metres up to her house, where I found a piece of wood about a centimetre thick. I asked Chhiring to cut it to the right length. I took her local dressing down but left the paste on so as not to upset her too much. I laid her arm on the wood and wrapped it with a self-adhesive stretchy bandage. I gave her a couple of days supply of painkillers.

Chhiring did all the translation for me. The lady's name was Pema Drolma. She was a sixty-one-year-old widow. Her arm had been broken a few days earlier when a donkey trapped her limb between itself and a wall. She had no one to take her to Dunai, which was at least a week's round trip. I tried to emphasise that it needed a plaster cast, but I think that she was just resigned to it healing on its own. The possible outcome for her limb wasn't pleasant to think about but the healing process would take a long time and be chronically painful, with a high chance of poor function.

SUNDAY, 15 MAY

Ringmo (3648 metres; 11,968 feet) to Phoksumdo Khola (3712 metres; 12,178 feet), 9.1 kilometres via high point approximately 4000 metres (13,123 feet)

Another marvellous night's sleep then a breakfast coffee while once again enjoying the pleasing lake vista.

Then it was time to leave Ringmo and set off, on that beautiful clear morning, along 'the devil's pathway'. Apparently, only a couple of days before, a bit fell off and the way had been closed for a few hours.

For Alex and Michael this was new but it was still a thrill for me even though I'd done the traverse of this spectacular place before. The precarious trail dropped down into the valley coming off a Kanjiroba glacier and which is full of trees. I went off to a stream to fill up my bottles with water. The others went higher and I tried to get up to them but the trees and thorns were too dense. I struggled for half an hour to get across to the main path. Gradually I got above the tree line, covered in scratches, and reached the main trail distinctly tired after the unnecessary exertion. It was a long climb up to the ridge with no hope of catching the others. At the highest point on a ridge, where there is a cairn, Ian had waited for me. Then it was a quick drop down a rocky trail into the tree line once more and all the way down to the end of the lake.

Lunch was taken picnic fashion, with the fare spread out on tarpaulins by the side of the lake. After lunch we had a pleasant level 5-kilometre walk up the valley to the 'rock' campsite under Kanjiroba. As we approached the campsite there came the thunderous sounds of a couple of large avalanches plummeting down from the several hanging glaciers adorning the vast face of the Kanjirobas.

We had tea and biscuits at 16.00, when Ian, Alasdair and I worked out a plan for tomorrow. It was a case of what was the best way towards the Kang La.

Before dinner at 18.30, for several minutes the combined noises of jangling pony bells, the roar of the kerosene stove from the kitchen tent, the occasional thunder of an avalanche off Kanjiroba and the explosive flatulence from various tents made for a distinctive but peculiar Nepalese symphony.

After dinner we took our mugs of tea over to the campfire which the boys had started. The new plan for the next day, at least 'Plan C', was to head up to Snowfields camp, then next day over the Kang La, down to the south of Crystal Mountain and over the pass which is part of the *kora*. It would be a sensational route.

38

WHERE'S THE KANG LA?

MONDAY, 16 MAY

Phoksumdo Khola (3712 metres; 12,178 feet)
to Valley Camp (4301 metres; 14,110 feet)
8.5 kilometres

It was a frosty morning at our 'forest camp', the air rendered hazy by the trapped layer of smoke from our overnight campfire. The massive white bulwark of Kanjiroba was free of cloud and simply magnificent as it towered over us filling our western horizon.

As I stood sipping my coffee, taking in the scene, I noticed small frost-covered plants all round our campsite instantly recognisable as rhubarb but a miniature version of our domestic type. This was a native Himalayan rhubarb (*Rheum emodi*), which David Snellgrove had come across in this same valley in 1956. He said of this plant, 'When we stopped for our morning meal, we cooked it with sugar and mixing it with condensed milk, placed it in the snow to cool. It provided a dish, which in those harsh circumstances seemed to us sheer luxury.' Sharp-eyed Wangchhu also spotted some wild garlic, the stalks of which were destined for our evening meal.

We departed at 8.00, enjoying the slight warmth of the sun which had only just popped over the ridge of the mountain to the east of us. The level walk along the river was most pleasant, accompanied on our left by the cliffs of the Kanjirobas. Within a kilometre or so we walked past the entrance to the gorge, that of the Tuk Kyaksa Khola, which was our route two years previously.

A gradual climb northwards led us to another tributary and we crossed this by a small bridge then a steep zigzag climb up to a meadow, giving us a clear view north into the valley of the Ghyampo Kapuwa Khola. The stream ran steeply over many cascades and the trail traversed along its right bank towards the head of the valley. Many plants were in flower and there was an abundance of the native iris, *Iris decora*, and the small native rhubarb.

I stopped for an early snack lunch at 11.30. The rest of the team was still behind, so I followed the mules a little higher before we turned into the valley and started the walk slightly downhill and into the depths of the gorge.

I got to what I took to be Matthiessen's 'Cave Camp' in time to be greeted by Ade and Chandra. Their group had camped there overnight but I could see no sign of a cave. Some of his porters had been up to the Kang La to find it was not blocked by snow so open for crossing.

Even though it was 13.00 his group was all packed up and about to leave on the uphill slog to Snowfields camp with the intention of crossing the pass next morning.

I followed them for a short while, as our boys and ponies had gone on to our chosen campsite at the head of the valley. This was the place where I assumed Snellgrove had camped and which was now a revolting wasteland of rubbish left by locals on their trips to the Tibetan border or on the *yarsa gumba* hunt. Most of the discarded bottles, tins and clothes were Chinese. The rest of our group came in half an hour after me. They told me they'd seen some snow leopard scat. We were most definitely in the area which Alex and Michael's conservationist, authoritarian, bureaucrat from Nepalgunj and the National Park Office had told us was one of the best habitats for snow leopards. I was on tenterhooks.

We took in plenty of chai and soup and afternoon tea. One of the pony boys, Punna, showed us a couple of *yarsa gumba* he'd found on the hillside just above camp. The boys got a small fire going but it was early to tent for everyone as the temperature plunged and we endured a bitterly cold night.

The plan for tomorrow was to go up to Snowfields camp then over to Shey next day. Brilliant.

Alasdair and I had talked about it a lot and on this trek we were looking forward to getting over the real Kang La and also, hopefully, around the Crystal Mountain *kora*. It was looking good so far.

TUESDAY, 17 MAY

Valley Camp (4301 metres; 14,110 feet)
to High Camp (4874 metres; 15,990 feet)
4.6 kilometres

Even though it was well below freezing outside I had a reasonable sleep. It was a fantastically clear morning. Breakfast was porridge and granola but, for the only time on the trip, Wangchhu was off his egg game and the scrambled egg was inedible.

Ian asked us to photograph the rubbish around camp so he could make some waves about it in the Nepali media after the trip.

We set off at 8.00. Ahead of us was a steep climb straight up the side of the mountain. The slope was greater than forty-five degrees but we took it slowly with several stops. It was initially a couple of hundred metres up to a large boulder, then on another hundred to a massive rock buttress.

We'd just gone past the rocks of the buttress when Ian stopped us. There, in the sandy surface of the trail, for about 100 metres beyond us were fresh snow leopard tracks. They'd probably been made within the hour as they hadn't yet dried out; the soil was still damp and darker than the previous afternoon's footprints left by Ade's group. After a short gap the prints returned for another 50 metres. We advanced even more slowly and looked carefully from within a few metres out to the nearby ridge lines but there was no sign of the cat. As George Schaller said to Matthiessen on the trail above Phoksumdo, when they'd just spotted fresh signs of snow leopard, 'It might be close by, watching us and we'd never see it.' Thinking of that left me with an eerie sensation that on this morning, high on the mountainside, the elusive animal was exceptionally close. It seemed that we might commune with the spirit of the snow leopard, through its signs and our own imaginations, though we might be destined to never encounter the physical form of such an enigmatic creature.

After the steep climb up of greater than 300 metres a long traverse went deep into the valley to what we thought was 'Snowfields camp'. Ian even said as much as he'd been this way when he and Sarita had visited Shey for the festival in 2012. They'd camped at this level stretch of, currently snow-free, ground and then headed east up to what he understood to be the Kang La. We were clearly not going that way, as Wangchhu and the pony boys with the mules continued further north and higher into the widening valley. It was quite windy and getting rapidly cooler as we gained height so we didn't stop in the valley but went about a further kilometre up a side valley where we established camp on a knoll soon after 1.00 p.m.

The tents were going up. I yelled down to Alex, 'Hey! We're up here but it's easier to go around,' pointing to my left. He suddenly went off like a rocket: 'Don't ruin my trek. Stop telling us stuff. Just let us enjoy our trek.' Then he stormed straight at me. The egregious outburst of pure fury was rendered slightly amusing as he was completely blue in the face with anger but so out of breath he couldn't actually get his words out. I tried to calm him down. 'Hey, relax. Just chill. We're all here for a good time.' He went off to the far side of the campsite and sat by himself for half an hour to quieten down. I realised that he had been fairly quiet and the medic in me knew that the altitude can make people less communicative. It can be an indicator of developing problems.

We talked in quite civil fashion together only a short time later and he was calm but gave no explanation for his outburst and certainly didn't apologise. I gave him the benefit of the doubt reasoning that the hypoxia, headache and tiredness can make anyone a bit friable. I'd seen it before. Matthiessen himself had said, of his own anger issues, 'I remember my first visit to high altitudes, in the Andes, when I was so volatile that any sudden noise inspired fury.' Alex had had his mad Matthiessen moment. We both moved on. I did, however, resolve that for the rest of the trip I'd just stay ahead during the daytime marches and allow him the space he desired and that strategy worked out remarkably well.

After a cup of tea he told me about his father, who'd died about seven years before, following a serious illness. I think that combined with the anniversary of his wife's death and some difficult times recently he really did want this trip to be a peaceful journey, a meditation and a catharsis. My deliberate interactions to check on how everyone was feeling and performing simply grated on him, although they were my best indicator of the first signs of altitude sickness.

Tea and biscuits at 15.00. It began snowing heavily. Alex and I, now friends again, expressed our concerns about Michael's fluid intake. He may well have been developing a serious problem. During tea he sounded confused. He thought we were talking about Kilimanjaro but we hadn't even mentioned it. There was no doubt that the altitude was exerting its inexorable effects on the team.

In my tent I read *Into the Silence* before dinner at 18.00. The snow had stopped but the now-clear sky meant it was extremely cold. It was early to bed at 4800 metres.

WEDNESDAY, 18 MAY

High Camp (4874 metres; 15,990 feet)
to Shey Gompa (4388 metres; 14,396 feet)
via pass at 5235 metres (17,175 feet)

I woke every hour during the night. I had developed a bit of a headache, but I had drunk plenty. A couple of ibuprofen helped.

A beautiful morning ensued and today was the day we were to reach Shey Gompa. We set off after an outdoor breakfast. Ian pointed at a valley well to the east of where we were and about 2 kilometres away, and said, 'When we went to Shey for the festival in 2012 we went up that valley and over the pass that way.' I thought that must be the way Ade and Chandra had taken their group the day before. So was that the Kang La?

Directly from our campsite we took the traverse across the river and dropped into the next valley. We crossed that river and started to climb up towards a huge rock buttress. We made our way round the back of the crag to gain a smooth pebbly ridge, and after about two hours' walking arrived onto what we thought was the Kang La. Just as the others came up to the low cairn marking the pass a large eagle swooped low over our heads and descended with motionless wings into the valley ahead, as if showing us the way.

The view from this vantage point was special. Before us lay a long deep valley which we clearly had to negotiate. Directly behind us was a 'real' mountain. It was large, rocky, pointy and covered in snowfields, icy overhangs, flutes and funnels. The map told us it was 5670 metres (18,602 feet) high, yet it was apparently unnamed. To the west we had an unparalleled view of the Kanjiroba massif. Beyond that and further north stood an isolated chisel-shaped and completely snow-decorated peak called Tsho Karpo Kang. This was quite a landmark and visually striking, standing at its 6556 metres (21,509 feet).

As we sat at the pass and had a snack and a drink, Ian said, 'So you reckon the Black Pond is down here?'

'Yes,' I said, 'it's just down on our left.'

'Well I reckon it's on our right way over in the next valley.'

As it turned out he was absolutely correct, but at the time we were a little confused as to where exactly we were and how we were going to get to Shey.

We dropped down into another valley, that of the Mendokrin Khola.

There was still plenty of snow in patches. We followed a high trail on the right bank of the river. Suddenly we had a surprisingly clear and unexpected view of our objective, Danphe Sail, still quite far to the north, which was somewhat confusing. Where were we?

The light was beginning to dawn. We were on the Crystal Mountain *kora*, heading clockwise around it, with Crystal Mountain itself at 5576 metres (18,294 feet) high on our right.

There is sparse information available about the *kora*. Snellgrove and Matthiessen didn't go round it. Akai Kawaguchi hinted that he did, but his book gave no detail. In 1977 Joel Ziskin certainly did circumambulate the *kora*, but his *National Geographic* account gave little detail of the route and landmarks.

Corneille Jest and his companion Karma did the *kora* in 1961 as part of their giant *kora* of Dolpo itself, and his account carries quite a lot of detail. They set off from Shey, past the half dozen water-driven prayer wheels and up the valley towards Kang La. 'The entire path is marked out regularly by small piles of white stones,' he wrote. 'After an hour there is a large rock with a pile of stones on top. This is a place for prostration and from there the path heads north between two cliffs.'

Jest mentions the high point of the *kora* and descent into a valley, which is where we had just joined. If the *kora* is envisaged as a clock face, Shey sits at 3 o'clock, and we joined the circuit about 8 o'clock.

As soon as we began our walk down the valley we encountered *mani* stones and *chortens*. Marietta Kind, in *The Bon Landscape of Dolpo,* gives more precise details. She makes the point that it is debatable as to the origin of the *kora,* with claims from both Buddhist and Bon camps. It is certainly ancient and the Bonpo, somewhat under sufferance, deign to follow the *kora* in the usual Buddhist clockwise fashion.

One of the first *chortens* we encountered was a shrine which Kind tells us encloses the 'Dragon Footprint' of the mount of Treton Nyima Senge. The Bon canon would have us believe that the Buddhists appropriated this character and altered his name to Drutob Senge Yeshe and his mount to snow lion. From the *chorten* the trail dropped down to a flat area enclosed within a natural amphitheatre, with Crystal Mountain towering at its head. Several large rocks here are said to represent various deities. The trail leads out of this bowl by a steep climb up to an outstanding and prominent crag. Jest says this rock represents the Palace of Drolma in her twenty-one manifestations. Marietta Kind calls the ascent up to it the *mtho ris skas lam,* translated as 'Stairways to Heaven'.

I climbed the Stairways to Heaven and reached the flat top of the crag to the astonishing sight of many dozens of small square structures up to about knee height. They were constructed of the flat stones easily found all around the crag. Jest tells that they represent small houses and are called *khangpa.* He and Karma burned juniper here and built their own 'house'. Marietta Kind maintains that the small 'houses' are built to assist the soul in ascending to heaven after death and to provide a better rebirth. They are also called *Namsche Tönsha.*

From the Palace of Drolma the trail climbed and traversed some frighteningly steep slopes. The scree was loose and wet. In places the chutes of snow which had to be crossed were perilously steep and exposed. A slip here would certainly have been fatal. I was amazed at how the mules, which were just ahead of me, were able to cross ice, snow and rock, regardless of severity, without even appearing to break their stride. I must confess that in one or two places I was grateful that Ramesh lent me a hand for security.

I kept going. The afternoon wore on. No sign of Shey. I eventually came to a large square *mani* wall on a pass where it was clearly all downhill from that point and the direction was south. This relatively flat, high area is meadow-like, and Kind says it is the *mkha' 'gro 'bro ra*, the Dancing Ground of the Dakinis. Here pilgrims sing and dance before their descent into Shey.

Another twenty minutes' walk and way below me, on my left, I could see a deep ochre-coloured cliff, and perched in its centre was Tsakhang Monastery. I now knew exactly where I was. Shey Gompa itself soon came into view and I could even see the rows of tents belonging to Ade's group.

I got down as quickly as I could, arriving at the river at 15.35, just in time to stop the unloading of the mules. I hailed Wangchhu and together we crossed the bridge and went up to where Ade was camped. There was plenty of room and no problem camping there.

I had a chat with Chandra, who confirmed that the campsite was good, then settled in for tea with Ade and Ken.

'How come you came down that way? We came down the valley back there,' Ade said, pointing in the opposite direction from that which I'd descended. 'It was easy. Much easier than the way we came last time,' he said, referring to our trip two years before. So had Ade come over the actual Kang La this time?

I was still uncertain as to where we'd been over the last couple of days but we'd definitely done more than half the *kora*. So where the hell was the real Kang La?

In 1956 Snellgrove made his journey over 'the Phoksumdo Pass' to get to Shey. He described travelling up the valley of the Phoksumdo Khola. He mentioned the primulas and willow catkins that we'd seen at the same time of year. He said, 'Then it forked and we began to climb up the course of the right hand stream, which was now leading us due north.' Eventually the gorge opened to a smooth glacial valley and he camped under cliffs at its head. Next day he ascended the last stage to the pass, when his advance was slow because of the 'fine slaty scree which caused loss of height at every step'. The pass was a snow cornice and after cutting steps down it a long glissade brought them to the river that runs northwards to Shey.

Matthiessen writes much about crossing the pass to Shey. Schaller wasted a day by trying to cross too high, to the west, and they had to do many trips to ferry their supplies. The pair walked up the Phoksumdo Khola to where 'the Kang stream comes out of the north'. They entered a valley of 'warped birches and gaunt willows'. After several hours they reached a 'chasm in the northern walls' where the water descends from the Kang La ice fields. Near there they established 'Cave Camp'. Unsure of the route as 'maps of the region are more imaginative than precise', Matthiessen refers to the 1956 'scholar of Tibetan Buddhism' – Snellgrove – who made camp higher up at the head of the canyon. The next day they discovered a faint path following a series of waterfalls at the valley's head. Beyond this, in a large snow-filled valley they established Snowfields camp, where there was nothing but 'snow and silence, wind and blue'. The three-hour ascent from there to the pass was entirely in knee-deep snow. Their crossing of the pass was to the east of 'Black Pond'.

In their guide to Dolpo, my friends Sian Pritchard-Jones and Bob Gibbons were unequivocal about the route. The Nagdalo La and the Kang La are one and the same. The way that we'd climbed with Ade and Chandra two years before was the Kang La and the same way that Snellgrove and Matthiessen and Schaller had gone years before. It was absolutely confirmed when I looked at my copy of Snellgrove's *Himalayan Pilgrimage* and easily matched his photograph looking back down the final scree field leading up to Kang La in 1956 with my own photograph taken in 2014. Alasdair and I had already been over the Kang La and now we had notched up over half a *kora*.

39
SHEY GOMPA IDYLL

I sat recovering with Ade and American Ken outside their mess tent, and over tea Ade said, 'See the old man in the green top? He's a lama and he was the one beaten up five weeks ago by the robbers.' Apparently Shey had been burgled. The monk, whose name was Tenzin Chogyal, was assaulted and forced to open the *gompa* doors – and five small Buddha statues were stolen. There was now a Nepali police presence, with four young policemen stationed next to the *gompa* for a five-month stretch. Ade's group hadn't been allowed to see inside the main temple and had been told there had been earthquake damage and it was unsafe to go in. I suspected that might have just been an excuse to avoid a large number of people milling around inside.

Alasdair arrived at the Shey campsite about an hour after me and joined us for tea. Like me he'd been puzzled by the route we'd taken. The others rolled in half an hour after that, Michael once again unequivocal about having just done 'the hardest thing I've ever done'. The word around camp was that the pony boy, Punna, had brought us the long way round Crystal Mountain as it was easier on the mules than any of the possible 'Kang Las'.

It became sharply cold in the late afternoon the instant the sun went down behind Crystal Mountain. Dinner, after this long day, was most welcome. The hot face towel was an absolute treat and dessert was a luscious deep-fried apple pie. Surely this place was, at least at the culinary level, truly a Shangri La?

THURSDAY, 19 MAY

I started this rest day at Shey with a superb sleep, which is restorative and essential at altitude.

Behind our tents about 20 metres away was the huge warren engineered by the local marmots. The fearless creatures often popped their heads up to check us out, and the youngsters spent much time tumbling around in playful wrestling.

Ade's lot were all packing up as they were heading off to make for Namgung that day. That would be the last we saw of Ade and Chandra on this trip, so we said our goodbyes. They departed soon after breakfast and as soon as they'd rounded the corner on the trail east I wandered over to the cluster of ruddy buildings that made up Shey Monastery. One of the four young policemen spoke a little English and was keen to have a chat. The four of them were terminally bored. They were from Kathmandu but here in Upper Dolpo they had no friends, no entertainment, no phones. They had been there only one month so far. I felt a little sorry for them. I said we would like to see in the *gompa* if that was possible. The one with the English took me round to the abbot's house, behind the main building. There was a chained barking dog in the entrance courtyard. Through the low entry there was a notched log ladder leading to the main room upstairs. There, sitting cross-legged in the corner having his breakfast was my old friend the lama, Karma Tsondru Rinpoche, the head monk who'd taken young Dorje's green balloon and wandered off with it two years before. I sat next to him while he supped on his yak butter tea. He was rather affable and more than happy to escort us up to Tsakhang Gompa.

We arranged a time of 9.30 to head up to Tsakhang. He showed up at our campsite just before that and I was able to show him, on my small iPad, the photos I had taken of him two years earlier. He was quite amused. Then we crossed the river and, following the trail, started the slow relaxing plod up to that incredible place. On the way the fairly rotund Rinpoche took frequent rests. On subsequent trekking days I would tell myself to 'just go at the Rinpoche's pace' and it would enable me to keep on moving. We can learn from many people.

Often our stops on this day's pilgrimage would be at a shrine. We thus were shown by the Rinpoche a hoof print of a horse in a rock, then a rock with the marks left by the knees and forehead of Drutob Senge Yeshe himself. A third shrine displayed an ancient footprint.

At last we reached the high point, the Rigsum Gompo La, the Pass of the Three Protectors, and could look across to Shey Tsakhang Gompa in all its ancient splendour. In a short time we were approaching the buildings and came across an old man, the caretaker lama, who sat on a rock, walking stick by his side, spinning his prayer wheel. He turned out to be the father of the young lama we'd met two years earlier, Phurpa Tinley, the father of Dorje – hence this old fellow was young Dorje's grandfather. He told us that Dorje was now at school in Bhijer.

It was indeed special to be once again at this tranquil place, to stoop under the main entrance portal and climb up the log stairway to the small landing. At the top, the dark, cold, fireless kitchen. Off that the tiny sleeping area. Across the landing, the temple area with its statues, books and *thangkas*. The Rinpoche sat in the lama's chair waiting patiently for us. In front of him an open prayer book surrounded by the paraphernalia of bell, *dorje* and cymbal. An aged and dust-covered ceremonial drum hung, just within reach, above.

We spent some time enjoying the ambiance before the long plod back. As we left Karma Tsondru pointed out, across the valley, three prominent crags each dropping hundreds of metres below the trail along which we'd come. These were the Three Protectors mentioned by Corneille Jest as being just before the pass at the end of the *kora* and which gave the Rigsum Gompo La its name. In the valley directly below the *gompa* Alasdair managed to find the large ammonite fossil in a rock on the trail that Dorje had shown us previously. Alex and Michael were impressed and, even though I'd seen it before, I still felt the wonder of knowing that all before us was once deep under an ocean. I'd also recently found out that throughout the Hindu world these black fossils were revered as symbols of the god Vishnu and were known as *shila* or *shaligram*.

Back at camp, as we were waiting for lunch, Punna the pony boy and Ramesh started arguing, and then the fight was on. It happened without warning and became quite heated. One upended the other into our pile of stores. Rocks were picked up and used. Shirts were torn. Blood was drawn. They had to be separated. We had no idea what it was about, but it was certainly an unexpected spectacle. Chhiring, as the boss, soon had things under control.

Lunch was, as always, most welcome, then about 14.30 Alex, Alasdair, Alex and I went over to the *gompa* and I hung a long chain of prayer flags above the *mani* wall in honour and memory of David Snellgrove.

We started talking to a couple of the police and the old lama, Tenzin, who'd been attacked during the robbery. Ade's group hadn't been allowed to enter the *gompa*. They'd been told there was earthquake damage but I knew that the earthquakes hadn't affected places this far west. As there were just the three of us they said we could go in, but no photography. I was happy with my photographs from our previous visit so didn't feel this was any imposition. We were let in and the dismal gloom was suddenly dispelled by several electric light bulbs running off the small panel of solar panels on the roof. We had a fun half-hour revisiting this iconic place, with Tenzin and the police quite happy to chat. Alasdair spotted a splendid *kangling*, this particular leg bone flute being partially encased in silver. I asked the monk about the skull chalice which Snellgrove had seen. He said it was there, but kept hidden.

I'd forgotten how impressive the quite recent wall paintings were. The entire right wall, continuing round on to the back wall to the right of the entrance, displayed a splendid and bright series of highly skilled paintings depicting the life of the Buddha.

It was a pleasant afternoon in the tent catching up on the diary. Around teatime, some locals came over to check us out. There was a woman with a baby and a young girl of about ten. The woman turned out to be the wife of Phurpa Tinley and was Dorje's mother. She too enjoyed seeing the photos of herself and her son that I'd taken on the previous trip.

At 17.00 I was asked to see a local girl about eighteen years old, who had dental pain. She had a rotten molar tooth on her lower left jaw but was complaining of pain in her right jaw. She had no sign of swelling or infection. I gave her some ibuprofen and paracetamol for the next three nights and advised her to go to the next dental clinic in Saldang, whenever that might be.

40

TO SAMLING AND BHIJER

Northward, beyond Somdo mountain, on a hidden plateau above the canyons, lies the old B'on stronghold at Samling.

—Peter Matthiessen, *The Snow Leopard*

FRIDAY, 20 MAY

Shey Gompa (4388 metres; 14,396 feet)
to Tora (4672 metres; 15,328 feet)
via pass at 4870 metres (15,977 feet)
11.2 kilometres

After my best sleep of the entire trip I woke to find the valley of Shey with 5 centimetres of snow blanketing the ground, our tents and the monastery itself. There was no wind, just a marked silence. Shey looked picturesque and peaceful.

Over morning coffee we heard that the fight between Punna and Ramesh had broken out again during the night and Alasdair had had to tell them to pack it in. I didn't hear a thing, but Nepalese law dictated that the police should be informed that threats had been issued. Representation was to be made to the police over at the *gompa*.

It was time to leave Shey, and after breakfast we set off directly up the hill behind camp for a 500-metre climb. As we got higher the snow rapidly disappeared. At this altitude the air is totally dry. At the first hint of sun the snow melts but evaporates before it has time to turn to slush. It just seems to magically vanish, leaving quite dry earth and grass behind. After an hour we could look across the steep valley of the Shey River and found ourselves looking down on Tsakhang Gompa in its cliff setting.

There followed a long traverse along the western flank of a mountain that Snellgrove called 'the Purple Mountain', Muk-po Rong (Tibetan: *smug-po'i rong*), 5605 metres (18,389 feet), which he was told was over 21,000 feet on the Survey of India map. That would be 6400 metres, and there are certainly no mountains quite that high in the area.

On our way we saw little wildlife. There were no herds of sheep and the birds kept their distance. A lone marmot raised his head out of a burrow and screeched a warning to us to be on our way.

After a couple of hours we began a long descent down to the bottom of the valley of the Den Khola to reach a *doksa* called 'Yak Yak Kharka' where we had lunch. The pasta and fried Spam weighed heavily on the belly afterwards when we faced a long uphill haul of 300 metres in just over 1 kilometre to a pass. A small cairn with a single green flag marked the pass with simply stunning views back of the way we'd come and beyond to Crystal Mountain itself. Just beyond the cairn, on the brow of the pass, a pair of faint trails crossed at right angles. In the centre I came across a pile of snow leopard scat. There were about twenty lots of droppings of various ages: some fresh, some old and crumbling. It was clearly a place where the animal liked to leave its mark and where it was a frequent visitor. I looked carefully around in the forlorn hope of seeing any sign of the elusive feline as the area in all directions was rounded and flat with not even a boulder for cover. The cat was long gone.

There followed a whole series of high traverses across treacherous loose scree set at an angle of about fifty degrees. Way below to our left were rugged uncrossable canyons plunging down to the Shey River almost half a kilometre beneath our flimsy path.

Ahead of me, a few hundred metres away, in the next cirque, I spotted a large herd of yaks being driven directly in my direction. I quickly scrambled off the trail onto a more level bit of mountain just as they reached me and I was thrilled to find myself surrounded by more than fifty of the beasts, who simply parted and ambled their way around this lone traveller. They were magnificent shaggy specimens. Only a few of the animals were burdened so they were probably being driven to Shey, or beyond, for sale. At the back were the drover, a gaggle of four giggling young girls, who were loath to pose for a photograph, and a man in his twenties, hair wrapped in the classic Tibetan red headband, who insisted on being photographed. We parted all smiles.

Within half an hour I gained the high point of this trail at a narrow pass with a large square *chorten* festooned with many prayer flags. Just as I reached the ridge another herd of yaks made its way around me. More of these beasts were carrying heavy burdens. I spotted sheepskins and tent poles and the black woven yak hair tents. This was a move by the *drogpa* of their whole living quarters and belongings. At the rear of this group of thirty or forty animals came a young girl of about ten and her father, who was leading a handsome brown horse on a long tether. Without stopping we said our '*Tashi delek*'s and moved on. I could now see into the next vast valley, that of the Yangu Khola, and sitting on an alp, high above the river, the dozen or so houses of our destination, the *doksa* of Tora about 3 kilometres away.

A third group of yaks went by on their way to Shey. All the yak herders were keen to chat – by which I mean '*Tashi delek*', '*Namaste*', then three or four words of English – and they also insisted on having photos taken. I was happy to oblige. I was having fun on this splendid, perfect day of trekking. At the bottom of the valley I reached the final group of herders and their yaks. This lot of yaks were the biggest and best beasts so far. Dark-haired animals with stunning sets of horns. They had intricate rugs and harnesses tied over their backs and red ribbons woven into their fur. Some sported huge bells around their necks which clanged sonorously as they lumbered by. The ten or so *drogpa* were in fine spirits. *Raksi* was offered. There was a definite carnival atmosphere.

I arrived at Tora, the *doksa* currently unoccupied, just after 17.00. In May 1956 Snellgrove had passed through on his way to the Shey Festival and described it as 'a small group of rough stone huts which are abandoned during the winter then rendered habitable again for the summer'. We'd been walking for well over eight hours at greater than 4000 metres altitude. I asked the kitchen boys for some milky sweet chai, put on my Crocs and settled into the mess tent. Alasdair arrived half an hour later and the others a few minutes after that. Everyone was glad to be in this rather pretty place but Alex had a quite bad headache, which had been going a few days, so he took himself straight off to have a sleep.

SATURDAY, 21 MAY

Tora (4672 metres; 15,328 feet)
to Bhijer (3846 metres; 12,618 feet)
8.6 kilometres

We woke to a cloudy cool morning, imbibed the essential coffee, then breakfasted outside. A group of four children, about ten or eleven years old, was heading to Shey entirely unaccompanied. They came over to our camp to check us out and we gave them some biscuits, then they happily skipped on their way.

Today we were heading to the ancient village of Bhijer. The kitchen boys and mules, with Alex and Michael, were heading the most direct way: straight over the pass then a steep drop down to the town itself.

Alasdair, Ian and myself, with Ramesh either leading or following, were planning to head down to the village of Tata then across to the famed Bon centre that is Samling Monastery.

The local yak herders were busy on the hillsides, and we passed a beautiful yak farm and spoke to the locals there. A little further on a woman with a hoe was irrigating her field of barley, the trickle of water being skilfully directed back and forth across the plot with adept use of her single tool.

We skirted around the top of the village of Tata, which Snellgrove calls 'Trä', as we were keen to press on and reach Samling. Across the valley was a sharp brown rocky peak dominating the whole area. This was 'the Copper Mountain' mentioned by both Snellgrove and Kind. We left Tata by way of a low pass surmounted by three new *chortens*, still under construction, and followed soon after by several *mani* walls. These were, in fact, mainly *matri* walls, with the occasional *matri dhokor*, as this was totally Bon territory. A 2-kilometre easy traverse led to a natural bowl in the mountainside and the ancient buildings and *chortens* of Samling Monastery. It was an imposing but arid place. There is no stream in the valley. It nevertheless had a beauty of its own. It seemed to be deserted apart from a lone figure accompanied by two white horses.

We walked past the *chortens* marking the southern boundary and up a gentle slope to the solitary inhabitant. He was a tall older man busy shovelling horse and yak dung into yellow bags. He wore a floppy red sun hat and a red jacket over a saffron undershirt. His beads were round his neck and over his face he wore a purple surgical-style face mask. I assumed it was to keep out the dust of his current task. Ramesh was able to communicate with him. The main temple was closed but he invited us into his house. This gentleman was Mr Nyima Gyaltsen, who is a *ngagpa*, a non-monastic lama, acting as a caretaker at the monastery. His son lived nearby in Tata. He led us to the low entrance to his dwelling. We entered a small courtyard to be greeted by four newborn goats and a tiny brown calf. A small wooden door was emphasised with bands of paint around it in delightful shades of yellow ochre, blue and brick red. Immediately through the door was a notched log ladder leading up to a rooftop area, then the main room off there.

This main room was a tiny dark chapel about 3 metres by 4 metres and clearly exceedingly old. There was minimal light filtering through the low doorway and a small window high on one wall. It gave the interior a tomb-like atmosphere which was augmented by the dull reds and browns of the decor and statues, covered as they were by apparent aeons of dust. A shelf contained more than twenty prayer books. *Thangkas* and coloured wall hangings were all around. A central shrine had a 1-metre-high statue, which I took to be of Tonpa Shenrab. Photographs were hung around the frame of the shrine of the current head of the Bon religion, Lobpon Tenzin Namdak. There was also a photograph of this venerable old man with the Dalai Lama. To the right of the shrine was a box about a metre long with a sheepskin draped over it. This was the *gomtri* or 'meditation box' in which the lama slept upright when on retreat. Next to it was a small shelf to hold the prayer books during reading. The other Buddhist paraphernalia were there: a conch shell, cymbals, a *damaru* two-headed drum and a fine *kangling* human femur flute, this latter encased in copper at one end and with a silver mouthpiece.

We lit butter lamps and smoky incense which added to the musty smell of those items. Nyima gave us some *tsampa*, which had been mixed with butter and allowed to dry into steel hard lumps. It was a rigorous chew. After leaving an offering of rupees on the altar we emerged into the bright daylight on the rooftop. The gentle old *ngagpa* had by now removed his mask and it was obvious that he had an extensive and severe condition called leukoplakia of his bottom lip which had already turned cancerous on the right side. That was the real reason he wore his mask.

Snellgrove was much enamoured with Samling and said of the place, 'Samling was to prove the main object of our travels and this old lama our truest friend' and 'We could have lived contentedly at Samling until the autumn: for a while I considered staying on here and foregoing much of the travel that still lay ahead'. As it transpired Snellgrove and his companions were to spend over three weeks at Samling, with visits to Bhijer and Shey during that time.

He was given access to all the old manuscripts in the monastery and settled in to begin translation. He was given as a gift two ancient Bon manuscripts, *The Tantra of Tibet* and *The Treatise on the Basic Traditions of the Great Perfection*. His translations, aided by two lamas who travelled to England to assist, led to the publication of his book *The Nine Ways of Bon* published in 1967.

Leaving the monastery we had a climb of 100 metres up the slope to a *chorten*. Catching our breath and looking back gave us a remarkable view of the Samling complex and, behind it on the other side of the Shey River, the Copper Mountain (*zangs-kyirong*). From this viewpoint the massive pyramidal rocky mountain, 5138 metres high (16,856 feet) with a deep gorge at its base concealing the hidden river, was at its most imposing. It is said to be the abode of the local god of Samling and Marietta Kind says that the *kora* of the mountain has been described but 'not yet opened', thus unofficial.

There was another long traverse before a steep drop down to Bhijer which, from our high vantage point, looked like a well-laid-out old place. Indeed Bhijer was quite ancient. It was also notable that, even among the widely varied spellings of place names in Nepal, it had possibly the widest variety of monikers – hence Bhijer, Bijer, Bicher, Pijor, Phijor, Phijorgaon, and even Vijer.

My guidebook-writing friends, Sian and Bob, told the story of how Bhijer was named. A 'roguish' mouse (*byi*) apparently controlled the whole area. A lama came to sort out the issue and in a rather un-Buddhist fashion crushed (*jer*) it against a cliff, hence Byi-jer. The synonym '*Phiger*' means dead rat. An equally credible origin for the name comes from the *Caragana gerardiana*, a yellow flowering shrub common to the area, for which the local name is *bijera* or *bitsera*.

The day was hot so drink and lunch on arrival were most welcome. Alex and Michael had got there a couple of hours before us and had been exploring. They'd visited the Buddhist *gompa* and a small clinic and, having dropped in to the Bon *gompa* earlier, had been told of an afternoon ceremony. The timing was perfect and after lunch Alex and I headed over to the recently built Bon *gompa*. As soon as we got across the stream running through Bhijer we could hear the drumming and chanting. We entered to find ourselves the only people in there besides a single monk. We took a seat on the broad wooden planks of the floor and listened to prayers for twenty minutes. It was easy to sit, breathe and be in the moment. The bespectacled lama was expert at drumming the small turquoise-coloured drum with his typically curved drumstick. The rate and rhythm of his beating the drum varied with the intensity of his deep-throated chanting to produce a hypnotic strain. The performance rose to a climactic crescendo and ended with a blowing of several long notes on a conch shell. We were both sorry it had ended. The musical priest removed his hat, stood and came over to us. He was of medium height and appeared in his fifties. He wore a modern red-and-black anorak over his traditional maroon robes. He welcomed us and introduced himself. He was the Spiritual Head and Lineage Master of Samling Monastery, Yangton Lama Sherab Tenzin Rinpoche. He was happy to show off his recently built *gompa*. The decoration was splendidly elaborate and, to my untrained eye, little different to many of the Buddhist temples I'd been in. There was a fine collection of prayer books filling a whole wall and surrounding a collection of small statues. *Torma* and butter lamps abounded. There were piles of books wrapped in plastic and I understood that they were for distribution to Bon monasteries in Tibet although the logistics and legality of that seemed rather difficult to me. Perhaps they were for local use. The Rinpoche was happy to chat and try out his English. He gave us each a pamphlet about Samling, Bon and Dolpo and his own role there. It told us that he was also an *amchi* and a local representative of the WWF Nepal. It was a pleasure to meet this venerable gentleman.

As we headed back across the stream to the main village and our campsite the sky was becoming grey and it certainly looked like a storm was brewing. At tea Ian suggested it was time we discussed our options as we were clearly running out of time. We'd already taken about three days longer to reach Bhijer than we had expected and we had to make a choice. We could turn south and keep on walking along the Panzang to Tsharka and then over to Jomsom or we could continue our attempt on the mountain and ultimately helicopter out. After a few minutes' consideration the unanimous decision was to crack on for Danphe Sail and worry about our exit later.

Critical decision made, Alasdair and I walked the couple of hundred metres down to the Buddhist *gompa* on the western edge of Bhijer.

We approached the entrance to the old ochre-coloured Buddhist monastery named Nesar, from the Tibetan *gNas-gsar dGon-pa*. A few women of the village sat outside, but upon entering the main temple we found the interior was deserted, dark and quiet. No lama was there, but a large prayer wheel about 2 metres high was demanding to be spun. We absorbed the tranquil atmosphere in what was clearly a remarkably old temple adorned with dull and ageing artefacts in contrast to the brightly lit and recently constructed Bon *gompa* I'd been in earlier. However, there was much to the story of this place. Snellgrove visited 'Phijor' while undertaking his three-week sojourn at Samling. He walked over the same way we had come and pitched his tent at the old Bonpo temple. He also visited this Buddhist temple, saying of it, 'At the northern end of the village is a little Sa-kya-pa temple, which we visited the following morning. It contains a complete set of the Tibetan Buddhist Canon and a fine gilt image of Maitreya. Repainting was in progress.'

Carbon dating has shown the wood of the pillars inside the temple to date to the late eleventh or early twelfth century. Alasdair and I had, without knowing it at the time, been treading slowly around in the gloomy interior of a 1000-year-old building.

Next door to the *gompa* was a modern building made of stone in traditional style, the Kunphen Shogtso Menkhang Dispensary. This was the small clinic that Alex and Michael had visited in the morning. We entered and spoke to the young doctor who was stationed there. His name was Dr Sagar Mahajan and he told us that he spends six months in Bhijer, between May and October, and six months in Kathmandu. This was his fourth stint in Dolpo. His salary is paid by the charity which he said also aids the Bon community. The doctor showed me his report of his previous stay and the sort of cases he had to deal with then we had a tour of the hospital. His small laboratory could perform many medical tests and his pharmacy was well stocked, but his was a lonely stay. His family were in Kathmandu and he had no easy way of contacting them.

Dinner that evening in Bhijer was chicken soup, sardines and mashed potatoes, which sounds prosaic when written but in reality was tasty, much appreciated and what our bodies craved at this altitude.

SUNDAY, 22 MAY

Bhijer (3846 metres; 12,618 feet)
to *doksa* (4448 metres; 14,593 feet)
via pass at 5117 metres (16,788 feet)
9.1 kilometres

Next morning was beautifully sunny and any sign of impending bad weather was gone. It was also my birthday and as a special treat for all I produced a tube of Vegemite which I'd brought specially for the occasion. Breakfast was taken outside – porridge, bread and cheese – and the Vegemite was a great success spread on the *chapati*.

We knew that the day would be a hard one as we had a massive range of hills to cross and we set off at 8.20 up the valley. Within ten minutes we'd reached the modern buildings of the Shree Mukporong Himal Primary School. I walked in the main gate of the white-walled structure and spoke to a group of four of the teachers. There were no children in attendance as, like many other institutions, they were closed for *yarsa gumba* season.

Another kilometre up the valley of the Yumchho Khola we approached a small settlement with a dozen or so terraced fields, just turning green. This was a place called Phulak and, much as we had gone 'Beyond the Snow Leopard' north of Samling two years earlier, we now turned uphill and went 'Beyond Himalayan Pilgrimage'. Snellgrove had come down this way from Karang in 1956 but he had travelled no further north. I felt like we were treading new ground, indeed the trail itself was rather faint and sometimes hard to follow. We were aiming for a 'low point' at more than 5100 metres on a long ridge running west to east between the Yambur Danda hills and the Kyala Lek massif. This was the only way across towards our goal.

The climb started and it didn't stop. We had an ascent of over 1200 metres, well over 4000 feet, of relentless uphill walking to gain the pass before dropping down towards the Panzang Valley.

The ascent was unremitting and the last couple of hours was on loose scree with barely a trail. At the pass there was a splendid view of our goal, Danphe Sail, now about 30 kilometres away. I took a couple of panorama shots looking back into Dolpo and ahead into Tibet. This was a remote place. I could see no sign of my companions behind or Wangchhu scouting ahead. I revelled in my splendid isolation for a few moments before stepping into a gap in the overhanging snow ridge and beginning my descent.

I got down first, found Wangchhu, then we had lunch just after 2.00 p.m. at a first campsite. I watched the train of mules come over the pass. When they caught us up Punna suggested we go further on to a *doksa*, where we arrived at 15.40. However, there was absolutely no water. Two of the boys were packed off with a barrel each to go to a stream, almost 2 kilometres away, to cart a heavy load of the essential fluid back to camp.

The others rolled in at 17.00. Michael didn't have to say it this time. The 1200-metre ascent to gain the pass, at well over 5000 metres, was possibly the hardest thing that most of the group had done.

There was still, in that early evening, nothing to drink. To eventual cheers from everyone the pair of porters returned, exhausted by their liquid burden. Quite soon, milky chai was produced along with ginger snap biscuits. Ginger snaps. I hadn't had those for thirty years. What a birthday treat.

Dinner, my birthday dinner, was prepared late in the evening under rather adverse conditions and was a simple fare of vegetable soup, mashed potatoes and curry but rarely can a meal have been so eagerly devoured.

Wangchhu and Chhiring, in a somewhat endearingly hesitant way, came into the mess tent and apologised to me for lack of a birthday cake. However, each gave me a *kata* as compensation and I was more than content. I'd had an extra special and memorable birthday.

41
TO KU AND BEYOND

MONDAY, 23 MAY

Doksa (4448 metres; 14,593 feet)
to Ku (3536 metres; 11,601 feet)
6.8 kilometres

It was a beautiful sunny morning for our coffee and porridge outside. We made a leisurely start, as it was apparently only a couple of hours downhill to the village of Ku. Our trail north gave us a sensational view towards Tibet, and I had a lucid impression of being in a dramatically remote location.

Ian, Alex and Chhiring were 100 metres ahead and had arrived at a *chorten*. This was the Yesi La. As I approached, Ian grinned and said, 'How's that for a breathtaking view?' and what he indicated was a staggeringly beautiful vista. Our destination village of Ku was just over 900 metres directly below us, its houses and fields laid out beneath us as if we were viewing a map. It was surrounded by rocky brown mountains on all sides, and down to our right ran the torrent of the Tara Khola emerging from a deep gash in the earth. Above all this was the vast blue Himalayan sky. Ten kilometres away, back up that pathless and impassable gorge, was Dora Sumdo, where the Panzang and the Nangkong met to form this new river.

Ku consisted of fewer than fifty houses on a triangular piece of cultivated land with its base along the river and its apex up a narrow valley through which a small stream ran. I set off down as quickly as possible and gradually more detail came into view. A long row of large *chortens* had been built alongside the stream at the top end of the village. Across the river, many caves, clearly human-made. The fields were just turning green with barley.

I saw our ponies pull into the area round the main group of *chortens*. There were many people gathered there. I thought it must be a ceremony of some sort. I dropped down and within ten minutes had joined the throng. Wangchhu already had the kettle fired up on a kerosene stove in the shade of a tree. There must have been at least forty people of all ages milling around and staring at us. The women were all dressed in typical Tibetan garb with their striped *chuba* skirts and thick waistcoat-type tops. All the ladies sported beads and earrings of coral and turquoise. There were *dzi* stones aplenty alongside beautiful amulets and brooches. The women's hairstyles were outstanding for virtually all sported their jet-black manes finely plaited into long shiny strands which were then fashioned into smooth, elegant loops down their backs. The children wore a mixture of the traditional Tibetan and modern Chinese clothes; one young fellow in a stripy jumper wished us 'Melcom'. There were few men and we suspected that, once again, the *yarsa gumba* hunt had lured them off the land.

It turned out that hardly any Westerners had passed through here in the last fifty years and there was no ceremony happening, this was just a 'come and look at the weird strangers' gathering.

The locals only spoke Tibetan but a couple of our porters were able to converse with them. As the tents went up and we had some lunch of spaghetti with sausage, chips and fried Spam, the locals thoroughly enjoyed the spectacle.

I took a short walk around the village. It was admirably well laid out with a fine irrigation system, fed by a stream, and immaculate fields some of which had just been planted. There were few animals, just young yaks and a handful of horses. Once again I guessed that the *yarsa gumba* season had taken many of the villagers, with their larger stock, away from home.

Some of the local kids, like youngsters anywhere, were paddling in a muddy pond formed behind a dam near our camp.

That afternoon the atmosphere changed. The sun became less intense and a massive circular rainbow formed around the slightly dimmed orb. This was a '22-degree halo', or 'sun halo', due to a layer of high-altitude ice crystals. This one was the biggest and most distinct I'd ever seen. A sign perhaps of an imminent change in the weather?

I went to the mess tent to read *Into the Silence*. For the hour I was there I was closely observed at all times by a group of locals peering into the entrance of the tent. The wind began to increase and dust was flying everywhere. At 16.00 we had tea of cheese and biscuits and each mouthful was carefully observed by groups of local women and children.

It was time to have a clean-up. I removed the t-shirt I'd worn since leaving Brisbane eighteen days before. Clean t-shirt, underpants and Icebreaker.

Dinner at 18.30 was also observed carefully by the locals.

TUESDAY, 24 MAY

Rest day at Ku

David Snellgrove may not have travelled as far as Ku but he was aware of its existence. In *Four Lamas of Dolpo* he states that the texts he translated refer to 'Inner and Outer Corners' of Dolpo. Yangtsher, being the oldest established monastery in the region, was the centre of the Inner Corner, which included the nearby monasteries of Zhogam and Margom and the five villages of Nyisal, Mo, Karang, Tiling and Ku. The Outer Corner was made up of everything else in the valleys of the Nangkong and the Panzang.

In the biography of the second of the Four Lamas, *Chos-skyabs dpal-bzang*, the 'Religious Protector Glorious and Good', who lived from 1476 to 1565 and established Yangtsher Monastery, Ku gets several mentions. The biography was written in 1534 when the lama was aged fifty-eight. A delegation of villagers from Po, Bhijer and Ku paid their respects to once again beg the lama to visit them at what they called 'the Isle of Gems'. He made the journey and gave teachings and initiations during which he gave a 'general consecration' for Po and Ku. The villagers said to him, 'We are very fortunate when good lamas come duly to see us. We who live in these distant parts and who are getting old cannot come to see you. We beg you, at all costs, to establish a community.'

The third lama, *dPal-ldan blos-gros*, 'Glorious Intellect', lived from 1467 to 1536. When he was sixty-seven, in 1534, he was living at Hrap and became seriously ill. To gain some merit he gave away many things to various lamas and monasteries. To the villagers of Tarap, Panzang, Nangkong, Ku and Bhijer, 'he gave away measures of grain and made general distributions on a large scale'.

It was therefore clear that this small, remote and picturesque village had been established for at least 500 years and I suspected that it had changed very little in that time.

Corneille Jest, on the other hand, did visit Ku as part of his Dolpo *kora* in 1961. He and Karma left Samling and walked to 'Pijor' – Bhijer. From there they went to the distant village of Po, to the north, then heading towards Karang they took the trail to Ku. They reached the summer grazing grounds of Ku, the *doksa* where we'd camped the day before. They then dropped down to the village and inspected the dilapidated temple. Upon leaving Ku Jest described the climb up to the Yesi La, where 'The view is magnificent'.

I had an unusually good sleep and much enjoyed the breakfast of coffee, porridge and Nutella pancake at 8.00 sitting outside on the base of a *chorten*, under the scrutiny of the infinitely curious *kuwa-pa*. One of our early visitors, among the many who came to give us 'the once over', was a fellow who was a teacher at the village school. We were invited to go and inspect the establishment at 10.00.

I wandered into the village. Across the river I spied several people leading horses into the valley which was to be our route north. We wouldn't be alone on the way up to Tibet. The horsemen were apparently some of many *yarsa gumba* hunters who weren't especially welcome in the village. The policemen in Bhijer had been notified and had established a presence in the village. It was said that a hundred people had already gone up the valley on the hunt and all were meant to pay a fee.

All our group went over to the school. It was a single-storey building on a flat piece of ground at the eastern edge of the village. It was made of a few wooden poles and the same rock as the cliffs behind and daubed with mud so it blended in. This was the Tashi Sumdo Primary School. Our young teacher friend, Tsewang Rinzin Choekhortshang, or Rinzin, spoke good English and was proud of what he'd achieved. He was only twenty-two years old and from Ku. His father had sent him to train as a teacher in India, but recently he'd been forced to return as his parents were unwell. The local VDC, Village Development Committee, was the one in Saldang, two days' walk away. They were prepared to fund two teachers, but the villagers had to build the school themselves at their own expense. Rinzin taught English and the other teacher, Pasang, taught Nepali. They were paid 13,000 rupees a month, about A$170. A third teacher was a local lama who taught Tibetan and who was paid by a Buddhist lama based in Malaysia. The VDC did pay a daily allowance of 5 rupees per child, about 20 Aussie cents, to supply a lunch of rice or potato.

Rinzin began his tour of the school in the kitchen. This was a bare room about 2 by 3 metres with a small wood-burning stove in a corner opposite the door. A pile of flat stones was a bench for pots. The walls were rendered smooth with mud and there was no window. A few thin strips of meat were hanging over a rope above the stove drying.

Next door was a similar-sized room where the two teachers lived, ate and slept. A tarpaulin covered the dirt floor and a mattress was in each of the far corners with a rug and other blankets on their beds. There were a couple of small backpacks and some simple drawings on the wall and some nursery rhymes in English.

There were two classrooms, each about 3 by 3 metres. They both had an unglazed, uncovered simple wooden window which was the only light. The dirt floors had a tarpaulin in each room. There were no desks or chairs or benches. The first classroom was adorned with a blackboard and a colourful poster of different types of fruit. The second room also lacked any furniture and possessed a blackboard and a single bright laminated poster entitled 'Good Habits 1'. The teachers were apparently doing some evening classes for the adults to teach basic reading and writing. There was a strong desire among the few hundred inhabitants of Ku to try and improve their lot.

Without too much need for discussion we invited Rinzin for tea at 13.30 to see if we could offer any help for the school.

Sitting outside our mess tent at the end of the row of large *chortens* we had a valuable meeting with Rinzin and about twenty villagers. We asked him directly what he needed and what he would like for his school. It was mainly stationery but he could envisage another classroom and he liked our suggestion of a couple of 'Himalayan stoves'. He said that 50,000 rupees, about A$650, would pay for a new classroom. That was essentially the cost of buying enough wooden poles, for no large trees grew in the vicinity, then transporting them from as far away as Dunai. The villagers would do all the building themselves. We had no hesitation in promising to help as much as we could. The finance would be easy, and Ian was 'our man in Nepal' to liaise with Rinzin.

To round off a perfect rest day we had apple pie and custard after dinner that evening. In the morning we were to enter the eerie and somewhat threatening canyon across the river which was our way north towards the Tibetan border and our goal.

WEDNESDAY, 25 MAY

Ku (3536 metres; 11,601 feet)
to Valley Camp (4166 metres; 13,667 feet)
10.5 kilometres

Through the village, over the narrow wooden bridge across the Tara Khola, past the caves and in less than twenty minutes we were into the gorge. Cliffs towered hundreds of metres above our heads, all carved out over the aeons by the torrent of the Jhyanglung Khola. The huge rock faces either side of us and, sometimes, above us were a warm orange/brown hue. If this massive cleft in the earth had been in Europe or North America it would have been a famous tourist destination and, most likely, a mecca for rock climbers. Today we were the only people in the valley but the distinct trail and well-engineered stepping stones across the water were testament to the fact that, for whatever reason, the local people often came this way.

Scattered about the first hundred metres or so of the gorge the trail was adorned by coarse spiny shrubs bearing a profusion of exquisite, delicate white flowers about 5 centimetres across. The centre of each four-petalled flower was lit up with bright yellow stamens. This was the silky rose, '*Rosa sericea*'. It was a surprising and delightful visual treat in an otherwise barren rocky landscape and a plant that only grows in the Himalaya between 2000 and 4500 metres.

About 1 kilometre up the valley a massive limestone landslip from a cliff high above the right bank had recently poured tens of thousands of tons of rock into the valley. It had initially obstructed the river and the stream now cascaded over and bubbled through the still white boulders.

After about three hours' walking we came to the end of the canyon and identified the valley we required leading east. We were unable to follow the river directly but after an hour of mooching around, Chhiring discovered our way, a high climbing trail which went steeply up about 200 metres then began its traverse high along the valley.

At last we dropped down and passed, surprisingly, several *mani* walls, to an open grassy area next to the river. Clearly this remote valley had some significance. We were now close to the north-leading valley which we had to take to the base of Danphe Sail but from our campsite that evening we were unable to see any of the mountain.

It was tents up then chai and biscuits. There were a few blue sheep around and Alex had spotted some snow leopard scat along the trail. Continuously scanning the hillsides was a forlorn task yet there always remained that glimmer of hope that we might get a surprise sighting of a snow leopard. I was beginning to feel that we were more likely to spot a yeti, but in my heart I would rather see the rare and beautiful snow leopard.

42
BASE CAMP SOJOURN

THURSDAY, 26 MAY

Valley Camp (4166 metres; 13,667 feet)
to Base Camp (5353 metres; 17,562 feet)
8.25 kilometres

It was a cloudy morning and I'd had a remarkable sleep. Perhaps, being at altitude, with the body physically stressed, it is a natural physiological response to require longer and deeper sleep. The inflatable mattress and warm sleeping bag which cocooned me guaranteed many hours of comfortable oblivion.

We left camp at 8.30, embarking on a splendid climb up the narrowing valley. Mid-morning I spotted a faint trail on the other side of the gully and crossed the stream to take it. I soon got higher and well ahead of the others, who'd stayed on the opposite side of the stream.

By midday I found myself on a boulder field several hundred metres across when, with little warning, it began to snow. Within minutes it was a near white-out. I quickly put on some more layers of clothes and my waterproof shell jacket and kept going, carefully and slowly, over the slippery boulders. Wangchhu had been scouting ahead and we met each other on his descent. I saw his bright red jacket materialise out of the wall of white about 20 metres ahead of me. After a few words he carried on down to meet the others and I kept heading upwards. The snow soon stopped but there was now a cold wind. We were close to 5000 metres and the going was necessarily slow with plenty of stops.

The trail climbed up and around a small rock face and I suddenly gained the first sight of Danphe Sail in several days. At the head of the valley opening up before me was a long snow slope, the top of the snow dome that was our mountain. I stopped to eat a snack lunch. Within ten minutes I spotted the mules coming but they were still way below, so I pulled on the backpack and kept on heading up.

Eventually I came to a frozen lake about the same time as Wangchhu caught up to me. It was strangely familiar. Long periods of gazing at this remote spot on Google Earth had made the landmarks well known to me, but now I was there the scale of the venture was apparent. Danphe Sail was huge. The dull cloudy light gave the mountain a flat appearance and it was by no means clear to my hypoxic mind what would be the best way up it. The ridges on the Tibetan border to each side of the mountain looked impossibly daunting.

The mules arrived and the tents started going up. Once the animals had unloaded they went straight back down to where there was grass. I sheltered from the icy breeze behind the kitchen tent. All around was fairly level for about a hundred metres. The ground was rocky with not a single blade of grass. Closer inspection at my feet revealed many small rock plants, mosses and lichens in rather pleasing shades of green, straw yellow and dull red.

The others arrived at camp about forty minutes after me and I was sorry to hear that Chhiring wasn't well: some gut upset. He went straight to his bed. The tents were most welcome and cosy and solid in the increasing wind.

There was little to do except rest. There was coffee and soup about 17.00 then dinner at 18.30. It was sixteen days since we'd left Nepalgunj, and it had been a fabulous but long walk in to our base camp. We'd gained almost 1200 metres in height during this day alone and everyone was justifiably tired, but happy to be close to our destination. We were keen for sleep.

FRIDAY, 27 MAY

This was our first full day at base camp and deemed to be a rest day.

I'd managed a satisfyingly good sleep. Not so the others. Ian said it was his worst night ever, due to breathing problems, but then we were over 5300 metres.

It was, however, a beautiful, clear morning.

Danphe Sail looked slightly less daunting than in the flat dull light of the previous evening. We had breakfast outdoors gazing up at the mountain while shovelling in the porridge. Wangchhu and Ian went scouting, heading off up some lateral moraine to the north-east. They'd been gone less than two hours when we spotted the tiny figure of Wangchhu high on the mountain just below the summit snowfield.

He left a 200-metre coiled rope up there which we would use as a fixed line in the days to come. The pair returned quite quickly and were back in camp before midday.

During the morning Alex, with the help of some of the boys, had built several low piles of stones and strung up some prayer flags on the twentieth anniversary of his wife's death. The flags, of five different colours, fluttered continuously in the ceaseless wind sending their printed sentiments up into the ether on the back of the Lungta (Tibetan: *rLung rta*), the Wind Horse.

Lunch was excellent pakora and potatoes, after which we got all our climbing gear out of the barrels, organised our harnesses and racks and went off, roped, to a small snowfield to practise jumaring and abseiling.

Things were going well so far and a restful afternoon was indulged in. However, the weather once again changed and as the day wore on the wind started getting up and cloud increased. By the time we'd had dinner it had begun to snow.

SATURDAY, 28 MAY

Our second day at base camp

Snow

I was up for coffee at 7.00. There was thick low cloud, seemingly just above our heads, and heavy snow.

Wangchhu and Chhiring set off to fix ropes but within the hour had returned as it was simply not possible to climb.

Over our breakfast porridge we discussed the plan, always evolving, which was to sit tight for twenty-four hours and see what the weather would do.

During the morning the snow gradually stopped and the few centimetres which had lain around the tents quickly disappeared, but the low scudding cloud remained.

I sat in the mess tent reading. It was markedly unusual to be learning of Mallory and Somervell stuck in weather at camp III below Everest North Col in 1922 when I was in a not-dissimilar position in the Himalaya in 2016.

Lunch was sherpa stew, and incredibly good it was too. I had started looking forward to this concoction of Wangchhu's, which was much like a slightly spicy Irish stew with noodles.

In a throwback to Schaller's coffee story, we were now down to our last jar of instant coffee. Alasdair and Michael asked Ramesh for the 'Nescoffee'. They put it into their cups of hot water to find coffee grounds floating on the surface. To keep them happy, the instant being almost finished, Ramesh had added some of our precious ground filter coffee to top up the instant coffee jar.

Supplies in general were getting a little low. There was now only 'mint tea', a bit of 'Nescoffee' and one jar of chocolate powder but afternoon tea came with popcorn, which was a luxurious treat.

Things were otherwise getting desperate. Alasdair, Alex and Michael were reduced to playing cards. At least the weather gradually cleared.

For dinner we were presented with papadums and spaghetti. Ian wasn't happy so he went over to the kitchen tent and got some more sherpa stew. Then, to everyone's surprise, Alasdair announced, 'Guys, I've got something here you might like' and he produced individually wrapped slices of his mother's homemade Christmas cake. It was the real deal complete with marzipan and icing. We were amazed and definitely most appreciative.

By 20.00 the evening was absolutely clear and still. Mars and Jupiter were high in the sky. The constellation of Ursa Major, the Great Bear, was floating just above Danphe Sail. It was certainly going to be an intensely cold night.

SUNDAY, 29 MAY

Day three at base camp and, after the clarity of weather the previous evening, we now woke to more low cloud, gusting cold wind and snow flurries.

One of the kitchen boys, Rajendra, had a headache and was vomiting. He was also sleepy, so I gave him some Diamox and he was sent down with Ramesh to where the mules were, 1000 metres lower down the valley.

Wangchhu and Chhiring left at 6.15 to go fix the rope. We were to get our climbing gear together ready to move up to ABC, which was 150 to 200 metres higher, to bivouac there with a view to an early start upwards next morning.

I was packed and ready to go up when we spotted the pair returning at the top of the lateral moraine about half a kilometre away from camp.

They'd had a tough time of it. The rock was simply covered in thin ice, known as verglas, and unclimbable. Some of the ridges were especially treacherous. Chhiring shook his head and said, 'Very much windy. Too dangerous.' If it was too difficult for them it would be impossible for the rest of us.

We unpacked our gear back into the tents to wait out the day. We had little choice. Tomorrow we'd get the ponies back and begin the journey out.

The afternoon brought a further drop in temperature, well below zero, and an intensely strong, gusty wind was blasting up the valley from the south. The tents stood up to it staunchly but it was clear that this weather pattern was well established and Danphe Sail was off the agenda.

We were looking forward to the evening meal. Chhiring brought it over to the mess tent: more sherpa stew, but then he reappeared and put on the table a mystery dish. Alex investigated. He had a sniff. 'It's beef bourgignon.' Alasdair had again come up trumps and had given Wangchhu a couple of packets of the freeze-dried luxury to boil up. It was superb.

And so to bed knowing we were moving off the hill in the morning.

MONDAY, 30 MAY

Base Camp (5353 metres; 17,562 feet)
to Green Camp (4455 metres; 14,616 feet)
6.7 kilometres

Day four at base camp.

A weird night. I developed the Cheyne-Stokes irregular breathing for the first time on the trip. I'd taken some tablets to try and clear a blocked nose and they contained codeine. It was probably sufficiently strong to affect the pattern of breathing so, not worth it in the end.

That morning there was less wind but it remained cloudy and snowy. Danphe Sail was shrouded by cloud down to below the snow line. It was a good call to start making the move down.

Then suddenly there was a fuss and urgency among the boys. Chhiring was cursing. Wangchhu was missing. Having been told to leave it behind, he had gone up the mountain alone to retrieve the 200 metres of rope he'd deposited three days before just at the snow line. He'd been away since soon after 5.00 and we could now see him, a tiny black dot, against the snow during breaks in the cloud.

Chhiring was donning his climbing gear. He was half angry and half fearful. He said to me, 'He hasn't moved for the last hour.'

We knew Wangchhu had gone up with no extra climbing gear, certainly no crampons or harness. Chhiring borrowed my harness and ice axe to take up to him, then with a couple of the boys started heading upwards.

During lulls in the wind we could hear shouts from Wangchhu but couldn't make out what he was saying.

Ian and Alasdair got into their climbing gear and followed Chhiring up the moraine.

Alex and I got into support mode. I got together the medical and resuscitation kit. We gathered tarpaulins, sleeping bags, hot water and food and just before 10.00 we also started up towards ABC. Michael was to stay at camp awaiting the mules and the pony boys. By now Wangchhu had been in the same spot for almost three hours.

As we gained the top of the moraine, about 10.45, I could see that Chhiring had almost reached Wangchhu. They were 300 or 400 metres above us but for the next half hour there was hardly any movement between the two. At last we could see that they were together. Chhiring had managed to get a rope across to him. The pair spent time getting a climbing harness and crampons onto Wangchhu then together they started rapidly abseiling down.

One of the kitchen boys, Jaya, had stayed high. He'd started up and said to Chhiring, 'That's my cook up there,' but he didn't have crampons and Chhiring told him to wait below the snow. Just before 12.00 the three of them reached us at ABC. Wangchhu was much relieved and visibly upset. Chhiring told me that he'd lost his gloves so I was concerned about his fingers. I examined them. They were cold and white and he couldn't feel them but he was able to move them. We needed to get him down quickly.

We learned what had happened. Wangchhu reached the snow slope he'd been on only a few days earlier but the conditions had changed dramatically. The snow was soft and slippery. It was extremely steep and his crampon-less feet slipped. He lost his footing and went over the edge. He was just able to grab onto a rock which enabled him to halt his fall. He found himself stranded on a thin edge of rock with steep blue ice below and unable to climb back up the steep snow slope above. His gloves were gone. As we emerged from our tents that morning, he was able to shout down and alert us to his dangerous predicament.

At the bleak rocky place that was our ABC, Wangchhu and Chhiring had a hot drink and a snack to eat, then we started down to base camp. A mere half-hour later we had Wangchhu sitting in the mess tent with his hands in a bowl of hot water. When I entered he said, 'Bill, I am so sorry for this trouble.' I said, 'Wangchhu. It's no problem. We are all so pleased that you are safe.' He and I both knew that he'd been incredibly close to death. He said he had only been able to think of his wife and children while he waited, and he had truly believed that he was going to die. His fingers were by now pink but painful. I gave him some strong painkillers. There was a welcome supply of soup ready for everyone before 'the off'.

By now the mules had arrived. It was after 13.00 and everyone was keen to descend. The weather continued cold, grey and snowy.

And so, with mixed feelings, we set off away from our goal. It had seemed so achievable, but it was simply not to be. Within three hours we were at the bottom of the valley setting up camp on a flat verdant area about 1000 metres lower, sipping hot sweet coffee in a warmer temperature with no wind.

Our futile sojourn at Danphe Sail base camp was over.

43
RAPID EXIT

TUESDAY, 31 MAY

Green Camp (4455 metres; 14,616 feet)
to Ku (3536 metres; 11,601 feet)
12.1 kilometres

Today was to be our last day of walking. All we had to do was get back down the gorge to Ku and then arrange a helicopter. I would have liked to carry on and climb up the great ridge out of Ku and trek the two days to Saldang. However, I knew that the rest of the group was not keen to give that a go and it was not something to be done alone so I too would be on the helicopter ride out.

From our camp back to Ku was virtually all downhill and involved traversing the incredible gorge through which we'd ascended. The day was sunny and it was pure pleasure to negotiate my way down the spectacular path just behind our mules. The animals were also happy, as they were by now rested, well fed and could sense the end of their load-carrying endeavours.

Within a few hours I emerged from the shadows of the chasm, next to the caves, and could look directly across the Tara Khola to Ku itself. The mules were already across the stream and the kitchen boys had just arrived. On this occasion we were to set up camp on the green riverbank just below the *gompa*.

The rest of the team rolled in over the next hour, throwing off their day-packs for the final time. We sat on the rocks in the afternoon sun above the river and watched the slow procession of villagers and *yarsa gumba* hunters, with their horses, moving back and forth over the stream.

In the evening we would be having the traditional end-of-trek ceremony whereby our Nepalese friends, who'd looked after us so well, would be given their tips and a share of whatever gear and clothing we no longer wanted. We'd already chipped in a certain number of rupees each and this was divided up by some 'olde tip formula for ye trekking' whereby the guides got more than the porters, with the pony boys and kitchen boys somewhere between. After dinner all the spare gear was laid out on a tarpaulin. It was a fine collection of backpacks, water bottles, umbrellas, socks, a few shirts and a hat or two. Ian had the bright idea of the boys taking cards to determine their turn at picking from the pile. It appealed to their gambling instincts and it was a great success, with Ramesh plucking two backpacks from the heap. Generally everyone was more than satisfied with their prizes and before long the *raksi* was brought out. We were joined by one or two of the people from the village as we raised mugs of the hooch and said our 'thank yous' to our new friends, with whom we'd had such a good time over the previous month.

WEDNESDAY, 1 JUNE

The helicopter arrived about 8.30 after the pilot initially missed us and flew up the wrong valley heading directly for Tibet. We heard him and saw him way off to the west. He'd been unable to find us so turned back and dropped in to Bhijer. There he picked up an old man who showed him the way. The co-opted guide now faced the long walk back over the high pass to Bhijer and demanded 1000 rupees for his trouble. Ian was happy to oblige him.

The helicopter ride was spectacular, as we essentially followed the route by which we had trekked in. We flew over Bhijer, then Samling, Shey and Phoksumdo, the lake looking no less 'Phoksumdo blue' from high up than from lakeside. Then it was straight down the valley to Dunai, where we were to change helicopters for a longer flight to Pokhara.

There was still an issue with the cloudy weather, as we flew insanely close to Dhaulagiri, across the Kali Gandaki Valley and then along the south of the Annapurna massif without once glimpsing any sign of these Himalayan giants. The machine dropped into the airport at Pokhara and we were made acutely aware that we were far from Dolpo and out of the mountains. It was, to my mind, a rather sad moment. When Peter Matthiessen was about to leave Shey he was also saddened, saying, 'Having got here at last, I do not wish to leave the Crystal Mountain. I am in pain about it, truly, so much so that I have to smile, or I might weep.'

The Hotel Family Home would be our base until we had a flight back to Kathmandu. The first stop was lunch at our old hotel on Lakeside, the Hotel Landmark, and that traditional end-of-trek highlight, the first beer. Now it so happened that our companions Alasdair, Alex and Michael had all renounced the demon alcohol for a variety of reasons. Nevertheless, ignoring the exhortations of such exalted beings as W.C. Fields, John Wayne and Sir Les Patterson to 'not trust a man who doesn't drink', Ian and I allowed them to look on as we poured, sipped, relished and thoroughly enjoyed that extra-special post-trek ale.

Some of us went to a local barber in the afternoon for a trim as a prerequisite to rejoining what many think of as 'civilisation' and the evening visit to the Moondance restaurant to reprise the magnificent boar stew. And glorious it was.

Alex and Michael were planning to stay on in Pokhara for a few days to relax and get stuck into some yoga, but next day, Thursday, 2 June, Ian, Alasdair and I had a morning flight to Kathmandu and were back in time for lunch and a good clean-up.

With the Hotel Tibet as a base the following few days were a whirlwind of meetings with people and shopping for books and gifts.

On Friday, 3 June, Ade and his team arrived back at the Hotel Tibet quite early in the morning. Ade was surprised to see us there and we were able to swap notes about the rest of our respective journeys since we'd parted at Shey. K-too restaurant was visited and we caught up with Sarita and her sisters Gita and Sangita. It was special to see Gita as we'd been through the earthquake episode together in Sindhupalchowk a year before.

Alasdair arranged for an earlier flight back to Sydney but not before we'd both added to our *thangka* collections.

Alex and Michael returned from their few days in Pokhara and we once again hit the restaurants of Kathmandu. Michael was by now much less rotund, svelte even, having shed about 10 kilograms. He and Alex thanked me in all sincerity for the pee bottle advice of which they'd initially been so dismissive.

Then it was back to Australia.

*

Once settled at home in Brisbane I could get back online and make contact with various people.

I was able to get in touch via email with Geshe Tsuphu Lama, the Kathmandu-based son of Yangton Lama Sherab Tenzin Rinpoche, the Bon Rinpoche whom we met in Bhijer. He gave me interesting information about Samling, Bhijer and the current state of Bon in Nepal.

My friend the Dolpo Maniwa Rinpoche, Dungse Ogyen Gyaltsen, had been in Saldang, and I was sorry we hadn't managed to get there to meet up with him. However, on his return to Kathmandu, he was able to give me many of the details about the robbery of statues from Shey Gompa a few weeks before our visit.

I was, of course, in touch with Ian. Less than two weeks after my return he and Sarita hosted a dinner in Kathmandu, which was attended by two lamas from Dolpo. They had heard from Shey, just the week before, that one of the four policemen stationed there who we'd befriended had become unwell. A helicopter was dispatched but, in the day or two it took to reach Shey, the young man had succumbed to his illness and died: a testament to the precarious nature of life in Dolpo and a reminder of the fragility of existence in remote places.

Naturally we discussed our plans to get some support for the school at Ku: after all, they had so little. We hoped to help them with supplies and maybe get the Himalayan Stove Project to supply a new cooking range for the children.

By November 2016 the Great Stupa at Boudhanath had undergone its post-earthquake renovation and the new superstructure meant that, once more, the enormous Buddha eyes could gaze benevolently in the four cardinal directions, spreading their message of compassion across the Kathmandu Valley.

Peter Matthiessen also returned to Kathmandu and, to end his account in *The Snow Leopard*, he sought a final meeting with his friend Tukten at the

Great Stupa at Boudhanath. But Tukten Sherpa was not to be found. 'Under the Bodhi Eye I get on my bicycle again and return along grey December roads to Kathmandu' was the final sentence of his journey's narrative.

My own feeling is not that a journey had ended but that I was involved in an apparently endless cycle of travel, of learning, meeting people and, hopefully, spreading the word about what a beautiful, fascinating and sensitive planet we live on. It is, in my view, the fundamental nature of existence and samsara.

It also seems to me that many people who travel to exotic places are somehow searching for something. They seek answers or solutions to their issues. To a large extent I think that Peter Matthiessen was reaching out. Perhaps he thought that a visit to Crystal Mountain would cement his evolving Buddhist nature and provide some certainty of belief. He was the first to admit that was not the outcome. He explained in his zen conclusion about the snow leopard – 'Have you seen the snow leopard? No! Isn't that wonderful?' – when he said:

> If the snow leopard should manifest itself, then I am ready to see the snow leopard. If not, then somehow (and I don't understand the instinct, even now) I am not ready to perceive it, in the same way I am not ready to resolve my koan; and in the not-seeing I am content.
>
> That the snow leopard is, that it is here, that its frosty eyes watch us from the mountainside – that is enough.

Peter Matthiessen said more, when he was musing on the geographical place and the concept of 'Dolpo':

> I like to imagine that this archaic kingdom might be none other than the Kingdom of Sh'ang-Sh'ung that the B'on-pos claim as the home of their religion. That Sh'ang-Sh'ung is deemed 'mythical' may be discounted: the Land of Dolpo is not found in the geographies, and it seems mythical even to such people as myself, who like to imagine they have been here.

I too liked to imagine I had been there.

I knew for certain I would return.

2019

DOLPO, THIRD TIME AROUND

44
THIRD TIME AROUND

6 OCTOBER 2019

Juphal (2475 metres; 8120 feet)
to Dunai at (2160 metres; 7086 feet)
12 kilometres

It was 6 October 2019 and my son George's twenty-ninth birthday. We sat that evening on the verandah at the Blue Sheep hotel in Dunai, and my old friend Chhiring presented George with his birthday cake. Chhiring was guiding us once more around Dolpo and the cake had been made by our cook, Ram Gurung. It was good to be back.

Our group was small. George and I were joined by a couple from England, Peter and Brenda. They weren't a married couple, both having families back in the UK, but were old friends and enjoyed walking and travelling together. They had both turned seventy but had trekked frequently and recently in the Alps. This was their first time in the Himalaya.

Earlier that day we had climbed out of the plane at Juphal and Peter was ecstatic. 'That's the first flight I've ever done with absolutely no descent.' He was a retired British Airways pilot and was most impressed that the newly surfaced runway at Juphal was simply an uphill continuation of the small plane's flightpath all the way from Nepalgunj.

I had naturally warned the group, in no uncertain terms, about the hotel we were to stay in on arrival in the 'Gunj. We pulled up, after sunset, in front of a modern, glitzy, brightly lit, brand new edifice. The large entrance led to a grand staircase. There was an immaculate dining room. The swimming pool was lit up, clear and a perfect blue. 'Well,' said Peter referring to my previous descriptions, 'if this is a shithole I'd like to see the places you normally stay in.' In the intervening years since my other visit the Hotel Siddhartha had been transmogrified, essentially by being rebuilt, into a shining example of modern, prestigious accommodation. I can highly recommend it. However, its extravagant, Gunjian luxuries were only to be enjoyed for a few hours before our early morning, ascent only, plane ride to Juphal.

The walk into Dunai was familiar and surprisingly warm. The road into town now bypassed the *kani chorten* but the bazaar was its usual bustling self and it was good to eventually reach the Blue Sheep hotel at the far end of town and get some refreshment.

We met the rest of our team there. Chhiring had travelled with us from Kathmandu but his nephew, Pimba, was waiting for us in Dunai. I knew Pimba from a winter circuit of Dhaulagiri that I'd done the year before. He was an indefatigable and cheerful young man and I was glad he was with us. We met Ram Gurung, our cook, for the first time when he brought out George's birthday cake. We also had two porters and a father and son team of 'pony boys' who owned and looked after the team of eight mules that would be our main transport. After a bit of discussion, and with Chhiring highly recommending it, we decided that a horse would also be an advantage in case Brenda found the going a bit hard at times. She could always get some respite from the trail but we could all get a little help with some of the river crossings that we knew we would have to confront.

7 OCTOBER

Dunai (2160 metres; 7086 feet)
to Chhepka (2672 metres; 8766 feet)
14.6 kilometres

Our small group left Dunai by walking back through the bazaar then onto the old road so we could admire the antiquated *kani chorten* with its vibrant internal decoration.

My previous trips to Dolpo, in 2014 and 2016, had both started in May and were springtime extravaganzas. David Snellgrove started his first Dolpo journey, via Dunai, in April. Here we were in October and I was reminded that Matthiessen, who was here in the month of October, had written, 'I wonder if anywhere on earth there is a river more beautiful than the upper Suli Gad in early autumn.' As we walked, even up the lower reaches of that river, I had to concur. We had a perfect day and a well-trodden pathway. It was weather for shorts, my well-travelled blue-and-white-hibiscus board shorts. The burned-out bridges of a few years before had been replaced. Some were new modern ones, but some replacements were traditional wooden cantilevered constructions. As we crossed these back and forth over the glacial blue-water torrent, we kicked our way through the newly fallen leaves carpeting the trail. At one point we entered a copse of walnut trees (*Juglans regia*), known locally as *okhar*, the abundant walnuts scattered everywhere across our path.

Eventually we crossed for the last time to the left bank of the river and started climbing up through the cool scented pine forest to our first campsite at Chhepka. About 100 metres before the gentle drop into the village I saw a baby yak stumble off the trail and somersault a few metres down a boulder. I knew the village was literally one minute away so I ran in to get help. By the time I returned a few minutes later with a couple of young villagers the yak had been restored to the trail. Chhiring had simply jumped down, put his shoulder under the young animal and given it a bunk up the steep bank and it hopped up unharmed.

Not such a good result for the young goat which greeted us near our campsite. It lay by its butcher in its bright red dismembered glory next to its drying pelt having just been slaughtered that hour. We had a fresh meat curry for dinner that evening.

8 OCTOBER

Chhepka (2672 metres; 8766 feet)
to Amchi Hospital (3134 metres; 10,282 feet)
13 kilometres

The stroll in the hills continued next morning by merely following the trail along the perfect upper Suli Gad. Peter and Brenda were doing well and enjoying the walk. A leisurely outdoor lunch at Rechi was in glorious sunshine but straight after lunch, this being the mountains, cloud rapidly came over and the initially light rain grew steadily heavier. By the time we passed the Tapriza school it was torrential but we planned to stop at Amchi Hospital. We arrived at the hospital-hotel complex at Chunuwar and were welcomed in out of the rain. 'Would you like some tea?' we were asked. We were shivering and grouped around the fire. The tea which materialised was Tibetan butter tea, which I love. I guzzled down six cups of the stuff and it was a great and warming treat.

Most unexpectedly, at about 4.00 p.m. the sun came out. The tents were put up and our sleeping bags hung out to air. In the pale evening sunlight, on a green and brown cliff about 50 metres behind Chunawar a group of five *bharal*, the blue sheep, put on a performance. They delicately and adeptly moved their way up and across the essentially vertical cliff face. It was mesmerising to watch them, knowing that they wouldn't fall but marvelling at how such a feat was even possible.

9 OCTOBER

Amchi Hospital (3134 metres; 10,282 feet)
to Ringmo (3648 metres; 11,968 feet)
5.2 kilometres

Next morning was bright and sunny as we set off up the gentle slope to the *doksa* of Polam at 3397 metres. There were no nomads in residence, which did bode the question were these traditional over-wintering quarters even in use these days? The whole encampment was seriously overgrown with grass and shrubs.

Just beyond Polam began the long series of zigzags taking us a further 300 metres up to the viewpoint with its pergola. Once again I beheld Nepal's highest waterfall spewing the waters of the lake 167 metres down to the valley floor. A short clamber up to the actual highest point on the trail took us to the small cairn with its hundreds of prayer flags. From there it was the strange transition from a precarious, rocky and exposed scramble into a gently sloping, tree canopied tunnel with soft leaves underfoot leading down the 2 kilometres into Ringmo. We had glimpses of the implausibly blue waters of the lake and George, Peter and Brenda, not having been here before, were suitably impressed. Even more so once we gained our campsite at the lake's edge.

George and I took a walk along the water's margin towards the stream that is the outlet of the lake. A young girl was crouched on a rock doing her washing. Just beyond, a small group of yaks was crossing the stream just before the water became white in the shallow rapids. A mother yak, black with an enormous white bushy tail, was carefully shepherding her two small offspring safely through the water.

We were now well over 3500 metres and were due an acclimatisation day. Next morning we would visit the Thasung Tsholing Gompa a short way around the lake.

10 OCTOBER

The white of the beech trees against the unreal blue of the lake still served to make our spirits soar. The eastern flank of Kanjiroba hovered as a white pyramid above all. Passing the column of crumbling *chortens*, 'the Eleven Lama Dungten', we approached the Bon monastery. As usual it was deserted but as we stood in front of the *gompa* entrance a monk suddenly came across the courtyard to greet us. He was a man in his thirties with a wispy beard and moustache; his dark red robe was layered with a warm orange sweater and an orange down jacket over that. An orange beanie completed the ensemble. This fellow turned out to be the deputy head of the monastery, Lama Lodoe, and more importantly he had the keys! That I could recite the Bon mantra 'Om Matri Muye Sale Du' brought a smile to his face.

David Snellgrove had visited Tsholing Gompa in 1956 and had lengthy talks with the Lama of Kham. Peter Matthiessen was disappointed to find the place locked up when he visited on his way to Shey. On our visit we entered the main community *gompa*, which had been built as recently as 1996. The wall paintings were fresh but the interior was not especially elaborate. Lodoe then asked if we'd like to see the old *gompa*. I was desperately keen as I hadn't been into that building and it was the place Snellgrove had seen. The old temple was right next to the new building. Lodoe opened the door and we stepped down into a dark, square room. To our right was the old altar but most striking was a pair of clearly ancient statues. They were covered in dust and adorned with some old *katas*. On the left was a white plaster ten-armed character with multiple coloured crowns sitting in a cross-legged position. On the right a more grotesque figure made of wood with a demonic face. He had nine pairs of arms, the main pair in front embracing a female *dakini* type of figure in the *yab-yum* position. She had bright orange hair. I was later to find out from a book called *Bon in Nepal* by a Bon lama called Nagru Geshe Gelek Jinpa that these statues were 'holy objects of devotion'. The white plaster statue was a representation of a Bon deity called Kunzang Gyallwa Düpa and the wooden figure 'a very old, powerful statue of Walse Ngampa'.

In the afternoon I led the others through the woods to the east of Ringmo to get the view of the Phoksumdo waterfall from that side. It didn't disappoint and this is one of the best places to see Nepal's finest and highest cascade. On the way back to camp we saw many families out in the fields digging up the potato crop.

Next morning was to be our procession along the Devil's Pathway.

11 OCTOBER

Ringmo (3648 metres; 11,968 feet)
to Phoksumdo Khola (3712 metres; 12,178 feet)
via high point approximately 4000 metres (13,123 feet)
9.1 kilometres

It was another crystal-clear autumnal morning with the temperature just a few degrees below zero. We set off along the ever-precarious narrow trail perched above the lake. George, Peter and Brenda hadn't been this way before and they loved its spectacular course. It's a special and unique kind of walk in the hills.

The view back towards Ringmo from the *chorten* at the high point is one of the highlights of a trek in Dolpo. There was then the tree-lined trail heading on down to the north end of the lake, where it was time for a lunch stop. There were a few nomad tents and many yaks already there.

From the lunch stop to the 'river camp' was only a few kilometres of level walking but could be difficult if the river was high or there had been recent rain. Snellgrove had some difficulty on this leg, but in this autumn fine weather it was pure joy. The feature marking the campsite we were heading for was a large boulder with a small *chorten* on top. Usually it was hidden until you were right on top of it. On this visit it could be seen from at least 1 kilometre away, as many of the shrubs and trees around it had been cleared. The blazing fire we had overnight may suggest one explanation for the gradual clearance.

Sitting outside the mess tent having afternoon tea we were quite suddenly passed by a dozen large yaks, bells tinkling and much snorting. Each was burdened by a pair of massive logs, twice as long as the animal itself, carefully balanced so as not to trail on the ground. Some of the logs had been dressed squarely into beams for houses but many were still round and covered in bark. Four more magnificent shaggy beasts went by a few minutes later, these carrying bundles of much shorter wooden poles. Where, we wondered, were these destined? Surely not Shey.

12 OCTOBER

Phoksumdo Khola (3712 metres; 12,178 feet)
to High Camp (4700 metres; 15,419 feet)
8.2 kilometres

It was –1°C in the tent in the morning but brilliant clear sunshine outside. The fire from last night was still smouldering and the layer of cold air near the ground was trapping the smoke. The pristine white glaciers of the Kanjiroba massif towered over us but we'd seen no avalanches as yet.

Less than an hour up the valley and we came to the sharp right-hand turn into the dark canyon of the Tuk Kyaksa Khola. This was the cataract that our group had climbed up in 2014 and I now knew to be the traditional way to the Kang La. It was a strenuous clamber back and forth among the waterfalls before emerging, a couple of hours later, into a widening valley above the tree line. The train of yaks with the massive beams passed us as we had a snack lunch. We plodded on as we were gaining 1000 metres in this single day. This went against all the current advice about daily height gains while acclimatising but there was no other way to gain the Kang La and access to Shey. It is certainly the case that many trekkers run into trouble on this leg of the trek. On this particular day we were all in fine fettle, George and I feeling great, Peter and Brenda going only marginally slower, also feeling good. All of us exhausted but happy.

Camp was established and at the head of the valley we could see the yak train making its ponderous way up past the waterfall cliff and on towards Matthiessen's 'Snowfields camp'. It was sherpa stew that evening and time to break out the down jacket.

13 OCTOBER

High Camp (4700 metres; 15,419 feet)
to Shey Gompa (4388 metres; 14,396 feet)
via Kang La at (5360 metres; 17,585 feet)
9.4 kilometres

It was a frigid morning at this height but we had another 600 metres to climb to get over the Kang La. We soon gained the cliff but the waterfall was dry at this time of year. I wondered if the cliff was the site of Matthiessen's 'Cave camp'. Beyond the rock wall the valley opened up in an easterly direction but was almost completely free of snow. On my 2014 visit, in the spring, it truly was a massive snowfield.

The loose trail was a gradual wend up to the ridge but was fairly easy-going with the short steps and frequent stops. The cairn at the 'summit' of the Kang La only came into view about 100 metres before reaching it. Then, there we were. Short of breath. Prayer flags flapping noisily in the stiff breeze. The snow cornice before us and the view right into Tibet, a mere 30 kilometres away. Danphe Sail stood magnificently Matterhorn-like on the horizon. We had climbed up 1600 metres from the Phoksumdo Khola in a little over twenty-four hours and it was time to head down.

The permanent snow on the north side of the pass is treacherous underfoot but the thin icy trail zigzagged down to a path free of snow several hundred metres below the cairn. All that remained was the steady downhill trail past the Black Pond, along the valley of the Hubalung Khola to Shel Sumdo and the tranquillity of Shey Gompa. We arrived soon after two in the afternoon at that oasis of peace in a tumultuous world, looked over by Shel Ri, the Crystal Mountain.

45
LAMA STEPS

14 OCTOBER

Lama Karma Tsondru Rinpoche was just leaving his house behind the main *gompa* at Shey. My old friend was heading off to lead an Italian freelance film-maker up to Tsakhang Gompa and he didn't mind if we followed. He'd taken one look at me then George and his face broke into a large grin. He pointed to me, then back to George and nodded, letting us know that he recognised that we were father and son. He seemed quite amused at his own astuteness.

We went over to our campsite to collect Peter and Brenda and with Chhiring we set off to catch up the lama. There was no denying that over the preceding few years he'd gained substantial extra weight and the poor fellow's knees were suffering. We caught up with him resting at the second significant landmark on the climb up to Tsakhang, the rock with the marks left by the knees and forehead of Drutob Senge Yeshe. We chatted to the Italian photographer then set off with the lama and her at the Rinpoche's pace. I was instantly reminded that on my previous excursion with Lama Tsondru I'd taken his slow, tiny-stepped gait as an example and now he was even slower. Yet here he was still climbing up to this remote monastery. I promised myself that in future, whenever I found the going tough, I would force myself to simply take 'lama steps' – short, unhurried footsteps with a breath between each – and frequent stops and that would get me as far and as high as I would ever need, just like the lama.

We passed the remaining rocky landmarks on the ascent to reach the Rigsum Gompo La, the Pass of the Three Protectors, with its unobstructed vista directly across to the buildings of Tsakhang sitting flush in the massive cliff face opposite.

This was my third visit to this *gompa* and it was easy to simply enjoy the peace and tranquillity of this picturesque site under the gaze of the Crystal Mountain. We left Karma Tsondru in the temple room of the *gompa*, where he was performing a *puja* to be filmed for Italian television. We made our way back to camp for tea.

Later that afternoon, as we were waiting for dinner, Karma Tsondru came over to our campsite for a chat. Chhiring was able to translate for us. The lama's knees were giving him terrible trouble. Did we have any medicine to help? I gave him a box of paracetamol and recommended he take a regular dose for the next three days to see if the pain eased. We carried on a pleasant conversation about life at Shey. How was young Dorje doing at school and was his father in Shey? The lama's face changed and he became intensely serious. Phurpa Tinley, the young lama who was Dorje's father, had been killed in an avalanche in March about seven months before. Dorje was now at school in Bhijer. That was devastating news. Once again the fragility of life in the Himalaya was confirmed. Om Mani Padme Hum.

TUESDAY, 15 OCTOBER

Shey Gompa (4388 metres; 14,396 feet)
to Tora (4672 metres; 15,328 feet)
via pass at 4870 metres (15,977 feet)
11.2 kilometres

It was another perfect day as we set off directly uphill from our campsite. The marmots squeaked as we plodded past their burrows. I found I was having to invoke my 'lama steps' approach to trekking right away as the going seemed especially hard. After half an hour of struggle I sat down and ate some chocolate and drank half a litre of water. Within ten minutes I was back to normal. This was one of many times that, having 'hit the wall', the clear answer is to hydrate and get some energy supply into the system. The body's demands are great at altitude and the margin between 'well' and 'no good' is dangerously slim.

Chhiring came trotting up on the horse. He'd been chatting to Karma Tsondru and now rejoined the group. He handed over our horse to Brenda who was also feeling the altitude and appreciated a break from walking. It was a long level trail across moorland at 4500 metres with views across to Crystal Mountain before the steady drop down to a yak pasture. Suddenly we were being overtaken in a narrow gully by dozens of yaks. We tried to move to one side but they streamed around us. We heard whistling and right next to us was a young woman we instantly named 'Yak Girl'. She was probably in her twenties, slim, jet-black hair and an enormous smile showing off a gold capped upper incisor. She spoke no English but chatted away to us in her own tongue in an obviously friendly way. She wore a full-length dress of a thick charcoal grey material with multicoloured trim, a *chuba* over that and tied at the waist with a blue cloth. Over her shoulders she sported a well-worn fleece jacket in a plum colour. She was on a mission to get her yaks moving. In her right hand was a thick wooden pole almost as high as her shoulder. She waved this around over her head and whistled and made loud 'whooping' noises. The beasts got the message and kept moving at high speed. She crossed the bottom of the gully and started up the opposite bank towards a grassy upland then she and her fifty or so yaks were gone.

We had a lunch in that valley then started up towards a cairn on a minor pass above us. Once there I had a look around. In the spring season of more than three years before a pair of animal trails had crossed at right angles near this cairn. At that time there was clear evidence of snow leopard activity, with piles of scat, from the grey, crumbly and dry to the clearly fresh. There had obviously been animals there from a day or two to several weeks before. On this occasion, in the autumn, there were no signs of animal comings and goings. I couldn't even detect the trails.

From this cairn at the low pass we had a long traverse of almost 2 kilometres across loose scree towards Bhijer. The land fell away at a steep angle to our left, plummeting dramatically down to the Tartan Khola over 1000 metres below us. As soon as we started on the lofty trail we saw travellers coming towards us from the direction of Bhijer. A herd of magnificent yaks went by us on either side of the narrow track. At the end of the long traverse stood a *chorten* and we were a mere few hundred metres from it when a group of Western trekkers came our way. It was led by my friend Jamie MacGuinness, a well-known climber and owner of Project Himalaya Treks. I had known he was in Dolpo, but the odds of meeting on the trail were extremely slim. Yet here we were. It was great to see him. We swapped travel tales. He had planned to drop in to Ku but couldn't fit it in this trip. We were both having enjoyable and healthy journeys and looked forward to that next beer at Sam's. Then, ships in the night, we were on our separate ways again.

A few minutes further on we were at the *chorten*, and we could see down to the *doksa* at Tora on the other side of the valley of the Yangu Khola. It was about 2 kilometres to finish off a long trekking day, all of which was well over 4000 metres. Refreshment was most welcome.

46
BHIJER AND BEYOND

16 OCTOBER

Tora (4672 metres; 15,328 feet)
to Bhijer (3846 metres; 12,618 feet)
via Tra La pass at 4800 metres (15,748 feet)
5 kilometres

We chose the short route to Bhijer. About 1 kilometre up to the Tra La, the pass just above us at 4550 metres, then a long steep march of 4 kilometres down to Bhijer at 3846 metres, so dropping over 700 metres.

Our campsite in Bhijer was at the eastern end of the village between a row of ancient *chortens* and the briskly flowing stream of the Yamchho Khola. As soon as we'd settled in, I was keen to visit the Buddhist Nesar Gompa at the other end of the village.

George and I wandered down through this delightful and ancient settlement. Upon entering the grounds of the small *gompa* we met three older men sitting outside the temple entrance. We said '*Namaste*,' but it was clear they spoke no English. I was wondering if there would be a doctor in residence at the adjacent clinic, the Kunphen Shogtso Menkhang. We were greeted by a tiny woman in her thirties dressed in traditional Tibetan garb. She had a pleasant round face with a large, seemingly permanent, smile. Her English was excellent and she introduced herself as Tsewang 'Dolpotsang' Gurung. She was trained as an *amchi* and spending six months in Bhijer. She told me that there was no doctor in residence but the daughter of the head lama was a nurse, trained in Western medicine and midwifery. She was out attending a birth in a village up the valley. We had a look around Tsewang's traditional dispensary and we had a good conversation about the overlap between old and new methods in medicine. We both agreed that caring and compassion were massive aspects of our jobs.

Since my previous visit in 2016 I'd learned much about this remote enclave of Buddhism, Nesar Monastery in Bhijer on the border with Tibet. Way back in June 1978 an American called Tom Pritzker, along with his wife and a friend, travelled for 700 kilometres through western Nepal, their object being to explore the region known as Dolpo. Matthiessen had been there five years before but *The Snow Leopard* hadn't yet been published. Pritzker and co. were relying on the writings of David Snellgrove and advice from a Kathmandu-based friend called Ted Worcester, a Tibetologist, who had visited Dolpo. They reached Samling but were warned against the hostile villagers of Bhijer and so never visited. Many years later Tom and his wife, Margot, had a family of three sons and Tom was keen to show them the part of the Himalaya he was so enamoured with. The family of five travelled with a couple from Switzerland called Chino and Elizabeth Roncoroni and a Nancy Jo Johnson. In 1999, when they made their next trip into Dolpo, Tom noticed fewer young people in the villages, smaller yak trains and, even then, to his eye, smaller glaciers. Having reached Samling they were keen to see Bhijer. They dropped in to Nesar Gompa and realised its antiquity. They were keen to hire a horse in Bhijer to help the final stage of their journey and were taken to the house of the head lama, Lama Tenzin. He verified the age of the monastery and agreed to rent them his horse. As was usual, he would accompany them so he could return with his horse. A week later, over dinner, Lama Tenzin said that he realised that these visitors had a special interest in and respect for Tibetan culture. Would they be interested in a library of old manuscripts in Nesar Gompa which had been sealed up by a wall just behind the altar? He was prepared to break down the wall to let them study the documents. One year later Chino Roncoroni organised an expedition to return to Bhijer and record the find. When the wall was broken down everyone was amazed. Six hundred and forty-two ancient Tibetan manuscripts, each with 500 to 600 pages, were recovered, and restoration and translation undertaken. Of the 320,000 manuscript pages 150 were illuminated leaves. The discovery of the manuscripts and their contents is documented in the book *Hidden Treasures of the Himalayas: Tibetan Manuscripts, Paintings and Sculptures of Dolpo* by Amy Heller, who spent ten years working on the discovery. This lavish book reveals the splendour of the thousands of pages of handwritten and illustrated leaves. The direct comparison to European medieval illuminated manuscripts is easy to make given the beauty and complexity of the artwork but rather than the ecclesiastical Christian portraits we can see the whole pantheon of Buddhist theology and symbology in brilliant colour. There are hundreds of depictions of Sakyamuni Buddha, Avalokiteshvara, Tara, demons, *dakinis*, the eight auspicious symbols, monks, farmers, archers, elephants, horses, characters without end. While carbon dating has shown the wood of the pillars inside the temple dates from the late eleventh or early twelfth century, the documents themselves range from the late eleventh to the sixteenth century.

Knowing all this I was keen to have a better look inside the *gompa* than Alasdair and I had managed three years earlier. Tsewang took us to the temple entrance, and it so happened that one of the three men we'd spoken to on the way in was Lama Tenzin Gyaltsen himself. He was a fit-looking man with a swarthy complexion. His hair was still completely black, tied back in a ponytail, and he sported a gold upper incisor. His loose-fitting red pants and yellow shirt completed his piratical look. He was extremely friendly and welcoming. Tsewang translated for us and the lama was more than willing to show us inside the *gompa*. This time we had lights and I could see the 'fine gilt image of Maitreya', as described by Snellgrove, a 130-centimetre-high clay figure, sitting on a 21-centimetre-high lotus base, glinting in the light. Behind the statue were the hundreds of manuscripts on their shelves, to above head height. Both statue and library were now secured within an iron bar cage but there was a gate to the right so the books could be easily accessed. Tenzin already had one of the loose-leaf books out so we could see it, and he read from it in the classic chanting way.

We had just returned to our camp for a spot of tea when I saw my friend Rinzin walking past. 'Hey, Rinzin!' I called out. 'Come and have some tea.' Tsewang Rinzin Choekhortshang was the young teacher who had welcomed us to Ku and its school three years before. We had managed to stay in touch when he was in Kathmandu and it transpired he was now working at the school in Bhijer. We had a good chat, but he was off to see his mother and soon had to leave.

17 OCTOBER

Bhijer (3846 metres; 12,618 feet) to lake camp below pass at 5080 metres (16,666 feet) via the cheese factory at 4200 metres (13,780 feet)

Next morning, as we were breaking camp, we were visited by Tashi Bhuti, Lama Tenzin Gyaltsen's daughter, who was working hard in Bhijer as a nurse and had just returned from attending the delivery of a baby.

We started our trek that day by following the Yamchho Khola upstream and soon came to the Shree Mukporong Himal Primary School. This was where Rinzin was currently working, and he gave us a wave as we passed. The children in their blue uniforms were all outside playing and it sounded like any playground across the world. The school had been started in 1971 but in 2005 had received much help from the Pritzkin and Roncoroni families. This was at the same time as they sponsored the documentation of the Nesar manuscripts and the building of the Kunphen Shogtso Menkhang clinic.

After half an hour we passed through the *kani chorten* at the edge of Bhijer. It was a busy morning on the trail. Several groups of locals passed us on their horses, always with a '*Tashi delek*'. It was harvest time and a man went by laden with a vast pile of cut straw held onto his back by his forehead strap. After an hour or so we saw a cloud of dust on the trail rapidly approaching us. We didn't have long to wait before a herd of almost 200 goats came storming down the trail directly at us. No more than 20 metres before they were about to run into us, they veered to our right and leapt, lemming-like, in a great curtain of fine powder, over a low wall and into a recently harvested field.

A stunningly beautiful Dolpo woman on a horse passed us going down towards Bhijer. She smiled and asked, in the most impeccable English, 'Are you visiting my brother at the cheese factory?' We promised that we would, fully expecting some ancient shed. Within a short time the magnificence of the Mukporong Himal Yak Cheese dairy farm revealed itself. A recently, and well, constructed wooden beam and stone building with a bright red metal roof and verandah round two sides, it was situated at a place called Phalang, at an altitude of 4200 metres, 500 metres above Bhijer. It had been built in 2016 with the financial support of the Roncoroni and Pritzken families and began producing the yak cheese, more correctly *nak* cheese, in 2017.

We were greeted by a young man called Yeshe Gurung, who ran the dairy. He had been trained by cheesemakers from Switzerland. He asked us to don apron, boots, mask and hat before entering the building. During the tour Yeshe explained how the milk was sourced from local farmers, up to 200 litres a day during the short season. The milk was tested then heated and the culture added. The cheese was poured into moulds lined with a stencil to imprint 'Upper Dolpo' around the rim of the cheese. The wheel of cheese was then rubbed with salt and left to mature for at least three months. Most of the product was prepurchased by some exclusive hotel restaurant outlets in Kathmandu. That entailed, for the cheese, a four-day journey on the back of a mule then a three-day truck ride to Kathmandu.

'Surreal' is the only word to describe this experience of observing a traditional process done so well in a modern facility in such a remote location. The proof of the pudding is, of course, in the eating. We bought half a wheel of the yellow-rinded cheese and divided it into three. For the next week, George, Peter and I carried a great wedge of cheese each in our backpacks to have the occasional bite from during the day or when arriving in camp. It was marvellous. Creamy and firm, with a slight salty tang. It is now without doubt my favourite cheese in the world.

The trail continued ever upwards, with the mountains either side of the Neng La pass ahead of us gaining more prominence. Behind us the red roof of the dairy became ever tinier and the fringe of Bhijer seemed impossibly far below. The trail passed between two massive crags then into a wider valley. At last, one of our porters was coming our way with a flask of hot lemon to get us the last kilometre in to camp. We reached a pair of huts with a small lake below the unnamed, distinctly pointy rocky summit standing at 5770 metres at the western end of the Nangla Lek. An extra-friendly dog had followed us all the way from Bhijer and he was happy to hang around camp to get our scraps.

We'd climbed up 1230 metres in one day over a distance of 7.5 kilometres, but we were acclimatised and now we had cheese.

47
ONCE MORE UP THE PANZANG

FRIDAY, 18 OCTOBER

Lake camp below pass at 5080 metres (16,666 feet)
to Saldang (3770 metres; 12,368 feet)
via Neng La at 5368 metres (17,660 feet)
10 kilometres

We woke to find a white world of snow. Several centimetres had settled overnight and a steady fall continued. George was thrilled. He'd seen the white stuff but had never felt the pure joy of standing in gently falling snowflakes. Of our canine friend there was no sign.

After packing up and breakfast we had a steady ascent of 300 metres over a distance of less than 2 kilometres to gain the pass, the Neng La at 5368 metres (17,612 feet). There were white-out conditions at the pass, the hundreds of prayer flags noisily flapping to destruction in the wind. We quickly dropped into the shelter of the valley below. Snellgrove had passed this way, but travelling in the opposite direction to us, as he travelled from Saldang on his way to Samling Monastery in 1956. We were now heading down to Saldang through knee-deep snow. Brenda wisely chose to ride the horse down most of the way.

After a couple of hours the valley floor levelled out and the snow ceased. We were walking on a gently undulating high-altitude moorland as we approached the scattered houses of upper Saldang. To our left I could see the house of the now departed Thinle Lhondup which I'd visited in 2014. We marched on down into the centre of Saldang to a campsite next to the village school. There, enjoying afternoon tea, we observed a group of half a dozen villagers threshing the newly harvested barley with medieval-looking flails, two sticks joined by a leather strap. The people sang in harmony as they got into a united rhythm and pummelled the grain. Peter couldn't resist and went down to join in, and they were happy to let him have a go.

SATURDAY, 19 OCTOBER

Saldang (3770 metres; 12,368 feet)
to Khomas (4060 metres; 13,320 feet)
9.4 kilometres

We had been hearing rumours of a road running from Saldang to Khomas. I couldn't imagine why there would be, but we planned to take the old established trail anyway. Walking down from our campsite in Saldang took us past a building where there was a pile of square-cut beams. These were the very beams that had passed us on the backs of the yaks at the river camp above Phoksumdo Lake. We had last seen them as they were heading up towards the Kang La as we settled into our high camp.

A bit further on and we passed the Saldang Gompa, the Samye Choling Monastery, and dropped down to the bridge across the Nagon Khola. A series of gentle zigzags up the other side gave us the full view back to Saldang, which is a widely scattered settlement throughout the length and height of the valley.

The trail continued east on a day with high cloud and above freezing temperatures. We passed a couple of large herds of goats being looked after, as seemed common, by young girls about ten years of age.

There was a rocky pass at our high point with a bit of a clamber up, but this was a pleasurable day of trekking. After only four hours we were looking down on Khomas, where there was a bright red new metal roof on the *gompa* and a bright blue one on the school. We were to camp near some *chortens* next to the school. Khomas was a pleasant place. Plenty of children came to check us out and the adjacent fields were full of people with scythes harvesting and groups of Dolpo-pa threshing, all the while singing.

There was one other group of travellers from Europe, who were spending a few days in Khomas doing some charitable work. All in all it was quite a busy place.

On the afternoon of our arrival there was to be a welcome by the locals for the charity work team. There would be music and dancing in the grounds of the school. About 3.00 p.m. we joined the small crowd.

A man in traditional costume played the *dramyin*, a Tibetan guitar with, usually, six strings. He wore a white wool hat over hair braided with a red tasselled headband. His white silk embroidered jacket had red sleeves and over that was a plum-coloured overcoat, right arm out, with the sleeve hanging behind him. His high boots were of multicoloured felt with woven feet and soles. The women of the village were equally spectacular. They wore their best patterned *chubas*, the Tibetan wrap-around skirts. Over that, they wore a geometric-patterned apron in bright colours then over the whole ensemble, around their shoulders, a square folded blanket held at the front by a large silver clasp. The clasps were about 30 centimetres across and resembled the traditional *dorje* symbol. In the centre was a large bead of turquoise with a pink coral sphere to each side. All the ladies had shiny black hair tied back. They all sported their best earrings and necklaces, a fine display of silver, turquoise, coral and *dzi* stones. The half-dozen women held hands in a large circle with the many girls of the village and swayed and rotated the ring as they sang their chants. There were bells and gentle drums. Young boys ran around misbehaving simply because they could. It was a most pleasant colourful entertainment.

The evening was peaceful as we settled into our sleeping bags. Then the cats started mewing. Inevitably the dogs were barking. There were even cows mooing. Then there were raised voices from the charity workers' camp about 50 metres away. The argument became full blown. The shouting became screaming. It went on for half an hour or so, seemed to reach a climax, then there was a sudden silence.

SUNDAY, 20 OCTOBER

Khomas (4060 metres; 13,320 feet)
to Shimen (3876 metres; 12,716 feet)
8.6 kilometres

The morning in Khomas was overcast, so not particularly cold. All was quiet in the other camp. As we walked by, one of the European contingent explained that one of their kitchen boys had got drunk and aggressive. The protracted argy-bargy had been solved by judicious use of one of the chairs from their mess tent. The chair was now wrecked and I couldn't resist looking in on the tent, where there was a whimpering creature now feeling sorry for himself with a sore head and clearly much pain elsewhere.

Our day's walk, like the previous day, was exceptionally pleasant high-altitude trekking. No serious ascent or descent. More herds of well-fed goats until, after about 6 kilometres, we stood at the minor pass of the Shimen La at 4270 metres (14,010 feet) looking down into the Panzang Valley and the village of Shimen. Its abundant trees, mainly willows, so admired by Snellgrove, were still a bright green this late in the year. We dropped down and crossed the river by a narrow bridge, then we were in the village proper. There is a small *gompa* and many *chortens* above the village where the valley drops down from the Mu La and the stream joins the Panzang. Here, among the cluster of houses, were four or five motorbikes! I was astonished. This was different from my previous visit five years before.

We camped at the southern edge of the village in a dusty field. From Shimen all we had to do was trek south all the way to the Kali Gandaki.

MONDAY, 21 OCTOBER

Shimen (3876 metres; 12,716 feet)
to Tinje (4153 metres; 13,625 feet)
14 kilometres

Leaving Shimen next morning was an easy stroll along the Panzang past the purported 'longest *mani* wall in the world'. I was searching my memory trying to remember if the trail was this level and wide on my previous walk. After less than 2 kilometres the answer was revealed. It was clear that the old trail had been wiped out and there was now a grey gravel roadway wide enough to take a truck. There was no traffic on this new road but it stretched as far as the eye could see down the valley, replacing the old trail. Where the Panzang flowed through a narrow gorge we had to bear left and climb up to the level alp of Mendo. Of nomads and their goats there was no sign at this time of year. The pasture was deserted and the gash in the earth that was the new road skirted around the border of the grassland. As we walked across this pleasant idyll, deep in the valley, the peace was disturbed by the coughing sound of a struggling motorbike, which slowly overtook us, also on its way south.

A little further on we approached the Bon Pu Gompa on the opposite bank. The road stretched ahead on our side of the river, clearly extending the full length of the valley. The new gouge in the land necessarily had to follow the contours of the mountainsides and in places I could see the old trail, clearly becoming more overgrown, many metres to one side. There was little movement on the new road, but we were passed by a dozen yaks heading in the opposite direction each carrying a pair of huge wooden beams heading up to Shimen or beyond.

Late morning had us arriving at the collection of *chortens* that overlooked the village of Phalma. We sheltered from the wind among the crumbling monuments and over hot lemon juice I once again relished the view down the valley to the sacred mountain, Kula (6060 metres; 19,881 feet).

Another few kilometres and we strolled into Tinje where camp was being set up in the grounds of a house in the centre of the village. Just across the way a group of nomads had set up their tent. Not a traditional yak one but a large canvas edifice. Inside there was bedding along each side of the tent and boxes of Chinese beer were stacked at the back. A centrally placed iron stove made it especially cosy. We were welcomed in for tea and met the sisters running the show. Ram had arranged for us to eat our meals in the tent, and over dinner the elder sister started negotiations with me to set up the younger one with George. Apparently they would be more than happy to have George marry the younger sister, stay for six months then get back to Australia for the rest of the year! It was excellent banter and we had a fun evening. We never did agree on the price of the dowry.

TUESDAY, 22 OCTOBER

Tinje (4153 metres; 13,625 feet)
to Rapka (4508 metres; 14,790 feet)
17 kilometres

Next morning was –7°C in the tent as we said goodbye to George's prospective bride. Passing through Tinje we could see the large ancient tower that is one of the few remaining frontier forts.

We went through the *kani chorten* on the bridge to the south of town and it was a short clamber up to the level part of the valley where the old CIA airstrip was located. The new manufactured trail went round the edge of this strange spot, but much other development was going on and I couldn't see any of the old stone markers at the end of the grassy runway.

The valley opened out as we progressed, leaving Kula to our left, and apart from a couple of river crossings the day was uneventful and pleasant. We kept walking up the valley of the Kehein Khola. A good campsite with plenty of water also provided enough firewood for a welcome night-time campfire under a star-studded canopy.

WEDNESDAY, 23 OCTOBER

Rapka (4508 metres; 14,790 feet)
to Lake Camp (4929 metres; 16,171 feet)
11.9 kilometres

A bright, intensely cold day. It was –9°C in my tent when I woke.

The valley led to a place where the river was wide and the water partially frozen. I managed to find a place to cross without falling in. The road, still recently excavated, carried on up the valley of the Lakhyan Khola, but bridges and fords were not part of the current road-making scheme. We ended up at the edge of a fast and treacherous-looking river. Some of the porters were game to wade across, but I had no qualms about jumping on our trusty horse and being ferried across. Another couple of less threatening river crossings later and I recognised where the Mo La was at the end of the valley. The new trail wended its way towards that point, but we decided to camp at a small lake about 1 kilometre short of the pass where the mules could eat and be watered and we had some shelter from the chill wind at about 4900 metres. Directly across the lake and towering over all was the jagged 5745-metre-high point of a range called the Dhakraltyo Lek, which I knew to be pre-eminent when looking back from Tsharka.

THURSDAY, 24 OCTOBER

Lake Camp (4929 metres; 16,171 feet)
to Tsharka (4321 metres; 14,176 feet)
11.8 kilometres

From our lakeside campsite it was a gentle walk up that final kilometre, along the grey dust and stones of the newly excavated roadway, to the cairn at the top of the Mo La at 5030 metres (16,502 feet). It was a calm day with good visibility and looking down towards Tsharka it was clear that the old, direct, up-and-down trail through many gulleys had been superseded by the long back and forth sweeping curves of the contour-hugging roadway. I hurried down the easy walkway of the new thoroughfare eager to reach one of my favourite places in Dolpo. On the edge of Tsharka the road had been carved appallingly close to the *kani chorten* and several older *chortens* in what could easily be construed as deliberate disrespect. Even more galling was the huge, bright yellow, caterpillar-tracked excavator parked incongruously next to the ancient and crumbling artefacts.

Once into Tsharka I made my way through the old buildings and across a bridge and straight to the Karnali Hotel. I was greeted by the matriarch, who recognised me or perhaps the *dzi* stone I was wearing that she'd sold me three years before. Her daughter Tsewang Wangmo had just finished teaching for the day and we had a good catch-up over some masala tea. Tsewang was now married and had a daughter of her own who was almost three. I asked Tsewang about the new road. What did the locals think? 'They have mixed feelings,' she replied. 'It is good and bad!'

In the enclosure next to our campsite was a herd of around a hundred goats and it was milking time. In the traditional way, two rows of the long-horned shaggy goats were tethered head-to-head with a length of rope woven between the horns. Thus immobilised the family went around with a pail and did the milking.

That evening we ate in our friend's hotel and drank plenty of freshly prepared yak butter tea in the warm smoky atmosphere of the Tibetan living room. Luxury!

FRIDAY, 25 OCTOBER

Tsharka (4321 metres; 14,176 feet)
to Kharka (4932 metres; 16,181 feet)
20.2 kilometres

We left Tsharka early, waving goodbye to Tsewang and her daughter as we passed their house. We had far to walk on this day. The road seemed particularly intrusive on this south side of the village and was extremely close to the houses.

Within a few kilometres we reached the place called Naljyang Sumna, where the trail dropped steeply to a long suspension bridge over the Tsharka Tulsi Khola with a daunting scramble up the other side. Our plan was to follow the next stream, the Thasan Khola, as it led inexorably, steadily south and upwards towards our highest pass. We had a couple more river crossings, which always add that element of adventure. The horse yet again proved invaluable. We were hoping to reach a place called Malum Sumna but the day was proving short and, as the sun got lower, then slipped behind the mountains, it grew intensely cold. As the light was fading we called a halt and got the tents up. Everyone was happy to get into sleeping bags and have food in our tents. As the last glimmer of light was leaving we heard voices and a party of five young women went by. They had become separated from one of their group and she was somewhere behind with their cook. We had a chat. They were from Denmark, I believe. Their plan was to get across to Hidden Valley then down to the Dhaulagiri base camp. I tried to persuade them to camp where they were, as it was so late, but they seemed intent on reaching what little shelter there was at Malum Sumna. It was pitch black as they set off under the light of their head torches. It was too cold for us to linger out in the open and our group was all wrapped up in our tents and heading off to sleep at the end of a protracted day, where we had walked over 20 kilometres – and there was no more yak cheese.

SATURDAY, 26 OCTOBER

Kharka (4932 metres; 16,181 feet)
to Juniper camp (4245 metres; 13,927 feet)
via the Jungben La (5561 metres; 18,244 feet)
13.5 kilometres

After an uncomfortable disturbed sleep because of the cold, we woke with the valley still in shadow. It was –11°C inside my tent. George and I downed a quick cup of hot tea before setting off ahead of the others in search of the sun, which we could see shining into the valley about 1 kilometre upstream. A few minutes in the sun made a world of difference to our morning. Across the river was a small stone building that was Malum Sumna. Getting across the river was a balancing act. It was about 30 metres wide at this point and shallow, running between many boulders. The water was frozen in patches and running rapidly under the ice. The boulders themselves were covered in a glassy layer of thin clear ice. It took some time to get across. A couple of the European trekkers came out of the shelter. They had done this river crossing in the dark after leaving us. 'Did you get wet feet last night?' I asked. 'Oh yes. All of us,' one of the women replied. Apparently they'd heard from their missing companion and were soon to be reunited with their cook. I wished them luck for the rest of their trek to Dhaulagiri.

The rest of our group caught up with us and we followed the stream as it gently curved round the base of the mountain. Three kilometres up the valley we bore right up the riverbank to reach the minor pass called the Niwar La, at 5100 metres. Ahead of us, another 2 kilometres away, was the Jungben La. I could see the trail leading up to the pass. This was Kamaguchi's valley of the headless and legless skeletons. The trail divided almost a kilometre below the pass into half a dozen parallel paths created by the frequent animal and human traffic passing this way. At well over 5000 metres altitude, it was a long struggle of 'one step, one breath' to get to the cairn. There were impressive views of Dhaulagiri 20 kilometres to the south on our way up but it was blowing a gale on the pass.

We didn't linger on the Jungben La but enjoyed the rapid descent on the zigzag trail down to the campsite at 5100 metres on the south side of the pass. I'd camped there in snow in 2014 but this day, after a hot drink and snack, we trekked on. There was the small pass with a *chorten* after a level 2-kilometre trail with exceptional views of the snow-covered peaks of Tashikang and its more easterly companion Tsartse towering over the village of Sangda. It was here that I'd hung some prayer flags in memory of my father five years previously. The drop down from that point was treacherous and steep, the trail loose gravel and unstable underfoot. The river at the valley floor was a long way below at 3870 metres so a drop of 1200 metres from this pass. Fortunately the aim was to stop at a campsite halfway down in a patch of ancient juniper trees. It took less than an hour to get to a tin shed with a few other groups camped around it. We were now at about 4200 metres but that was 1300 metres lower than the Jungben La and we could wallow in the luxury of plenty of oxygen.

SUNDAY, 27 OCTOBER

Juniper camp (4245 metres; 13,927 feet)
to camp above Sangda (4480 metres; 14,698 feet)
16.3 kilometres

From Juniper camp it was a steady 0.5-kilometre descent through the gnarly, scented old trees until the final precipitous drop down to the river. The day was calm and bright and from the modern bridge over the stream the trail undulated in an easterly direction towards Sangda. Now that breathing wasn't an issue this was exceptionally pleasant trekking. To our left across the valley we could see the grey and ochre eroded water channels near the old settlement of Ghok, which Snellgrove considered to be the original settlement of the people of Sangda. Looking back we could see the trail down which we'd come that morning. A yak train of over twenty beasts resembled a long line of ants. Above that, impossibly high and steep, was the narrow yellow trail down from the high pass of yesterday. Had we really come that far?

We rolled in to Sangda for lunch. Chhiring was of a mind to get a bit more distance along to make the final day easier. I was inclined to agree, so after a quick snack we started the daunting task of the 400-metre climb up directly from Sangda to regain the trail. It was just as hard as I remembered but we stopped frequently. The tiny settlement of Sangda grew steadily smaller as we ascended and it seemed, as always, to be perched precariously above the massive valley below it. Unmissable and jarring to the eye was the new road. We crossed its tortuous trail once on the way up, and when we reached the *chorten* at 400 metres above Sangda we were firmly upon it. Looking down we could observe its trail sweeping back and forth all over the hillside as it hugged the contours. This would be a game changer for Sangda, but the big question in my mind was 'where next?' Trucks and jeeps could get up here from Jomsom so, therefore, even from Kathmandu. We'd also seen the huge amount of work that had gone into constructing the road from Shimen to Tinje to Tsharka and it was clearly headed south from there. Could the intention be to somehow gouge a trail over or near the Jungben La? It would be difficult engineering-wise but precedents for new ambitious roads were being set all over the Himalaya.

The afternoon wore on and Ram and co. set up camp on a level grassy area in a great curve of the new road. Sitting in my tent I could see what was on the gravel highway. An occasional motorbike went by. Some people on horses passed. Only one massive and glaringly noisy truck, rocking back and forth, slowly rolled past on its way to Sangda. As the sun got low in the sky a yak train of a dozen beautiful, large, unburdened animals sauntered by. They were untroubled, magnificent, black and white and brown. They had long horns and a natural shaggy skirt of hair around the lower half. I revelled in the sight of these lumbering primeval-looking beasts and cherished the moment.

MONDAY, 28 OCTOBER

Camp above Sangda (4480 metres; 14,698 feet)
to Kagbeni (2838 metres; 9311 feet)
14 kilometres

All we had to do on this last day of trekking was follow the road.

To our left the eroded and chaotic landscape of Mustang stretched far below us. Directly ahead, across the giant gorge of the Kali Gandaki was the Thorung La, not much higher than us at 5416 metres. Directly below it and much lower than us was the holy pilgrimage site of Muktinath.

As the kilometres slipped by we started heading a little more south and the Nilgiris and the summit of Annapurna, all snow-covered and glistening pure white, came into view to delight our senses.

The new road allowed us to drop, with the occasional short cut across its wide curves, straight down into lower Mustang. George and I crossed the bridge into Kagbeni, where the Kali Gandaki is narrow and fast-flowing. We walked past Yak Donalds, which is a yak-burger joint and where we were promised 'Guest is God'. And then there we were at trek's end at the Paradise Trekkers Home lodge. It was mere minutes before the traditional end-of-trek beer was being downed.

We had a bit more journey to undertake to get us back to Kathmandu. We had, next day, an opportunity to visit the sacred village of Muktinath at 3762 metres (12,343 feet) halfway up from Kagbeni to the Thorung La. The tarmac road leading up there from Jomsom allows an annual influx of many thousands of pilgrims, a significant proportion of whom fly into Jomsom from India then take a jeep directly up to the Hindu temple. That sudden exposure to altitude would test anyone's faith.

A night in Jomsom, pre-flight, was followed by two nights in Pokhara which allowed us to say our farewells to Peter and Brenda as well as have a go at paragliding over Phuwa Tal.

And so I'd been to Dolpo for a third time.

There are, of course, no conclusions to be drawn. All places change, progress, evolve. Some places, sadly, decline. George Schaller said, when reviewing Ken Bauer's *High Frontiers*, 'Cultures are dynamic, constantly in flux, even in the most remote regions such as the Tibetan enclave of Dolpo in Nepal.' In *High Frontiers* Bauer professed early in the book that it was a 'case study of change', maintaining that the 1959 closure of the border with Tibet, after the Chinese invasion, had profound effects on the pastoral yak-herding lifestyle. Bauer then wrote in his 2014 essay 'High Frontiers: Dolpo Revisited' that 'the current *yarsa gumba* trade props up the economy of Dolpo and means that the people return annually'. However, since that was written the situation had morphed once more. There was a massive drop in the overseas price of *yarsa gumba* in the 2010s but that has started to rise again. The 2019 price in Beijing was about $83,000 per kilogram and in early 2023 that was back up to $110,000 per kilogram: always more expensive than gold itself. But more significantly for the poor Nepali collecting the caterpillar fungus there would appear to be a dramatic reduction in numbers of the hybrid organism. It is thought that overharvesting has most likely disturbed the life cycle with massively lower numbers currently developing each year. The possible influence of climate change has not gone unnoticed. Throughout the whole of the Himalaya the inhabitants are aware of less snowfall, glacial retreat, the drying up of streams, alteration of the usual flora and the change in distribution and behaviour of the natural animal populations.

On top of this, since Ken Bauer's 2014 review, I have seen with my own eyes the changes in even such a short time. This last journey through Dolpo in 2019 revealed that a mere handful of heavy industrial machines can tear a network of roadways through the pristine mountainsides. It's hard to get information on these new roads and how extensive they are planned to be. There is absolutely no doubt that the pace of change is increasing exponentially. It makes it harder, but not impossible, for the Dolpo-pa to retain their distinctive cultural identity.

David Snellgrove wrote, after making a summer return visit to Dolpo following his winter 1960–61 sojourn, 'It seemed absurd to be there in summer when all the tracks and passes were open, and yet to be cut off from news of the outside world. At the same time it was extraordinary, even wonderful, to reflect that here was one part of the world where conditions of life still continued not only as they had been in Dolpo a thousand years before perhaps, but also much as they had been everywhere else in the world until a hundred years ago. Maybe one gains in historical perspective by living even a short while in just such circumstances oneself.'

I do believe that the opportunity to dwell 'in just such circumstances', with its window into the past, is even now evading us in remarkable Dolpo.

2020

PANDEMIC

48
IN PANDEMIC TIMES

I got the phone call from Sarita on the afternoon of 16 March 2020 just after our descent from the 5357-metre summit of Gokyo Ri. 'Bill, you have to get back to Kathmandu as soon as possible. I've changed your flight out of Kathmandu as the whole country is closing down.' The race was on. The pandemic had been declared by the World Health Organization on 11 March 2020, a few days after my arrival in Nepal, and the immediate future was suddenly uncertain. All we knew was that international travel was to cease and, from the Nepalese point of view, the April–May 2020 tourist season would not be happening.

My friend and guide Kinga Sherpa and I prepared our gear and the next morning began the long walk back to Lukla from Gokyo. We spent the first night at Dole, the second night in Namche and the third evening, in pouring rain and power cuts, at Lukla. If the flights were cancelled next morning I would miss my flight out of Kathmandu, with a potential prolonged stay in Nepal.

The heavens cleared. Next morning three planes were allowed to land. Priority, I found out later, was given to foreigners such as myself who may have had connecting flights to catch. My Nepalese friends, Aashma and Sabina, were stranded for two more days in Lukla. Ian Wall picked me up at the domestic airport and we arranged my farewell beer for that evening. I was to get the final Thai Airways flight out of Kathmandu next morning.

The Tribhuvan Airport was riotous that next day. People were desperate to get onto any flight out of the country. At least fifty people were on standby for my already full flight. A French anaesthetist and his wife, who I'd met in Lukla, were on the flight to Bangkok, completely the opposite direction for them, but it was the only way they could ultimately get home to France. I had a short wait at a virtually deserted Bangkok airport for my final leg to Brisbane. The departure boards were a long list of red 'cancelled' notices against more than 90 per cent of the scheduled flights. A mere handful of planes were to reach final destinations.

I arrived back in Australia to start my two weeks of self-isolation at our house in Maleny. The world had changed for everyone. Thus began the two years of universally imposed travel bans. Video calls and online social media replaced our usual human interactions. Much to my chagrin it seemed that the opinions of the bigots counted as much as the factual scientific learning and experience of the real experts. It was a two-year exercise in diminished mobility and intellectual frustration. Friends were lost because of their knee-jerk attraction to nutjob cures and dismissal of considerate and proven practices such as social distancing and simply wearing a mask. After a few months, the hospital I worked at started doing a little more than just emergency work. Australia, because of its isolation and travel ban, didn't experience the mayhem we saw on the news in places like New York and European centres. The bodies being burned in car-park funeral pyres in Delhi made an indelible visual impression.

International travel was still banned, to and from Australia, almost two years into the pandemic, but we could get around locally. The hills in the Sunshine Coast hinterland are gentle and rolling. It is dairy-farming country. Paula and I had a regular 5.5-kilometre circuit alongside the Obi Obi creek, where we'd walk Portia and Phoebe, our two English staffies. In late 2021 I started to notice that the hills weren't so easy to get up. I'd sometimes wake in the early hours with indigestion. It didn't take long for me to realise that these were cardiac symptoms. My father had died aged sixty-seven from heart disease, having had his first infarct in his late forties. Unlike him I wasn't overweight and had never smoked. I had watched my cholesterol and blood pressure carefully and had been on statins and hypotensive medication for a few years, but I knew it was now time to get investigated. My ECG was fine but a 'calcium score' was equivocal. My cardiologist recommended, given the family history, doing an angiogram.

In late September the angiogram was abandoned after only a few minutes as the stenoses in the arteries were obvious and clearly not amenable to stent placements. Bypass surgery was required and was scheduled for the following week. I was able to choose my preferred team of surgeon and anaesthetist, the superb Dr Bruce Garlick and Dr John Keys, both of whom I'd known since they were registrars. One week later I opened my eyes in the hospital intensive care unit, after a triple bypass, with a grinning Paula only a few inches from my face saying exuberantly and loudly, 'Hello, darl!' I was back in the land of the living.

There's no doubt it hurt a bit but that, as I would remind myself constantly, was so much better than suddenly dropping dead. A week of gradual mobilisation in hospital had me walking slowly around the ward with the physiotherapist. When I could handle one flight of stairs I was ready for home.

Everything was necessarily at a snail's pace but I had a plan. I got home and poured a glass of red wine and posed for a photo to post to Instagram and Facebook. Time for family and friends to know. The post read:

> Some of you may recall the British adventurer Sir Ranulph Fiennes, the first man to reach both poles in a single circumpolar adventure.
> At the age of 59 he suffered a cardiac arrest, had cardiac bypass surgery and was in a coma for 4 days.
> 16 weeks after the operation he ran 7 full marathons in 7 days on 7 different continents.
> He climbed Everest, on his third attempt, 6 years after his surgery.
> His autobiography is titled 'Mad, Bad and Dangerous to Know'.
>
> Now, let me tell you about my week. After a couple of weeks of tests for a bit of shortness of breath, going hard uphill, and some noticeable lower chest discomfort, I had my coronary artery bypass done at the Wesley last Friday. Exactly 1 week later, I'm back home and feeling great. I had no heart attack so the heart muscle is pumping well. What I have now is another twenty years instead of sudden death in the next couple of years. My message to you all is that it's too easy to put down new symptoms to 'getting older' or 'lack of exercise in the pandemic' or 'a few extra kilos'. Just get things checked out BEFORE the crushing chest pain or the cardiac arrest.

> Sir Ranulph is a bit special, as well as mad, but one has to have an agenda.
>
> I'll be up the Glasshouse mountains before my fourteen-week mark. Tasmania trekking in February. The Oxfam 100-kilometre walk next June and the anniversary of the surgery, next 24 September, at Everest Basecamp.

I was fully aware that I had dodged a bullet. It was now important to maximise my newly acquired time to get the most contact with my family and friends and to achieve as much as possible.

I started by walking 50 metres up the street and back each day. Then, a few days later, round the block. Breathing became less painful. The sternum and ribs take a few weeks to heal. After a couple of weeks I could slowly walk 1 kilometre. At the three-week mark I walked the 2-kilometre trail around the Mary Cairncross Reserve near Maleny. There were twice weekly rehab sessions in the hospital gym starting after four weeks. At six weeks Paula and I walked up one of the Glasshouse Mountains. It was Mount Ngungun, a 3-kilometre circuit and only a 200-metre ascent, but I felt great. At the eight-week mark it was time to get back on the rowing machine, and the sternum held together. In the new year I was doing walks up to 10 kilometres and we'd booked the trip to Tasmania. In early March Paula and I walked the Three Capes Trek with no problems. Sadly, the Oxfam 100-kilometre walk in June was cancelled due to poor weather, but the planned trip to Nepal was going ahead. My son George and son-in-law Brady Duggan were joining me, Brady on his first trip to the Himalaya. Would he end up carrying me, or me him?

In early September 2022 I arrived back in Kathmandu. George and Brady joined me a couple of days later and we managed to get one of the few flights to Lukla. It was still the tail end of the monsoon, so the weather was warm and wet. Chhiring was once more to be our guide, so just four friends walking in the hills. We got to Everest Base Camp on 17 September, exactly one week before the anniversary of my surgery. We'd met a Geordie woman on the trail called Melissa, who lived in Wallsend, and she insisted we pose with her Geordie flag: black and white stripes and the Newcastle Brown Ale star with the motto 'Newcastle Born and Bred'. It turned out that her grandmother had been a year behind me at Rutherford School, Newcastle, back in the late 1960s!

We walked back from Base Camp by crossing the Cho La, surely one of the best trails in the Himalaya, then over the Ngozumpa glacier to Gokyo. On my previous trip the lakes had been completely frozen over, but this time the sun shone on those Nepalese lochs possessed of an ethereal blue almost rivalling Phoksumdo itself.

My previous return from Gokyo had been a dash to catch one of the last flights out of Nepal. This time we could enjoy the trail with its myriad wildflowers, dozens of yaks and not too many other trekkers. The weather was brighter, as the last of the monsoon cleared away and we had glorious sunshine on our way down the Ngozumpa glacier to Macchermo. The night after that we were at Mong La luxuriating in the view of the sunset on Ama Dablam and looking directly across at Tengboche Monastery. Next day we took the less direct route to Namche passing through Khumjung and Khunde. We ended up being the first customers at the brand-new coffee shop of Ang Phurba and his wife in Khumjung. Ang, now in his seventies, was for many years a sirdar for Doug Scott's climbing expeditions and he'd summited several major peaks.

George and I both suffered our boots falling apart a couple of days before Namche, so it was a pleasure to be able to buy new ones there and then drink to their longevity in the 'World's Highest Irish Pub' in mid-town Namche that evening.

Two more days had us back in Lukla, where the wet weather with low cloud had returned. One couple in our lodge had been waiting four days in vain for a plane out. Once again it was Sarita to the rescue. She had traded in our plane tickets and for a little extra we could helicopter out. All that entailed was an early morning start and a two-hour walk directly downhill to a place below the cloud level where the helicopters could creep in. The plan worked beautifully, and we were back in Kathmandu, showered and in Sam's that evening.

So, the big question was where would my next trip take me? Well, even before the Base-Camp trek that event had been well planned.

In early June 2022 I had a phone call from my friend Margaret Gee in Sydney. Would I like to come to Ladakh in winter to try and see a snow leopard. I didn't even have to think about it and instantly said, 'Yes.' In January

2020, over two years before, Margaret had a trip to Ladakh with a couple of friends and they managed to spot a snow leopard. The sighting was less than a minute, but left her keen to go back. She was proposing that she get together a small group of like-minded friends and go with the same people who had guided her before. She put me in touch with Tsering Norboo, a tour guide with much Himalayan experience, and Jigmet Dadul, who had worked for twenty years with the Snow Leopard Conservancy India Trust. These were first-rate guides and the flights were arranged.

Having achieved the trek to Everest Base Camp I had only twelve weeks back in Queensland before leaving, on New Year's Day 2023, for India and the quest to see a snow leopard.

2023

LADAKH IN WINTER, ONCE MORE

49
LADAKH A DECADE ON

Leh in the clear winter light is a stunning, albeit chilly place. With its ancient castle, Buddhist *gompas* and *chortens*, Moslem mosques and minarets it still conjures up a quintessential multicultural and busy marketplace. It has always been a link on the trade route from the Indian south and west up to places like Yarkand and Kashgar on the main Silk Roads to its north.

It was ten years exactly since my initial trip to Ladakh when I'd seen the snow leopard prints in the fresh snow. Our group of six had foregathered in the Novotel at Delhi Airport the night before. Margaret Gee had arrived with her old friend Payza Pelzang, a tour guide from Bhutan. Dave and Kate Nixon, a GP and his wife from Taupo in New Zealand, were longstanding friends of Margaret and had worked in Nepal and Bhutan. David Raubenheimer, the sixth member of the group, was a professor of nutritional ecology in Sydney. He'd studied the snow leopard food chain in Nepal but had never seen one of the cats.

The arrival into Ladakh was similar to my first trip, being the early morning flight from Delhi watching the sun rise onto the hundreds of snow-covered peaks in Kashmir below us. The landing had us banking low over Spituk Monastery, as we turned into the Kushok Bakula Rimpochee Airport. Yet again it was –15°C, so it had a familiar feel. The only difference on this occasion was the compulsory PCR test for foreigners, reflecting our pandemic era.

We were met at the airport by Tsering Norboo, known as 'Norboo', who was to be our guide and trek leader. A very experienced man, he had worked for over twenty years as a guide in the Himalaya and was a native Ladakhi. Margaret knew him from her previous trip to Ladakh and was instrumental in making sure that this excellent leader would be looking after us during our endeavours. We were whisked off in two cars to our hotel, the rather luxurious Grand Dragon Hotel near the old centre of Leh. It was time to put up our feet and acclimatise. At 3500 metres Leh is at a similar altitude to Namche Bazar and Lhasa. The first day in all these places is gruelling. Walking upstairs is noticeably difficult and bending over to tie shoelaces requires the occasional upright 'breather'. I decided on a very slow walk into the centre of Leh, remembering the trekking philosophy of 'lama steps' and getting there in the end. On my new Apple watch my oxygen saturation was 89 per cent.

The old town was quiet but there was still a crowd of about 100 people sitting in front of the Soma Gompa, seemingly oblivious to the sub-zero air. The lamas inside the temple were chanting and their prayers were broadcast to the people sitting outside, in the ineffectual sunlight, over a tinny-sounding loudspeaker system. I joined the audience on the steps facing the *gompa* and enjoyed listening to the ancient Tara mantra 'Om Tare Tuttare Ture Svaha' for about twenty minutes.

We were joined at dinner in the evening by Jigmet Dadul, who was to be our wildlife guide for the trip. Jigmet is a striking man. He is of average height and has a round face but his luxuriant hair has a streak of white in a wave from the front and he sports a dapper white 'Van Dyke' goatee and moustache. He is softly spoken and has a ready smile. He and Norboo were boys together in their village to the east of Leh. Jigmet has worked for the Snow Leopard Conservancy India Trust for over twenty years, and he is a recognised expert and skilled spotter of Himalayan wildlife.

The drive next day from Leh to the mountain hamlet of Ulley was only a couple of hours. We were to follow the Indus River downstream then a long climb up a tortuous gravelled road to the village sitting at 4000 metres altitude.

It was a perfect Ladakhi winter's day when we set off mid-morning. Clear blue sky and –15°C with unimpaired views across to the Stok range and with the Ladakh mountain range ahead of us. We had stopped briefly about 10 kilometres outside of Leh when Jigmet asked, 'Do you like petroglyphs?' 'Oh yes,' I answered, jumping with eagerness out of the car. The land both sides of the road was flat and dry and scattered with hundreds of large boulders. We approached the 1- to 2-metre-high rocks and I was impressed to see on many of them, etched into their chocolate-brown surfaces, the ochre outlines of antelopes and yaks and stick-figure people carrying spears and bows. They were beautiful in their simplicity. These ancient artworks were created by the people of the so-called Indus Valley Civilisation who lived in this part of India from 3300 BCE to 1300 BCE. These rock-art drawings were almost 5000 years old.

The road led us on through the Indus Valley and we had a brief stop at a viewpoint to admire the confluence of the pale blue and clear water of the Zanskar River with the muddy waters of the Indus. Both river edges were lined by ice sheets and lumps of pancake ice hurried downstream.

Another hour along the valley we stopped at the narrow entrance to a rocky gorge. After a five-minute walk up the trail Jigmet knelt at a large rock. Pointing down at the ground he said, 'This hollow is where the snow leopard makes its scrape and up here on the overhang is where the animal sprays and leaves its scent.' We could envisage the animal being right there, but the nearby bony remains of a kill informed us that it had been about two weeks since the last feline visit.

We left the surfaced road just past the village of Yargthang and started the 6-kilometre climb up to Ulley. The road was narrow, merely loose gravel and wound back and forth as we gradually gained height up the valley. It was not long after two in the afternoon when we caught sight of the small collection of houses that is Ulley.

We had less than 1 kilometre to go when Jigmet, who was sitting in the front of the car, yelled, 'Stop!'

The driver slammed on the brake.

'Wolf,' said Jigmet.

And there it was, no more than 50 metres directly ahead of us. It was quickly running uphill away from the road to our left. Years of childhood indoctrination as to the ways and looks of the 'big bad wolf' left no doubt as to what I was seeing. It was followed by another unmistakeable shaggy beast and then another. There were at least three animals running swiftly up a ridge, then, as we drove around the next corner, we saw the reason. We had disturbed them on a kill. In the middle of the road lay a young *dzo*, the yak-cattle crossbreed. It was clearly dead and was surrounded by blood.

I knelt over the poor animal and felt its face. It was still warm. The foot-long tear in its lower abdomen, guts bulging out, gave testament to the way a wolf pack will kill. Where some predators go for the throat, the wolves surround the prey and hang onto its limbs to effectively immobilise it. Then some pack members tear at the lower belly to spill the guts and the animal has a protracted death as the feeding begins. This poor beast had been attacked about 10 metres above the road, and the trail of blood showed us where victim and attackers had rolled down into the trail before being disturbed by us.

We motored on the last short distance into Ulley. It is a small group of square-built houses either side of a narrow stream which was largely frozen at this time of year, the ice the colour and opacity of candles. There was next to no snow lying in or round the village. There was much talk of climate change, as the lack of snowfall this year and last meant little water to allow for the spring crops to thrive. A row of old and crumbling *chortens* in the centre of the settlement sat above a collection of modern prayer wheels. The large building which was to be our homestay was owned by a local widowed lady called Nilza Angmo. Her son, also called Norboo, lived there for most of the year and he would help us with spotting the animals. We called him 'young Norboo'. Also waiting for us was Jigmet's son Gyaltsen, who was following in his father's footsteps as a wildlife spotter and snow leopard expert.

As soon as we arrived our team set up the spotting scopes and scanned the ridge behind the house for signs of the wolf pack. Sure enough, they were there. I saw four of the unmistakably lupine outlines of the beasts silhouetted on the skyline about 100 metres above Ulley. Watching us watching them.

50
THE SNOW LEOPARDS

8 JANUARY

Breakfast was in the highly traditional main living room with its central iron stove and seats/beds around the sides. The fireplace, burning twigs, was only just taking the chill off the air.

After our meal and plenty of coffee we loaded ourselves into our pair of cars and set off down the trail. We were keen to see the site of the previous day's kill by the wolf pack, so we stopped a mere couple of hundred metres outside of the village to explore. The carcass of the *dzo* had been dragged off the trail further down the hill. We could see its eviscerated remains about 10 metres below us. All around us, in the soft sandy dirt of the track, the paw prints of the wolves overlay our tyre tracks of the previous day. A lot of animals had eaten their fill overnight.

We carried on down the 6 kilometres of dusty track. The cars had just reached the tarmac road at the bottom of the valley trail below Ulley when Jigmet got the call on his walkie-talkie. His face broke into a grin. 'There are snow leopards.' Our driver turned around and we drove a tad faster back up the hill than we had come down.

'Young Norboo said that there are two snow leopards and they were watching the car as we drove down,' said Jigmet. He had promised Norboo 1000 rupees if he spotted the snow leopards for us.

We piled out of the pair of vehicles, and the four spotting scopes were set up in minutes. I was fully expecting to be disappointed; that the animals would be long gone. After all, people rarely saw the snow leopard. I peered through the eyepiece of the scope which had been set up by Jigmet, and there they were. Across the narrow valley, a few hundred metres away, lying side by side. The two large cats were unmistakeable in their profiles, and they were watching all that moved in the valley from their rocky perch directly opposite us.

What a feeling! This wasn't the adrenaline rush one might expect of a quick glimpse. The beasts were luxuriating in the bright winter sun and I could equally indulge myself in simply watching them. It was a supremely tranquil moment. I was in the presence of something that was much anticipated and yet hardly to be expected. The mere presence of the animals elevated, indeed consecrated, the very place we were standing. The already beautiful and otherworldly Himalaya were even further enhanced in my mind's eye. It was ultimately calming and satisfying to be communing with these elegant and ethereal creatures.

We congratulated each other on our good fortune. Margaret said that she was especially happy for me, as she knew how close I'd been to a sighting in the past. Our human group settled in to observe the feline pair for as long as we could. Occasionally one of the cats would raise its head, look around and then settle down again. I saw a flick of the impressive spotted tail of one. I had been watching for about ten minutes, when there was sudden movement behind the pair and to everyone's amazement a third snow leopard head popped up! We were watching a mother and her two mature cubs. The newly apparent mother stood and turned around to be facing the same direction as her offspring. She lowered her head and started to lick one of the cubs behind its ears. This was a dream.

We had morning tea brought down from the house and sat near our scopes in dread of missing any action. At one point the mother stood up, tail waving. She turned around and lay down at full stretch. A minute later she rolled onto her back, stretching, and extended all four limbs into the air. Relaxing, she started a prolonged lick of her enormous front paws. I could make out the black pads and the impressive claws as she licked between them. Grooming done, and still on her back, she gave a huge yawn. Her tongue poked out and she displayed her four magnificent fangs. We'd been watching a mother cat playing with and grooming her kittens and herself.

Suddenly, with one yawn, the efficient huntress and killing machine was revealed. It was simply awesome in the true sense of the word.

Jigmet assured us that the family's modus operandi would be to rest up during the day then, as evening approached, to begin patrolling their territory and, most likely, hunting. We could spend the rest of the short winter day observing them in their rocky eyrie.

We had lunch delivered to us as the animals luxuriated in their untroubled repose on their rock perch. After our feed Jigmet suggested we move closer, so we walked about 300 metres downhill in the direction of the leopard trio. We set up the scopes again and continued to watch for another couple of hours. At one point the three beauties were lying together facing us. Their three faces, right next to each other, were in a line, looking straight at us. A triptych portrait of ethereal feline perfection staring directly at me for over five minutes. I had spent time in the Baltoro, which author Galen Rowell described as 'The Throne Room of the Mountain Gods'. This was better. This valley in remote Ladakh was more than sanctified by the presence of these divine beings.

Little else happened that afternoon but we remained enthralled. Jigmet even suggested that we try to hide behind large rocks for a short time in case we were making the animals stay put. The sun disappeared behind a ridge, and we were in shadow while the dying rays remained on the cats. It was bitterly cold. All day long it had been around –12°C to –15°C but it was now plummeting towards –20°C. The cold invaded our limbs. It was time to leave the beasts and head back to our home up the hill in Ulley. Dave, Kate, Margaret and I walked back up to the cars, but David stayed on with Jigmet and Norboo. He was rewarded in less than fifteen minutes by seeing the three cats slowly mobilise themselves and amble off with their unhurried loping gait up a gully and out of sight.

What a remarkable day. We had watched the snow leopards for a total of six hours. We were all a little shellshocked and overwhelmed by such a feast for the senses. Over dinner we talked about and dissected the day's events, still hardly able to believe our extreme good fortune. Sleep came easily.

9 JANUARY

Next morning we were having a latish breakfast around 8.00 when we got the word from Norboo, 'The snow leopards are there!' Gyaltsen was watching not too far down the valley, so we decided to walk, checking the wolf-pack kill site on the way. Now the carcass of the *dzo* was even more diminished and to my delight the wolf tracks on the road were mixed in with fresh snow leopard paw prints. The wolves had been back for a feed, but at some point the cats had been there to claim their share.

Gyaltsen, David and I carried on down the hill and, with little fanfare, Gyaltsen pointed out a snow leopard high on the ridge across the valley. It was tiny at that distance. The sun was behind it, so it was merely a silhouette but, unmistakably, a solitary snow leopard. It turned its head a couple of times before moving off the ridge away from us and disappearing out of sight. The stark image was indelibly imprinted in my mind. What a thrill. A brief sighting but a real one. Was it one of the three from the previous day or was this a new beast? We were learning that ridge lines are favourite places for animals to linger as it gave them expansive views far below and to both sides of them, whether predator or potential prey. In less than two days I'd seen yaks, *bharal*, wolves and now a snow leopard, all taking the high ground of the ridges.

A short walk further on we had another brief sighting. About 400 metres away and walking slowly up the valley were two snow leopards. They were clearly in no hurry. Possibly well fed. David and I saw them for less than a minute before they entered a gully and we lost sight of them.

Were these the same animals as the day before? The question was answered less than ten minutes later when we came across Norboo and Jigmet with spotting scopes set up watching our family of three from the previous day reclining on their new perch, settled in for the day. We had just seen six separate snow leopards in under an hour! What more could we expect?

We settled in to observe our family of cats. The two cubs, essentially fully grown, were more active than the previous day. They played a little and moved around the slope with an occasional leap. At one point a pair of magpies flew teasingly close to the family. These were the Eurasian magpies (*Pica pica*) with their distinct white chest and wing tips and, unlike the

Australian magpie (*Gymnorhina tibicen*), an elegant diamond-shaped tail with the feathers displaying an iridescent emerald sheen. The birds were fearless and swooped close to the young cats. Jigmet said it was common to have these birds follow the leopards as scavengers. The pair settled on a rocky outcrop about 20 metres from the leopard family. One of the cubs wanted to play, and keeping its body close to the ground began to slowly creep towards its feathered friends, silently stalking them. Halfway there it gently raised itself up and then, spring-like, made its giant leap. It flew up towards the magpies, but the birds were well prepared, took off and soared over the cat's head. Game over.

The three leopards found a triangle of level snow and appeared to settle down for a well-earned rest. We'd watched for an hour and a half and Jigmet assured us that they were now set for the day. Gyaltsen and young Norboo would stay watching and let us know of any subsequent activity.

I went for a walk around Ulley village before lunch. There were several ibex around, all potential prey for our three leopards. Mid-afternoon we returned down the hill to resume our sojourn with the cats. For another hour there was only slight activity but the novelty of watching head lifting and tail flicking was never going to wear off. Then, at about 4.00 in the afternoon it was all happening. The mother cat stretched and stood up. The cubs followed suit. They looked around but ignored us as we were about 400 metres away. All three started moving downhill towards an area of loose eroded gullies dropping down to the river. The cubs led, occasionally having a short jog or jumping up onto a rock. Constantly they looked around and seemed to sniff the air. They were hunting. Just before the gullies the mother cat approached a large boulder about 2 metres high by 3 long. She walked in front of it and sniffed at the ground at the corner. With her paw she made a scrape. She then slowly and elegantly turned around, raised her tail and sprayed the rock behind her at her head height. Job done, the three of them moved onto the loose scree of the gully below them and started moving at speed. We got glimpses of them as they shot past the rocks and boulders, then suddenly they were in the trees at the bottom of the valley and they were gone. The show was over, but we'd had another three hours that day of unadulterated *Panthera* exhibitionism.

51
DÉNOUEMENT

Were we destined to see snow leopards every day? Unlikely, but we carried on looking.

The days assumed a more usual routine of finding a promising spot then settling in to scan the slopes for any sign of animal life. The art of patience was a positive thing. It was also a time, simply standing there, for introspection. A time for contemplation on where we were, what we'd seen, what we might yet see and the interconnectedness of all things. It was a frigidly cold form of meditation standing at the scope.

10 JANUARY

Our third day based at Ulley. The day was cold with some high-altitude cloud filtering a weak sun. Perhaps a change in weather was coming. We drove in our two vehicles to the next valley over to the west where the village of Shukpachan was situated. This valley was known for its ancient juniper trees and its massive, gold-painted statue of the Buddha, raised high above the settlement. We enjoyed a long walk into the village and then, after lunch, a long walk out the other side, but there were few animals of any description to be seen, barring the domestic yaks and *dzos*. We did, however, get some good views a long way down a side valley to the Indus.

11 JANUARY

On the fourth day we woke to find Nilza sitting outside the house in the sub-zero conditions making *rotis* on a hot-stone fired by yak dung. I think she made enough to last for several days. After breakfast we went a couple of kilometres up the valley to an old farmhouse with a young family in residence. There were a few *bharal* on the nearby hillside and we saw some ibex a little further away, but there was no sign of either wolves or snow leopards. However, the family did have a pair of exquisite white pashmina goats which they shepherded into their enclosure. This was a 2-metre-high stone built space with a stout wooden door. The edifice was roofed over with beams of whole willow tree trunks about 15 centimetres in diameter and these covered with a strong metal mesh. These anti-predator measures were sponsored by the Snow Leopard Conservancy India Trust based in Leh and were highly effective defences.

Inside the farmhouse was a splendid large kitchen with a massive stove. Just behind this room was a storeroom with boxes of grain and *tsampa*, onions and potatoes and, more excitingly for David and me, an ancient wood and iron muzzle-loading flintlock rifle standing in the corner.

Snow was threatening in the afternoon, so after a walk back to our abode along the frozen river it was simply time to rug up and read and stay warm.

12 JANUARY

There had been a light smattering of snow overnight but the sky was now free of cloud and had taken on the intense blue of altitude. It was, naturally, well below freezing.

Our plan for the day was to drop down to the tarmac road and turn east towards the village of Yangthang. From there we could head north on a gravel road up to the village of Saspochey sitting directly east of Ulley behind a high rocky ridge.

A few minutes before reaching Yangthang another dead yak was spotted lying about 20 metres off the road. The scopes revealed at least three wolves relaxing on the slope opposite, about 500 metres from us. The carcass demonstrated a classic wolf-pack kill. It was lying on its right side and had been totally eviscerated. I noticed that even the costal cartilage had been chewed off leaving the sharp bony ends of the ribs poking straight out. I looked even closer and, sure enough, in their feeding frenzy the wolves had snagged the ends of the ribs and the pointed bones carried small clumps of grey wolf fur. More disturbingly, a few metres away from the remains of the yak, David had come across the stomach of the beast. It had been dragged there and ripped open to reveal a mixture of grass and plastic. There were recognisable containers and lids and plastic bags, which the poor animal had ingested and then just kept accumulating in its double stomach. Even in this remote place human detritus continues to offend and even threaten nature itself.

We ate an early lunch at Saspochey and a walk up a deserted gully that was the beginning of a tenuous trail across the ridge to Ulley in the next valley. Jigmet spotted a herd of over thirty ibex on the opposite side of the valley to us, but they were quite distant. Their lack of agitation implied that they didn't feel threatened by any predators at that time.

The day became windy and the wind chill factor rendered simply standing at the scope unbearable. It was time to retreat back to Ulley.

That evening Norboo invited Margaret, Payza and me to the house of his friend Tsewang Norboo and his wife Dolma. This couple ran the well-known Snow Leopard Lodge in Ulley. Margaret had stayed with them on her previous trip to Ladakh. We were made most welcome in their comfortably warm kitchen/dining/living room. Dolma stoked up her stove with more willow twigs and put the kettle on. She then got her traditional wooden-tube mixer and plunger and rustled up some yak butter tea. I was most appreciative, but Margaret declined. It is, naturally, not everyone's cup of tea. I was already on my second cup when Norboo opened his wooden container of *tsampa* and suggested I add some to my tea. I'd never had it like that before, but it was a revelation. The rich nutty taste of the roasted barley flour added to the flavours of the salty yak butter tea and the resultant smooth paste was exquisite.

13 JANUARY

On our sixth day in Ulley we woke to an overcast sky. Norboo announced that we would drive past the village of Shukpachan and walk down through the gorge, the Hemis Chhu Valley, which leads right down to the Indus.

Early on we saw some distant urials. The urial (*Ovis orientalis*) is a variety of mountain sheep living around the 4000-metre mark. The males are reddish-brown and carry magnificent horns, most commonly curving downwards and forwards. They are a vulnerable species and it's estimated that there are only about 2000 to 2500 in the whole of Ladakh and eastern Kashmir.

As I walked down the gorge, I turned a bend in the road and spotted a group of a dozen or more *bharal* only about 100 metres from me. There was a large male and several females and young. Another smaller group came over a ridge to join them and the male of this group immediately approached and locked horns with the larger male I'd first seen. They half-heartedly wrestled for a couple of minutes and then found grazing more interesting.

We crossed the Indus and drove up a spectacular valley to the village of Mangue for lunch. We watched the nearby slopes for almost two hours but there was no activity and so we started our return to Ulley by travelling further up the Indus then into the valley leading to a place called Sumdo near Yangthang. The valley was initially wide and flat, and we stopped the cars near some large boulders which displayed some good examples of the 4000-year-old petroglyphs. I could easily make out dozens of animals with long horns, short horns, curved ones and even one that looked like a reindeer. There were stick figure people carrying spears and bows. On some of the boulders were stylised drawings of Buddhist *stupas* and some real examples of these were nearby. The drawings, given the time of emergence of Buddhism in northern India, must have been much younger than the Indus Valley Civilisation drawings by 1000 or 2000 years, but they were still well over 2000 years old.

14 JANUARY

This was to be our last full day at Ulley and the wildlife-viewing benefactress that was Ladakh would continue dishing out her bounty to we mere observers.

On this bright, cold, winter, Ladhaki day with a centimetre or two of fresh snow on the trail we set off walking downhill. Every few hundred metres

Jigmet, Gyaltsen and Norboo would stop and scan through the scopes. I had binoculars but didn't spot any movement. A few lammergeiers soared noiselessly overhead, dark silhouettes against the intense dark blue of the sky. About 2 kilometres down the trail Jigmet pointed out a side track. We scrambled down a steep slope into a dry gully where the path levelled out and led into a gradually widening canyon, the start of the Spango Valley. One kilometre into the rocky ravine was a level area with some rough stone shelters used by the yak herders. We stopped for an early lunch and set up the scopes. Gyaltsen and young Norboo had gone on ahead. I decided to head up the main valley and try and catch up with the two spotters. The trail was level and well-marked and the going was easy at just over 4000 metres. There was no sign of my two friends and when I was 1 kilometre up the valley, with no one else about, it occurred to me that there was a slight possibility that the wolves may be getting a little peckish, so I beat a hasty retreat.

Two hundred metres up a side valley we could see a small three-roomed retreat built into the side of a cliff. This, Jigmet told me, was the retreat of the Rinpoche Sras. The Rinpoche was particularly eminent and had immersed himself in a three-year retreat in this hermitage. The old fellow had died, only four weeks before our visit, on 8 December 2022 at the age of ninety-four.

In fact Rinpoche Sras was a remarkable man. Born in Ladakh in 1928 he was recognised as a *tulku*, a reincarnation of the previous Sras Rinpoche, by the thirteenth Dalai Lama. When he was twenty he travelled to Tibet and studied at Drepung Monastery in Lhasa. He received his ordination from the ninety-fourth Ganden Tripa, the then current head of the Gelugpa. With the Chinese invasion in 1959 he fled to India with the fourteenth Dalai Lama. Many years later he was named as the Abbot of the Drepung Loseling Monastery in Karnataka, India. In 2009 he was appointed, under his full name of Thubten Nyima Lungtok Tenzin Norbu, as the 102nd Ganden Tripa and was still in post, albeit in India, at the time of my 2015 visit to Ganden Monastery just outside Lhasa.

I met up with Jigmet and he told me the others had already gone up to the meditation *gompa*. He'd never been there himself so the two of us set off. A hundred metres or so up the side valley, just before the climb up to the tiny *gompa*, we saw another dead yak. This carcass was hollowed out and desiccated and had acquired a thin layer of snow. It was another wolf-pack kill. The wolves in Ladakh appeared to be remarkably well nourished.

Ahead of us the hermitage was perched on a 20-metre-high cliff. At its base were a couple of leafless trees and a steep and narrow path led behind the cliff and up to the rear of the building. It was well constructed of stone, with small wooden-framed windows on three sides. At its front was a terrace about 5 by 3 metres and here we met up with Dave and Kate, Payza and David. From the terrace, doors opened to three rooms and to a staircase leading up to the roof. Prayer flags were draped under the eaves but there was no furniture. It effused an aura of tranquillity. It took little imagination to picture the old and eminent lama leaving the monastery in India, of which he was head, to come to this most remote of valleys and incarcerate himself for three years. This was a prolonged tantric meditation he undertook on the Yamantaka mandala, the destroyer of death.

I enjoyed the idea that I had visited Ganden in Tibet at the time when this Rinpoche was its titular head. I had been blessed by a monk there by being tapped on the head with the cloth case containing the yellow hat of Tsongkhapa himself, as well as the slippers of the thirteenth Dalai Lama. I had delighted in Younghusband's tale of his meeting the eighty-sixth Ganden Tripa, Lobsang Gyeltshen, his 'Ti-Rimpoche' who he thought to be the embodiment of the lama in Kipling's novel *Kim*, and who gave him his treasured Buddha statue. Now here I was on the verandah of the tiny retreat where Rinpoche Sras, the 102nd Ganden Tripa, had meditated and I felt somehow that I had come full circle. The endless knot. Everything is most certainly connected.

As we lingered on the Rinpoche's verandah Jigmet got a call on the walkie-talkie. Gyaltsen said that there was a snow leopard up the valley. We had to be quick. We moved as rapidly as we could out of the *gompa* and rushed down the 200 metres to the main valley. The scopes had been set up. I looked up the valley towards the natural amphitheatre that was its end. A large dark urial was moving awkwardly uphill to the right. Half a minute later a snow leopard appeared at the left-hand side of the valley and moved excruciatingly slowly across its floor. In one minute it reached a group of rough boulders and appeared to lie down there among the rocks. The urial continued limping its way uphill.

Gyaltsen and Norboo joined us. They had been spotting up near the end of the valley a little beyond where I'd turned back. With no warning the two animals, leopard and prey, fell tumbling from above their position, rolling towards the dry valley floor. The attack continued but both creatures had been injured. The urial was able to hobble away and we saw it begin to climb uphill. The leopard had a rest before slinking off to find the security of the rocks to recover.

It was by now mid-afternoon and we settled in to wait for the reappearance of the snow leopard. We knew exactly where it was resting. We'd been joined by another group of travellers who were also staying in Ulley at the Snow Leopard Lodge. We were now a crowd of almost twenty. Less than an hour went by when there was a gasp from one of the other observers. 'Snow leopard! On the ridge!' The scopes were swung upwards and there it was, smoothly walking down from the crest of the ridge at the top end of the valley. It looked like it was stalking. There were certainly plenty of animals, at least a dozen urials, to tempt it. About 50 metres below the crest-line it found a rocky outcrop to use as a perch and it sat there just watching. Its head moved from side to side. It was in no hurry. After twenty minutes it lay down and we lost sight of it. Every few minutes it would raise its head but quickly settle down again. The first snow leopard must still have been licking its wounds as it hadn't reappeared.

Once again the time passed all too quickly and we found ourselves in the dark, cold shadow of a high ridge behind us. The snow leopards and the herd of urials were still luxuriating in the late afternoon sun. We were freezing. It was time to start heading back up to Ulley.

*

Our time in Ladakh was finished. Next day it was back to Leh then on to Delhi and beyond. Ulley had served up a visual feast of eight different snow leopards in our week there. It was almost too much to comprehend and absorb. Had it really happened? We had the photographs, of course, but I also had a warm inner glow of satisfaction and a series of unforgettable images in my head.

My long journey. A lifetime of loving the outdoors and the mountains. A career in medicine involving, as it necessarily does, a greater than normal degree of empathy and compassion towards my fellow man. An academic interest in the physiology of high-altitude regions, with their low ambient oxygen level and frequently adverse climatic conditions. The travels which provoked in me a love of the Buddhist ethos and the communities I was welcomed into. It seemed like these many aspects of a life were coming together, thankfully not to a conclusion, but to a remarkably satisfying zenith epitomised by these hours of communing with the legendary *Panthera uncia.*

The French author Sylvain Tesson wrote *The Art of Patience: Seeking the Snow Leopard in Tibet.* He had travelled with photographer Vincent Munier to a remote part of the Tibetan plateau to the north of Lhasa. The resulting documentary on the snow leopard was the award-winning *The Velvet Queen.* In his book Tesson spoke of his emotions after first seeing the snow leopard. He referred to his sightings as 'apparitions'. Of his first snow leopard observation he said, 'I had waited for this vision; it had come. Henceforth nothing would ever be the same in this place made fruitful by the presence. Not even in my innermost self.'

Beyond the snow leopard, beyond the actuality that is the flesh and blood and fur of the beast, lies a whole realm of snow leopard beliefs. We idealise and idolise the concept of an animal we easily label as otherworldly and yet, when seen 'in the flesh' it even surpasses one's unrealistic expectations. It is truly a divine creature.

There are few people, in a world of 8 billion, who have seen a snow leopard in the wild. Most have simply had a glimpse of the *Panthera uncia.* I feel more than fortunate to have had 'quality time' with the enigmatic cats.

Many people view Buddhism as being a little negative, even nihilistic, in its outlook. The emphasis on 'suffering, ageing, illness and death' is, however, meant to focus one's attention on enjoying the current moment and not to dwell on past and future problematic issues. It allows for a fatalistic outlook but sanctions pleasure in the present juncture. Built in is acceptance of one's fortune, good or bad. Peter Matthiessen found himself having little choice but to accept his lack of a sighting of the snow leopard, and, 'Have you seen the snow leopard? No! Isn't that wonderful?' definitely works as a philosophy.

What if we hadn't actually seen a snow leopard on our Ladakhi adventure? What of it? Could we also as easily have sought solace in the Zen ruminations of Matthiessen and his ilk? It quite simply 'is what it is'. Equally profoundly, as my three-year-old grand-daughter Pippa recently quoted to me, 'You get what you get and you don't get upset.' But I certainly had no need to get upset. After all, I had seen not one but several snow leopards.

Buddhism allows one to live in the moment, to engage in tranquillity regardless of what preceded or will follow that moment. But 'the moment' need not be unemotional. It can be ecstatic. Matthiessen was right to memorialise his moment despite not seeing the snow leopard. My own moment was neither more nor less important than Peter Matthiessen's but I can paraphrase the great storyteller.

Have you seen the snow leopard? Yes! It is beyond wonderful!

ACKNOWLEDGEMENTS

The writing of this book has been satisfyingly self-indulgent as it has allowed me, as I put down my recollections, to relive some remarkable and memorable journeys.

I'd like to begin by thanking all my travelling companions over the years especially the guides and porters who looked after me so well in sometimes seriously adverse conditions. Many are mentioned in the text. Thank you all. Without you I would have had no stories to tell.

The research into the history of the Himalaya, and especially Dolpo, was fascinating and I am grateful to all the travellers, climbers, explorers and historians who wrote down their accounts to serve as my inspiration and guide.

Once I'd begun my writing I found a true mentor in Margaret Gee. She knows well the literary landscape and has always been forthcoming with advice and good suggestions.

The team at Black Inc. has looked after me especially well. Special thanks to Sophy Williams, Amelia Willis and Kirstie Innes-Will for guiding me through the process of getting my thoughts into published form. Also the design and marketing teams are the 'total package'.

Finally, infinite thanks to my wife Paula. Her support was everything. She would let me get on with writing and supply endless cups of tea. I am forever grateful that she would let me disappear to 'parts unknown' for weeks on end and rarely complain about the smelly gear on my return. She is the love of my life.

GLOSSARY

A note on place names used in this book

Many northern Nepali places have traditional Tibetan names and when first written, or placed on maps, were subject to various linguistic and grammatical distortions.

For example, the village of Tsharka. The classical Tibetan name (Tib.) is *tshar-ka*. The Survey of India (SI), on its 1930s maps, calls it Chharkabhot, where the suffix *bhot* means 'Tibetan'. The situation was further complicated by the other suffix, *gaon*, meaning 'village'. Thus Tsharka became (SI) Chharkabhotgaon.

Similarly, the village of Ku is seen on some maps as 'Kugaon'.

The Tibetan (Tib.) gSal-mdangs becomes (SI) Sāldānggāon but most commonly Saldang.

Tibetan (Tib.) gSang-dag becomes (SI) Sangdāh but more commonly Sangdak. I have used Sangda even though its most recent incarnation on the Dolpo map is Santa. Locals still often call it Paling.

Throughout I have generally stayed with those names used by David Snellgrove, who had much insight into the linguistic origins of most names of people and places.

amchi a practitioner of traditional Tibetan herbal and holistic medicine

beyul a sacred and hidden valley offering refuge

bharal the Himalayan blue sheep, *Pseudois nayaur*

chang locally brewed beer made from barley, rice or millet

chapati unleavened bread cooked on a hot plate, finished with a layer of oil

chorten Tibetan for the Sanskrit *stupa*: a memorial mound, often highly stylised

chuba traditional wrap-around Tibetan skirt

dakini a spirit or demon in female form

damaru a small two-sided drum

dhauiliya or *dok-pa*, the primitive wooden carved effigies placed on houses to protect against evil spirits

dhokor in a flower shape, e.g. *mani dhokor*

dok-pa a *dhauiliya*; the primitive wooden carved effigies placed on houses to protect against evil spirits

doksa seasonal settlement

dorje Tibetan for Sanskrit *vajra*, 'thunderbolt' symbolising diamond-like hardness

dramyin a Tibetan six-stringed lute

dri the female yak, often called *nak*

drogpa nomads

dzo a yak and domestic cow hybrid

dzong a fort, often on a hill or crag

gompa Tibetan *dgon-pa*, a strongly built ecclesiastical building

gomtri a wooden crib for meditation

kalachakra Buddhist symbol involving ten interlocking letters in Sanskrit

kangling a flute made from a human femur – from Tib. *kang* (leg) and *ling* (flute)

kani chorten a *chorten* with a passageway through at the entrance to a village

kata ceremonial silk scarf

kora a ritual circumambulation of a place of holy significance

lassi a yoghurt-like drink

mani stone	a stone carved with the six symbols of the mantra 'Om Mani Padme Hum'
mani dhokor	a *mani* stone carved in circular, rosette form
momo	filled steamed dumplings
naan	unleavened bread made with plain flour and fat cooked on a hot plate
nak	female yak, also called *dri*
ngagpa	a Buddhist or Bon practitioner who is not ordained
puja	a ceremony of blessing especially before starting an endeavour
rakshasi	an ogress
rakshasa	an ogre
raksi	locally fermented spirit made from barley, rice, potato or millet
roti	unleavened bread cooked on a hot plate
sirdar	an old army rank but used to denote the, usually, local leader of an expedition, now known as 'guide'
stupa	Sanskrit for the Tibetan *chorten*, a memorial mound, often highly stylised
tashi delek	Tibetan greeting: roughly 'blessings and good luck'
thangka	a Tibetan religious painting
torma	ornamental figures created from yak butter
trapa	aspirant monk
trisul	Trident symbol
tsampa	roast barley flour
yab-yum	a symbolic sexual linking of a male deity and his consort in Tibetan art to symbolise the union of wisdom and compassion

BIBLIOGRAPHY

Allen, Charles. *The Buddha and Dr. Führer: An Archaeological Scandal.* London: Haus Publishing, 2008.

Allen, Charles. *The Search for Shangri-La: A Journey into Tibetan History.* London: Little, Brown, 1999.

Baker, Ian, and Thomas Laird. *The Dalai Lama's Secret Temple: Tantric Wall Paintings from Tibet.* New York: Thames & Hudson, 2000.

Baker, Ian. *The Heart of the World: A Journey to the Last Secret Place.* New York: Penguin, 2004.

Bauer, Kenneth M. *High Frontiers: Dolpo and the Changing World of Himalayan Pastoralists.* New York: Columbia UP, 2004.

Bell, Charles. *Grammar Of Colloquial Tibetan.* Abingdon, Oxfordshire: Routledge, 2017.

Bernstein, Richard. *Ultimate Journey.* New York: Random House, 2001.

Blofeld, John. *The Tantric Mysticism of Tibet; a Practical Guide.* New York: Dutton, 1970.

Craig, Mary. *Tears of Blood: A Cry for Tibet.* Washington, D.C.: Counterpoint, 1999.

Davis, Wade. *Into the Silence: The Great War, Mallory, and the Conquest of Everest.* New York: Alfred A. Knopf, 2011.

Dolma, Dorje. *Yak Girl: Growing up in the Remote Dolpo Region of Nepal.* Varanasi: Pilgrims, 2018.

Fiennes, Ranulph. *Mad, Bad and Dangerous to Know*. London: Hodder and Stoughton, 2019.

Fleming. *News from Tartary a Journey from Peking to Kashmir*. London: Cape, 1937.

French, Patrick. *Tibet, Tibet: A Personal History of a Lost Land*. New York: Knopf, 2003.

French, Patrick. *Younghusband: The Last Great Imperial Adventurer*. London: HarperCollins, 1994.

Hedin, Sven Anders. *Trans-Himalaya: Discoveries and Adventures in Tibet*. London: Macmillan, 1910.

Heller, Amy. *Hidden Treasures of the Himalayas: Tibetan Manuscripts, Paintings and Sculptures of Dolpo*. Chicago: Serindia Publications, 2009.

Hesse, Hermann. *Siddhartha*. New York: Bantam, 1981.

Hopkirk, Peter. *The Great Game: On Secret Service in High Asia*. London: Murray, 1990.

Hopkirk, Peter. *Trespassers on the Roof of the World: The Race for Lhasa*. London: J. Murray, 1982.

Jest, Corneille, and Margaret Stein. *Tales of the Turquoise: A Pilgrimage in Dolpo*. Ithaca, NY: Snow Lion Publications, 1998.

Jinpa, Gelek. *Bön in Nepal: Traces of The Great Zhang Zhung Ancestors in the Himalayas: The Light of the History of Existence*. New Delhi: Heritage Publishers, 2013.

Kawaguchi, Ekai. *Three Years in Tibet, with the Original Japanese Illustrations*. Adyar, Madras: Theosophist Office, 1909.

Kind, Marietta. *Mendrub: A Bonpo Ritual for the Benefit of All Living Beings and for the Empowerment of Medicine Performed in Tsho, Dolpo*. Kathmandu: WWF Nepal Program, 2002.

Kind, Marietta. *The Bon Landscape of Dolpo: Pilgrimages, Monasteries, Biographies and the Emergence of Bon*. Bern: P. Lang, 2012.

Kipling, Rudyard. *Kim*. London: Macmillan, 1901.

Landon, Perceval, Herbert James Walton, William Frederick Travers O'Connor, and Francis Edward Younghusband. *The Opening of Tibet: An Account of Lhasa and the Country and People of Central Tibet and of the Progress of the Mission Sent There by the English Government in the Year 1903–4*. New York: Doubleday, 1905.

Matthiessen, Peter. *The Snow Leopard*. New York: Viking, 1978.

Pritchard-Jones, Siân, and Bob Gibbons. *Trekking around Upper & Lower Dolpo*. Kathmandu: Himalayan Map House, 2014.

Rinpoche, Namgyal, and Cherry Bird. *Dolpo, the Hidden Land*. Kathmandu: SNV/Nepal, 2005.

Roberts, John B., and Elizabeth A. Roberts. *Freeing Tibet: 50 Years of Struggle, Resilience, and Hope*. New York: AMACOM, 2009.

Schaller, George B., and Jean Pruchnik. *Stones of Silence: Journeys in the Himalaya*. New York: Viking, 1980.

Service, Robert W. *Collected Poems of Robert Service*. New York: Putnam, 1989.

Shipton, Eric Earle. *That Untravelled World: An Autobiography*. London: Hodder & Stoughton, 1970.

Sinclair, William Boyd., and Robert E. Crozier. *Jump to the Land of God; the Adventures of a United States Air Force Crew in Tibet*. Caldwell, ID: Caxton Printers, 1965.

Singer, Peter. *The Life You Can Save: Acting Now to End World Poverty*. New York: Random House, 2009.

Snellgrove, David L. *Buddhist Himālaya: Travels and Studies in Quest of the Origins and Nature of Tibetan Religion*. Oxford: Cassirer, 1957.

Snellgrove, David L. *Himalayan Pilgrimage: A Study of Tibetan Religion*. Oxford: B. Cassirer, 1961.

Snellgrove, David L. *The Nine Ways of Bon; Excerpts from GZi-brjid*. London: Oxford U.P., 1967.

Snellgrove, David L. *Four Lamas of Dolpo: Tibetan Biographies*. Oxford: Bruno Cassirer, 1967.

Tesson, Sylvain. *The Art of Patience: Seeking the Snow Leopard in Tibet*. London: Penguin Books. 2023

Younghusband, Francis Edward. *India and Tibet: A History of the Relations Which Have Subsisted between the Two Countries from the Time of Warren Hastings to 1910: With a Particular Account of the Mission to Lhasa of 1904*. London: J. Murray, 1910.

Ziskin, Joel F. "Trek to Nepal's Sacred Crystal Mountain." *National Geographic* April (1977).

www.ingramcontent.com/pod-product-compliance
Ingram Content Group UK Ltd.
Pitfield, Milton Keynes, MK11 3LW, UK
UKHW021839270726
14058UKWH00002B/242

9 781760 645229